CASENOTE® Legal Briefs®

TORTS

Keyed to Courses Using

Prosser, Wade, Schwartz, Kelly, and Partlett's
Torts: Cases and Materials
Fourteenth Edition

Authored by: Publisher's Editorial Staff

Wolters Kluwer

Published by Wolters Kluwer in New York.

Wolters Kluwer Legal & Regulatory U.S. serves customers worldwide with CCH, Aspen Publishers, and Kluwer Law International products. (www.WKLegaledu.com)

To contact Customer Service, e-mail customer.service@wolterskluwer.com, call 1-800-234-1660, fax 1-800-901-9075, or mail correspondence to:

Wolters Kluwer
Attn: Order Department
P.O. Box 990
Frederick, MD 21705

Printed in the United States of America.

1 2 3 4 5 6 7 8 9 0

ISBN 978-1-5438-3183-2

About Wolters Kluwer Legal & Regulatory U.S.

Wolters Kluwer Legal & Regulatory U.S. delivers expert content and solutions in the areas of law, corporate compliance, health compliance, reimbursement, and legal education. Its practical solutions help customers successfully navigate the demands of a changing environment to drive their daily activities, enhance decision quality, and inspire confident outcomes.

Serving customers worldwide, its legal and regulatory portfolio includes products under the Aspen Publishers, CCH Incorporated, Kluwer Law International, ftwilliam.com, and MediRegs names. They are regarded as exceptional and trusted resources for general legal and practice-specific knowledge, compliance and risk management, dynamic workflow solutions, and expert commentary.

Format for the Casenote® Legal Brief

Nature of Case: This section identifies the form of action (e.g., breach of contract, negligence, battery), the type of proceeding (e.g., demurrer, appeal from trial court's jury instructions) or the relief sought (e.g., damages, injunction, criminal sanctions).

Party ID: Quick identification of the relationship between the parties.

Fact Summary: This is included to refresh your memory and can be used as a quick reminder of the facts.

Rule of Law: Summarizes the general principle of law that the case illustrates. It may be used for instant recall of the court's holding and for classroom discussion or home review.

Facts: This section contains all relevant facts of the case, including the contentions of the parties and the lower court holdings. It is written in a logical order to give you a clear understanding of the case. The plaintiff and defendant are identified by their proper names throughout and are always labeled with a (P) or (D).

Issue: The issue is a concise question that brings out the essence of the opinion as it relates to the section of the casebook in which the case appears. Both substantive and procedural issues are included if relevant to the decision.

Palsgraf v. Long Island R.R. Co.

Injured bystander (P) v. Railroad company (D)

N.Y. Ct. App., 248 N.Y. 339, 162 N.E. 99 (1928).

NATURE OF CASE: Appeal from judgment affirming verdict for plaintiff seeking damages for personal injury.

FACT SUMMARY: Helen Palsgraf (P) was injured on R.R.'s (D) train platform when R.R.'s (D) guard helped a passenger aboard a moving train, causing his package to fall on the tracks. The package contained fireworks which exploded, creating a shock that tipped a scale onto Palsgraf (P).

RULE OF LAW

The risk reasonably to be perceived defines the duty to be obeyed.

FACTS: Helen Palsgraf (P) purchased a ticket to Rockaway Beach from R.R. (D) and was waiting on the train platform. As she waited, two men ran to catch a train that was pulling out from the platform. The first man jumped aboard, but the second man, who appeared as if he might fall, was helped aboard by the guard on the train who had kept the door open so they could jump aboard. A guard on the platform also helped by pushing him onto the train. The man was carrying a package wrapped in newspaper. In the process, the man dropped his package, which fell on the tracks. The package contained fireworks and exploded. The shock of the explosion was apparently of great enough strength to tip over some scales at the other end of the platform, which fell on Palsgraf (P) and injured her. A jury awarded her damages, and R.R. (D) appealed.

ISSUE: Does the risk reasonably to be perceived define the duty to be obeyed?

HOLDING AND DECISION: (Cardozo, C.J.) Yes. The risk reasonably to be perceived defines the duty to be obeyed. If there is no foreseeable hazard to the injured party as the result of a seemingly innocent act, the act does not become a tort because it happened to be a wrong as to another. If the wrong was not willful, the plaintiff must show that the act as to her had such great and apparent possibilities of danger as to entitle her to protection. Negligence in the abstract is not enough upon which to base liability. Negligence is a relative concept, evolving out of the common law doctrine of trespass on the case. To establish liability, the defendant must owe a legal duty of reasonable care to the injured party. A cause of action in tort will lie where harm, though unintended, could have been averted or avoided by observance of such a duty. The scope of the duty is limited by the range of danger that a reasonable person could foresee. In this case, there was nothing to suggest from the appearance of the parcel or otherwise that the parcel contained fireworks. The guard could not reasonably have had any warning of a threat to Palsgraf (P), and R.R. (D) therefore cannot be held liable. Judgment is reversed in favor of R.R. (D).

DISSENT: (Andrews, J.) The concept that there is no negligence unless R.R. (D) owes a legal duty to take care as to Palsgraf (P) herself is too narrow. Everyone owes to the world at large the duty of refraining from those acts that may unreasonably threaten the safety of others. If the guard's action was negligent as to those nearby, it was also negligent as to those outside what might be termed the "danger zone." For Palsgraf (P) to recover, R.R.'s (D) negligence must have been the proximate cause of her injury, a question of fact for the jury.

ANALYSIS

The majority defined the limit of the defendant's liability in terms of the danger that a reasonable person in defendant's situation would have perceived. The dissent argued that the limitation should not be placed on liability, but rather on damages. Judge Andrews suggested that only injuries that would not have happened but for R.R.'s (D) negligence should be compensable. Both the majority and dissent recognized the policy-driven need to limit liability for negligent acts, seeking, in the words of Judge Andrews, to define a framework "that will be practical and in keeping with the general understanding of mankind." The Restatement (Second) of Torts has accepted Judge Cardozo's view.

Quicknotes

FORESEEABILITY A reasonable expectation that change is the probable result of certain acts or omissions.

NEGLIGENCE Conduct falling below the standard of care that a reasonable person would demonstrate under similar conditions.

PROXIMATE CAUSE The natural sequence of events without which an injury would not have been sustained.

Concurrence/Dissent: All concurrences and dissents are briefed whenever they are included by the casebook author.

Analysis: This last paragraph gives you a broad understanding of where the case "fits in" with other cases in the section of the book and with the entire course. It is a hornbook-style discussion indicating whether the case is a majority or minority opinion and comparing the principal case with other cases in the casebook. It may also provide analysis from restatements, uniform codes, and law review articles.

Holding and Decision: This section offers a clear and in-depth discussion of the rule of the case and the court's rationale. It is written in easy-to-understand language and answers the issue presented by applying the law to the facts of the case. When relevant, it includes a thorough discussion of the exceptions to the case as listed by the court, any major cites to the other cases on point, and the names of the judges who wrote the decisions.

Quicknotes: Conveniently defines legal terms found in the case.

Note to Students

Wolters Kluwer Legal & Regulatory U.S. is proud to offer *Casenote® Legal Briefs*—continuing thirty years of publishing America's best-selling legal briefs.

Casenote® Legal Briefs are designed to help you save time when briefing assigned cases. Organized under convenient headings, they show you how to abstract the basic facts and holdings from the text of the actual opinions handed down by the courts. Used as part of a rigorous study regimen, they can help you spend more time analyzing and critiquing points of law than on copying bits and pieces of judicial opinions into your notebook or outline.

Casenote® Legal Briefs should never be used as a substitute for assigned casebook readings. They work best when read as a follow-up to reviewing the underlying opinions themselves. Students who try to avoid reading and digesting the judicial opinions in their casebooks or online sources will end up shortchanging themselves in the long run. The ability to absorb, critique, and restate the dynamic and complex elements of case law decisions is crucial to your success in law school and beyond. It cannot be developed vicariously.

Casenote® Legal Briefs represents but one of the many offerings in Legal Education's Study Aid Timeline, which includes:

- *Casenote® Legal Briefs*
- *Emanuel® Law Outlines*
- Emanuel® *Law in a Flash* Flash Cards
- Emanuel® *CrunchTime®* Series

Each of these series is designed to provide you with easy-to-understand explanations of complex points of law. Each volume offers guidance on the principles of legal analysis and, consulted regularly, will hone your ability to spot relevant issues. We have titles that will help you prepare for class, prepare for your exams, and enhance your general comprehension of the law along the way.

To find out more about our law school tools for success, visit us at *www.WKLegaledu.com* or email us at *legaledu@wolterskluwer.com*. We'll be happy to assist you.

How to Brief a Case

A. Decide on a Format and Stick to It

Structure is essential to a good brief. It enables you to arrange systematically the related parts that are scattered throughout most cases, thus making manageable and understandable what might otherwise seem to be an endless and unfathomable sea of information. There are, of course, an unlimited number of formats that can be utilized. However, it is best to find one that suits your needs and stick to it. Consistency breeds both efficiency and the security that when called upon you will know where to look in your brief for the information you are asked to give.

Any format, as long as it presents the essential elements of a case in an organized fashion, can be used. Experience, however, has led *Casenote® Legal Briefs* to develop and utilize the following format because of its logical flow and universal applicability.

NATURE OF CASE: This is a brief statement of the legal character and procedural status of the case (e.g., "Appeal of a burglary conviction").

There are many different alternatives open to a litigant dissatisfied with a court ruling. The key to determining which one has been used is to discover *who is asking this court for what.*

This first entry in the brief should be kept as *short as possible.* Use the court's terminology if you understand it. But since jurisdictions vary as to the titles of pleadings, the best entry is the one that addresses who wants what in this proceeding, not the one that sounds most like the court's language.

RULE OF LAW: A statement of the general principle of law that the case illustrates (e.g., "An acceptance that varies any term of the offer is considered a rejection and counteroffer").

Determining the rule of law of a case is a procedure similar to determining the issue of the case. Avoid being fooled by red herrings; there may be a few rules of law mentioned in the case excerpt, but usually only one is *the* rule with which the casebook editor is concerned. The techniques used to locate the issue, described below, may also be utilized to find the rule of law. Generally, your best guide is simply the chapter heading. It is a clue to the point the casebook editor seeks to make and should be kept in mind when reading every case in the respective section.

FACTS: A synopsis of only the essential facts of the case, i.e., those bearing upon or leading up to the issue.

The facts entry should be a short statement of the events and transactions that led one party to initiate legal proceedings against another in the first place. While some cases conveniently state the salient facts at the beginning of the decision, in other instances they will have to be culled from hiding places throughout the text, even from concurring and dissenting opinions. Some of the "facts" will often be in dispute and should be so noted. Conflicting evidence may be briefly pointed up. "Hard" facts must be included. Both must be *relevant* in order to be listed in the facts entry. It is impossible to tell what is relevant until the entire case is read, as the ultimate determination of the rights and liabilities of the parties may turn on something buried deep in the opinion.

Generally, the facts entry should not be longer than three to five *short* sentences.

It is often helpful to identify the role played by a party in a given context. For example, in a construction contract case the identification of a party as the "contractor" or "builder" alleviates the need to tell that that party was the one who was supposed to have built the house.

It is always helpful, and a good general practice, to identify the "plaintiff" and the "defendant." This may seem elementary and uncomplicated, but, especially in view of the creative editing practiced by some casebook editors, it is sometimes a difficult or even impossible task. Bear in mind that the *party presently* seeking something from this court may not be the plaintiff, and that sometimes only the cross-claim of a defendant is treated in the excerpt. Confusing or misaligning the parties can ruin your analysis and understanding of the case.

ISSUE: A statement of the general legal question answered by or illustrated in the case. For clarity, the issue is best put in the form of a question capable of a "yes" or "no" answer. In reality, the issue is simply the Rule of Law put in the form of a question (e.g., "May an offer be accepted by performance?").

The major problem presented in discerning what is *the* issue in the case is that an opinion usually purports to raise and answer several questions. However, except for rare cases, only one such question is really the issue in the case. Collateral issues not necessary to the resolution of the matter in controversy are handled by the court by language known as *"obiter dictum"* or merely *"dictum."* While dicta may be included later in the brief, they have no place under the issue heading.

To find the issue, ask *who wants what* and then go on to ask *why did that party succeed or fail in getting it.* Once this is determined, the "why" should be turned into a question.

The complexity of the issues in the cases will vary, but in all cases a single-sentence question should sum up the issue. *In a few cases,* there will be two, or even more rarely, three issues of equal importance to the resolution of the case. Each should be expressed in a single-sentence question.

Since many issues are resolved by a court in coming to a final disposition of a case, the casebook editor will reproduce the portion of the opinion containing the issue or issues most relevant to the area of law under scrutiny. A noted law professor gave this advice: "Close the book; look at the title on the cover." Chances are, if it is Property, you need not concern yourself with whether, for example, the federal government's treatment of the plaintiff's land really raises a federal question sufficient to support jurisdiction on this ground in federal court.

The same rule applies to chapter headings designating sub-areas within the subjects. They tip you off as to what the text is designed to teach. The cases are arranged in a casebook to show a progression or development of the law, so that the preceding cases may also help.

It is also most important to remember to *read the notes and questions* at the end of a case to determine what the editors wanted you to have gleaned from it.

HOLDING AND DECISION: This section should succinctly explain the rationale of the court in arriving at its decision. In capsulizing the "reasoning" of the court, it should always include an application of the general rule or rules of law to the specific facts of the case. Hidden justifications come to light in this entry: the reasons for the state of the law, the public policies, the biases and prejudices, those considerations that influence the justices' thinking and, ultimately, the outcome of the case. At the end, there should be a short indication of the disposition or procedural resolution of the case (e.g., "Decision of the trial court for Mr. Smith (P) reversed").

The foregoing format is designed to help you "digest" the reams of case material with which you will be faced in your law school career. Once mastered by practice, it will place at your fingertips the information the authors of your casebooks have sought to impart to you in case-by-case illustration and analysis.

B. Be as Economical as Possible in Briefing Cases

Once armed with a format that encourages succinctness, it is as important to be economical with regard to the time spent on the actual reading of the case as it is to be economical in the writing of the brief itself. This does not mean "skimming" a case. Rather, it means reading the case with an "eye" trained to recognize into which "section" of your brief a particular passage or line fits and having a system for quickly and precisely marking the case so that the passages fitting any one particular part of the brief can be easily identified and brought together in a concise and accurate manner when the brief is actually written.

It is of no use to simply repeat everything in the opinion of the court; record only enough information to trigger your recollection of what the court said. Nevertheless, an accurate statement of the "law of the case," i.e., the legal principle applied to the facts, is absolutely essential to class preparation and to learning the law under the case method.

To that end, it is important to develop a "shorthand" that you can use to make marginal notations. These notations will tell you at a glance in which section of the brief you will be placing that particular passage or portion of the opinion.

Some students prefer to underline all the salient portions of the opinion (with a pencil or colored underliner marker), making marginal notations as they go along. Others prefer the color-coded method of underlining, utilizing different colors of markers to underline the salient portions of the case, each separate color being used to represent a different section of the brief. For example, blue underlining could be used for passages relating to the rule of law, yellow for those relating to the issue, and green for those relating to the holding and decision, etc. While it has its advocates, the color-coded method can be confusing and time-consuming (all that time spent on changing colored markers). Furthermore, it can interfere with the continuity and concentration many students deem essential to the reading of a case for maximum comprehension. In the end, however, it is a matter of personal preference and style. Just remember, whatever method you use, underlining must be used sparingly or its value is lost.

If you take the marginal notation route, an efficient and easy method is to go along underlining the key portions of the case and placing in the margin alongside them the following "markers" to indicate where a particular passage or line "belongs" in the brief you will write:

N	(NATURE OF CASE)
RL	(RULE OF LAW)
I	(ISSUE)
HL	(HOLDING AND DECISION, relates to the RULE OF LAW behind the decision)
HR	(HOLDING AND DECISION, gives the RATIONALE or reasoning behind the decision)
HA	(HOLDING AND DECISION, applies the general principle(s) of law to the facts of the case to arrive at the decision)

Remember that a particular passage may well contain information necessary to more than one part of your brief, in which case you simply note that in the margin. If you are using the color-coded underlining method instead of marginal notation, simply make asterisks or checks in the margin next to the passage in question in the colors that indicate the additional sections of the brief where it might be utilized.

The economy of utilizing "shorthand" in marking cases for briefing can be maintained in the actual brief writing process itself by utilizing "law student shorthand" within the brief. There are many commonly used words and phrases for which abbreviations can be substituted in your briefs (and in your class notes also). You can develop abbreviations that are personal to you and which will save you a lot of time. A reference list of briefing abbreviations can be found on page x of this book.

C. Use Both the Briefing Process and the Brief as a Learning Tool

Now that you have a format and the tools for briefing cases efficiently, the most important thing is to make the time spent in briefing profitable to you and to make the most advantageous use of the briefs you create. Of course, the briefs are invaluable for classroom reference when you are called upon to explain or analyze a particular case. However, they are also useful in reviewing for exams. A quick glance at the fact summary should bring the case to mind, and a rereading of the rule of law should enable you to go over the underlying legal concept in your mind, how it was applied in that particular case, and how it might apply in other factual settings.

As to the value to be derived from engaging in the briefing process itself, there is an immediate benefit that arises from being forced to sift through the essential facts and reasoning from the court's opinion and to succinctly express them in your own words in your brief. The process ensures that you understand the case and the point that it illustrates, and that means you will be ready to absorb further analysis and information brought forth in class. It also ensures you will have something to say when called upon in class. The briefing process helps develop a mental agility for getting to the *gist* of a case and for identifying, expounding on, and applying the legal concepts and issues found there. The briefing process is the mental process on which you must rely in taking law school examinations; it is also the mental process upon which lawyers rely in serving their clients and in making a living.

Abbreviations for Briefs

acceptance	acp
affirmed	aff
answer	ans
assumption of risk	a/r
attorney	atty
beyond a reasonable doubt	b/r/d
bona fide purchaser	BFP
breach of contract	br/k
cause of action	c/a
common law	c/l
Constitution	Con
constitutional	con
contract	K
contributory negligence	c/n
cross	x
cross-complaint	x/c
cross-examination	x/ex
cruel and unusual punishment	c/u/p
defendant	D
dismissed	dis
double jeopardy	d/j
due process	d/p
equal protection	e/p
equity	eq
evidence	ev
exclude	exc
exclusionary rule	exc/r
felony	f/n
freedom of speech	f/s
good faith	g/f
habeas corpus	h/c
hearsay	hr
husband	H
injunction	inj
in loco parentis	ILP
inter vivos	I/v
joint tenancy	j/t
judgment	judgt
jurisdiction	jur
last clear chance	LCC
long-arm statute	LAS
majority view	maj
meeting of minds	MOM
minority view	min
Miranda rule	Mir/r
Miranda warnings	Mir/w
negligence	neg
notice	ntc
nuisance	nus
obligation	ob
obscene	obs
offer	O
offeree	OE
offeror	OR
ordinance	ord
pain and suffering	p/s
parol evidence	p/e
plaintiff	P
prima facie	p/f
probable cause	p/c
proximate cause	px/c
real property	r/p
reasonable doubt	r/d
reasonable man	r/m
rebuttable presumption	rb/p
remanded	rem
res ipsa loquitur	RIL
respondeat superior	r/s
Restatement	RS
reversed	rev
Rule Against Perpetuities	RAP
search and seizure	s/s
search warrant	s/w
self-defense	s/d
specific performance	s/p
statute	S
statute of frauds	S/F
statute of limitations	S/L
summary judgment	s/j
tenancy at will	t/w
tenancy in common	t/c
tenant	t
third party	TP
third party beneficiary	TPB
transferred intent	TI
unconscionable	uncon
unconstitutional	unconst
undue influence	u/e
Uniform Commercial Code	UCC
unilateral	uni
vendee	VE
vendor	VR
versus	v
void for vagueness	VFV
weight of authority	w/a
weight of the evidence	w/e
wife	W
with	w/
within	w/i
without	w/o
without prejudice	w/o/p
wrongful death	wr/d

Table of Cases

CHAPTER 1

Development of Liability Based upon Fault

Quick Reference Rules of Law

Hulle v. Orynge (The Case of Thorns)

[Parties not identified.]

K.B., Y.B.M. 6 Edw.4, fol.7, pl.18 (1466)

NATURE OF CASE: Action for damages due to a trespass.

FACT SUMMARY: [Facts not stated in casebook excerpt.]

RULE OF LAW

Every trespass on land that causes damage is actionable.

FACTS: [Facts not stated in casebook excerpt.]

ISSUE: Is every trespass that causes damage actionable?

HOLDING AND DECISION: (Brian, arguing as counsel) Yes. Every trespass that causes damage is actionable. Fault is not required for liability. If a person does something, he must do it in a manner that does not cause damage or injury to another person. Every unwarranted invasion of property is actionable, irrespective of the intent of the tortfeasor. For example, if timber from *A*'s lot falls on *B*'s house and damages it, *A* is liable. Similarly, if *A* injures *B* with a stick that *A* is using in self-defense against *C*, *A* is liable to *B*.

ANALYSIS

The tortfeasor is held strictly liable in a trespass case, even if the trespass is innocent. [Note that the attorney's opinion seems to have been adopted by the court; subsequent to this case, he became a Chief Justice of the Court of Common Pleas.] But see *Weaver v. Ward,* King's Bench, Hobart 134, 80 Eng. Rep. 284 (1616), where no trespass was found in an action brought for accidental trespass of assault and battery as between skirmishing soldiers.

Quicknotes

LIABILITY Any obligation or responsibility.

TRESPASS Unlawful interference with, or damage to, the real or personal property of another.

Weaver v. Ward

Injured soldier (P) v. Shooting soldier (D)

K. B., Hobart 134, 80 Eng. Rep. 284 (1616)

NATURE OF CASE: Action to recover damages for assault and battery.

FACT SUMMARY: During a military exercise, Ward's (D) musket accidentally discharged, injuring Weaver (P).

RULE OF LAW

An actor is liable for injury directly caused by his act unless he can prove himself utterly without fault.

FACTS: Ward (D) and Weaver (P) were participants in a military exercise. During the exercise, Ward's (D) musket accidentally discharged, injuring Weaver (P). Ward (D) contended that the accidental nature of his action should be a defense. The lower court held, as a matter of law, that a showing of accident alone is not a defense to an injury caused by Ward (D). The court gave judgment for Weaver (P) by sustaining his demurrer to the answer.

ISSUE: Is an actor excused from liability for the consequence of his act if he can prove that the injury occurred utterly without his fault?

HOLDING AND DECISION: [Judge not stated in casebook excerpt.] Yes. The court held that an actor would be excused from liability if he could show the lack of any fault. However, the court considered the voluntary nature of the act of firing the musket as involving an aspect of fault and affirmed the judgment for Weaver (P). Apparently, the court would have found differently were the action of firing found to be involuntary.

ANALYSIS

This is one of the first cases clearly recognizing that some form of fault may be necessary for imposition of liability upon an actor. Modernly, the test for imposition of liability under a fault-based negligence theory is whether a reasonable person might have taken the defendant's action. If a reasonable person might have acted as the defendant's did, then there is no negligence, no fault, and, consequently, no liability.

Quicknotes

ACTION OF TRESPASS An action to recover damages resulting from the wrongful interference with a party's person, property or rights.

Brown v. Kendall

Injured dog owner (P) v. Stick-wielding dog owner (D)

Mass. Sup. Jud. Ct., 60 Mass. (6 Cush.) 292 (1850)

NATURE OF CASE: Trespass for assault and battery.

FACT SUMMARY: Kendall (D), while attempting to separate his dog from Brown's (P) dog, when the two dogs were fighting, accidentally struck Brown (P) with a stick.

RULE OF LAW

If in the prosecution of a lawful act, a casualty purely accidental arises, i.e., the injury was unavoidable, and the conduct of the defendant was free from blame, no action can be supported for an injury arising therefrom.

FACTS: Two dogs, owned by Brown (P) and Kendall (D) respectively, were fighting. Kendall (D) attempted to separate the dogs with a stick. When he raised the stick to strike the dogs, Kendall (D) stepped back to avoid the dogs as they approached him, and he accidentally struck Brown (P), who was behind him, in the eye, inflicting a serious injury. Brown (P) brought an action in trespass for assault and battery. The trial court instructed the jury that if it was not a necessary act, and Kendall (D) was not in duty bound to part the dogs, he was responsible for the consequences of the blow, unless it appeared he exercised extraordinary care, so the accident was inevitable. It further instructed that if Kendall (D) had no duty to separate the dogs, then the burden of proving extraordinary care was on him, as well as showing alternatively lack of ordinary care on the part of Brown (P). Following Kendall's (D) death, his executrix (D) took exception to the instructions.

ISSUE: If in the prosecution of a lawful act, a casualty purely accidental arises, can an action be supported for an injury arising therefrom?

HOLDING AND DECISION: (Shaw, C.J.) No. If in the prosecution of a lawful act, a casualty purely accidental arises, i.e., the injury was unavoidable, and the conduct of the defendant was free from blame, no action can be supposed for an injury arising therefrom. The instructions that should have been given are to the effect that Brown (P) could not recover: (1) if at the time of the accident both Kendall (D) and he were using ordinary care; (2) if Kendall (D) was using ordinary care and Brown (P) was not; or (3) if neither were using ordinary care. What constitutes ordinary care will vary with the circumstances, but, generally, it means that kind and degree of care which prudent and cautious people would use. Such is required under the circumstances and is necessary to guard against probable danger. An inevitable accident is one the defendant could not avoid by the use of the kind and degree of care necessary under the circumstances. Because the instructions to the jury placed the burden on Kendall (D) to show that he used extraordinary care or that Brown (P) failed to use ordinary care, rather than having placed the burden of proof on Brown (P) to prove his case, a new trial must be ordered.

ANALYSIS

This case established that some form of fault, negligent or intentional, must form the basis of liability. Consequently, the loss from an unavoidable accident will stay where it falls. This case is also interesting because its discussion includes the concept of contributory negligence, which was fully accepted by the Massachusetts court, but which is losing favor to the concept of comparative negligence today.

Quicknotes

BILL OF EXCEPTIONS A writing setting forth the objections to a ruling, decision or instruction of the trial court for appeal.

COMPARATIVE NEGLIGENCE Doctrine whereby the court in assessing the appropriate measure of damages compares the relative fault of the parties and reduces the amount of damages to be collected by the plaintiff in proportion to his or her degree of fault.

CONTRIBUTORY NEGLIGENCE Behavior on the part of an injured plaintiff falling below the standard of ordinary care that contributes to the defendant's negligence, resulting in the plaintiff's injury.

DICTA Plural of dictum. Statement by a judge in a legal opinion that is not necessary for the resolution of the action.

TRESPASS VI ET ARMIS Action to recover for damages resulting from the direct or immediate injury inflicted by one party against the person or property of another.

Cohen v. Petty

Injured passenger (P) v. Driver (D)

D.C. Ct. App., 62 App. D.C. 187, 65 F.2d 820 (1933)

NATURE OF CASE: Action for injury negligently inflicted.

FACT SUMMARY: Petty (D) suffered a fainting spell while driving which caused an accident in which Cohen (P) was injured.

RULE OF LAW

When injury results from an unforeseeable event there is no liability.

FACTS: Petty's (D) guest, Cohen (P), was injured when Petty (D) lost control of his car and it crashed. The evidence was that the loss of control was due to a fainting spell and that Petty (D) had never before experienced such fainting. The trial court directed a verdict in Petty's (D) favor and Cohen (P) appealed.

ISSUE: Is an actor liable for injury caused when an unforeseeable event causes him to lose control of his actions?

HOLDING AND DECISION: (Groner, J.) No. So long as the loss of control was not foreseeable, there is no negligence. Petty (D) had never fainted before and, consequently, the fainting was unforeseeable. Negligence is the failure to employ that degree of care that a reasonable man would use under the circumstances. If an event is unforeseeable, then a reasonable man would be unable to take any care to prevent it and would be under no duty to do so. There is no liability for the consequences of an unforeseeable event. Affirmed.

ANALYSIS

An unavoidable accident is one that could not have been prevented by the exercise of reasonable care. If an occurrence is unforeseeable it cannot be prevented. However, had Petty (D) known that he was subject to fainting spells, foreseeability would exist and driving would have become an unreasonable risk and injury therefrom would have resulted in liability. The case indicates that negligence is to be judged in terms of risk foreseeability.

Quicknotes

BINDING INSTRUCTIONS A jury instruction informing jurors how to resolve an action if specified circumstances are determined to exist.

FORESEEABILITY A reasonable expectation that an act or omission would result in injury.

Spano v. Perini Corp.

Garage and car owner (P) v. Blasting company (D)

N.Y. Ct. App., 25 N.Y.2d 11, 250 N.E.2d 31, *on remand*, 33 A.D.2d 516, 304 N.Y.S.2d 15 (1969)

NATURE OF CASE: Property damage based on strict liability.

FACT SUMMARY: Blasting by Perini Corp. (D), while building a tunnel, wrecked Spano's (P) garage on nearby property.

RULE OF LAW

(1) One who engages in blasting is responsible for damage caused without any showing of fault.
(2) Proof of trespass is not necessary to recovery in strict liability.

FACTS: Spano (P) owned a garage, which was wrecked by shock waves from a dynamite blast set off by Perini Corp. (D) on nearby property. There was no physical trespass caused by the blast nor was there any proof of negligence on the part of the defendant. In addition to the foregoing, suit was also brought for damages to Davis's (P) automobile, which had been in the garage at the time of the blast. The two suits were consolidated and judgment was for Spano (P) and Davis (P). Perini Corp. (D) appealed, and the appellate court reversed. Davis (P) and Spano (P) appealed.

ISSUE:

(1) Is one who engages in blasting responsible for damage caused without any showing of fault?
(2) Is proof of trespass necessary to recovery in strict liability?

HOLDING AND DECISION: (Fuld, C.J.)

(1) Yes. One who engages in blasting is responsible for damage caused without any showing of fault. This case recognizes that, under the doctrine of strict liability, an actor is liable for damage caused by abnormally dangerous activity without regard to fault. The rationale is that one who engages in an abnormally dangerous activity should bear the loss as opposed to the injured and innocent victim.
(2) No. Proof of trespass is not necessary to recovery in strict liability. The early common law would have distinguished between the physical invasion, which was a trespass, and the concussion, which would be a nuisance. For purposes of strict liability, the distinction has been abandoned.

Remanded.

ANALYSIS

This case indicates the traditional approach to strict liability. If an activity cannot be made safe even by the exercise of utmost care, then strict liability applies. This is the majority view. In many jurisdictions, the protection of strict liability has been extended to food, drugs, and products. In those jurisdictions, if a defect exists in the product when it left the manufacturer, the manufacturer will be absolutely liable.

Quicknotes

STRICT LIABILITY Liability for all injuries proximately caused by a party's conducting of certain inherently dangerous activities without regard to negligence or fault.

CHAPTER 2

Intentional Interference with Person or Property

Quick Reference Rules of Law

Garratt v. Dailey

Arthritic woman (P) v. Five-year-old boy (D)

Wash. Sup. Ct., 46 Wash. 2d 197, 279 P.2d 1091 (1955)

NATURE OF CASE: Action to recover damages for battery

FACT SUMMARY: Brian Dailey (D) pulled a chair out from under Ruth Garratt (P) as she began to sit down in it.

RULE OF LAW
The intent necessary for the commission of a battery is present when the person acts, knowing with substantial certainty that the harmful contact will occur.

FACTS: Ruth Garratt (P) alleged that Brian Dailey (D), who was five years old, pulled a chair out from under her as she was sitting down, thereby causing her to fall and break her hip. Brian Dailey (D) alleged that he picked up the chair and sat down in it, and then noticed that Ruth Garratt (P) was about to sit down where the chair had been. However, upon a second appeal, it was found that he knew when he moved the chair that Ruth Garratt (P) was about to sit down in it.

ISSUE: Is an intent to harm another necessary for the commission of a battery, when the defendant knows that his actions will result in an offensive contact?

HOLDING AND DECISION: (Hill, J.) No. While battery requires an intentional infliction of a harmful bodily contact, this does not mean that there must be an intent (or desire) to cause harm or even to cause the contact. A harmful bodily contact is inflicted intentionally when the person knows with substantial certainty that the contact will occur. In this case, the trial court ultimately found that Brian Dailey (D) moved the chair from under Ruth Garratt (P) while she was in the process of sitting down, and that he therefore knew with substantial certainty that she would attempt to sit down where the chair had been and that she would fall (come into contact with the ground). Brian Daily's (D) intent to cause a harmful bodily contact is inferred from his knowledge that the contact would occur. Remanded.

ANALYSIS

This decision's holding regarding the nature of the intent needed for a battery is representative of the nature of intent required for any intentional tort (such as assault, false imprisonment, trespass). Thus, the general view of intent is that where a reasonable person in the position of the defendant would believe that a certain result was substantially certain to follow his acts, the defendant will be considered to intend that result.

Quicknotes

BATTERY Unlawful contact with the body of another person.

Wagner v. State

Injured (P) v. State government (D)

Utah Sup. Ct., 2005 UT 54, 122 P.3d 599 (2005)

NATURE OF CASE: Certiorari review of granted motion to dismiss.

FACT SUMMARY: Wagner (P) was attacked by a mentally handicapped man in the custody and care of a state (D) agency.

RULE OF LAW

The intentional tort of battery requires only an intent to contact with that contact legally harmful or offensive, but does not require an intent to cause harm thereby.

FACTS: Tracy Wagner (P) was in line at a K-Mart when Sam Giese, a mentally incapacitated patient of the Utah State Development Center (USDC) (D), attacked her and caused injuries. Giese was at K-Mart with a caretaker who was taking him out as part of a treatment program. Giese had a history of violence. Wagner (P) and her husband, Robert, sued USDC (D) and the Utah Department of Human Services (the Department) (D) for failure to properly supervise Giese while under their care. USDC (D) and the Department (D) moved to dismiss the claim based on Rule 12(b)(6) for failure to state a claim because the state (D) retains immunity for the intentional tort of battery. The Wagners (P) stated the claim was not one of battery but one of negligence. The court granted the state's (D) motion and the Wagners (P) appealed. The court of appeals affirmed and the Wagners (P) filed a petition for certiorari. This court granted the petition and issued a writ of certiorari.

ISSUE: Does the intentional tort of battery require only an intent to contact with that contact legally harmful or offensive, but does not require an intent to cause harm thereby?

HOLDING AND DECISION: (Wilkins, C.J.) Yes. The intentional tort of battery requires only an intent to contact with that contact legally harmful or offensive, but does not require an intent to cause harm thereby. Reviewing a 12(b)(6) motion requires reviewing the facts in the light most favorable to the non-movant. Here, the state's (D) position is Giese intended to make contact with Wagner (P) and the contact was offensive as a matter of law, so it constituted battery for which the state (D) was immune. The Wagners (P) argued battery requires an intent to make contact and an intent to cause harm. They contend Giese was not mentally competent to form the intent to cause harm, so his contact could not have constituted a battery. Determining the definition of battery necessarily determines whether the state has retained immunity for Giese's actions. The Restatement (Second) of Torts is adopted in Utah and requires only the intention to make contact. The intention is that of contact and not that of the consequence of the contact. The intent of the act is demonstrated by a person pulling a trigger in a vast desert. The act is that of pulling the trigger while the consequence might be the intentional tort of battery if the person intended to shoot an individual or negligence if the bullet hits a person unexpectedly appearing in the vast desert. The Wagners' (P) argument would provide a complete defense to battery if the actor did not intend to commit harm. The court here overrules *Matheson v. Pearson*, 619 P.2d 321 (Utah 1980), which was decided prior to Utah adopting the Restatement (Second) of Torts and contradicts later decided cases. The "harmful or offensive" contact cannot be viewed from the perspective of the actor but must be from the objective perspective of the court. Society has not simply consented to violent contacts from mentally handicapped people merely because those individuals cannot form the legal intent to harm. It might not be appropriate for the state (D) to have retained immunity in these situations, but that is not for the court to decide. Affirmed.

ANALYSIS

The Utah court confirms the law as one of "single intent" which is only intent to make contact. Some courts do not follow the Restatement (Second) of Torts and apply "dual intent" which is intent to make contact and intent for that contact to be harmful or offensive. Consent to the contact may be an affirmative defense in both instances. Determination of the jurisdiction as "single" or "dual" intent is important to analysis of any intentional tort case.

Quicknotes

BATTERY Unlawful contact with the body of another person.

INTENTIONAL TORT A legal wrong resulting in a breach of duty, which is intentionally or purposefully committed by the wrongdoer.

Ranson v. Kitner

Dog owner (P) v. Hunters (D)

Ill. App. Ct., 31 Ill. App. 241 (1889)

NATURE OF CASE: Appeal from award of damages for injury to personal property.

FACT SUMMARY: Appellants (D), while hunting wolves, killed appellee's (P) dog, believing it to have been a wolf.

RULE OF LAW
Mistake does not absolve an actor from liability for the harm caused by his or her intentional act.

FACTS: While hunting wolves, the appellants (D) spotted the appellee's (P) dog. Due to the dog's striking resemblance to a wolf, they mistakenly killed it. The appellee (P) sued the appellants (D) to recover the value of the dog, and the trial court awarded the appellee (P) $50 in damages. The appellants (D) appealed, arguing that they should not have been held liable for the harm caused by their conduct because they had acted in good faith.

ISSUE: Does mistake absolve an actor from liability for the harm caused by his intentional act?

HOLDING AND DECISION: (Conger, J.) No. Mistake does not absolve an actor from liability for the harm caused by his intentional act. The appellants (D) intended to kill the animal, and their good-faith belief that it was a wolf does not relieve them from liability for the consequences of their act. Affirmed.

ANALYSIS

The general rule is that mistake is no defense to an intentional tort. Because intent is held to be present when a result is substantially certain to occur, without regard to the actor's desire, the actor's belief as to the nature of the result of his or her conduct is normally irrelevant. Thus, in the case at hand, the tortfeasors were liable for killing the dog, despite the fact that they meant only to kill wolves, because they intended to kill the animal that was the victim of their hunt. All the same, it remained a loss for the dog's owner regardless of the tortfeasors' good-faith mistake.

Quicknotes

MISTAKE An act or failure to perform due to a lack of knowledge or a misconception as to a law or fact.

McGuire v. Almy

Nurse (P) v. Violent ward (D)

Mass. Sup. Jud. Ct., 297 Mass. 323, 8 N.E.2d 760 (1937)

NATURE OF CASE: Action for damages for assault and battery.

FACT SUMMARY: Almy (D), an insane ward, injured her nurse, McGuire (P), during a rage.

RULE OF LAW

An insane person may be capable of entertaining the intent to commit a battery.

FACTS: McGuire (P), a registered nurse, had been hired to give 24-hour care to Almy (D), an insane person. Almy (D) had a violent attack during which she broke furniture and warned McGuire (P) not to enter her room or she would be killed. After entering, McGuire (P) approached Almy (D), who stood in striking position with a piece of furniture raised above her head. When McGuire (P) grabbed for the hand with the weapon, Almy (D) struck her. There was a jury verdict for McGuire (P). Almy (D) appealed the denial of her motion for a directed verdict.

ISSUE: May an insane person be liable for a battery?

HOLDING AND DECISION: (Qua, J.) Yes. An insane person is to be judged by the same standards as a normal person. Intent to do the act is the key to a battery, not the intent to harm. If an insane person can entertain that intent, then he can be liable for battery. The standard applies even though an insane person's acts may be uncontrollable. The loss is placed on the insane actor rather than on the innocent victim. Judgment for the plaintiff.

ANALYSIS

This case represents a basic policy decision that is generally accepted. The policy reasons are: (1) the loss is better borne by the actor than the victim; (2) liability will encourage closer surveillance by custodians; and (3) insanity is easily feigned. The counter-argument is that one should not be liable for acts not within his control. This is not generally accepted.

Quicknotes

BATTERY Unlawful contact with the body of another person.

DIRECTED VERDICT A verdict ordered by the court in a jury trial.

Talmage v. Smith

Blinded boy (P) v. Property owner (D)

Mich. Sup. Ct., 101 Mich. 370, 59 N.W. 656 (1894)

NATURE OF CASE: Action for damages for trespass to person.

FACT SUMMARY: Smith (D) threw a stick at a boy, but instead hit Talmage (P).

RULE OF LAW

When one intends to harm another, it is no defense that an unintended person was harmed instead.

FACTS: Talmage (P) and several other boys were playing on the roofs of sheds on Smith's (D) property. Smith (D) ordered the boys to get down, but before they had succeeded in doing so, Smith (D) took a stick and threw it, hitting Talmage (P) in the eye with such force that the sight in that eye was lost. There was evidence that Smith (D) threw the stick intending to hit Byron Smith, another boy on the roof, and not Talmage (P).

ISSUE: When the defendant intends to harm one person but accidentally harms another person instead of the original intended victim, can the defendant be held liable for a battery to the second person?

HOLDING AND DECISION: (Montgomery, J.) Yes. When a defendant acts with the intention to inflict an unwarranted injury on someone, it does not matter that a person other than the one intended was harmed. Therefore, in this case, Smith (D) could not be relieved from liability because he hit Talmage (P) with the stick, instead of Byron Smith, the boy he intended to hit. Affirmed.

ANALYSIS

This decision provides an example of the prominent doctrine of "transferred intent." This doctrine holds that once there is an intent to commit an intentional tort, for example, battery, it does not matter that the person harmed was not the one intended. The intent is transferred from the person intended to the one actually harmed. The doctrine of "transferred intent" may perhaps represent the most peculiar aspect of "intent" in intentional interferences with persons or property, in that a defendant may be liable for harming another (or his property) even if he or she had no desire to harm, or even knowledge that such harm would occur to that person (or property). The reason for the doctrine may be because of the feeling that when the defendant does act intentionally with respect to one person, the defendant is morally "at fault" and should not escape liability because of the fortuitous circumstance of injuring an unintended victim.

Quicknotes

TRESPASS UPON THE PERSON Cause of action to recover from any injuries to the plaintiff's person, resulting from the direct and immediate injury inflicted by another party.

Cole v. Turner

[Parties not identified.]

Nisi Prius, 6 Modern Rep. 149, 90 Eng. Rep. 958 (1704)

NATURE OF CASE: Action for assault and battery.

FACT SUMMARY: [Facts not stated in casebook excerpt.]

RULE OF LAW

The least touching of another in anger is a battery. An unintentional touching without violence is not a battery. The use of violence in a rude manner is a battery. An attempt to pass through a narrow way resulting in a struggle sufficient to do injury is a battery.

FACTS: [Facts not stated in casebook excerpt.]

ISSUE: [Issue not stated in casebook excerpt.]

HOLDING AND DECISION: (Holt, C.J.) An unintentional touching without violence is not a battery. The use of violence in a rude manner is a battery. An attempt to pass through a narrow way resulting in a struggle sufficient to do injury is a battery.

ANALYSIS

The interest protected by an action for battery is the interest in freedom from intentional and unpermitted contacts with the plaintiff's person. Consequently, an unintentional or socially acceptable contact is not a battery. The gist of the action for battery is not the actor's wrongful intent but the absence of consent to the contact.

Quicknotes

BATTERY Unlawful contact with the body of another person.

NISI PRIUS A court having original jurisdiction over a matter.

Wallace v. Rosen

Student's mother (P) v. Teacher (D)

Ind. Ct. App., 765 N.E.2d 192 (2002)

NATURE OF CASE: Suit to recover damages for an alleged battery.

FACT SUMMARY: A high-school teacher touched a student's mother to encourage her to leave the school building during a fire drill. The student's mother fell down a stairway and alleged that the teacher's touching of her was a battery that caused the injuries she incurred in her fall.

RULE OF LAW

Intentionally touching another person cannot constitute battery if the touching does not occur in a rude, insolent, or angry manner.

FACTS: Mable Wallace (P) went to an Indianapolis high school to deliver homework to her daughter, who was a student at the school. Wallace (P) stopped to talk to her daughter near the top of a stairway in the school, and two of her daughter's friends joined them. Then the school initiated a fire drill. Students used the stairway to file out of the building. Wallace (P), though, moved to the landing at the top of the stairway, where she interfered with students as they tried to leave the building. Teacher Harriet Rosen (D) noticed Wallace (P) and the three students with whom she was speaking at the top of the stairway. Wallace (P) did not hear Rosen (D) tell the group to "move it," so Rosen (D) touched Wallace (P) on the back to get Wallace's (P) attention. Wallace (P), who was recovering from foot surgery at the time, then fell down the stairs. At trial Rosen (D) admitted touching Wallace (P) on her back but denied pushing her. After the evidence closed, the trial judge refused to give the jury Wallace's (P) tendered instruction on battery, which in pertinent part defined battery as "the knowing or intentional touching of one person by another in a rude, insolent, or angry manner." The jury returned a verdict for Rosen (D) and the school district that employed her. Wallace (P) appealed, challenging, in part, the trial judge's refusal to instruct the jury on battery as Wallace (P) requested at trial.

ISSUE: Can intentionally touching another person constitute battery if the touching does not occur in a rude, insolent, or angry manner?

HOLDING AND DECISION: (Kirsch, J.) No. Intentionally touching another person cannot constitute battery if the touching does not occur in a rude, insolent, or angry manner. Battery requires intent—but it also requires more. In tort law, intent need not mean that a defendant behaves with hostility or wants to harm the plaintiff. What tortious intent does require is an intent to violate another person's interests in a legally prohibited way. When the alleged tort is battery, as in Rosen's (D) touching of Wallace (P) here, the alleged touching must have occurred both intentionally and in a rude, insolent, or angry manner. In today's crowded world, some touching is normal and necessary. The test for determining the tortious manner of an intentional touching, then, is whether it would offend an ordinary person who is not unduly sensitive about her personal dignity. Here, reviewing the evidence in the light most favorable to the judgment, Rosen (D) merely touched Wallace's (P) shoulder and turned her toward the stairway during a fire drill. Such a touching cannot be the rude, insolent, or angry intentional touching that the law of battery requires. The evidence therefore supports the trial judge's discretionary rejection of Wallace's tendered instruction. Affirmed.

ANALYSIS

One of the concurring opinions in *Wallace*, Judge Sullivan's, would have affirmed the trial court's refusal of Wallace's (P) tendered instruction because the instruction's last portion would have instructed the jury that a reckless touching, and not necessarily an intentional touching, can constitute battery. As Judge Sullivan wrote, "[t]he alleged battery here was either an intentional touching in a rude, insolent, or angry manner, or it was no battery at all." 765 N.E.2d at 202. This distinction between mental states is a vestige of the ancient relationship between tort law and criminal law, with the contemporary law of battery requiring, as Judge Sullivan emphasized, a more culpable state of mind as a basis for liability.

Quicknotes

BATTERY Unlawful contact with the body of another person.

INTENT The state of mind that exists when one's purpose is to commit a criminal act.

Fisher v. Carrousel Motor Hotel, Inc.

Guest (P) v. Motor hotel (D)

Tex. Sup. Ct., 424 S.W.2d 627 (1967)

NATURE OF CASE: Action to recover damages for battery.

FACT SUMMARY: Fisher (P), while in line at a buffet luncheon, had his plate snatched from his hands by an employee of the Carrousel Motor Hotel (D), who also insulted him.

RULE OF LAW

A battery may be committed even though there is no physical contact with the person's body, so long as there is contact with something that is attached to, or closely identified with, the body.

FACTS: Fisher (P), a black man, was attending a meeting at the Carrousel Motor Hotel (Hotel) (D). While he was standing in a buffet lunch line, holding his plate, an employee of Hotel (D) came up to Fisher (P) and snatched his plate from his hands, shouting at the same time that Hotel (D) would not serve a black man. While Fisher (P) was not physically injured, the incident was highly offensive to him, and he sued Hotel (D) for damages for battery. A jury found for plaintiff, but the trial court handed down judgment for the defendants notwithstanding the verdict. The court of appeals affirmed and plaintiff appealed to the state supreme court.

ISSUE: Is there a battery when there is no actual physical contact with the plaintiff's body, but only with something held in the plaintiff's hands?

HOLDING AND DECISION: (Greenhill, J.) Yes. Any offensive contact with a person's body or anything closely identified with the body is a battery. The reason for this is that battery involves an offense to the person's dignity, not just a physical injury. Therefore, an unpermitted invasion of the person's body is not necessary, because an unpermitted contact with something closely identified with the body, such as with something held in the hands, may be just as offensive as an unpermitted contact with the person. In this case, the snatching of the plate Fisher (P) held in his hands, in an offensive manner, was an unpermitted, offensive contact with something closely connected to Fisher's (P) body, and was therefore a battery. Reversed.

ANALYSIS

This decision is representative of the prevailing view that actual physical contact with the body is not necessary for battery. It should be noted that actual physical injury of the plaintiff is not a requirement of battery. The rationale for this is the same reason for not requiring actual physical contact with the person: battery protects not only a person's interest in not being physically harmed, but also protects a person's personal integrity. An unpermitted, offensive contact with the person or anything identified with the person, violates a person's integrity, even if one is not harmed. A battery, therefore, entitles the plaintiff to recover damages for mental disturbance—such as fright, or humiliation or embarrassment. Thus, in this decision, Fisher (P) recovered damages for the humiliation he suffered as a result of the battery.

Quicknotes

BATTERY Unlawful contact with the body of another person.

HARMFUL OR OFFENSIVE CONTACT Contact that causes injury or annoyance to another individual.

I de S et ux. v. W de S

Tavern owner and wife (P) v. Attacker (D)

Assizes, Y.B. Lib. Ass. fol. 99, pl. 60 (1348)

NATURE OF CASE: Action to recover damages for trespass, because of an assault made upon the plaintiff.

FACT SUMMARY: W (D) struck at I's wife M (P) with a hatchet, but missed her.

RULE OF LAW

An act that causes another to be fearful of a harmful or offensive contact is known as an assault, and the plaintiff may recover damages, even though there is no actual physical contact or physical harm.

FACTS: W (D) was beating with a hatchet upon the door of I's (P) tavern, which was closed for the night. When I's (P) wife M (P) put her head out the window and ordered W (D) to stop, he struck at her with the hatchet. W (D) claimed there was no trespass for which the woman (P) could recover, since he did not actually harm her.

ISSUE: Is an act that causes another to be fearful of a harmful or offensive contact known as an assault, and may the plaintiff may recover damages, even though there is no actual physical contact or physical harm?

HOLDING AND DECISION: (Thorpe, C.J.) Yes. An act that causes another to be fearful of a harmful or offensive contact is known as an assault, and the plaintiff may recover damages, even though there is no actual physical contact or physical harm. In this case, W (D) struck at I's (P) wife M (P) with a hatchet, thereby frightening her. The harm was in the assault itself, and she is entitled to recover damages from W (D).

ANALYSIS

This case was one of the earliest decisions to recognize a mental, as opposed to physical, injury, and the need to compensate the plaintiff for such an injury. Thus, the law of assault developed to protect a person's interest in freedom from being fearful of a harmful or offensive contact upon his person, as opposed to battery, which protected a person from the injury itself.

Quicknotes

ASSAULT The intentional placing of another in fear of immediate bodily injury.

Western Union Telegraph Co. v. Hill

Company employing agent (D) v. Husband and wife (P)

Ala. Ct. App., 25 Ala. App. 540, 150 So. 709 (1933)

NATURE OF CASE: Action to recover damages for assault.

FACT SUMMARY: Sapp allegedly made a grab for Hill's (P) wife over a counter, the dimensions of which made contact virtually impossible.

RULE OF LAW

There can be no assault unless there is an apparent ability to carry out a threatened contact.

FACTS: Sapp was an employee of Western Union Telegraph Co. (Western Union) (D). When Mrs. Hill (P) came to the office to have her clock repaired, Sapp, who had been drinking, suggested illicit sexual relations. Mrs. Hill (P) claimed that Sapp then made a grab for her shoulder over the counter, but she jumped back. The counter was 4 /2" high, coming to Sapp's armpits, and so wide that by stretching over it Sapp's fingers barely reached the end of it. The photographs showed it was unlikely that Sapp could have reached Mrs. Hill (P). Judgment went for Hill (P) and Western Union (D) appealed, claiming there was no apparent ability to carry out the threat as a matter of law.

ISSUE: Can an assault be committed where the actor lacks the apparent ability to carry out his threat?

HOLDING AND DECISION: (Samford, J.) No. The apprehension raised by the alleged threat must be a reasonable one based on an apparent ability to carry out an immediate battery. The court found that there was a sufficient conflict in the evidence to raise a jury question on the existence of an apparent ability to carry out the battery. The case was reversed on other grounds relating to the liability of the corporation for the acts of its employees.

ANALYSIS

This case illustrates the principle that the apprehension raised must be a reasonable one. Only an apparent ability to commit a battery could raise a reasonable fear and consequently only those may be redressed by the action for assault. The requirement of a reasonable fear is a policy limitation designed to guard against insubstantial or feigned fears as a ground for litigation. Alabama Code § 8264—Damages for injuries to person or reputation—all damages that the wife may be entitled to recover for injuries to her person or reputation, are her separate property. Section 8268—How wife sues; and must be sued—The wife must sue alone, at law or in equity, upon all contracts made by or with her, or for the recovery of her separate property, or for injuries to such property, or for its rents, income, or profits, or for all injuries to her person or reputation; and upon all contracts made by her, or engagements into which she enters, and for all torts committed by her, she must be sued as if she were sole. Prior to the enactment of the above statutes (1928) the wife could not sue alone for personal injuries but had to sue jointly with her husband and for his sole benefit.

Quicknotes

APPREHENSION Fear; anticipation of harm or injury.

ASSAULT The intentional placing of another in fear of immediate bodily injury.

BATTERY Unlawful contact with the body of another person.

EQUITY Fairness; justice; the determination of a matter consistent with principles of fairness and not in strict compliance with rules of law.

Big Town Nursing Home, Inc. v. Newman

Nursing home (D) v. Confined retiree (P)

Tex. Civ. App. Ct., 461 S.W.2d 195 (1970)

NATURE OF CASE: Appeal from award of damages for false imprisonment.

FACT SUMMARY: Big Town Nursing Home, Inc. (D) appealed from a judgment for Newman (P) for actual and exemplary damages in his false imprisonment action, arguing that the award of exemplary damages was improper in this case.

RULE OF LAW

One can be held liable for exemplary damages in a false imprisonment action if the false imprisonment is done intentionally in violation of the rights of the plaintiff.

FACTS: Newman (P) was taken to Big Town Nursing Home, Inc. (Big Town) (D) by his nephew on September 19, 1968. The admission papers provided that he would not be kept in Big Town (D) for any length of time against his will. Three days later, Newman (P) decided he wanted to leave and attempted to call a taxi. He was prevented from leaving by Big Town's (D) employees. Newman (P) was advised that he could not leave or use the phone and his grip and clothes were locked up. He attempted to leave on several occasions, but was caught and brought back against his will each time. He was locked up in Wing 3, a ward for senile patients, incorrigibles, alcoholics, etc. Payment of Newman's (P) social security checks was changed without his authorization. When he finally escaped on November 11, 1968, he had lost 30 pounds. He sued Big Town (D) for false imprisonment and received an award for actual and exemplary damages. Big Town (D) appealed this decision, arguing that the award of exemplary damages was improper in the case.

ISSUE: Can one be held liable for exemplary damages in a false imprisonment case if the false imprisonment is done intentionally in violation of the rights of the plaintiff?

HOLDING AND DECISION: (McDonald, C.J.) Yes. One can be held liable for exemplary damages in a false imprisonment action if the false imprisonment is done intentionally in violation of the rights of the plaintiff. False imprisonment is the direct restraint by one person of the physical liberty of another without adequate justification. The entire course of Big Town's (D) conduct was to prevent Newman (P) from leaving, in violation of his admission papers. There was no court order for Newman's (P) commitment, and the admissions papers clearly indicated to Big Town (D) Newman's (P) right to leave at will. Since Big Town (D) acted intentionally in violation of Newman's (P) rights, the award of exemplary damages was proper. [Newman (P) accepted a remittitur suggested by the court.] Affirmed as modified.

ANALYSIS

Whether or not an action for false imprisonment will succeed depends upon whether or not there is a reasonable means of escape available to the person confined. If an individual could remain imprisoned without risk of physical harm, there is authority for the proposition that one cannot recover for injuries suffered in making an unreasonably dangerous escape.

Quicknotes

EXEMPLARY DAMAGES Damages exceeding the actual injury suffered for the purposes of punishment, deterrence and comfort to plaintiff.

FALSE IMPRISONMENT Intentional tort whereby the victim is unlawfully restrained.

REMITTITUR The authority of the court to reduce the amount of damages awarded by the jury.

Parvi v. City of Kingston

Inebriated complainant (P) v. Municipality (D)

N.Y. Ct. App., 41 N.Y.2d 553, 362 N.E.2d 960 (1977)

NATURE OF CASE: Appeal from dismissal of false imprisonment action.

FACT SUMMARY: Parvi (P), who was picked up by police while intoxicated and driven by them to an abandoned golf course to "sleep it off," was unable to recall whether he was aware of his confinement at the time.

RULE OF LAW

A plaintiff's present recollection of a previous consciousness of confinement is not required to make out a prima facie case for false imprisonment.

FACTS: Parvi (P) was found by police in downtown Kingston (D), New York, in an intoxicated state. He told the officers he had nowhere to go, and they drove him to an abandoned golf course outside of town to "sleep it off." Parvi (P) brought an action for false imprisonment against the City (D) on the ground that the officers had confined him. The testimony as to whether Parvi (P) willingly went to the golf course conflicted. Parvi (P) testified that he could not presently recall whether he was conscious of being confined at the time he was taken out of town. The trial court dismissed the complaint and Parvi (P) appealed.

ISSUE: Is a plaintiff's present recollection of previous consciousness of confinement required to make out a prima facie case for false imprisonment?

HOLDING AND DECISION: (Fuchsberg, J.) No. While there is some division of authority in the United States as to the necessity of proof of consciousness of confinement in false imprisonment actions, the law of New York is settled on that point. False imprisonment, as a dignitary tort, is not suffered unless the victim knows the invasion or confinement. The trial court dismissed the case on the ground that Parvi (P) could not recall on the witness stand that he had been aware of his confinement when he was removed to the golf course. However, a plaintiff's present recollection of previous consciousness of confinement is not required to make out the prima facie case for false imprisonment. It may well be that the alcohol or Parvi's (P) injuries wiped out the memory of a consciousness that existed at the time the officers picked him up. This is not the same as saying he was unaware of the dignitary invasion when it occurred. Reversed and remanded.

DISSENT: (Breitel, C.J.) Parvi (P) has no memory of the entire incident and admitted that his only knowledge of it stemmed from subsequent conversations. He thus failed to make out even a prima facie case for false imprisonment.

ANALYSIS

There remains some question among the various jurisdictions as to whether the action for false imprisonment will lie in the absence of knowledge of the confinement. A substantial number of states require such knowledge. The Restatement (Second) of Torts provides that the action will lie without such knowledge if the plaintiff suffers some actual injury or damage from the confinement.

Quicknotes

FALSE IMPRISONMENT Intentional tort whereby the victim is unlawfully restrained.

PRIMA FACIE CASE An action where the plaintiff introduces sufficient evidence to submit the issue to the judge or jury for determination.

SINA QUA NON Without which not; a necessary element or requirement.

Hardy v. LaBelle's Distributing Co.

Accused employee (P) v. Department store (D)

Mont. Sup. Ct., 203 Mont. 263, 661 P.2d 35 (1983)

NATURE OF CASE: Appeal from denial of damages for false imprisonment.

FACT SUMMARY: Hardy (P) contended she was falsely imprisoned by LaBelle's Distributing Co. (D) when interrogated about an alleged theft.

RULE OF LAW

False imprisonment exists upon the unlawful restraint of an individual against his or her will.

FACTS: Hardy (P), a temporary employee of LaBelle's Distributing Co. (LaBelle) (D), was asked by another employee to tour the store. She was taken to the manager's office where she was detained and informed that she had been accused of stealing a watch. Other employees and at least one uniformed police officer were present in the office. Hardy (P) denied the accusations and voluntarily underwent a polygraph examination. She passed and was given an apology. She brought suit for false imprisonment, contending that she had been detained against her will. At trial, Hardy (P) testified that she voluntarily stayed in the office to attempt to exonerate herself. The jury returned a verdict for LaBelle (D), and Hardy (P) appealed.

ISSUE: Is false imprisonment the unlawful restraint of an individual against his will?

HOLDING AND DECISION: (Gulbrandson, J.) Yes. False imprisonment is the unlawful restraint of an individual against his will. In this case, Hardy (P) admitted that she felt restrained from leaving the office, yet would have stayed anyway to exonerate herself. Thus, she was not restrained against her will and was not falsely imprisoned. Affirmed.

ANALYSIS

False imprisonment requires actual confinement, either through physical force or threats. The plaintiff also must know of the confinement. Thus, if an unconscious individual is confined, yet released before he or she awakens, no cause of action exists. Further, the existence of a safe, reasonable avenue of escape must be known by the plaintiff before such can be used by the defendant to preclude his or her liability.

Quicknotes

FALSE IMPRISONMENT Intentional tort whereby the victim is unlawfully restrained.

Enright v. Groves

Dog-at-large owner (P) v. Policeman and municipality (D)

Colo. Ct. App., 39 Colo. App. 39, 560 P.2d 851 (1977)

NATURE OF CASE: Appeal from award of damages for false imprisonment.

FACT SUMMARY: Officer Groves (D) appealed an award of damages to Mrs. Enright (P), whom he arrested for failure to produce her driver's license during his investigation of a "dog leash" ordinance violation.

RULE OF LAW

A claim for false arrest will not lie if an officer has a valid warrant or probable cause to believe that an offense has been committed and that the person who was arrested committed it.

FACTS: Groves (D), a uniformed police officer for the City of Ft. Collins (D), observed a dog running loose in violation of the Ft. Collins (D) "dog leash" ordinance. He saw the dog approach Mrs. Enright's (P) house, and he asked her 11-year-old son if the dog was his. The son replied that it was his dog, and that his mother was sitting in the car parked at the curb. Mrs. Enright (P) got out of the car and spoke with Groves (D). Groves (D) demanded her driver's license. Enright (P) gave her name and address but refused to produce her license. Groves (D) ordered her to produce her license or go to jail. She responded, "Isn't this ridiculous?" whereupon Groves (D) said, "Let's go," and arrested her. Enright (P), who was convicted of violating the "dog leash" ordinance, sought and was awarded $1,500 damages for false imprisonment. Groves (D) and Ft. Collins (D) appealed arguing that there was probable cause for the arrest, and that Enright (P) was convicted.

ISSUE: Will a claim for false arrest lie if an officer has a valid warrant or probable cause to believe that an offense has been committed and that the person who was arrested committed it?

HOLDING AND DECISION: (Smith, J.) No. A claim for false arrest will not lie if an officer has a valid warrant or probable cause to believe that an offense has been committed and that the person who was arrested committed it. Conviction of the crime for which one is specifically arrested is a complete defense to a subsequent claim for false arrest. In this case, Groves (D) did not arrest Enright (P) for violation of the "dog leash" ordinance. He arrested her for failure to produce her driver's license upon demand. No statute or case law requires a citizen to produce a driver's license upon demand unless that person is the driver of a vehicle and the demand is made in that connection. Enright (P) was not driving when the demand and arrest were made. Accordingly, Groves (D) was without authority to demand her license and to use force in arresting Enright (P). Affirmed.

ANALYSIS

In *Whitman v. Atchison, T. & S. F. R. Co.*, 85 Kan. 150, 116 (1911), P. 234, a case of false imprisonment was made where the plaintiff, who fell and broke his leg while attempting to leave defendant's train, was detained by defendant's conductor. The conductor claimed that the law required him to have the injured plaintiff fill out a statement about the accident, but the plaintiff was unreasonably delayed for 20 minutes in getting medical help while in considerable pain. Note that a plaintiff can also hold a private citizen who aids a police officer in the making of a false arrest liable for damages. See Annot., 98 A. L. R. 3d 542 (1980).

Quicknotes

FALSE ARREST The illegal arrest or restraint of a person's liberty.

PROBABLE CAUSE A reasonable basis for believing that a crime has been committed.

Whittaker v. Sandford

Former cult member (P) v. Religious cult leader (D)

Me. Sup. Jud. Ct., 110 Me. 77, 85 A. 399 (1912)

NATURE OF CASE: Suit to recover damages for false imprisonment.

FACT SUMMARY: After crossing the Atlantic, the defendant failed to meet the terms of his agreement with plaintiff, thus making it impossible for plaintiff to reach shore, detaining her for over a month.

RULE OF LAW

(1) To commit a false imprisonment it is not necessary that the tortfeasor actually apply physical force to the person of the plaintiff, but that plaintiff be physically constrained.

(2) A false imprisonment occurs when there is an intentional breach of an obligation to take active steps to release plaintiff.

FACTS: Plaintiff and defendant agreed that plaintiff would travel on defendant's yacht across the Atlantic, on the condition that defendant would not attempt to detain plaintiff on board for any purpose, particularly that of reconverting plaintiff to the religious movement with which defendant was affiliated. Upon arrival in port, defendant refused to furnish a boat so that plaintiff was detained on defendant's yacht for over a month.

ISSUE:

(1) Is a false imprisonment committed when defendant exerts no physical force on plaintiff's person but obstructs plaintiff from leaving a confined area?

(2) Is a false imprisonment committed when there is a breach of a promise to take active steps to release plaintiff?

HOLDING AND DECISION: (Savage, J.)

(1) Yes. Even though defendant does not actually lay hands on plaintiff, there is still a false imprisonment because plaintiff's freedom of movement is limited.

(2) Yes. When defendant breaches his duty to take active measures to release plaintiff, defendant commits the tort of false imprisonment.

Verdict on liability affirmed.

ANALYSIS

In the holding, Judge Savage cites another example of false imprisonment: "If one should, without right, turn the key in a door, and thereby prevent a person in the room from leaving, it would be the simplest form of unlawful imprisonment. The restraint is physical. The four walls and the locked door are physical impediments to escape."

Quicknotes

FALSE IMPRISONMENT Intentional tort whereby the victim is unlawfully restrained.

State Rubbish Collectors Assn. v. Siliznoff

Trash collectors' union (P) v. Holdout (D)

Cal. Sup. Ct., 38 Cal. 2d 330, 240 P.2d 282 (1952)

NATURE OF CASE: Appeal from damages awarded on cross-complaint alleging damages for mental suffering.

FACT SUMMARY: The State Rubbish Collectors Assn. ("the Association") (P) threatened to beat up Siliznoff (D), destroy his truck, or force him out of business unless he joined the Association (P) and paid dues to it.

RULE OF LAW

A complaint based on mental suffering caused by the outrageous conduct of defendant will be sustained if there was no privilege to act in such a manner.

FACTS: Siliznoff (D) had collected rubbish from a certain brewery while he was not a member of the State Rubbish Collectors Assn. ("the Association") (P). This action prompted the Association (P) to threaten to inflict bodily harm on Siliznoff (D), ruin his truck, or destroy his business unless he joined the ranks of their membership and paid them dues. The Association (D) sued to collect on notes it had forced Siliznoff (D) to sign, and he counterclaimed for damages for the emotional distress caused by the Association's (P) threats. The jury found for Siliznoff, and the Association (P) appealed.

ISSUE: Is a defendant who makes extremely anti-social threats on a plaintiff, but who inflicts mental, not physical, injury, liable in a tort suit based on mental suffering?

HOLDING AND DECISION: (Traynor, J.) Yes. In the absence of a privilege, any conduct of a defendant which exceeds the bounds of societal decency and causes extreme mental suffering, but no physical injury, constitutes the basis for a cause of action in mental suffering. The foundation of this opinion is that because mental suffering is an inherent element of the damages suffered in battery, assault, false imprisonment, and defamation, it is anomalous to deny recovery in cases in which the defendant's intentional misconduct fell short of producing some physical injury but produced intense mental distress. Affirmed.

ANALYSIS

The case represents a breakthrough in the tort law; traditionally, recovery was only allowed for physical injury, and words of force that caused damage were not recognized as an invasion into an area protected by the tort law. One of the main reasons such claims were not recognized as valid was the absence of tangible physical injury and the existence of any injury was hard to prove.

Quicknotes

INTENTIONAL INFLICTION OF EMOTIONAL DISTRESS Intentional and extreme behavior on the part of the wrongdoer with the intent to cause the victim to suffer from severe emotional distress, or acting with reckless indifference, resulting in the victim's suffering from severe emotional distress.

Slocum v. Food Fair Stores of Florida

Insulted customer (P) v. Grocery store (D)

Fla. Sup. Ct., 100 So. 2d 396 (1958)

NATURE OF CASE: Suit to recover damages for mental suffering.

FACT SUMMARY: While shopping in Food Fair Stores of Florida (D), Slocum (P) was given an abusive reply to inquiries made to a grocery clerk. The rude remarks aggravated her heart condition and caused her emotional distress.

RULE OF LAW

No recovery is allowed for mental suffering when the abuse, insult, or profanity is not accompanied with serious threats to life or other affronts that amount to more than mere annoyances.

FACTS: While shopping in Food Fair Stores of Florida (Food Fair) (D), Slocum (P) inquired into the price of an item and was met with a rude and malicious reply by a store employee. The remark upset Slocum (P) mentally and allegedly caused a heart attack.

ISSUE: Is abusive language that causes mental anguish enough to maintain a cause of action for emotional distress?

HOLDING AND DECISION: (Drew, J.) No. Defendants are not liable for mere insults, indignities, or even threats regardless of the consequences these words may have for plaintiffs. In this case, Food Fair's (D) agent only refused to help Slocum (P) in a rude manner and made an adolescent comment about her bodily odor. This is enough to cause only little distress in the reasonable person. In order to recover, there must be severe emotional distress as an outgrowth of the conduct. The purpose of this is that if trivial insults were actionable at law then there could well be a curtailment of free speech, for those who fear legal repercussions for expressing disrespectful opinions might be deterred from speaking. Affirmed.

ANALYSIS

Most jurisdictions accept the rule that there can be no recovery for mental suffering inflicted by petty insults. The judges expect that most individuals who interact in society are hardened and are thus prepared to deal with uncomplimentary affronts. Therefore, no tort remedy is necessary for the reasonable person. Further, courts see mental suffering as being much less quantitative and, hence, much less susceptible of proof than claims for physical injury so that there is a likelihood of many fictitious claims arising.

Quicknotes

ACTIONABLE Unlawful activity from which a cause of action may arise.

BUSINESS INVITEE A party invited onto another's property in order to conduct business to whom the owner owes a duty of care to protect against known dangers and those capable of discovery through reasonable care.

COMMON CARRIER An entity whose business is the transport of persons or property.

IN TOTO In whole.

RESPONDEAT SUPERIOR Rule that the principal is responsible for tortious acts committed by its agents in the scope of their agency or authority.

Harris v. Jones

Stutterer (P) v. Supervisor and employer (D)

Md. Ct. App., 281 Md. 560, 380 A.2d 611 (1977)

NATURE OF CASE: Appeal from denial of damages for intentional infliction of emotional distress.

FACT SUMMARY: Harris (P) sued his employer, General Motors (D), and a supervisor, Jones (D), for damages resulting from insulting and cruel behavior that allegedly worsened his stuttering condition.

RULE OF LAW

In order to recover damages resulting from the intentional infliction of emotional distress, a plaintiff must show that the distress suffered was "severe."

FACTS: Harris (P) worked at a General Motors (D) plant. He was a lifelong stutterer, was very self-conscious about the fact and, hence, also suffered from bad nerves. Harris (P) charged that Jones (D), a supervisor at the plant, "maliciously and cruelly" ridiculed him, causing him acute nervousness and resulting in an increase in his stuttering. Furthermore, Harris (P) charged that General Motors (D) had ratified Jones's (D) conduct. At trial for intentional infliction of emotional distress, a jury found for Harris (P) and awarded damages. The court then dismissed the verdict and entered judgment for Jones (D) and General Motors (D). Harris (P) appealed.

ISSUE: In order to recover damages resulting from the intentional infliction of emotional distress, must a plaintiff prove that the distress suffered was "severe"?

HOLDING AND DECISION: (Murphy, C.J.) Yes. In order to recover damages resulting from the intentional infliction of emotional distress, a plaintiff must show that the distress suffered was "severe." Maryland is among the 37 jurisdictions recognizing that the intentional infliction of emotional distress, standing alone, may constitute a valid tort action. However, in order for such an action to lie, four separate elements must be shown: (1) the conduct must be intentional or reckless; (2) the conduct must be extreme and outrageous; (3) there must be a causal connection between the wrongful conduct and the emotional distress; and (4) the emotional distress must be severe. In the instant action, Harris (P) was not able to show the fourth element. He admitted that both his speech impediment and nervous conduct existed prior to his subjection to Jones's (D) insults. However, he contended, Jones's (D) conduct served to aggravate his problems. While this might be true, there is no evidence that such aggravation reached the level of severity required by the law governing the tort of intentional infliction of emotional distress. Absent such evidence, an action cannot lie. Thus, the judgment notwithstanding the verdict was properly granted. Affirmed.

ANALYSIS

Section 46 of the Restatement (Second) of Torts discusses the second element of intentional infliction of emotional distress, that of whether the defendant's conduct was extreme and outrageous, in comment D: "Liability has been found only where the conduct has been so outrageous in character, and so extreme in degree, as to go beyond all possible bounds of decency, and to be regarded as atrocious, and utterly intolerable in a civilized community." As such, mere insults, indignities, "or other trivialities" are not actionable.

Quicknotes

INTENTIONAL INFLICTION OF EMOTIONAL DISTRESS Intentional and extreme behavior on the part of the wrongdoer with the intent to cause the victim to suffer from severe emotional distress, or acting with reckless indifference, resulting in the victim's suffering from severe emotional distress.

JUDGMENT N.O.V. A judgment entered by the trial judge reversing a jury verdict if the jury's determination has no basis in law or fact.

Taylor v. Vallelunga

Victim's daughter (P) v. Assailant (D)

Cal. Ct. App., 171 Cal. App. 2d 107, 339 P.2d 910 (1959)

NATURE OF CASE: Suit to recover damages for battery and mental suffering caused by the battery.

FACT SUMMARY: Unknown to Vallelunga (D), Taylor (P) watched a physical attack upon her father by Vallelunga (D) and as a result suffered mental anguish.

RULE OF LAW

In order to recover damages for mental suffering that is the result of defendant's injury of a third person, the plaintiff must show that defendant reasonably anticipated mental stress would be inflicted on the plaintiff.

FACTS: Taylor (P) witnessed the beating of her father by Vallelunga (D), which caused her mental anguish. Taylor's (P) presence at the scene of the assault was unknown to Vallelunga (D) and he had no intent to inflict the severe emotional upset on Taylor (P).

ISSUE: Can damages for mental distress brought about by injury to a third person be recovered from one who had no cognizance of the presence of the emotionally upset plaintiff and no intent to cause that plaintiff mental injury?

HOLDING AND DECISION: (O'Donnell, J.) No. The defendant who does harm to a third party must be aware of plaintiff's presence and intend to cause the mental distress in plaintiff; otherwise, as in this case, plaintiff has no cause of action for the tort of mental suffering. Affirmed.

ANALYSIS

Most courts have analogous holdings to the present one, in disallowing recovery in situations where defendant has no knowledge of plaintiff's presence and no intent to injure the plaintiff mentally. These decisions have been rationalized by the doctrine of substantial certainty, i.e., given the injury to a third person there was a foreseeability of some mental effect on plaintiff. In cases where defendant has knowledge of plaintiff's presence and injures a third person, recovery for mental suffering is granted.

Quicknotes

GENERAL DEMURRER The assertion that the opposing party's pleadings are insufficient and that the objecting party should not be made to answer.

Dougherty v. Stepp

Landowner (P) v. Surveyor (D)

N.C. Sup. Ct., 18 N.C. 371 (1835)

NATURE OF CASE: Action to recover damages for trespass.

FACT SUMMARY: Stepp (D) entered the enclosed property of Dougherty (P) without permission.

RULE OF LAW

Every unprivileged entry onto the land of another is a trespass regardless of the amount of damages.

FACTS: Stepp (D) entered the enclosed property of Dougherty (P) without consent. While on the property, Stepp (D) surveyed the land. However, the surveying techniques involved no marking of trees or cutting of bushes. Dougherty (P) sued Stepp (D) for trespass. The jury found for Stepp (D), and Dougherty (P) appealed.

ISSUE: Is every unprivileged entry onto the land of another a trespass regardless of the amount of damages?

HOLDING AND DECISION: (Ruffin, C.J.) Yes. Every unprivileged entry onto the land of another is a trespass regardless of the amount of damages. An action for trespass can be maintained without proof of any actual damage. From every entry against the will of the landowner, the law implies some damage; "if nothing more, the treading down the grass or herbage." Reversed and new trial granted.

ANALYSIS

The purpose of this decision is that at common law the trespass action was a safeguard against the repeated trespasser. Without the deterrent of legal liability for mere entry on the land without damage, the trespasser could after numerous entries onto the land claim an easement by prescription. The case also presents the old rule that a person is strictly liable for trespass, i.e., if he enters the land of another without permission, he is liable regardless of his intent or negligence in doing so. The present rule is that liability for trespass exists only if there is intentional or negligent intrusion.

Quicknotes

PRESCRIPTIVE EASEMENT A manner of acquiring an easement in another's property by continuous and uninterrupted use in satisfaction of the statutory requirements of adverse possession.

TRESPASS QUARE CLAUSUM FREGIT Action for damages sustained as a result of the defendant's illegal entry onto plaintiff's property.

Herrin v. Sutherland

Property owner (P) v. Hunter (D)

Mont. Sup. Ct., 74 Mont. 587, 241 P. 328 (1925)

NATURE OF CASE: Suit to recover damages for trespass.

FACT SUMMARY: While hunting, the defendant fired shots over the property and possessions of the plaintiff.

RULE OF LAW

A trespass to the land occurs when bullets or other foreign particles violate the airspace above the land.

FACTS: While hunting, the defendant repeatedly fired his shotgun at game birds in flight over the plaintiff's property. These shots deprived plaintiff of the quiet, peaceful enjoyment of his home and property.

ISSUE: Does a trespass to the land occur when bullets or other foreign particles violate the airspace above the land?

HOLDING AND DECISION: (Callaway, C.J.) Yes. If an alien object disturbs the airspace reasonably close to the surface of the land, a trespass is deemed to have been committed. The basis of the ruling is that the court envisions both the areas above and below the surface of the land as being legally protected from any unlawful intrusion. If these areas were not safeguarded by trespass laws, the property owner could not fully enjoy the premises. Further, the court fears that material crossing over the land in the airspace closely annexed to the property poses a potential source of danger to both persons and property. Affirmed.

ANALYSIS

The case is one among many that stands for the proposition that trespass occurs not only when there is a contact with or other entry onto the land, but also when there is intrusion in the space directly above the land. The case stands between the common-law notion that the owner's right to possession extends infinitely upward and the more modern view that only the airspace immediately above the land is protected by trespass laws.

Quicknotes

AIR SPACE The area that exists directly above real estate.

DEFAULT Failure to carry out a legal obligation.

NOMINAL Small; trivial; with reference to name only.

TRESPASS Unlawful interference with, or damage to, the real or personal property of another.

Rogers v. Board of Road Comm'rs for Kent County

Decedent's wife (P) v. Snow fencer (D)

Mich. Sup. Ct., 319 Mich. 661, 30 N.W.2d 358 (1947)

NATURE OF CASE: Suit to recover damages for death based on negligence and trespass.

FACT SUMMARY: After the license of the Board of Road Commissioners ("the Board") (D) to place a snow fence on Rogers's (P) property had expired, Rogers's (P) husband fatally injured himself due to the presence of the Board's (D) fencepost.

RULE OF LAW

Failure to remove a structure upon expiration of the license allowing the structure on plaintiff's land is a continuing trespass.

FACTS: Two years prior to the date of the fatal injury of Rogers's (P) husband, the Board of Road Commissioners for Kent County ("the Board") (D) obtained a license to place a winter snow fence on Rogers's (P) property on the condition it be removed at the end of each winter season. In clear violation of the condition of the license, the complete fence was not taken down by the summer and thus, as a result, Rogers's (P) husband, as he mowed the field, hit the fence, which caused him to fall and sustain a fatal injury. Rogers claimed trespass and negligence by the Board (D). The Board (P) filed a motion to dismiss based on the pleadings and on the ground of governmental immunity. The lower court dismissed the case, ruling that the action was based on negligence, there was no basis for any finding of trespass, and that the defense of governmental immunity applied to the facts presented in Rogers's (P) declaration. Rogers (P) appealed.

ISSUE: Is failure to remove a structure upon expiration of the license allowing the structure on plaintiff's land is a continuing trespass?

HOLDING AND DECISION: (Reid, J.) Yes. Failure to remove a structure upon expiration of the license allowing the structure on plaintiff's land is a continuing trespass. Although at one point there may have been a justification for the structure's presence on the land, after this justification is ended, any injury inflicted by the presence of that structure, whether negligent or not, is a trespass. Thus, even though the fence was licensed to be there during the winter, this license having terminated with the advent of the summer, any injury resulting from its unlawful presence entitled the landowner to damages for trespass. The court's decision reflects the concern of the law for the exclusiveness of possession. Reversed and remanded.

ANALYSIS

The case belongs to a line of precedents that hold that once a trespass has been committed the intruder is liable for all the consequences of his trespass. His liability encompasses all tangible damage inflicted on the land itself, the person of the possessor and his family, and his chattels. The liability flows regardless of the foreseeability of the event. The reasoning that justifies such a rule is that the liability is based on the doctrine of transferred intent, not negligence, that is, the intent to enter the land unlawfully is transferred to establish a basis of liability for all other injuries caused. Hence, the fact that such harms could not be anticipated is irrelevant to building or attacking liability.

Quicknotes

CHATTEL An article of personal property, as distinguished from real property; a thing personal and moveable.

NEGLIGENCE Conduct falling below the standard of care that a reasonable person would demonstrate under similar conditions.

TRANSFERRED INTENT When a perpetrator acts with the intent to commit a crime against one person, and instead commits that crime against another person, the perpetrator's intent is transferred to the actual victim for the purposes of liability.

Glidden v. Szybiak

Wounded child (P) v. Dog owner (D)

N.H. Sup. Ct., 95 N.H. 318, 63 A.2d 233 (1949)

NATURE OF CASE: Suit to recover damages with a defense of trespass to chattel.

FACT SUMMARY: Elaine Glidden (P), a four-year-old child, played with and disturbed a dog belonging to Jane Szybiak (D), whereupon the dog bit Glidden (P).

RULE OF LAW

In order for a cause of action based upon trespass to chattels to be sustained, chattel owner must prove more than nominal damages to and intentional interference with the chattel.

FACTS: Four-year-old Elaine Glidden (P) encountered the dog, Toby, owned by Jane Szybiak (D), on the porch of a store. Glidden (P) played with and eventually provoked the dog, which snapped at her and inflicted wounds. Glidden (P) sued. Szybiak (D) argued that Glidden (P) was barred from recovery because she was trespassing at the time of her injury.

ISSUE: Can there be a defense of trespass to chattels when there are neither more than nominal damages nor intentional interference involving the chattel?

HOLDING AND DECISION: (Branch, C.J.) Yes. In order for a cause of action based upon trespass to chattels to be sustained, the chattel owner must prove more than nominal damages to and intentional interference with the chattel. In this case, a trespass to chattels did not exist because there was no significant damage to the chattel. Since a trespass did not occur due to the fact that there was no willful intent to interfere with or do damage to the chattel, i.e., the dog, Szybiak (D) could not rely on an affirmative defense of trespass to chattel. Judgment for the plaintiff.

ANALYSIS

This case represents a departure from the common-law view that no actual damage was necessary to sustain an action for trespass to chattels. Although a technical tort (a tort without actual damages) may be allowed to protect real property from trespass, the inviolability of personal property is not recognized by most contemporary courts.

Quicknotes

NOMINAL DAMAGES A small sum awarded to a plaintiff in order to recognize that he sustained an injury that is either slight or incapable of being established.

TRESPASS Unlawful interference with, or damage to, the real or personal property of another.

TRESPASS TO CHATTELS Action for damages sustained as a result of defendant's unlawful interference with plaintiff's personal property.

CompuServe Inc. v. Cyber Promotions, Inc.

Online service provider (P) v. Advertising company (D)

962 F. Supp. 1015 (S.D. Ohio 1997)

NATURE OF CASE: Application for preliminary injunction.

FACT SUMMARY: CompuServe, Inc. (P) sought a preliminary injunction to restrain Cyber Promotions, Inc. (D) from sending unsolicited e-mails to its subscribers.

RULE OF LAW

An action claiming trespass to chattels allows recovery for interference with the possession of chattels that are not sufficiently important to rise to the level of conversion and requires the defendant to pay the full value of the thing with which he has interfered.

FACTS: Cyber Promotions, Inc. (Cyber) (D) is in the business of sending unsolicited e-mail advertisements on behalf of itself and its clients to Internet users. CompuServe, Inc. (P), a national commercial online computer service, notified Cyber (D) that it was prohibited from sending its e-mails to CompuServe's (P) subscribers and requested that it cease doing so. Cyber (D) instead increased the number of e-mails it sent to CompuServe (P) subscribers. CompuServe (P) sought a preliminary injunction preventing Cyber (D) from sending the unsolicited e-mail advertisements to its subscribers, claiming Cyber's (D) transmission of electronic messages to its computer equipment is actionable under the common-law theory of trespass to chattels.

ISSUE: Does an action claiming trespass to chattels allow recovery for interference with the possession of chattels?

HOLDING AND DECISION: (Graham, J.) Yes. An action claiming trespass to chattels allows recovery for interference with the possession of chattels that are not sufficiently important to rise to the level of conversion and requires the defendant to pay the full value of the thing with which he has interfered. The Restatement § 217(b) provides that a trespass to chattel is committed where the defendant intentionally uses or intermeddles with the chattel in possession of another. The comments define "intermeddling" as intentional physical contact. Electronic signals have been held to satisfy the definition of intermeddling. Here it is clear that CompuServe (P) has a possessory interest in its computer systems and that Cyber (D) has intentionally contacted such systems with its electronic signals. Cyber (D) argued that under the Restatement (Second) of Torts § 221, physical dispossession or substantial interference is required in order for the claim to be actionable. However, § 218 makes clear that an interference or intermeddling not meeting the § 221 definition is still actionable. Here Cyber's (D) mailings to CompuServe (P) subscribers demand disk space and drain CompuServe's processing powers, resulting in a diminution in value of its property. Motion for preliminary injunction granted.

ANALYSIS

CompuServe (P) also argued that it suffered harm under § 218(d) to a legally protected interest, namely its goodwill and business reputation. Due to the large number of e-mail advertisements received, many of CompuServe's (P) customers closed their accounts. The court held that CompuServe's § 218(d) claim was actionable and rejected Cyber's (D) defense that CompuServe (P) was precluded from bringing suit in trespass since it connected itself with the Internet in the first place.

Quicknotes

CHATTEL An article of personal property, as distinguished from real property; a thing personal and moveable.

PRELIMINARY INJUNCTION A judicial mandate issued to require or restrain a party from certain conduct; used to preserve a trial's subject matter or to prevent threatened injury.

TRESPASS Unlawful interference with, or damage to, the real or personal property of another.

Pearson v. Dodd

Columnist (D) v. U.S. Senator (P)

410 F.2d 701 (D.C. Cir.), *cert. denied*, 395 U.S. 947 (1969)

NATURE OF CASE: Appeal from partial summary judgment awarding damages for conversion.

FACT SUMMARY: Pearson (D) appealed from a grant of partial summary judgment for conversion, contending his actions in obtaining copies of certain information and publishing newspaper articles using this information did not amount to a conversion.

RULE OF LAW

The publication of information that does not amount to literary property, scientific invention, or secret plans formulated for the conduct of commerce, without an actual physical conversion of the documents containing the information, does not amount to conversion.

FACTS: Two former employees of Senator Dodd (P) secretly and without authority removed documents from Dodd's (P) files, copied and replaced them, and turned the copies over to Pearson (D). The information contained therein included contents of letters to Dodd (P) from supplicants and office records of an unknown nature. Pearson (D) published articles containing information obtained from the copies. Dodd (P) sued Pearson (D) on theories of conversion and invasion of privacy. The district court granted partial summary judgment in favor of Dodd (P) on the theory of conversion, and denied partial summary judgment in favor of Dodd (P) on the theory of invasion of privacy. From the court's grant of partial summary judgment on the theory of conversion, Pearson (D) appealed the court's grant of partial summary judgment on the conversion claim.

ISSUE: Does the publication of information that does not amount to literary property, scientific invention, or secret plans formulated for the conduct of commerce, absent an actual physical conversion of the documents containing the information, amount to conversion?

HOLDING AND DECISION: (Skelly Wright, J.) No. The publication of information that does not amount to literary property, scientific invention, or secret plans formulated for the conduct of commerce, without an actual physical conversion of the documents containing the information, does not amount to conversion. The measure of damages in a conversion action is the value of the goods converted. Because of the stringent measure of damages, not all interferences with property rights amount to conversions. It is clear from the facts that there has been no physical conversion of the actual original documents. Ideas or information is generally not protected by the law of conversion, but exceptions are made for literary work and scientific research, and information which has been gathered and can be sold as a commodity. The information contained herein does not appear to be this type of property. Since there was no actual conversion of the original documents, and the information utilized by Pearson (D) is not of the type normally protected by the law of conversion, the grant of partial summary judgment to Dodd (P) was improper. Reversed.

ANALYSIS

Most actions brought for conversion involve settling title to disputed goods. Although there is authority for the proposition that a conversion may occur when one who is authorized to use a chattel exceeds the authorization, this view must be tempered in that the unauthorized use must involve a conversion adverse to the rights of the owner.

Quicknotes

CONVERSION The act of depriving an owner of his property without permission or justification.

INVASION OF PRIVACY The violation of an individual's right to be protected against unwarranted interference in his personal affairs, falling into one of four categories: (1) appropriating the individual's likeness or name for commercial benefit; (2) intrusion into the individual's seclusion; (3) public disclosure of private facts regarding the individual; and (4) disclosure of facts placing the individual in a false light.

PARTIAL SUMMARY JUDGMENT Judgment rendered by a court in response to a motion by one of the parties, claiming that the lack of a question of material fact in respect to one of the issues warrants disposition of that issue without going to thc jury.

TRESPASS TO CHATTELS Action for damages sustained as a result of defendant's unlawful interference with plaintiff's personal property.

TROVER An action for damages resulting from the unlawful conversion of, or to recover possession of, personal property.

CHAPTER 3

Privileges

Quick Reference Rules of Law

O'Brien v. Cunard S.S. Co.

Vaccinated passenger (P) v. Steamship company (D)

Mass. Sup. Jud. Ct., 154 Mass. 272, 28 N.E. 266 (1891)

NATURE OF CASE: Action to recover damages for assault and negligence.

FACT SUMMARY: O'Brien (P) held out her arm without objection to the doctor employed by Cunard S.S. Co. (D) to be vaccinated.

RULE OF LAW
Silence and inaction may imply consent to defendant's acts if the circumstances are such that a reasonable person would speak if he or she objected.

FACTS: In order to save its passengers the trouble of being quarantined when they reached the shores of the United States, the Cunard S.S. Co. (the Steamship Company) (D) provided smallpox vaccinations on board ship. The Steamship Company (D) gave notice of this quarantine procedure and of its service in several languages. O'Brien (P) formed a part of the line of women who waited to have the doctor employed by the Steamship Company (D) inject her. Due to her presence in the line and her lack of objection to the vaccination, the doctor assumed that O'Brien (P) consented to receiving the smallpox vaccination. O'Brien (P) alleged that contamination of the vaccine or the site caused ulceration at the site and blistering on her body.

ISSUE: Do silence and inaction imply consent to defendant's acts if the circumstances are such that a reasonable person would speak if he or she objected?

HOLDING AND DECISION: (Knowlton, J.) Yes. Silence and inaction may imply consent to defendant's acts if the circumstances are such that a reasonable person would speak if he or she objected. In this case, consent will be implied from the plaintiff's conduct. In this case, the court looks to the facts that the plaintiff waited in the line designated for those who wished to be vaccinated and passively allowed the doctor to inject her. Affirmed.

ANALYSIS

The case represents the great weight of authority that in determining whether there was consent the court must be guided by the overt words and acts of the plaintiff; subjective states of mind will not be considered.

Quicknotes

CONSENT A voluntary and willful agreement by an individual possessing sufficient mental capacity to undertake an action suggested by another.

Hackbart v. Cincinnati Bengals, Inc.

Football player (P) v. Opposing team (D)

601 F.2d 516 (10th Cir.), *cert. denied,* 444 U.S. 931 (1979)

NATURE OF CASE: Appeal from denial of damages for battery.

FACT SUMMARY: Hackbart (P), a player for the Denver Broncos, was intentionally injured by a member of the Cincinnati Bengals (D) during a professional football game.

RULE OF LAW

An injury inflicted by one player upon another during a professional football game may give rise to liability where the cause of the injury was an intentional blow.

FACTS: Hackbart (P), a member of the Denver Broncos football team, brought suit for injuries arising out of an intentionally administered blow during a regular season game. The blow was administered to the back of Hackbart's (P) head by Charles "Booby" Clark, a member of the opposing team, the Cincinnati Bengals (D). The trial court, noting the violent nature of football and that incidents such as the one complained of by Hackbart (P) are not unusual, ruled that as a matter of law, liability could not issue in such a situation. Hackbart (P) appealed.

ISSUE: May an intentionally inflicted blow by an opposing player during a professional football game give rise to liability for injuries caused thereby?

HOLDING AND DECISION: (Doyle, J.) Yes. A review of the National Football League rules shows that an intentional blow to the head, such as the one complained of here, is clearly prohibited in a professional football game. As such, liability can result from the infliction of such a blow that gives rise to injuries in an opposing ballplayer. The trial court erroneously made its determination based on its observation regarding the violent nature of football as a sport rather than limiting its analysis to the evidence bearing on the liability of the Cincinnati Bengals (D) for the actions of its player. Reversed and remanded.

ANALYSIS

Not only cases involving injured players have arisen in the sporting context. In *Lang v. Amateur Softball Association of America,* 520 P.2d 659 (Okla. 1974), a fan injured by a softball thrown wildly over a fence by a pitcher warming up sued for damages. The court found that the defendant had utilized reasonable care to protect the fans, and that the spectators had impliedly assumed the risk of being hit when they entered the ballpark.

Quicknotes

ASSAULT The intentional placing of another in fear of immediate bodily injury.

ASSUMPTION OF RISK DOCTRINE An affirmative defense to a negligence suit by the defendant contending that the plaintiff knowingly and voluntarily subjected himself to the hazardous condition wholly absolving the defendant of liability for injuries incurred.

BATTERY Unlawful contact with the body of another person.

INTENT The state of mind that exists when one's purpose is to commit a criminal act.

NEGLIGENCE Conduct falling below the standard of care that a reasonable person would demonstrate under similar conditions.

RECKLESSNESS The conscious disregard of substantial and justifiable risk.

Mohr v. Williams

Patient (P) v. Ear specialist (D)

Minn. Sup. Ct., 95 Minn. 261, 104 N.W. 12 (1905)

NATURE OF CASE: Action to recover damages for battery.

FACT SUMMARY: Without Mohr's (P) permission in writing, or orally, Williams (D) operated on her ear.

RULE OF LAW

If the defendant's actions exceed the consent given, and the defendant does a substantially different act than the one authorized, then the defendant is liable.

FACTS: Mohr (P) was admitted to surgery so that her right ear might be operated upon by defendant. When Mohr (P) was unconscious, Williams (D) discovered the right ear was not that serious, but the left was infected. Thus, without awakening Mohr (P), Williams (D) operated on the left ear. Williams (D) only had permission to operate on the right ear. The operation was successful but Mohr (P) nevertheless brought an action for battery. The jury awarded her $14,322, but the trial judge found the award excessive and granted a new trial. Both parties appealed.

ISSUE: If the defendant's actions exceed the consent given, and the defendant does a substantially different act than the one authorized, is the defendant is liable?

HOLDING AND DECISION: (Brown, J.) Yes. If the defendant's actions exceed the consent given, and the defendant does a substantially different act than the one authorized, then the defendant is liable. Unless the physician discovers a condition that endangers the life of his patient during the operation to which the plaintiff consented, there is no consent to a different operation. In this case, the diseased condition of Mohr's (P) left ear was not discovered in the course of the authorized operation but by independent examination after the operation was found to be unnecessary and, further, it was not an eminently dangerous condition. Affirmed.

ANALYSIS

The case falls into the majority view. However, doctors have circumvented the problem of this decision by requiring the patient to give blanket consent to any remedy the physician thinks best.

Quicknotes

BATTERY Unlawful contact with the body of another person.

CONSENT A voluntary and willful agreement by an individual possessing sufficient mental capacity to undertake an action suggested by another.

De May v. Roberts

Doctor (D) and friend (D) v. Woman in labor (P)

Mich. Sup. Ct., 46 Mich. 160, 9 N.W. 146 (1881)

NATURE OF CASE: Action to recover damages for deceit, invasion of privacy, assault, and battery.

FACT SUMMARY: Dr. De May (D) arrived to deliver Roberts's (P) baby and introduced Scattergood (D) into the maternity room on the pretense that Scattergood (D) was Dr. De May's (D) assistant. Roberts (P) alleged that Scattergood (D) watched all that occurred, intruding on her privacy and indecently and wrongfully assaulting her.

RULE OF LAW

(1) There exists no privilege of consent when the plaintiff has consented under a mistaken belief that has been instilled by defendant's deceit.

(2) An assault is perpetrated by the inducement of consent through misrepresentation.

FACTS: Dr. De May (D) entered Roberts's (P) bedroom where she was in labor, in order to perform delivery. With Dr. De May (D) was Scattergood (D), who appeared to be his assistant and whom Dr. De May (D) knew to be untrained professionally, as well as unmarried. The evidence disclosed that Scattergood (D) was present in Roberts's (P) room during labor and that he also took hold of Roberts's (P) hand and held her during a paroxysm of pain. Roberts (P), therefore, contended that Dr. De May's (D) deceit in passing off Scattergood (D) as a physician's aid caused an intrusion upon her privacy. Furthermore, Roberts (P) contended that Scattergood (D) assaulted her when he did indecently, wrongfully, and unlawfully place hands upon her.

ISSUE:

(1) Is there consent when the defendant has misrepresented facts to a plaintiff and this misrepresentation has caused the plaintiff to consent?

(2) Has an assault been committed when the defendant induced plaintiff's consent by means of misrepresentation?

HOLDING AND DECISION: (Martson, C.J.)

(1) No. Consent gained through the defendant's misrepresentation is invalid. In this case, defendant De May (D) introduced Scattergood (D) as a professional. Because Roberts (P) believed Scattergood (D) was examining her, Roberts (P) acquiesced to his presence at her bedside and to his laying his hands upon her. There can be no genuine consent where there is no understanding of the nature of the act to which one consents.

(2) Yes. An assault has been committed when misrepresentation induced plaintiff's consent, for the defense of consent does not exist in favor of one who has obtained that consent by misrepresentation. The policy behind this principle is that a variety of torts could be defended and justified by the commission of another tort, i.e., to gain consent to commit the first tort assault, a wrongdoer could induce consent by means of misrepresentation, another tort. Affirmed.

ANALYSIS

Both holdings of this case seem to represent the mainstream of judicial authority. The case is also typical of early cases that did not recognize a remedy for the infliction of mental suffering unless it could be brought within the scope of some already existing tort remedy. Since it was possible without much pretense to grant recovery on a traditional assault theory, the court avoided granting relief on the then less acceptable doctrine of mental suffering. The case is an early forerunner of right to privacy as a basis of tort liability.

Quicknotes

ASSAULT The intentional placing of another in fear of immediate bodily injury.

CONSENT A voluntary and willful agreement by an individual possessing sufficient mental capacity to undertake an action suggested by another.

MISREPRESENTATION A statement or conduct by one party to another that constitutes a false representation of fact.

PARTURITION The act of giving birth to a child.

Katko v. Briney

Spring gun victim (P) v. Property owner (D)

Iowa Sup. Ct., 183 N.W.2d 657 (1971)

NATURE OF CASE: Appeal from judgment for plaintiff in action to recover compensatory and punitive damages due to physical injury caused by the firing of a spring gun set up by Briney (D).

FACT SUMMARY: In order to protect an uninhabited house, Briney (D) installed a mechanical spring gun whose fire was triggered by the opening of a door; Katko (P) opened the door and the gun fired, severely injuring him.

RULE OF LAW

A landowner does not have a privilege to install, for the purpose of protecting his uninhabited property against unlawful intrusions, a mechanism the sole function of which is the infliction of death or serious harm upon intruders.

FACTS: To guard an unoccupied, isolated house, which had been entered unlawfully on previous occasions, against future unlawful entries, Briney (D) took several precautions such as boarding up the house, posting no trespass signs, and setting up a shotgun trap. There was no warning of the spring gun device, which was rigged so that it would fire when a door was opened. When Katko (P), a trespasser, opened the door, the gun blast seriously wounded him, blowing away a substantial portion of his leg. The wound left Katko (P) permanently disfigured with a shortened leg. A jury returned a verdict for Katko (P), and Briney (D) appealed. The state's highest court granted review.

ISSUE: Does a landowner have a privilege to install, for the purpose of protecting his uninhabited property against unlawful intrusions, a mechanism the sole function of which is the infliction of death or serious harm upon intruders?

HOLDING AND DECISION: (Moore, C.J.) No. A landowner does not have a privilege to install, for the purpose of protecting his uninhabited property against unlawful intrusions, a mechanism the sole function of which is the infliction of death or serious harm upon intruders. The fact that an intruder is acting unlawfully does not justify the maintenance of a mechanical device to protect property that can cause great physical injury. Such a man-killing mechanical device is only permissible if the intruder is committing a violent felony and endangering the lives of the occupants. Affirmed.

DISSENT: (Larson, J.) The majority errs on several points. First, the trial court erred by failing to instruct the jury that it could find that the shotgun installation was not made with the intent to strike or injure an intruder such as Katko (P) but was made for the purpose of frightening away any intruder. Therefore, the matter should have been remanded on the matter of intent. Second, the majority's rule of law has never before been applied to a burglar, but only in the case of vineyard trespassers, and, third, punitive damages should not be allowed where the injured party's conduct was criminal, as was Katko's (P) here.

ANALYSIS

The use of a mechanical device cannot expand the privilege to use physical violence in defense of property. There is a severe limitation on this privilege, for there is no right, whether by mechanical means or by the landowner's hand, to use force that may be lethal. This privilege to use physical force exists only after the landowner's mild methods of expulsion (verbal requests or constrained physical acts) have been met with resistance or when the violence directed at the land is redirected at its occupants. The amount of force that may be utilized cannot exceed the apparent necessities of protecting the land in possession. The necessities are those that would be perceived by a reasonable individual in the property owner's position.

Quicknotes

COMPENSATORY DAMAGES Measure of damages necessary to compensate victim for actual injuries suffered.

PUNITIVE DAMAGES Damages exceeding the actual injury suffered for the purposes of punishment of the defendant, deterrence of the wrongful behavior or comfort to the plaintiff.

SPRING GUN A gun that is set to fire when triggered by an external force.

Bonkowski v. Arlan's Department Store

Shopper (P) v. Department store (D)

Mich. Ct. App., 12 Mich. App. 88, 162 N.W.2d 347 (1968)

NATURE OF CASE: Action to recover damages for false arrest and slander.

FACT SUMMARY: On the grounds of a reasonable suspicion, Arlan's Department Store's (D) detective detained Mrs. Bonkowski (P), and the detention resulted in Mrs. Bonkowski's (P) mental suffering.

RULE OF LAW

A privilege exists by which a shopkeeper is able to detain for a reasonable investigation a person whom the shopkeeper reasonably suspects has unlawfully taken merchandise.

FACTS: On the basis of a report that Mrs. Bonkowski (P) was shoplifting, Arlan's Department Store's (D) detective detained her outside the store and made her reveal the contents of her purse. Mrs. Bonkowski (P) produced sales slips for the items from the store, and this satisfied the detective that she had committed no theft. As a result of this detention, Mrs. Bonkowski (P) suffered psychological trauma.

ISSUE: Does a privilege exist by which a shopkeeper is able to detain for reasonable investigation a person whom the shopkeeper reasonably suspects has unlawfully taken merchandise?

HOLDING AND DECISION: (Fitzgerald, J.) Yes. If the merchant or the merchant's agent reasonably believes the individual has unlawfully taken goods held for sale in the merchant's store, then the merchant enjoys the privilege to detain that individual for a reasonable investigation. The court's reasoning in allowing this privilege is that it guards the shopkeeper from the dilemma of either allowing the suspected person to walk away free, thus assuming the burden of loss for the stolen item himself, or the equally unpalatable choice of arresting the suspect, thus assuming the risk of paying damages in an action for false arrest. Reversed and remanded.

ANALYSIS

The case conforms to a line of cases that hold that a businessman who reasonably suspects a customer of theft may, in order to make reasonable inquiries, hold that person for a short time if that customer has not left the store. The case at bar broadens this principle to allow detention of a customer who has already left the premises.

Quicknotes

JUDGMENT NOTWITHSTANDING THE VERDICT A judgment entered by the trial judge reversing a jury verdict if the jury's determination has no basis in law or fact.

LARCENY The illegal taking of another's property with the intent to deprive the owner thereof.

REMITTITUR The authority of the court to reduce the amount of damages awarded by the jury.

SLANDER Defamatory statement communicated orally.

Surocco v. Geary

Property owner (P) v. Mayor (D)

Cal. Sup. Ct., 3 Cal. 69, 58 Am. Dec. 385 (1853)

NATURE OF CASE: Action to recover damages for buildings and goods destroyed by a gunpowder blast.

FACT SUMMARY: During a fire, Geary (D) blew up buildings owned by Surocco (P) in order to prevent a fire from spreading.

RULE OF LAW

An individual is not personally liable for the damage he creates when, in good faith and under apparent necessity, he destroys the property of another in order to save the surrounding area.

FACTS: To halt the spread of a conflagration that endangered a whole town, Geary (D) destroyed, by means of a gunpowder blast, Surocco's (P) store and house and the goods therein. This destruction was accomplished while Surocco (P) still had time to empty the buildings of goods.

ISSUE: Is an individual personally liable for the damage he creates when, in good faith and under apparent necessity, he destroys the property of another in order to save the surrounding area?

HOLDING AND DECISION: (Murray, C.J.) No. An individual is not personally liable for the damage he creates when, in good faith and under apparent necessity, he destroys the property of another in order to save the surrounding area. The right to destroy property is justified if it is done to prevent a fire or other disaster from proliferating and is done in the good-faith belief that it is a necessity. The purpose of sanctioning this privilege to destroy property in times of emergency is to insure the safety of the entire community, which could be jeopardized if the owner had a right to recover against the individual who saved the community. This right to recovery might deter the community's savior from acting. Reversed.

ANALYSIS

The case is one of a series that condone the individual who acts to avert peril that threatens the public. Such an individual is not liable to the owner whose property has been ruined as long as the individual reasonably believed that such a deed was necessary to prevent a public disaster. There is another body of case law dealing with necessity in which no public interest is at stake. The privilege to protect a private interest is narrowly circumscribed. One may trespass or damage property with immunity from tort liability only to save one's own life or the life of another.

Quicknotes

EXIGENT CIRCUMSTANCES Circumstances requiring an extraordinary or immediate response; an exception to the prohibition on a warrantless arrest or search when police officers believe probable cause to exist and there is no time for obtaining a warrant.

NECESSITY DEFENSE A defense to liability for unlawful activity where the conduct is unavoidable and is justified by preventing the occurrence of a more serious harm.

Vincent v. Lake Erie Transp. Co.

Dock owner (P) v. Steamship company (D)

Minn. Sup. Ct., 109 Minn. 456, 124 N.W. 221 (1910)

NATURE OF CASE: Appeal from an award of damages in an action for trespass.

FACT SUMMARY: The crew of the *Reynolds*, a ship owned by the Lake Erie Transportation Co. (D), kept that ship tied to a dock belonging to Vincent (P) during a violent storm causing damage to the dock.

RULE OF LAW

The private necessity of avoiding destruction or damage to one's property gives rise to a privilege to invade the property of another, but this privilege is limited to entry and compensation must be made for any damage resulting from it.

FACTS: The steamship *Reynolds*, owned by Lake Erie Transportation Co. (Lake Erie) (D), was moored to Vincent's (P) dock for the purpose of discharging cargo. When a violent storm developed, instead of cutting the ship loose from the dock, the crew kept it tied up, with $500 damage resulting to the dock. Vincent (P) sued to recover for this damage. Upon judgment for Vincent (P), Lake Erie (D) appealed contending that the defense of necessity insulated them from liability.

ISSUE: Does the defense of private necessity relieve one of liability for damage done while protecting one's property?

HOLDING AND DECISION: (O'Brien, J.) No. The defense of private necessity does not relieve one of liability for damage done while protecting one's property. The private necessity of avoiding destruction or damage to one's property gives rise to a privilege to invade the property of another, but this privilege is limited to entry, and compensation must be made for any damage resulting from it. It is true that normal property rights may be suspended where nonhuman conditions such as storms get out of control. In the landmark case of *Ploof v. Putnam*, 81 Vt. 471, 71 A. 188 (1908), however, the Vermont Supreme Court pointed out that where injury to property results from an emergency trespass, the damages must be compensated for, even though the trespass itself is privileged. Here, the deliberate act of the crew in not cutting the ship loose, though not a trespass, nevertheless resulted in trespassory harm to the dock of Vincent (P). This must be compensated for. The judgment must be affirmed.

ANALYSIS

This case points out the general rule for the tort defense of private necessity. In addition to property, it, of course, also extends to situations in which nonhuman actions cause a threat of death or serious bodily injury to the trespassing party. The privilege may be extended to the breaking into of buildings including dwellings, and supersedes the right of the owner to protect his property. (Therefore, any force used to expel someone acting out of necessity is wrongful and actionable.) Of course, the trespass involved must not be disproportionate to the danger avoided. Private necessity, clearly, must be distinguished from public necessity. Unlike private necessity, public necessity carries with it a complete privilege (no liability for damages) whenever a trespass is necessary to avoid a public disaster (flood, etc.). Both public officers and private citizens may act in public necessity, and even deadly force may be justified in proper circumstances.

Quicknotes

ASSIGNMENT OF ERROR A complaint filed by an appellant setting forth the alleged errors of the trial court upon which he seeks a reversal.

PRIVATE NECESSITY A defense to liability for unlawful activity where the conduct is unavoidable and is justified by preventing the injury to life or health.

Sindle v. New York City Transit Authority

Injured student (P) v. Transit authority (D) and Bus driver (D)

N.Y. Ct. App., 33 N.Y.2d 293, 307 N.E.2d 245 (1973)

NATURE OF CASE: Appeal from an award of damages for false imprisonment.

FACT SUMMARY: Sindle (P), a 14-year-old boy, was detained on a bus while the bus driver Mooney (D) drove to the police station to report vandalism allegedly caused by children riding the bus. Sindle (P) was riding the bus but there is no evidence that Sindle (P) took part in any of the destruction. After the bus driver (D) locked the doors and took the bus occupants to the police station, Sindle (P) claimed false imprisonment. At trial, the New York City Transit Authority (D) and bus driver Mooney (D) unsuccessfully attempted to amend their answer to introduce the defense of justification.

RULE OF LAW

In a false imprisonment action, it is an abuse of discretion for the judge to deny the defendant's motion to amend its answer to claim the defense of justification.

FACTS: Students on a New York City Transit Authority (D) school bus were excessively loud and were vandalizing the bus. The bus driver Mooney (D) inspected the damage after having warned the students to quiet down and stop vandalizing the bus; he then decided to take the remaining students to a police station. Mooney (D) locked the doors, bypassed regular bus stops, and proceeded to the police station. Sindle (P), a 14-year-old boy riding the bus, joined with his father (P), and sought damages for negligence and false imprisonment. At trial, Sindle (P) waived the negligence claim. The court denied the New York City Transit Authority's (D) and Mooney's (D) motion to amend their answer to plead the defense of justification to the false imprisonment claim and excluded all evidence bearing on justification. The New York City Transit Authority (D) and Mooney (D) appealed an award of damages to Sindle (P).

ISSUE: In a false imprisonment action, is it an abuse of discretion for the judge to deny the defendant's motion to amend its answer to claim the defense of justification?

HOLDING AND DECISION: (Jasen, J.) Yes. In a false imprisonment action, it is an abuse of discretion for the judge to deny the defendant's motion to amend its answer to claim the defense of justification. It was the New York City Transit Authority's (D) and Mooney's (D) burden to prove justification, and Sindle (P) could not have been prejudiced by granting leave to amend the answer. It was unfair for the judge to deny the motion. Generally, restraint or detention, reasonable under the circumstances and in time and manner, imposed for the purpose of preventing another from inflicting personal injuries or interfering with or damaging real or personal property in one's lawful possession or custody, is not unlawful. The restraint or detention must be for the purpose of preventing personal injury or interfering with or damaging real or personal property. An example of a situation in which restraint or detention may be permissible is when a parent, guardian, or teacher uses physical force that is reasonably necessary to protect a child or maintain discipline. The school bus driver is analogous to one acting *in loco parentis* since he is entrusted with both the care of the students and the custody of personal property. The jury must determine whether he acted reasonably in light of all of the circumstances. These circumstances include (1) the need to protect the students and the property; (2) the bus driver's duty to aid the investigation of the students who caused the damage; (3) where and how the incident happened; and (4) the availability of other courses of action. Reversed and remitted for a new trial.

ANALYSIS

There are various types of situations in which justification is a valid defense to an intentional tort. For example, *Matter of Malone*, 105 A.D.2d 455 (1984), held that an attorney could raise the defense of justification because he had been acting in his official capacity as Inspector General of the New York State Department of Correctional Services when he advised his client to testify falsely. In order to protect the identity of a correction officer who stated he witnessed an incident, and thus protect him from retaliation for having broken the "code of silence" among correction officers, the attorney instructed the officer to testify falsely under oath at one point during the investigation. Also instructive is *Peterson v. Sorlien*, 299 N.W.2d 123 (Minn. 1980), *cert. denied*, 450 U.S. 1031 (1981). In that case, the plaintiff sued her parents for, *inter alia*, false imprisonment arising out of their effort to prompt her disaffiliation from a religious cult.

Quicknotes

FALSE IMPRISONMENT Intentional tort whereby the victim is unlawfully restrained.

IN LOCO PARENTIS In the place of a parent or instead of a parent.

Continued on next page.

JUSTIFICATION DEFENSE A reason recognized by law as an excuse for acting or failing to act.

NEGLIGENCE Conduct falling below the standard of care that a reasonable person would demonstrate under similar conditions.

CHAPTER 4

Negligence

Quick Reference Rules of Law

33. *Larson v. St. Francis Hotel.* The doctrine of res ipsa loquitur applies only where the cause of the injury is shown to be under the exclusive control and management of the defendant. *82*

34. *Cruz v. DaimlerChrysler Motors Corp.* A plaintiff cannot use the doctrine of res ipsa loquitur to raise an inference of the defendant's negligence where, although the injury-causing event at issue ordinarily does not occur in the absence of negligence, the plaintiff cannot present evidence that points the negligence to the defendant. *83*

35. *James v. Wormuth.* In a medical malpractice action based on a foreign object being left in a patient's body, the theory of res ipsa loquitur may not be used to establish a physician's negligence where the physician intentionally left the foreign object in the patient's body based on the physician's judgment that doing so would be in the patient's best interest. *84*

36. *Sullivan v. Crabtree.* The doctrine of res ipsa loquitur merely affords reasonable evidence, in the absence of an explanation that injury was caused by negligence. Even if the facts are unexplained in a res ipsa loquitur situation, the jury may still refuse to make a finding of negligence. *86*

Lubitz v. Wells

Injured nine-year-old (P) v. Golfer (D) and son (D)

Conn. Super. Ct., 19 Conn. Supp. 322, 113 A.2d 147 (1955)

NATURE OF CASE: Action to recover damages for negligence

FACT SUMMARY: Mr. Wells (D), father of defendant J. Wells, Jr. (D), left a golf club out in a place where children played, and his son (D) negligently failed to warn Lubitz (P) that he was intending to swing the club, thus injuring her.

RULE OF LAW

Conduct that is reasonable and has a low probability of resulting in harm to others is not negligence.

FACTS: The father (D) of J. Wells, Jr. (D) left a golf club out in his yard where both his son (D) and Lubitz (P) were playing. Wells, Jr. (D) swung the club without warning Lubitz (P) of his intention. As a result of his failure to warn her before swinging the golf club, Lubitz (P) was injured. Lubitz (P) sued the son (D) for his negligence in hitting her and sued the father (D) for his negligence in leaving the club in a position where it could inflict harm.

ISSUE: Is conduct that is reasonable and has a low probability of resulting in harm to others negligence?

HOLDING AND DECISION: (Troland, J.) No. Conduct that is reasonable and has a low probability of resulting in harm to others is not negligence. In this case the chance that the child would inflict injury by means of the golf club was not foreseeable. A person cannot be shouldered with responsibility for acts that portend no harm. It would be unfair and unreasonable to hold someone to a standard of conduct beyond that with which a prudent person could comply. Demurrer sustained.

ANALYSIS

The case conforms to the weight of authority; courts generally do not expect people to guard against events that cannot reasonably be expected to cause harm. If minute risks were taken seriously, activity would decrease out of fear of injury to others.

Quicknotes

DEMURRER The assertion that the opposing party's pleadings are insufficient and that the demurring party should not be made to answer.

Blyth v. Birmingham Waterworks Co.

Flooded property owner (P) v. Fire plug installer (D)

Ex., 11 Exch. 781, 156 Eng. Rep. 1047 (1856)

NATURE OF CASE: Appeal from an award of damages in action for negligence.

FACT SUMMARY: An extraordinarily severe frost caused a fire plug owned by Birmingham Waterworks Co. (D) to flood the property of Blyth (P).

RULE OF LAW

Negligence involves the creation of an "unreasonable" risk, by act or omission, which a reasonable and prudent man would not create.

FACTS: Birmingham Waterworks Co. (Waterworks) (D) installed water mains, including several fire plugs, in a street. The plugs worked well for 25 years. Then, during an extraordinarily cold frost one winter, one of the plugs got stopped up by ice, causing water from the pipes to flood and damage the property of Blyth (P). Blyth (P) sued for damages, alleging that Waterworks (D) was negligent for not taking adequate precautions to prepare for the contingency of this frost. Upon judgment for Blyth (P), Waterworks (D) appealed, contending that the frost was so extraordinary and unforeseeable that any damage resulted from mere accident.

ISSUE: Does negligence involve the creation of an "unreasonable" risk, by act or omission, which a reasonable and prudent man would not create?

HOLDING AND DECISION: (Alderson, B.) Yes. Negligence involves the creation of an "unreasonable" risk, by act or omission, which a reasonable and prudent man, guided upon those considerations that ordinarily regulate the conduct of human affairs, would not create. A reasonable person acts with reference to the average circumstances of ordinary times. He cannot be held liable, therefore, for extraordinary occurrences. Here, Waterworks (D) took all necessary precautions for ordinary frost. They cannot equitably be held responsible for a frost such as the one involved here as such a frost is seldom seen south of the polar regions. The judgment must be reversed. The rationale here is that making Waterworks (D) responsible for all harm caused, even inadvertently, would be to make them insurers of all people they deal with. Reversed.

ANALYSIS

This case points up the general rule for the negligence standard that all people owe: the objective "reasonable person under similar circumstances" test. If the conduct involved creates an "unreasonable risk" of harm, negligence can be found. Caution must be taken, however, to avoid confusing the foreseeability standard for standard of care (above) and the absence of this standard for proximate cause.

Quicknotes

NEGLIGENCE Conduct falling below the standard of care that a reasonable person would demonstrate under similar conditions.

PROXIMATE CAUSE The natural sequence of events without which an injury would not have been sustained.

REASONABLE PERSON STANDARD The standard of care exercised by a hypothetical person who possesses the intelligence, education, knowledge, attention, and judgment required by society of its members when governing behavior; the standard applies to a person's judgment when determining breach of a duty under the theory of negligence.

UNFORESEEABLE A result that was not likely to occur from a particular act or failure to act.

Pipher v. Parsell

Passenger (P) v. Driver (D)

Del. Sup. Ct., 930 A.2d 890 (2007)

NATURE OF CASE: Appeal from trial court's granting of judgment as a matter of law to defendant.

FACT SUMMARY: While three sixteen year olds were driving in Parsell's (D) pickup truck, a passenger, Biesel, reached over and grabbed the wheel. Thirty seconds later, Biesel grabbed the wheel again, causing an accident resulting in injuries to Pipher (P).

RULE OF LAW

When it is foreseeable that the actions of a passenger may interfere with a driver's ability to operate the vehicle safely, a driver's failure to prevent such conduct may constitute a breach of the driver's duty to other passengers and the public.

FACTS: Three sixteen year olds were driving in Parsell's (D) pickup truck. They were sitting in a row in the front seat. Parsell (D) was driving. Pipher (P) was in the middle and Johnese Biesel was on the right near the passenger side door. While traveling fifty five miles per hour, Biesel reached over and grabbed the wheel unexpectedly. Parsell (D) was able to control the vehicle. Thirty seconds later, Biesel grabbed the wheel again. The truck swerved off the road and into a tree. Pipher (P) suffered injuries. At trial, Parsell (D) admitted he could have reprimanded Biesel to not grab the wheel again. He also agreed that he could have placed Biesel in the back seat, or even demanded that she get out of the vehicle. The trial judge ruled as a matter of law that Parsell (D) had no duty to do anything after Biesel grabbed the wheel the first time.

ISSUE: When it is foreseeable that the actions of a passenger may interfere with a driver's ability to operate the vehicle safely, may the driver's failure to prevent such conduct constitute a breach of the driver's duty to other passengers and the public?

HOLDING AND DECISION: (Holland, J.) Yes. When it is foreseeable that the actions of a passenger may interfere with a driver's ability to operate the vehicle safely, a driver's failure to prevent such conduct may constitute a breach of the driver's duty to other passengers and the public. A driver owes other passengers and the public a duty of care because it is foreseeable that they may be injured if the driver, by failing to pay attention, gets into an accident. Pipher (P) argues on appeal that after Biesel grabbed the wheel the first time, Parsell (D) was on notice of a dangerous situation. He was under a duty to take steps to protect his passengers in light of that situation. The court agrees. Where a passenger's actions are not foreseeable, the driver is not negligent. However, a reasonable jury could conclude that Parsell (D) breached his duty to Pipher (P) by failing to prevent Biesel from grabbing the wheel again, just seconds after doing it the first time. The issues of breach and proximate cause all involve questions of fact that the trial court should have submitted to the jury. The judgment as a matter of law is reversed, and the case is remanded.

ANALYSIS

This case may be somewhat confusing to one attempting to learn the complex rules regarding duty, breach and causation. Specifically, the issue is whether breach of a duty occurred. There is no question a driver owes a duty of care to his passengers. Here, the court stated when the actions of another party are foreseeable, failure to prevent those future actions may constitute breach of a duty. Note the decision never actually states that Parsell (D) had a duty to prevent Biesel from grabbing the wheel. The decision only stated that Parsell's (D) failure to do so may constitute a breach of the duty. In addition, here the court uses foreseeability of a person's *actions* to assist in determination of a breach of duty. This is not to be confused with the foreseeability of possible *harm* to a plaintiff which is the focus of the proximate cause element of negligence.

Quicknotes

BREACH The violation of an obligation imposed pursuant to contract or law, by acting or failing to act.

DUTY OF CARE A principle of negligence requiring an individual to act in such a manner as to avoid injury to a person to whom he or she owes a duty.

FORESEEABILITY OF HARM An inquiry into the relatedness of events that contributed to the plaintiff's injury; whether the harm was foreseeable determines whether the tortfeasor's conduct was the proximate cause of the injury.

Chicago B. & Q.R. Co. v. Krayenbuhl

Railway (D) v. Injured boy (P)

Neb. Sup. Ct., 65 Neb. 889, 91 N.W. 880 (1902)

NATURE OF CASE: Appeal from an award of damages in an action for negligence.

FACT SUMMARY: Krayenbuhl (P), age 4, had his foot severed while playing on a railroad turntable belonging to Chicago B. & Q.R. Co. (D), a railroad company.

RULE OF LAW

When the owner of dangerous premises knows, or has good reason to believe, that children trespassers, so young as to be ignorant of the danger, will be attracted to and will resort to such premises, the owner under a duty of care to protect such children from the risks arising from such premises.

FACTS: Krayenbuhl (P), age 4, was known to have frequently trespassed upon the property of Chicago B. & Q.R. Co. ("the Railroad") (D) to play on its turntable with other children. Though company policy was that the turntable was to be padlocked by the foreman when not in use, this policy was frequently ignored. On the day in question, Krayenbuhl (P), along with other children, entered the premises of the Railroad (D), and either found the turntable unlocked or unlocked it. It was unguarded. In the process of playing on it, Krayenbuhl's (P) foot was severed above the ankle. He sued to recover for personal injuries. Upon judgment in his favor, the Railroad (D) appealed, contending that the fact of the child's status as a trespasser took the case out of negligence liability.

ISSUE: When the owner of dangerous premises knows, or has good reason to believe, that children trespassers, so young as to be ignorant of the danger, will be attracted to and will resort to such premises, is the owner under a duty of care to protect such children from the risks arising from such premises?

HOLDING AND DECISION: (Albert, Commr.) Yes. When the owner of dangerous premises knows, or has good reason to believe, that children trespassers, so young as to be ignorant of the danger, will be attracted to and will resort to such premises, the owner is under a duty of care to protect such children from the risks arising from such premises. As such, the risks so created are unreasonable and unjustified. Though there is no general duty of care to trespassers, such a duty may often arise from peculiar circumstances (e.g., one cannot set up a spring gun to repel trespassers). The so-called "turntable doctrine" herein described recognized the peculiar circumstance of child trespassers as one such exception to the general rule. Here, the failure of the Railroad (D) to take precautions (locks, guards, etc.) to prevent children from playing on their dangerous premises (turntable) is an omission to act while under a duty of care. Such is negligence. [Reversed on other grounds.]

ANALYSIS

This case points up the majority rule for children trespassers. It is more commonly called "the attractive nuisance doctrine" (rather than the "turntable" doctrine). Note that the duty of care here is higher than that normally imposed. The owner of land must not only maintain his premises such that no unreasonable risk is presented to those who have a right to be there, but he must also: (1) exercise due care to discover trespassing children, and (2) warn or, if necessary, protect them from the risks involved. Note also, however, that the doctrine is generally limited to cases involving artificial conditions on the land only (turntables, machinery, etc.). No special duty is owed where the condition or activity involved is natural (stream, etc.).

Quicknotes

ATTRACTIVE NUISANCE DOCTRINE The assignment of liability to an owner or occupier of land who permits a dangerous instrumentality to remain on the property, knowing it is likely to attract children who have access to it, and who fails to take reasonable steps to prevent such injury.

DUTY OF CARE A principle of negligence requiring an individual to act in such a manner as to avoid injury to a person to whom he or she owes an obligatory duty.

NEGLIGENCE Conduct falling below the standard of care that a reasonable person would demonstrate under similar conditions.

TRESPASS Unlawful interference with, or damage to, the real or personal property of another.

TURNTABLE DOCTRINE Requires persons who maintain a condition on their premises which is likely to attract children to take precautions as would a reasonably prudent person to prevent injury.

Davison v. Snohomish County

Accident victim (P) v. County (D)

Wash. Sup. Ct., 149 Wash. 109, 270 P. 422 (1928)

NATURE OF CASE: Suit to recover damages for negligence.

FACT SUMMARY: Davison (P) was injured on a Snohomish County (D) bridge due to the fact that there was a weak guardrail, improper banking, and dirt on the approach to the bridge.

RULE OF LAW

The burden in terms of monetary costs is too high for a public entity to protect against every anticipated accident.

FACTS: After Davison (P) crossed a bridge in Snohomish County ("the County") (D), his car skidded, struck a guardrail on a curve and broke through the guardrail. As a result of this accident, Davison (P) suffered severe injuries to his person and his automobile was also greatly damaged. Davison (P) alleged that the accident occurred because the guardrail was not sufficient in strength to hold the car, that there was dirt on the approach that contributed to the skidding, and that the approach to the bridge was improperly banked.

ISSUE: Is the burden in terms of monetary costs too high for a public entity to protect against every anticipated accident?

HOLDING AND DECISION: (Beals, J.) Yes. The burden in terms of monetary costs is too high for a public entity to protect against every anticipated accident. There is no duty on the part of a public body to assume the burden of safeguarding against all conceivable accidents. In this case, the fact that the guardrail was not as sturdy as it should have been to protect against a car running off the road is inconsequential. To insist on such a requirement would deter the county from opening roads to public access. In the era of the horse and buggy, if the county were to shield automobiles from leaving the road, the costs of maintaining and establishing such protection would be too prohibitive for the county's expense account. Further, the fact that the incline was too steep was also irrelevant when the margin by which it was banked is compared to the height of the entire slope. The County (D) would not be expected to correct the whole slope to correct such a marginal error. Also, the court considered the fact that there was dirt on the road irrelevant as to the proof of negligence. The County (D) cannot be held for ordinary accumulation of dirt. Reversed.

ANALYSIS

The case falls into a group of cases that consider the cost of the alternative courses of action which would prevent harm to the plaintiff. If the cost of prevention would halt the defendant from providing necessary services such as roads, then this cost should not be imposed. The converse is also considered, i.e., if the cost to post a warning or achieve some other safety measure is low, the defendant may be liable for not doing this inexpensive act.

Quicknotes

NEGLIGENCE Conduct falling below the standard of care that a reasonable person would demonstrate under similar conditions.

United States v. Carroll Towing Co.

State (D) v. Barge owner (P)

159 F.2d 169 (2d Cir. 1947)

NATURE OF CASE: Action to recover damages in admiralty for the sinking of a barge.

FACT SUMMARY: The attendant of the Conners Co. (P) barge left the vessel unwatched for 21 hours. During that period, the barge broke loose and sank.

RULE OF LAW

There is a duty of care to protect others from harm when the burden of taking adequate precautions is less than the product of the probability of the resulting harm and the magnitude of the harm.

FACTS: The attendant of the Conners Co. (P) barge left the vessel unwatched for 21 hours during the period when the harbor was full of vessels. During that 21-hour period, the barge broke loose from the pier through the negligence of Carroll Towing Co.'s (D) servant in shifting its mooring lines. The Conners Co. (P) barge sank. Conners Co. (P) sued Carroll Towing Co. (D) for negligence. The trial court divided the damages.

ISSUE: Is there a duty of care to protect others from harm when the burden of taking adequate precautions is less than the product of the probability of the resulting harm and the magnitude of the harm?

HOLDING AND DECISION: (Hand, J.) Yes. If the burden of preventing the injury is lower than the product of the probability of its occurring and the amount of harm that it will cause, then there is a breach of the duty of care and liability for negligence. In this case, the burden of preventing the accident was low; it only involved the watchman staying in the vicinity of the barge or recruiting someone else to stand by and watch it. The probability of the barge getting untied and striking another barge is undoubtedly a variable that changes with conditions, as is the amount of injury that will result. The existing conditions, the crowded harbor with barges constantly being moved about, made the probability of injury more than a negligible factor and made the magnitude of resulting injury an enormous figure. Thus, since the burden of preventing the collision was low and the product of the probability and the amount of injury projected is high, the fact that it occurred was a breach of duty. Affirmed.

ANALYSIS

This effort to formulate negligence, this "calculus of the risk," is an acceptable method of determining negligence. Behind this formula, however, is always the recognition that the measure of the reasonableness of the risk revolves around the specific circumstances of the situation. Conduct is relative to the particular occasion and need.

Quicknotes

DUTY OF CARE A principle of negligence requiring an individual to act in such a manner as to avoid injury to a person to whom he or she owes an obligatory duty.

NEGLIGENCE Conduct falling below the standard of care that a reasonable person would demonstrate under similar conditions.

Vaughan v. Menlove

Owner of burned cottages (P) v. Hay rick owner (D)

C.P., 3 Bing. (N.C) 468, 132 Eng. Rep. 490 (1837)

NATURE OF CASE: Action to recover damages for negligence.

FACT SUMMARY: Menlove (D) erected a hay rick near his neighbor Vaughan's (P) property, despite warnings that the hay rick was a fire hazard. Menlove (D) followed his own best judgment and allowed the hay rick to remain. It burned, destroying Vaughan's (P) cottages.

RULE OF LAW
The standard of care in determining gross negligence is the objective "reasonable person" standard.

FACTS: Hay rick owner (D) built a hay rick close to the boundary of his property. Persons in the community told him that this rick was susceptible to the dangers of fire. He ignored their warnings on the grounds that his stock was insured and because he made an aperture through the hay rick as a precaution against fire. Nonetheless, the hay rick burned, and the fire burned down Vaughan's (P) surrounding cottages.

ISSUE: Is the correct standard of care in a gross negligence action the objective "reasonable person" standard?

HOLDING AND DECISION: (Tindal, C.J.) Yes. The standard of care in determining gross negligence is the objective "reasonable person" standard. A jury should decide a negligence case on this standard, rather than the subjective standard of a person acting honestly and bona fide to the best of his judgment. Conduct in actions for negligence should be judged in terms of the "reasonable person" instead of judging in terms of the defendant's subjective intent. If the behavior of tort litigants were judged on a defendant's personal intent, torts would be subjective and highly variable among cases and therefore unfair. Rule discharged.

ANALYSIS

The "reasonable man" standard is almost universally accepted in negligence cases, even if it is called by another name. For example, in *Osborne v. Montgomery,* 203 Wis. 223 (1931), the court relied upon the "ordinarily prudent man." In *Warrington v. New York Power & Light Corp.,* 300 N.Y.S. 154 (1937), it was called the "typical prudent man," and in *Charbonneau v. MacRury,* 84 N.H. 501 (1931), the "average person of ordinary prudence."

Quicknotes

BONA FIDE In good faith.

CASE PRIMAE IMPRESSIONIS A new case that has no directly applicable precedent and must be decided entirely by reason as distinguished from authority.

HAY RICK A stack of hay.

NEGLIGENCE Conduct falling below the standard of care that a reasonable person would demonstrate under similar conditions.

REASONABLE PERSON STANDARD The standard of care exercised by a hypothetical person who possesses the intelligence, education, knowledge, attention and judgment required by society of its members when governing behavior; the standard applies to a person's judgment when determining breach of a duty under the theory of negligence.

RULE NISI Motion by one party to make a final ruling against the opponent, unless the opponent can show cause as to why such ruling should not be ordered.

Delair v. McAdoo

Car accident victim (P) v. Other driver (D)

Pa. Sup. Ct., 324 Pa. 392, 188 A. 181 (1936)

NATURE OF CASE: Action in trespass to recover damages for injury to person and property.

FACT SUMMARY: McAdoo (D), driving a car with dangerously worn tires, suffered a blow-out and crashed into Delair's (P) car.

RULE OF LAW

In exercising one's duty of due care for the safety of others, every automobile driver and owner is charged with such knowledge of the safe condition of his car as can be ascertained through a reasonable inspection.

FACTS: McAdoo (D), unaware of the dangerous condition of his tires, attempted to pass Delair (P), when McAdoo's (D) left rear tire blew out, causing his car to crash into Delair's (P) car. At trial, witnesses testified that McAdoo's (D) tire was worn through to the inside lining. McAdoo (D) denied this. Delair (P) claimed that McAdoo (D) was negligent in driving with defective tires.

ISSUE: In exercising one's duty of due care for the safety of others, is every automobile driver and owner charged with such knowledge of the safe condition of his car as can be ascertained through a reasonable inspection?

HOLDING AND DECISION: (Kephart, C.J.) Yes. Every adult in the community is held to general knowledge of certain facts, such as the law of gravity, and the effect of pulling a trigger on a gun. Included here is the knowledge that worn tires are dangerous and should not be used. In addition, the owner or operator of a motor vehicle is charged with knowledge of whether or not his car is safe to drive, if such knowledge can be gained through reasonable inspection. Here, the evidence indicated that McAdoo's (D) tire was clearly and visibly worn. The law will not permit him, in defense of negligence, to assert his ignorance of the conditions of the tire, or the danger it represents. Affirmed.

ANALYSIS

This case incorporates a phenomenon of modern society, the automobile, into that class of objects and activities about which everyone is deemed to possess a minimum amount of knowledge. Everyone, for instance, should be aware of the danger of driving at night without headlights. Moreover, if someone is engaged in a particular activity, or stands in particular relationship to another, or is merely a stranger in the community, he may be under an affirmative duty to learn further facts. For example, as in the above case, a driver must inspect his tires; a landlord must investigate his premises before letting and advise his tenant of dangerous conditions; and a traveling motorist must advise himself of local traffic violations.

Quicknotes

NEGLIGENCE Conduct falling below the standard of care that a reasonable person would demonstrate under similar conditions.

Trimarco v. Klein

Injured tenant (P) v. Apartment owner (D)

N.Y. Ct. App., 56 N.Y.2d 98, 436 N.E.2d 502 (1982)

NATURE OF CASE: Appeal from reversal of award of damages for negligence.

FACT SUMMARY: Klein's (D) tenant Trimarco (P) attempted to show that use of shatterproof glass for tub enclosures had become common over the years and that the regular glass enclosure on which he was injured, therefore, no longer met accepted safety standards.

RULE OF LAW

Evidence of custom and usage by others engaged in the same business is admissible as bearing on what is reasonable conduct under all the circumstances, which is the quintessential test of negligence.

FACTS: Trimarco (P), a tenant in Klein's (D) building, was injured when he fell through the glass door enclosing his tub. The glass looked like tempered glass but was just ordinary thin glass. In his negligence action, Trimarco (P) offered expert evidence that it had become common practice to use shatterproof glass in such enclosures so that by the date of his accident the glass door in his bathroom no longer conformed to accepted safety standards. The appellate division reversed a decision awarding Trimarco (P) damages, holding that even if the aforementioned evidence established a custom of using shatterproof glass in such enclosures, Klein (D) was nonetheless under no common-law duty to replace the glass unless he had prior notice of the danger (either from Trimarco (P) or from a similar accident in the building).

ISSUE: Is evidence of custom and usage by others engaged in the same business admissible as bearing on what is reasonable conduct under all the circumstances, which is the quintessential test of negligence?

HOLDING AND DECISION: (Fuchsberg, J.) Yes. The quintessential test of negligence is whether a party's conduct was reasonable under all the circumstances of a particular case. Because evidence of custom and usage by others engaged in the same business bears on what is reasonable conduct, it is admissible, although it is not necessarily a conclusive or even compelling test of negligence. Customs and usages run the gamut, like everything else. As Holmes put it, "what usually is done may be evidence of what ought to be done, but what ought to be done is fixed by a standard of reasonable prudence, whether it usually is complied with or not." The trial court followed these principles in admitting the evidence of custom and usage, and it should not have been reversed. However, a new trial must be had here because the trial judge erroneously admitted certain other evidence.

ANALYSIS

There is only one area in which the courts have been willing to let prevailing custom serve to define the standard of care that must be met to avoid a charge of negligence, and that area is malpractice. Even where the standard of care is not set by prevailing custom in a particular field of endeavor, custom may still be important in deciding whether the actor behaved as would a reasonable person.

Quicknotes

CUSTOM AND USAGE A customary practice that is so widespread that it has become mandatory and has the force of law.

NEGLIGENCE Conduct falling below the standard of care that a reasonable person would demonstrate under similar conditions.

PRIMA FACIE CASE An action where the plaintiff introduces sufficient evidence to submit the issue to the judge or jury for determination.

REASONABLE MAN STANDARD A hypothetical person whose judgment represents the standard to which society requires its members to act in their private affairs and in their dealings with others.

Cordas v. Peerless Transportation Co.

Victim of runaway cab (P) v. Cab owner (D)

N.Y.C. Ct., 27 N.Y.S.2d 198 (1941)

NATURE OF CASE: Action to recover damages for negligence.

FACT SUMMARY: While being threatened by a passenger with a gun who was being pursued by a crowd, a taxi driver, employee of Peerless Transportation Co. (D), jumped out of the cab. The cab proceeded to hit Cordas (P).

RULE OF LAW

A person is not necessarily negligent if, in an emergency, he acts to avoid injury to himself and in doing so injures bystanders.

FACTS: A man jumped into a taxi cab owned by Peerless Transportation Co. (D). He pointed a gun at the driver and commanded him to go. The driver was frightened and complied. The driver was further frightened when he heard the man's pursuers following and yelling "Stop Thief." The driver quickly threw the car out of gear, slammed on his brakes, pulled the emergency brake, and, although he thought the motor was still running, jumped out of the car. The car proceeded to injure Cordas (P).

ISSUE: Is a person necessarily negligent if, in an emergency, he acts to avoid injury to himself and in doing so injures bystanders?

HOLDING AND DECISION: (Carlin, J.) No. A person is not necessarily negligent if, in an emergency, he acts to avoid injury to himself and in doing so injures bystanders. A person in an emergency demanding prompt action is not required to exercise the mature judgment or due care required in normal circumstances as long as the emergency is not of the person's own making. Here, the driver is not liable. The law does not require heroism of the average reasonable person.

ANALYSIS

The basis of the emergency doctrine is that the actor has no time for deliberation and cannot be held to the same standard as one who had opportunity to reflect before acting. The limitations on the doctrine are that the emergency must arise suddenly and unexpectedly and not be caused by the actor's own negligence. However, it is not really a lesser standard of care which is required of an actor in an emergency. The actor's conduct is compared to the average reasonable person's conduct in similar circumstances with the emergency being part of the circumstances. The actor will not be held negligent if he did what the average reasonable person would or might do in similar circumstances.

Quicknotes

DUTY OF CARE A principle of negligence requiring an individual to act in such a manner as to avoid injury to a person to whom he or she owes an obligatory duty.

REASONABLE PERSON STANDARD The standard of care exercised by a hypothetical person who possesses the intelligence, education, knowledge, attention, and judgment required by society of its members when governing behavior; the standard applies to a person's judgment when determining breach of a duty under the theory of negligence.

Roberts v. State of Louisiana

Bumped man (P) v. Blind man's employer (D)

La. Ct. App., 396 So. 2d 566 (1981)

NATURE OF CASE: Appeal from dismissal of action for negligence.

FACT SUMMARY: Roberts (P) appealed from the dismissal of his action against the State of Louisiana (D), contending that Burson, a blind concession stand operator, was negligent in traversing the area of the concession stand without the use of a cane.

RULE OF LAW

The standard of care applicable to people with handicaps is that they must take those precautions that ordinary, reasonable persons would if they were similarly handicapped.

FACTS: Roberts (P) fell and allegedly injured his hip as a result of being bumped by Burson, a blind concession stand operator, as Burson was traversing the concession stand area, located in a state building. Roberts (P) sued the State of Louisiana (D) through the Louisiana Health and Human Resources Administration (D), contending that it was liable in respondeat superior and negligent in failing to supervise and oversee the safe operation of the concession stand. Although Burson was not named, Roberts (P), relying on expert testimony alone, argued that Burson was negligent in traversing the concession area without the use of his cane. The expert had not examined Burson. Burson testified that he often made short trips in familiar areas without the use of a cane, relying on his facial sense. There was additional testimony to the extent that the use of the facial sense was not unreasonable in those circumstances. The trial court dismissed Roberts's (P) action, and from this decision, he appealed.

ISSUE: Is the standard of care applicable to people with handicaps that they must take those precautions that ordinary, reasonable persons would if they were similarly handicapped?

HOLDING AND DECISION: (Laborde, J.) Yes. The standard of care applicable to people with handicaps is that they must take those precautions that ordinary, reasonable persons would if they were similarly handicapped. Burson introduced a great deal of evidence that the manner in which he was traversing the concession area was not unreasonable. Roberts (P) relied solely on the testimony of his expert, who had not examined Burson. Further, Roberts (P) did not demonstrate that Burson had engaged in any other acts which could be characterized as negligent. Roberts (P) has failed to meet his burden of showing that Burson was negligent, and as a result, the action against the State of Louisiana (D) must fail. Affirmed.

ANALYSIS

In essence, the standard applied to people with handicaps is not any different than the basic reasonable person standard; only the circumstance parameters within which the reasonable person acts have changed. This so-called handicapped standard applies both to individuals with physical handicaps, and individuals handicapped by their particular circumstances.

Quicknotes

NEGLIGENCE Conduct falling below the standard of care that a reasonable person would demonstrate under similar conditions.

RESPONDEAT SUPERIOR Rule that the principal is responsible for tortious acts committed by its agents in the scope of their agency or authority.

STANDARD OF CARE A uniform degree of behavior against which a person's conduct can be measured when determining liability in negligence cases.

Robinson v. Lindsay

Accident victim (P) v. Snowmobiler (D)

Wash. Sup. Ct., 92 Wash. 2d 410, 598 P.2d 392 (1979)

NATURE OF CASE: Appeal from order of new trial in negligence action.

FACT SUMMARY: Robinson (P) was injured in a snowmobile accident caused by Anderson (D), a minor.

RULE OF LAW

A child will be held to an adult standard of care when engaging in an inherently dangerous activity, such as the operation of a powerful motor vehicle.

FACTS: An action seeking damages for personal injuries was brought on behalf of Kelly Robinson (P), who lost full use of her thumb as a result of a snowmobile accident. Robinson (P) was 11 years old at the time of the accident. The driver of the snowmobile, Anderson (D), was 13 years old. At trial, the jury was instructed to consider Anderson (D) to be bound by a duty to exercise the same care that a reasonably careful child of the same age would exercise under similar circumstances. Robinson (P) objected to the instruction contending that a child engaged in a dangerous activity such as driving a snowmobile must be held to an adult standard of care. The judge agreed and, after the jury found for Anderson (D), ordered a new trial. Anderson (D) appealed.

ISSUE: Will a child be held to an adult standard of care when engaging in an inherently dangerous activity, such as the operation of a powerful motor vehicle?

HOLDING AND DECISION: (Utter, C.J.) Yes. A child will be held to an adult standard of care when engaging in an inherently dangerous activity, such as the operation of a powerful motor vehicle. It is true that, in general, a child is not held to adult standards of care in negligence actions. Instead, he is held only to the exercise of such degree of care and discretion as is reasonably to be expected from children of his age. However, an injustice would clearly result if a child who causes injuries while engaged in an inherently dangerous activity were permitted to defend himself by saying that he acted no more injudiciously than any other child his age would have acted. Accordingly, a general exception to the "children's standard of care" has been carved out. Thus, where a child engages in an inherently dangerous activity, he will be held to an adult standard of care. In the instant case, it is clear that Anderson (D) was engaged in an inherently dangerous activity. Snowmobiles may operate at very high speeds and they are the cause of hundreds of accidents each year. In operating such a machine, Anderson (D) must be held to the standard of care normally exercised by a reasonable adult. Accordingly, the new trial was properly ordered. Affirmed.

ANALYSIS

Occasionally, a court has attempted to adopt a specific age limit as a guideline for children's negligence. For example, Pennsylvania borrowed from the criminal law rules relating to intent, and held that a child under the age of seven is incapable of negligence as a matter of law. A child between the ages of seven and 14 is presumed incapable of negligence, but evidence may be introduced proving otherwise (for children between the ages of 14 and 18, the rebuttable presumption is reversed). See *Kuhns v. Brugger*, 390 Pa. 331 (1957).

Quicknotes

INHERENTLY DANGEROUS ACTIVITY An activity that is dangerous at all times so that precautions must be taken to avoid injury.

NEGLIGENCE Conduct falling below the standard of care that a reasonable person would demonstrate under similar conditions.

STANDARD OF CARE A uniform degree of behavior against which a person's conduct can be measured when determining liability in negligence cases.

Breunig v. American Family Ins. Co.

Injured trucker (P) v. Insurer (D)

Wis. Sup. Ct., 45 Wis. 2d 536, 173 N.W.2d 619 (1970)

NATURE OF CASE: Action for damages for personal injury from negligence.

FACT SUMMARY: While overcome by a sudden state of insanity, Erma Veith, insured by American Family Ins. Co. (D), drove her automobile into Breunig's (P) truck.

RULE OF LAW

A person seized with a sudden mental disability for which he had no warning will be excused from the general rule of holding an insane person liable for his negligence.

FACTS: A psychiatrist testified that Ms. Veith, insured by American Family Ins. Co. (D), told him that while she was driving she believed God was directing her car. She saw a truck coming and stepped on the accelerator in order to become airborne, because she knew she could fly. Instead of flying, she collided with Breunig's (P) truck. At the time of the collision, Ms. Veith's automobile was on the left side of the road.

ISSUE: Will a person seized with a sudden mental disability for which he had no warning be excused from the general rule of holding an insane person liable for his negligence?

HOLDING AND DECISION: (Hallows, C.J.) Yes. Sudden mental incapacity that strikes without warning is an exception to the general rule that an insane person will be held liable for negligence. Cases supporting the general rule generally involve preexisting or permanent insanity. The general rule is supported by the following policies: (1) where one of the two innocent persons must suffer a loss it should be borne by the one who occasioned it; (2) to induce those interested in the insane person's estate to restrain and control him/her; and (3) to deter persons from filing false claims of insanity to avoid liability. Sudden mental disability is equivalent to sudden physical disability such as heart attack, stroke, fainting, and epileptic seizure and should be treated alike and not under the general rule. Here, unless it is shown that Ms. Veith, insured by American Family Ins. Co. (D), had warning or knowledge that the mental disability would occur, she will not be held liable for acts she committed while suddenly mentally disabled. Affirmed.

ANALYSIS

In nearly all cases, an insane person is held liable for negligence without reference to his insanity. However, this rule has been criticized, as in this case. A transitory sudden mental disability is commonly regarded as a circumstance depriving the actor of control over his conduct and relieving him of liability.

Quicknotes

INSANITY An affirmative defense to a criminal prosecution that the defendant suffered from a mental illness, thereby relieving him of liability for his conduct.

Heath v. Swift Wings, Inc.

Estate administrator (P) v. Pilot (D)

N.C. Ct. App., 40 N.C. App. 158, 252 S.E.2d 526 (1979)

NATURE OF CASE: Appeal from denial of damages for negligence.

FACT SUMMARY: Heath (P) claimed that the jury was erroneously instructed regarding the issue of standard of care of a pilot (D) whose plane crashed.

RULE OF LAW

Even as to professionals, the standard of care is an objective one and may not be tailored to the individual characteristics of each defendant.

FACTS: The estates (P) of two persons killed in a small plane crash, sued the pilot (D) and others, alleging that the crash occurred as a result of negligence. On that issue, the jury was instructed that negligence in a case of this sort is the "failure to exercise that degree of ordinary care and caution, which an ordinary prudent pilot having the same training and experience as [the pilot of the plane at issue], would have used in the same or similar circumstances." The jury returned a verdict finding the pilot (D) not negligent. Heath (P) appealed, alleging, in part, that the jury instructions were improper.

ISSUE: Even as to professionals, is the standard of care an objective one and may it not be tailored to the individual characteristics of each defendant?

HOLDING AND DECISION: (Morris, C.J.) Yes. Even as to professionals, the standard of care is an objective one and may not be tailored to the individual characteristics of each defendant. It is true that a professional will be held to the requisite degree of learning, skill, and ability called for in his particular occupation. However, the standard imposed, although higher than that imposed upon a lay person, is still an objective one, i.e., all professionals engaged in a particular occupation or specialty are held to the standard of care commonly exercised by the reasonable practitioner in the field. To instruct a jury otherwise, as did the trial court here, is to impose a different standard of care upon each defendant, according to the particular level of training and experience attained. Such a practice would be untenable. Accordingly, a new trial must be had. New trial ordered.

ANALYSIS

A variation on the rule expressed in the *Heath* case occurs when a person engaging in a service represents that he possesses superior skill or training. In such a situation, the person is held to a higher standard, although it is still expressed in objective form. The same is true of specialists, who are held to exercise the reasonable care of the ordinary practitioner engaging in that particular specialty.

Quicknotes

PROFESSIONAL STANDARD OF CARE That degree of care as reasonable persons in the particular profession would exercise.

REASONABLY PRUDENT PERSON A hypothetical person whose judgment represents the standard to which society requires its members to act in their private affairs and in their dealings with others.

STANDARD OF CARE A uniform degree of behavior against which a person's conduct can be measured when determining liability in negligence cases.

Hodges v. Carter

Disappointed client (P) v. Attorneys (D)

N.C. Sup. Ct., 239 N.C. 517, 80 S.E.2d 144 (1954)

NATURE OF CASE: Appeal from dismissal of action for damages for negligence.

FACT SUMMARY: Hodges (P) engaged Topping (D) and Carter (D), attorneys, to bring suit against his insurers who did not pay a claim, but when the manner of service was invalidated by the state supreme court, Hodges (P) claimed his attorneys (D) were negligent.

RULE OF LAW

An attorney acting in good faith and with an honest belief that his actions are in the best interest of his client is not liable for mistaken advice in an area of unsettled law.

FACTS: Hodges' (P) drugstore and all property within were destroyed by fire. He filed claims with his four foreign insurers who refused to pay on the claims. Hodges (P) engaged Topping (D) and Carter (D), attorneys, to bring suit against the insurers. Service was made in the usual manner by mail to the commissioner of insurance of the State of North Carolina who forwarded copies by registered mail to each foreign insurance company. Each of the four foreign insurance companies appeared specially to challenge jurisdiction. The North Carolina Supreme Court held the manner of service, the standard method for over 20 years, to be invalid. Hodges (P) sought damages from Topping (D) and Carter (D) for alleged negligence in the method of service used and for failure to sue out alias summons within 60 days (as the statute of limitations had by then run barring action against the insurers). A non-suit was entered, and Hodges (P) appealed.

ISSUE: Is an attorney who acts in good faith and with an honest belief that his actions are in the best interest of his client liable for mistaken advice in an area of unsettled law?

HOLDING AND DECISION: (Barnhill, C.J.) No. An attorney acting in good faith and with an honest belief that his actions are in the best interest of his client is not liable for mistaken advice in an area of unsettled law. A lawyer will be held liable when a loss to a client is the proximate result of a want of a degree of knowledge and skill ordinarily possessed by others in the profession similarly situated, from an omission to use reasonable care and diligence, or from failure to exercise good faith in making a best judgment. Here, the manner of service used was a standard method for over two decades and had never been previously challenged. Topping (D) and Carter (D) had no reason to think otherwise. Affirmed.

ANALYSIS

As for use of best judgment, lawyers have not been held liable for errors in interpretation of the Rule Against Perpetuities. Similarly, doctors are given wide discretion in making a diagnosis. The best example of a lawyer's failure to use due care is the failure to file a suit before the statute of limitations runs; no exercise of judgment is involved.

Quicknotes

DICTUM Statement by a judge in a legal opinion that is not necessary for the resolution of the action.

DUE DILIGENCE The standard of care as would be taken by a reasonable person in accordance with the attendant facts and circumstances.

GOOD FAITH An honest intention to abstain from any unconscientious advantage of another.

INVOLUNTARY NONSUIT The termination of a case without prejudice due to the plaintiff's failure to make out a case.

SCINTILLA Doctrine whereby if there is the least bit of evidence regarding a material question of fact then that issue should be left for determination by the jury.

STATUTE OF LIMITATIONS A law prescribing the period in which a legal action may be commenced.

Boyce v. Brown

Patient (P) v. Physician (D)

Ariz. Sup. Ct., 51 Ariz. 416, 77 P.2d 455 (1938)

NATURE OF CASE: Appeal from a directed verdict denying damages for medical malpractice.

FACT SUMMARY: Boyce's (P) fractured ankle was set by surgery with the use of a metal screw by Dr. Brown (D), but several years later the ankle began to swell and the pin had to be removed.

RULE OF LAW

Negligence on the part of a physician or surgeon, by reason of his departure from the proper standard of practice, must be established by expert medical testimony, unless the negligence is so grossly apparent that a layman would have no difficulty in recognizing it.

FACTS: In 1927, Boyce (P) saw Dr. Brown (D) to reduce a fracture in her ankle. An operation was performed by which the bone fragments were positioned and secured by use of a metal screw placed in the bone. Dr. Brown (D) continued to see Boyce (P) until recovery was apparent. No serious contention was made that Dr. Brown (D) did not follow approved medical standards of the day. In 1934, Boyce (P) returned to Dr. Brown (D) complaining of swelling in the ankle. He taped the ankle and filed the edge of her arch support which was worn sharp. After removing the tape, the pain and swelling worsened. In 1936, Boyce (P) saw Dr. Kent, who found discoloration and swelling. An X-ray showed necrosis of the bone around the screw, which Dr. Kent removed. Recovery was complete. Boyce (P) alleged that Dr. Brown (D) was negligent in failing to take an X-ray. At trial, Dr. Kent testified as to what was proper to do in 1936 and was unable to express an opinion as to Boyce's (P) condition in 1934. A directed verdict was given Dr. Brown (D), and Boyce (P) appealed on the basis of Dr. Brown's (D) failure to X-ray, which was argued to be negligence inferable by a layman.

ISSUE: Must negligence on the part of a physician or surgeon, by reason of his departure from the proper standard of practice, be established by expert medical testimony, unless the negligence is so grossly apparent that a layman would have no difficulty in recognizing it?

HOLDING AND DECISION: (Lockwood, J.) Yes. Negligence on the part of a physician or surgeon, by reason of his departure from the proper standard of practice, must be established by expert medical testimony, unless the negligence is so grossly apparent that a layman would have no difficulty recognizing it. Boyce's (P) treatment in 1934 consisted of taping the ankle, filing down the worn arch support, and untaping the ankle. She did not return to Dr. Brown (D) in 1934. She waited two years before seeing Dr. Kent. No evidence showed whether the screw should have been removed prior to 1936 or whether earlier removal would have been justifiable. Dr. Kent also said that he might have suspected arthritis had Boyce (P) come to him in 1934 and would have taken an X-ray, but no testimony showed the standard of medical care for 1934. The failure to take an X-ray is not negligence that is so obvious it can be recognized by a layman. X-rays are not always an appropriate means of diagnosis. Affirmed.

ANALYSIS

The court mentioned five other rather lengthy rules applicable to malpractice to which the student should refer. Professional standard of care rules refer to the locality in which the professional practices, particularly in regard to the profession of medicine.

Quicknotes

DIRECTED VERDICT A verdict ordered by the court in a jury trial.

EXPERT TESTIMONY Testimonial evidence about a complex area of subject matter relevant to trial, presented by a person competent to inform the trier of fact due to specialized knowledge or training.

NEGLIGENCE Conduct falling below the standard of care that a reasonable person would demonstrate under similar conditions.

PROFESSIONAL STANDARD OF CARE That degree of care as reasonable persons in the particular profession would exercise.

Morrison v. MacNamara

Patient (P) v. Nationally certified lab (D)

D.C. Ct. App., 407 A.2d 555 (1979)

NATURE OF CASE: Appeal from ruling disallowing expert testimony in medical malpractice action.

FACT SUMMARY: Morrison (P) appealed from a ruling refusing to allow the testimony of his expert witness as to the standard of care to be utilized in administering a urethral smear test, arguing that since the laboratory administering the test was nationally certified, it should be held to a national standard of care.

RULE OF LAW

The standard of care applicable to board certified physicians, hospitals, medical laboratories, and other health care providers is measured by the national standard of care.

FACTS: Morrison (P) reported to MacNamara (D), a nationally certified medical laboratory, for a urethral smear test for trichomonas. The test was administered while Morrison (P) was standing. Morrison (P) had an adverse reaction to the test and fainted, suffering serious injuries when he fell. Morrison (P) sued MacNamara (D), contending that there was negligence in administering the test to him while he was standing. He sought to introduce the testimony of an expert witness to testify that the standard of care nationally was to administer the test while the patient was either sitting or lying down. The court refused to allow the testimony, but allowed testimony presented by MacNamara (D) from local doctors that the test was always administered in the area with the patient standing. Morrison (P) appealed from the ruling, arguing that since MacNamara (D) was nationally certified, it should be held to a national standard of care.

ISSUE: Is the standard of care applicable to board certified physicians, hospitals, medical laboratories, and other health care providers measured by the national standard of care?

HOLDING AND DECISION: (Newman, C.J.) Yes. The standard of care applicable to board certified physicians, hospitals, medical laboratories, and other health care providers is measured by the national standards of care. The so-called locality rule was premised on notions of disparity and access to advances in medical science between urban and rural areas. The locality rule has no relevance to medical practice in this jurisdiction, and may serve to foster substandard medical care by judging conduct against other practitioners in the community. The doctrine is peculiar to the medical world, and the premises behind the rule are outmoded. Varying geographical standards of care are no longer valid in view of standards of uniform proficiency established by national board certification. Since clinical laboratories perform similar duties as to physicians and hospitals, they owe similar duties in their care and treatment of patients. MacNamara (D) admits that they are a nationally certified medical laboratory and hold themselves out to the public as such. The court should have allowed Morrison's (P) expert's testimony on the national standard of care, and should have allowed the jury to resolve the conflict of expert testimony. Reversed.

ANALYSIS

As the factual basis for the so-called "locality rule" has been eroded, more and more jurisdictions are abandoning the doctrine, and the present case is indicative of this trend. An unfortunate by-product of the evolution of a national standard of care is the development of the professional expert witness in medical malpractice cases.

Quicknotes

EXPERT WITNESS A witness providing testimony at trial who is specially qualified regarding the particular subject matter involved.

NEGLIGENCE Conduct falling below the standard of care that a reasonable person would demonstrate under similar conditions.

STANDARD OF CARE A uniform degree of behavior against which a person's conduct can be measured when determining liability in negligence cases.

Scott v. Bradford

Patient (P) v. Surgeon (D)

Okla. Sup. Ct., 606 P.2d 554 (1979)

NATURE OF CASE: Appeal from defendant's verdict in medical malpractice action.

FACT SUMMARY: Scott (P) sued in medical malpractice, alleging that she was not properly informed of the risks involved in a proposed operation.

RULE OF LAW

A doctor is under a legal obligation to disclose sufficient information to a patient to enable him to make an informed decision regarding a proposed medical treatment.

FACTS: Scott (P) developed complications following surgery performed by Bradford (D). She subsequently sued Bradford (D) for malpractice, contending that he failed to advise her as to the risks involved in her surgery or as to alternative methods of treatment. Furthermore, she asserted that had she been so advised, she would have refused the surgery and thus avoided the resultant complications. The case was submitted to the jury, which was advised in broad terms of the physician's duty to disclose. A verdict for Bradford (D) was returned, and Scott (P) appealed, claiming the jury instructions had been erroneously framed.

ISSUE: Is a doctor under a legal obligation to disclose sufficient information to a patient to enable him to make an informed decision regarding a proposed medical treatment?

HOLDING AND DECISION: (Doolin, J.) Yes. A doctor is under a legal obligation to disclose sufficient information to a patient to enable him to make an informed decision regarding a proposed medical treatment. It is basic to our legal system that each person is considered to be his or her own master. Thus, a doctrine has evolved, known as the doctrine of informed consent, which prohibits a physician from substituting his judgment for that of the patient regarding treatment of the patient's medical problems. Instead, the doctor must adequately apprise the patient of all potential risks and consequences of a proposed procedure so that she may properly determine for herself whether she wishes to undergo the suggested treatment. Absent such appraisal, the doctor may be liable for any injuries caused by the unconsented-to treatment. In order to recover, a patient must prove: (1) the doctor failed to inform her adequately of a material risk before securing her consent to the proposed treatment; (2) had she been informed of the risks she would not have consented to the treatment; and (3) the non-disclosed risk of injury did in fact occur. In the instant case, factors (1) and (3) were shown by Scott (P). As to (2), she testified that she would not have undergone surgery had Bradford (D) advised her of the risks. The jury obviously disbelieved her since it rendered a verdict for Bradford (D). It appears that the jury was properly instructed as to the "informed consent" cause of action for medical malpractice. Affirmed.

ANALYSIS

The courts generally provide for three basic exceptions to the physician's duty to disclose. The first is where the risks are either already known by the patient or are so obvious that they ought to be known. The second is where full disclosure might be harmful to the patient, for example, where an emotionally upset patient would be unduly alarmed or shocked. Finally, an exception occurs where there is an emergency, and the patient is in no condition to determine for himself whether treatment is necessary.

Quicknotes

DOCTRINE OF INFORMED CONSENT Consent to a particular occurrence requiring full notification as to the consequence of that consent.

DUTY TO DISCLOSE The duty owed by a fiduciary to reveal those facts that have a material effect on the interests of the party that must be informed.

Moore v. The Regents of the University of California

Patient (P) v. Physician (D) and university regents (D)

Cal. Sup. Ct., 51 Cal. 3d 120, 793 P.2d 479 (1990)

NATURE OF CASE: Review of dismissal of action seeking damages for conversion, trespass, and personal injury.

FACT SUMMARY: Dr. Golde (D) developed and patented a genetic cell line using cells from his patient, Moore (P), without Moore's (P) consent.

RULE OF LAW

A physician has a duty to disclose to a patient intended research connected to the patient's treatment.

FACTS: Moore (P) was treated at UCLA Medical Center for a type of leukemia. Golde (D) was his treating physician. Tests revealed that Moore's (P) tissues had certain unique properties that made it valuable in genetic engineering research. Without informing Moore (P) of this area of inquiry, Golde (D) removed various tissues, including Moore's (P) blood and spleen, over a span of several years. Golde (D), largely as a result of this research, obtained certain biomedical patents potentially worth large sums of money. Moore (P) later brought a suit claiming a proprietary interest in his tissues, as well as conversion, trespass, and breach of fiduciary duty. The trial court dismissed for failure to state a claim. The court of appeals affirmed, and the California Supreme Court granted review.

ISSUE: Does a physician have a duty to disclose to a patient intended research connected to the patient's treatment?

HOLDING AND DECISION: (Panelli, J.) Yes. A physician has a duty to disclose to a patient intended research connected to the patient's treatment. As an inherent ancillary to a patient's right to control his own body, a patient is entitled to make an informed choice in deciding whether to consent to treatment. When a physician has a pecuniary interest in the treatment, the patient has a right to be told this. This is because a pecuniary interest may influence a doctor's decisions regarding treatment, and the patient should be allowed to consider this possible conflict of interest in deciding whether to consent to treatment. A failure on the part of Golde (D) to disclose his research and financial interests in Moore's (P) cells constituted a breach of fiduciary duty, if proved. Remanded.

ANALYSIS

This was a case closely watched by the medical community but not for the issue discussed here. Moore (P) had alleged conversion, claiming a proprietary interest in his tissues. This held far-reaching implications for the medical research community if upheld. However, the court rejected this claim, concluding that the common-law doctrine of conversion did not apply to cells.

Quicknotes

BREACH OF FIDUCIARY DUTY The failure of a fiduciary to observe the standard of care exercised by professionals of similar education and experience.

CONVERSION The act of depriving an owner of his property without permission or justification.

DOCTRINE OF INFORMED CONSENT Consent to a particular occurrence requiring full notification as to the consequence of that consent.

INTER ALIA Among other things.

PROPRIETARY INTEREST An owner's interest and rights in property.

Pokora v. Wabash Ry. Co.

Injured driver (P) v. Railroad (D)

292 U.S. 98 (1934)

NATURE OF CASE: Action to recover damages for personal injury from negligence.

FACT SUMMARY: Pokora (P) drove a truck across a railroad crossing and was hit by a train.

RULE OF LAW

Unless reasonable minds could not differ on the point, the standard by which negligence is measured is for the jury to decide. Failure to get out of a vehicle and look before crossing a railroad track is not contributory negligence as a matter of law.

FACTS: Pokora (P) drove a truck up to a railroad crossing at which Wabash Ry. Co. (D) had four tracks. Because of boxcars on the first track, Pokora (P) could not see the tracks to the north. Pokura (P) stopped, looked, and listened, but heard nothing. Pokora (P) did not get out of his truck to walk forward and look down the tracks. As Pokora (P) drove slowly onto the main track, he was struck by a train coming from the north. The trial court took the case from the jury and granted a directed verdict for the Wabash Ry. (D) on the ground that Pokora's (P) conduct was contributory negligence as a matter of law. The case was affirmed by the circuit court of appeals; the United States Supreme Court then granted certiorari.

ISSUE: Was Pokora's (P) failure to get out of the vehicle and walk forward to look down the track before driving forward contributory negligence as a matter of law?

HOLDING AND DECISION: (Cardozo, J.) No. It is for the jury to decide whether a plaintiff's conduct is contributory negligence unless the conduct is so obviously negligent that reasonable minds could not differ on the point. Whether one must stop, look, and listen or whether one must get out of the vehicle and reconnoiter depends on the situation. What is safe varies, and it is up to the jury to decide whether a particular conduct is safe for the particular situation. Reversed and remanded.

ANALYSIS

This case reaffirms the proposition that, unless reasonable minds could not differ, it is up to the jury to decide whether a particular conduct is safe or negligent. Justice Cardozo, writing for the Supreme Court, warns about the danger of framing inflexible standards of behavior that amount to rules of law applied by the judge. The Court then limits the stop, look, listen and/or get out rule enunciated by Justice Holmes in *B. & O. R. Co. v. Goodman* 275 U.S. 66 (1927).

Quicknotes

CONTRIBUTORY NEGLIGENCE Behavior on the part of an injured plaintiff falling below the standard of ordinary care that contributes to the defendant's negligence, resulting in the plaintiff's injury.

Osborne v. McMasters

Estate administrator (P) v. Clerk's employer (D)

Minn. Sup. Ct., 40 Minn. 103, 41 N.W. 543 (1889)

NATURE OF CASE: Action for damages for death of plaintiff's intestate.

FACT SUMMARY: McMasters' (D) clerk, in the course of his employment, sold poison without a label to Osborne's (P) intestate.

RULE OF LAW

When a statute imposes a legal duty, violation of the statute constitutes conclusive evidence of negligence, i.e., negligence per se.

FACTS: Osborne's (P) intestate bought a deadly poison from McMasters' (D) clerk, who was acting within the course of his employment at a drug store. The clerk sold the poison without labeling it "Poison," although a statute made it a crime to do so. The object of the statute was to protect the public. Osborne (P) claimed that a statute imposes a specific duty and that one who neglects to perform the duty is liable to those for whose protection or benefit the duty was imposed. McMasters (D) claimed that, since no common-law duty to label poison existed, failure to label according to statute was not conclusive evidence of negligence in a civil action arising from a common-law right.

ISSUE: When a statute imposes a legal duty, does violation of the statute constitute conclusive evidence of negligence, i.e., negligence per se?

HOLDING AND DECISION: (Mitchell, J.) Yes. When a statute imposes a legal duty, violation of the statute constitutes conclusive evidence of negligence, i.e., negligence per se. Where a statute or municipal ordinance imposes on any person a specific duty for the protection or benefit of others, if he neglects to perform that duty he is liable to those for whose protection or benefit it was imposed for any injuries which the statute was designed to prevent and which were proximately caused by such neglect. Negligence is the breach of a legal duty. It is immaterial whether the duty is imposed by the common law or by statute. The statute establishes a fixed standard by which the fact of negligence may be determined. Here, the master is civilly liable for the negligence of his servant committed in the course of his employment and resulting in injuries to third persons. Affirmed.

ANALYSIS

This case establishes the proposition that violation of a criminal statute is conclusive evidence of negligence in a civil action where the statute was passed to protect a class of people (here, the public) of which the plaintiff is a member. This is the majority view. Other courts, including California's, treat such violations as giving rise to a presumption of negligence, which becomes negligence as a matter of law unless rebutted. The presumption can only be rebutted by showing an excuse for the violation. A minority of about half a dozen states holds that the violation is only evidence of negligence, which the jury may accept or reject as it sees fit. A few states treat violations of statutes as negligence per se while violations of ordinances are only evidence of negligence. There is a similar conflict as to the effect of the regulations of administrative bodies, acting under statutory authority. Although such violations are sometimes treated as negligence per se, there is more of a tendency here to treat them merely as evidence of negligence.

Quicknotes

NEGLIGENCE PER SE Conduct amounting to negligence as a matter of law because it is either so contrary to ordinary prudence or it is in violation of statute.

PLAINTIFF'S INTESTATE In this case, the term refers to the dead woman.

Stachniewicz v. Mar-Cam Corp.

Bar patron (P) v. Bar owner (D)

Or. Sup. Ct., 259 Or. 583, 488 P.2d 436 (1971)

NATURE OF CASE: Damages for negligence per se.

FACT SUMMARY: Stachniewicz (P), who was injured in a barroom brawl, sought damages on grounds that the bar's owner, Mar-Cam Corp. (D), violated a statute prohibiting the serving of liquor to obviously intoxicated persons.

RULE OF LAW

A violation of a statute or regulation constitutes negligence as a matter of law when the violation results in injury to a member of the class of persons intended to be protected by the legislation and when the harm is of the kind which the statute or regulation was intended to prevent.

FACTS: A barroom fight erupted when American Indian patrons, sitting in a booth adjacent to the table where Stachniewicz (P) was seated with friends, were apparently offended by the refusal of one of the friends to permit his wife to dance with one of the Indians who was visibly intoxicated. Before the fight, the bartender, who had received complaints about insults from the Indians, warned Stachniewicz's (P) friends not to start any trouble with them. When police arrived, the Indians ran out a door with one of the friends in pursuit. The friend found Stachniewicz (P) lying just outside, his feet wedging the door open. He suffered retrograde amnesia and could not recall how he got there. At trial, Stachniewicz (P) contended that Mar-Cam Corp. (D) violated state regulations against serving liquor to visibly intoxicated persons and against boisterous or profane conduct or allowing visibly intoxicated persons on the premises. When the trial court did not find Mar-Cam's (D) action negligence per se, Stachniewicz (P) appealed.

ISSUE: Does a violation of a statute or regulation constitute negligence as a matter of law when the violation results in injury to a member of the class of persons intended to be protected by the legislation and when the harm is of the kind which the statute or regulation was intended to prevent?

HOLDING AND DECISION: (Holman, J.) Yes. A violation of a statute or regulation constitutes negligence as a matter of law when the violation results in injury to a member of the class of persons intended to be protected by the legislation and when the harm is of the kind which the statute or regulation was intended to prevent. Here, the regulation concerns matters having a direct relation to the start of fights that would create a likelihood of injury to customers. It can be assumed that the regulations were intended to insure the safety of bar patrons. It is an appropriate standard for awarding civil damages because Stachniewicz (P) was within the class of persons intended to be protected, bar patrons, and the harm suffered was the kind against which the statute was intended to protect. A jury could infer that his injuries were suffered as a result of the fight. Reversed and remanded.

ANALYSIS

Many states have "Dram Shop Acts" which create tort actions against liquor sellers in specifically defined cases. Oftentimes, state legislative history is scanty, which gives courts wide latitude in determining the class to be protected and the harm against which the class is to be protected. The court in the case above simply assumed those factors in reaching its decision.

Quicknotes

DRAM SHOP ACT Law that imposes liability upon the seller of alcoholic beverages for injuries to a third party resulting from the intoxication of the buyer.

NEGLIGENCE PER SE Conduct amounting to negligence as a matter of law because it is either so contrary to ordinary prudence or it is in violation of statute.

Perry v. S.N. and S.N.

Witnesses (D) v. Parents (P)

Tex. Sup. Ct., 973 S.W.2d 301 (1998)

NATURE OF CASE: Suit for damages resulting from injuries arising out of child abuse.

FACT SUMMARY: Parents (P) of a child who was abused at a day care center brought suit against alleged eyewitnesses to the abuse for failure to report the abuse pursuant to state statute.

RULE OF LAW

Violation of a mandatory child abuse reporting statute does not constitute negligence per se.

FACTS: B.N. and K.N. attended a day care center run by the Kellers (D). Their parents (P) brought suit against the Kellers (D) and three of their friends, Perry (D), White (D) and Quintero (D), alleging that during that period Daniel Keller (D) regularly abused their children physically and sexually. The parents (P) claimed that Perry (D), White (D) and Quintero (D) were negligent per se for violating a statute requiring any person that believes a child's physical or mental health or welfare has been or may adversely affected by abuse to file a report with the Department of Protective and Regulatory Services. They sought damages for pain, mental anguish, medical expenses and loss of income. Perry (D), White (D) and Quintero (D) moved for summary judgment for failure to state a cause of action. The trial court granted the motion and the court of appeal affirmed as to the negligence claims but reversed and remanded on the issues of negligence per se and gross negligence, holding that the violation of the statute was negligence per se.

ISSUE: Does the violation of a mandatory child abuse reporting statute constitute negligence per se?

HOLDING AND DECISION: (Phillips, C.J.) No. Violation of a mandatory child abuse reporting statute does not constitute negligence per se. The issue in negligence per se cases is whether the plaintiff belongs to the class the statute was intended to protect and whether the plaintiff's injury is of a type that the statute was designed to prevent. Here the legislature's intent was to protect children adversely affected by abuse or neglect. Here the children were clearly within the class of persons the statute was intended to protect and they suffered the type of injury the statute was designed to prevent. Next the court must determine whether the imposition of tort liability for violation of the statute is proper. Several factors may be considered in making this determination. First is whether there exists a relevant common-law duty. Here, negligence per se cause of action would derive the element of duty only from the Family Code. The court of appeals also mentioned several factors to be considered to deciding whether to apply negligence per se. These include whether the legislature has determined that compliance with criminal statutes is practicable and desirable and that the statutes give citizens notice of what conduct is required of them. With respect to notice, the court must consider whether the statute clearly defines the prohibited or required conduct. Here the statute imposes a duty to report when a person "has cause to believe" sexual abuse is occurring. This requirement does not clearly define what conduct is required in many situations. Next the court must consider whether applying negligence per se would create liability without fault. Here it would not because the statute only imposes liability for "knowing" failure to report. Third is whether negligence would impose liability disproportionate to the seriousness of the defendant's conduct. Here the penalty imposed for failure to report is far less than for abusers, weighing against the imposition of civil liability for nonreporters for damages resulting from the abuser's conduct. Last is whether the injury resulted directly or indirectly from violation of the statute. A majority of jurisdictions have held that failure to report child abuse is not negligence per se. Reversed.

ANALYSIS

The decision in this case rests on the issue of whether the defendants had a duty under tort law requiring the imposition of liability for failure to exercise that duty. A court will not impose civil liability for violation of a criminal statute without the existence of a corresponding common-law duty.

Quicknotes

CHILD ABUSE Conduct that is harmful to a child's physical or mental health.

NEGLIGENCE PER SE Conduct amounting to negligence as a matter of law because it is either so contrary to ordinary prudence or it is in violation of statute.

Martin v. Herzog

Unlit buggy rider (P) v. Car driver (D)

N.Y. Ct. App., 228 N.Y. 164, 126 N.E. 814 (1920)

NATURE OF CASE: Action for damages for death of plaintiff's intestate.

FACT SUMMARY: Martin (P) was killed in a collision between the buggy he was driving and Herzog's (D) automobile. Martin (P) was driving the buggy without lights, in violation of a criminal statute requiring lights.

RULE OF LAW

The unexcused omission to perform a statutory duty is negligence per se.

FACTS: Martin (P) was driving his buggy without lights when he was killed in a collision between the buggy and Herzog's (D) car. It was after dark and there was a criminal statute requiring lights. The trial judge refused Herzog's (D) request for an instruction that the absence of lights on Martin's (P) vehicle was prima facie evidence of contributory negligence, and instructed instead that the jury might consider the absence of lights as some evidence of negligence, but that it was not conclusive evidence. He granted Martin's (P) request for an instruction that the fact that Martin was driving without a light is not negligence in itself. The jury returned a verdict for Martin (P); the Appellate Division reversed; Martin (P) appealed to the court of appeals.

ISSUE: Is the unexcused omission of a statutory duty contributory negligence per se?

HOLDING AND DECISION: (Cardozo, J.) Yes. The unexcused omission of the statutory signals is more than just evidence of negligence; it is negligence in itself. Jurors have no power to relax the duty that one traveler on the highway owes under a statute to another traveler. It is error to instruct them that they have. The omission of lights, since it was unexcused, was negligence. However, a causal connection between the negligence and the injury must also be shown. Evidence of a collision occurring after dark between a car and an unlighted buggy is evidence from which a causal connection may be inferred between the collision and the lack of signals. If nothing is shown to break the connection, there is prima facie evidence of negligence contributing to the result. Affirmed.

ANALYSIS

This case states the position, followed by a great majority of the courts, that violation of a statute is negligence per se when a statute applies to the facts and the violation is unexcused. Note, however, that the court emphasizes that one must not confuse the question of negligence with that of the causal connection between the negligence and the injury, and that conduct that is negligent is not always contributory negligence.

Quicknotes

CONTRIBUTORY NEGLIGENCE Behavior on the part of an injured plaintiff falling below the standard of ordinary care that contributes to the defendant's negligence, resulting in the plaintiff's injury.

PRIMA FACIE An action in which the plaintiff introduces sufficient evidence to submit an issue to the judge or jury for determination.

STATUTORY DUTY An obligation owed by one individual to another pursuant to a particular statute.

Zeni v. Anderson

Injured pedestrian (P) v. Car driver (D)

Mich. Sup. Ct., 397 Mich. 117, 243 N.W.2d 270 (1976)

NATURE OF CASE: Appeal from reversal of award of damages for negligence.

FACT SUMMARY: Zeni (P) was struck by a car and injured while walking on a well-worn snow path with her back to oncoming traffic.

RULE OF LAW

Violation of a statute creates a presumption of negligence, which may be rebutted by a showing of adequate excuse for the violation.

FACTS: On a snowy morning, Zeni (P) was walking to work. Instead of using the snow-covered sidewalk, she traveled along a well-used pedestrian snow path, with her back to the oncoming traffic. A car driven by Anderson (D) struck Zeni (P), causing her severe injuries. There was evidence that Anderson (D) may have been traveling too close to the curb. At trial, the jury returned a verdict for Zeni (P), despite Anderson's (D) contentions that Zeni's (P) actions in walking in the street, rather than the sidewalk, constituted a violation of a state statute and as such was negligence per se, thus absolving Anderson (D) of liability. The court of appeals reversed. Zeni (P) appealed.

ISSUE: May the presumption of negligence arising from a statute violation be rebutted by evidence showing an adequate excuse for the violation?

HOLDING AND DECISION: (Williams, J.) Yes. Violation of a statute creates a presumption of negligence, which may be rebutted by a showing of adequate excuse for the violation. It would be unreasonable to adhere to a rigid, automatic rule of negligence per se in all cases involving statutory violations. This is because in some circumstances, the violator may have reasonable justification for not acting in accordance with the statute. As such, she must be able to offer proof of such justification in order to allow the jury to determine whether she is a deserving plaintiff or an "innocent" defendant, despite the technical statute violation. Accordingly, the fairest approach is to hold that the violation of a statute creates a rebuttable presumption of negligence which may be overcome by a showing of an adequate justification for the violation. In the instant case, the issue of the violation, along with Zeni's (P) excuse, was properly presented to the jury. As such, the judgment for Zeni (P) should be reinstated. Reversed.

ANALYSIS

Section 288A of the Restatement (Second) of Torts provides several valid excuses for the violation of a statute. These include: (1) where the actor's incapacity makes the violation reasonable; (2) where he is justifiably unaware of the need for compliance; (3) where he is unable due to the circumstances to comply with the statute; (4) where an emergency not caused by his own conduct makes it impossible to comply; and (5) where compliance would create a great risk to the actor or to others. The Restatement further notes that the list of excuses is meant to be illustrative and not exclusive.

Quicknotes

IRREBUTTABLE PRESUMPTION A rule of law inferred from the existence of a particular set of facts that is not subject to dispute.

NEGLIGENCE PER SE Conduct amounting to negligence as a matter of law because it is either so contrary to ordinary prudence or it is in violation of statute.

Goddard v. Boston & Maine R.R. Co.

Train passenger (P) v. Railroad company (D)

Mass. Sup. Jud. Ct., 179 Mass. 52, 60 N.E. 486 (1901)

NATURE OF CASE: Action for injuries sustained in a slip-and-fall.

FACT SUMMARY: A train passenger slipped on a banana skin and fell on a train-station platform shortly after he got off the train.

RULE OF LAW

A business owes no duty of reasonable care to ensure its patrons' safety unless the business has adequate notice that conditions on the premises are potentially dangerous.

FACTS: Goddard (P) got off a train at a station owned by the Boston & Maine Railroad Co. (D). Goddard (P) walked about the length of one train car on the platform. He then slipped and fell on a banana skin, sustaining injuries from his fall. The accident occurred shortly after Goddard's (P) train reached the station. Many passengers besides Goddard (P) were on the platform at the time. Goddard (P) sued the railroad company (D) for negligence. After the evidence at trial closed, the trial judge directed a verdict for the railroad company (D), and Goddard (P) appealed.

ISSUE: Does a business owe a duty of reasonable care to ensure its patrons' safety unless the business has adequate notice that conditions on the premises are potentially dangerous?

HOLDING AND DECISION: (Holmes, C.J.) No. A business owes no duty of reasonable care to ensure its patrons' safety unless the business has adequate notice that conditions on the premises are potentially dangerous. Although a banana skin was on the platform, one of the other passengers who were present could have dropped it there within a minute of the accident. Exceptions overruled.

ANALYSIS

The lesson in the law of negligence in Chief Justice Holmes's succinct opinion in *Goddard* is clear: In Massachusetts at the turn of the twentieth century, courts did not impose a duty of reasonable care on a business for an alleged failure to correct a dangerous situation unless the business had a reasonable opportunity to discover the condition. The practice lesson in *Goddard* is just as clear and perhaps more durable: A trier of fact cannot base a verdict on mere speculation, which is all that the evidence on how long the banana skin had been on the platform would permit a reasonable juror. As Chief Justice Holmes notes, the banana skin "may have been dropped within a minute" of Goddard's (P) fall, which is the same as saying that the skin also "may have been dropped" at a time sufficiently prior to the accident for the railroad company (D) to have owed Goddard (P) a particular duty of care. See, e.g., *Anderson v. Pre-Fab Transit Co.*, 409 N.E.2d 1157, 1160 (Ind. Ct. App. 1980) ("the 'might have' standard is not a correct statement of the burden of proof . . . [because it] invites the [trier of fact] to speculate"). Such inconclusive evidence cannot support a reasonable inference, and the trial judge therefore must direct a verdict for the defendant. When the burden of proof requires a preponderance of the evidence, a plaintiff must prove that an essential fact is more likely than not to have occurred as the law requires it to have occurred.

Quicknotes

BURDEN OF PROOF The duty of a party to introduce evidence to support a fact that is in dispute in an action.

DIRECTED VERDICT A verdict ordered by the court in a jury trial.

DUTY OF REASONABLE CARE Duty to exercise the degree of care as would a reasonably prudent person under like circumstances.

NEGLIGENCE Conduct falling below the standard of care that a reasonable person would demonstrate under similar conditions.

Anjou v. Boston Elevated Railway Co.

Slip-and-fall victim (P) v. Railroad (D)

Mass. Sup. Jud. Ct., 208 Mass. 273, 94 N.E. 386 (1911)

NATURE OF CASE: Action to recover damages for personal injuries due to negligence.

FACT SUMMARY: Anjou (P) was injured when she slipped on a dry, gritty, black banana peel lying on the platform at the Boston Elevated Railway Co.'s (D) station.

RULE OF LAW

Circumstantial evidence can sustain plaintiff's burden of proof of negligence only if a reasonable jury can draw from it the positive inference that defendant was negligent.

FACTS: Anjou (P) was a passenger who had just gotten off a train on the upper level of the Boston Elevated Railway Company's ("the Railway Co.") (D) Dudley Street terminal. She waited until the arriving crowd had left the platform and then asked a uniformed employee of the Railway Co. (D) for directions to another car. She followed this employee along a narrow platform toward a stairway he indicated. She slipped on a banana peel, fell, and was injured. Witnesses described the peel as dry, gritty, black, trampled over; and flattened down. The lower court directed a verdict for the Railway Co. (D).

ISSUE: Can circumstantial evidence sustain plaintiff's burden of proof of negligence only if a reasonable jury can draw from it the positive inference that defendant was negligent?

HOLDING AND DECISION: (Rugg, J.) Yes. Circumstantial evidence can sustain plaintiff's burden of proof of negligence only if a reasonable jury can draw from it the positive inference that defendant was negligent. The issue of negligence must go to the jury as a question of fact once the court decides that a reasonable jury can draw from the evidence the positive inference that defendant was negligent. In this case, the Railway Co. (D) (through its employees) had a duty to use reasonable care to keep its station safe for passengers. This included a duty to observe and remove anything on the platform that might interfere with passengers' safety. From the appearance and condition of the banana peel, a reasonable jury might draw the inference that it had been lying on the platform for a long time. From this inference, the jury might conclude that to leave the banana peel lying there for so long was negligence on the part of the Railway Co. (D). The issue of negligence should have been submitted to the jury, and the lower court erred in directing a verdict for the Railway Co. (D). (In this case, rather than remand for a new trial, judgment is given for Anjou (P) "in accordance with the terms of the report.")

ANALYSIS

The *Goddard,* 60 N.E. 410 (1901), case is distinguished. The question of negligence was thought to hinge on how long the Railway Co. (D) had allowed the banana peel to lie on the platform. In *Goddard,* there was no evidence to show how long it had been there, whereas in this case there was evidence to indicate it had been there for a long time. Other instances in which the presence of litter has been held to be a breach of defendant's duty of due care toward users of the premises include a self-service cafeteria (garbage on the floor) and a department store (gum on the stairs). In those cases, it was not necessary to introduce evidence to show how long the specific piece of litter had been there, as it was for the offending banana peel here.

Quicknotes

CIRCUMSTANTIAL EVIDENCE Evidence that though not directly observed supports the inference of principal facts.

DUTY OF REASONABLE CARE Duty to exercise the degree of care as would a reasonably prudent person under like circumstances.

NEGLIGENCE Conduct falling below the standard of care that a reasonable person would demonstrate under similar conditions.

REMAND To send back for additional scrutiny or deliberation.

Joye v. Great Atlantic and Pacific Tea Co.

Slip-and-fall victim (P) v. Store owner (D)

405 F.2d 464 (4th Cir. 1968)

NATURE OF CASE: Appeal from an award of damages for negligence.

FACT SUMMARY: Joye (P) was injured when he slipped and fell on a banana at Great Atlantic and Pacific Tea Co's A&P (D) supermarket.

RULE OF LAW

Without constructive notice of a dangerous condition, a defendant cannot be held liable for negligence.

FACTS: Joye (P) was injured when he slipped and fell on a banana in Great Atlantic and Pacific Tea Co.'s A&P (A&P) (D) supermarket. No direct evidence was offered as to how long the banana was on the floor before Joye (P) encountered it. The floor may not have been swept for as long as 35 minutes before the fall, and no one saw it until after Joye (P) fell. The banana was described as dark brown, having dirt and sand on it. The floor was dirty, and the banana was sticky about the edges. There was no evidence that A&P (D) put the banana on the floor or had actual notice of it. Joye (P) was awarded $10,000, and A&P (D) appealed arguing that it did not have constructive notice of the banana's being on the floor.

ISSUE: Can a defendant be held liable for negligence without constructive notice of the dangerous condition?

HOLDING AND DECISION: (Craven, J.) No. Without constructive notice of a dangerous condition, a defendant cannot be held liable for negligence. The case turns on the sufficiency of circumstantial evidence to establish constructive notice. From the evidence, a "jury could not tell whether the banana had been on A&P's (D) floor for 30 seconds or three days." Reversed.

ANALYSIS

This case seems to be difficult to reconcile with *Anjou v. Boston Elevated Railway Co.*, 94 N.E. 386 (1911). In both cases, brown, gritty bananas were involved. Liability may have ensued in *Anjou* on the basis of the higher duty to which common carriers are held. The court said that it was impossible to determine just how long the banana was on the floor, but the matter for determination would only seem to have been that the banana was on the floor for an unreasonably long time, which it would seem a jury could infer from the evidence.

Quicknotes

CIRCUMSTANTIAL EVIDENCE Evidence that though not directly observed supports the inference of principal facts.

CONSTRUCTIVE NOTICE Knowledge of a fact that is imputed to an individual who was under a duty to inquire and who could have learned of the fact through the exercise of reasonable prudence.

DANGEROUS CONDITION A condition of property that poses a reasonably foreseeable substantial risk of injury giving rise to liability for a public entity.

NEGLIGENCE Conduct falling below the standard of care that a reasonable person would demonstrate under similar conditions.

Ortega v. Kmart Corp.

Customer (P) v. Department store (D)

Cal. Sup. Ct., 26 Cal. 4th 1200, 36 P.3d 11 (2001)

NATURE OF CASE: Action for injuries sustained in a slip-and-fall.

FACT SUMMARY: A department-store customer sustained injuries when he slipped on a puddle of milk and fell. He could not prove how long the milk was on the floor before he slipped on it, but he did prove that the store probably had not checked the premises for at least 15-30 minutes before the accident.

RULE OF LAW

A store owner has a duty of reasonable care to inspect the store's premises within a reasonable period of time sufficient to permit discovery and correction of potentially dangerous conditions.

FACTS: While shopping in a Kmart (D) store, Ortega (P) slipped on a puddle of milk and fell, seriously injuring one of his knees. He sued Kmart (D) for his injuries, claiming that Kmart (D) was negligent for leaving the milk on the floor. Although Ortega (P) could not prove how long the milk was on the floor before he slipped on it, he could show that Kmart (D) had failed to inspect the premises within 15-30 minutes, and perhaps for as long as two hours, before the accident. Ortega (P) argued that such proof permitted jurors to infer that the milk had been on the floor long enough that Kmart's (D) employees should have discovered and removed the spill. Kmart (D), on the other hand, argued that Ortega (P) failed to show that the milk had been on the floor long enough to give the store constructive notice of the potentially dangerous condition. The jury awarded Ortega (P) $47,000. Kmart (D) appealed.

ISSUE: Does a store owner have a duty of reasonable care to inspect the store's premises within a reasonable period of time sufficient to permit discovery and correction of potentially dangerous conditions?

HOLDING AND DECISION: (Chin, J.) Yes. A store owner has a duty of reasonable care to inspect the store's premises within a reasonable period of time sufficient to permit discovery and correction of potentially dangerous conditions. Store owners owe their customers a duty to take reasonable measures to maintain reasonably safe premises. This duty is discharged by making reasonable inspections of those portions of the premises that are typically used by customers. If a plaintiff bases a negligence claim on a store's failure to correct a potentially dangerous condition, though, the evidence must show that the store had notice of the problem with enough time to remove the danger. Actual notice is not necessary: A store owner will be charged with constructive notice if the plaintiff shows that the potentially dangerous condition persisted long enough for a reasonably prudent store owner's employees to discover and correct the problem. The amount of time that suffices will vary from one case to another and is determined by the trier of fact. Plaintiffs can meet their burden on constructive notice by showing, as Ortega (P) did here, that the store's employees failed to inspect the premises within a reasonable period of time before an accident occurred. Affirmed.

ANALYSIS

Although it's tempting to see *Goddard v. Boston & Maine R. R. Co.*, 60 N.E. 410 (1901), as pro-business and *Ortega* as much less sympathetic toward business, it's also easy to reconcile the two decisions. In *Goddard*, the plaintiff showed only that the banana skin fell to the station platform only within some unspecified, wholly speculative timeframe. Here, the court in *Ortega* merely establishes some relatively specific guidelines for what timeframe suffices to show that a store owner has exercised reasonably prudent care in maintaining safe premises for customers.

Quicknotes

DUTY OF REASONABLE CARE Duty to exercise the degree of care as would a reasonably prudent person under like circumstances.

Jasko v. F.W. Woolworth Co.

Slip-and-fall victim (P) v. Department store (D)

Colo. Sup. Ct., 177 Colo. 418, 494 P.2d 839 (1972)

NATURE OF CASE: Appeal from denial of damages for negligence.

FACT SUMMARY: Jasko (P) was injured when she slipped and fell on a piece of pizza that fell on the floor near the counter where pieces of pizza were sold.

RULE OF LAW

When the operating methods of a proprietor are such that dangerous conditions are continuous or easily foreseeable, conventional notice requirements need not be met.

FACTS: Jasko (P) was injured when she fell on a piece of pizza that was on the terrazzo (tile) floor near the "Pizza Hoagie Counter" in an F.W. Woolworth Co. (Woolworth) (D) department store. Instead of showing actual or constructive notice to Woolworth (D) of the dangerous condition, Jasko (P) argued that Woolworth's (D) method of selling pizza slices on waxed paper to customers who stand while eating created a reasonable probability that food would drop to the floor, and that steps taken to constantly clean the floor showed that Woolworth (D) recognized the danger. Judgment was for Woolworth (D), and Jasko (P) appealed.

ISSUE: When the operating methods of a proprietor are such that dangerous conditions are continuous or easily foreseeable, must conventional notice requirements be met?

HOLDING AND DECISION: (Groves, J.) No. When the operating methods of a proprietor are such that dangerous conditions are continuous or easily foreseeable, conventional notice requirements need not be met. Basic notice requirements arise from the view that dangerous conditions are not ordinary, and in such a situation a storekeeper is allowed a reasonable time to discover and correct the condition unless it is the direct result of his or her employee's acts. When the danger is continuous or easily foreseeable, the logical basis for the notice requirement does not exist. As actual or constructive notice was not required to be proved, the decision is reversed and remanded.

ANALYSIS

Note that in any case, a plaintiff has two burdens of proof to satisfy. In order to avoid a directed verdict against him, a plaintiff must satisfy the burden of coming forward with evidence to establish the element of his case, that it is more probable than not that he is correct. The second burden is to convince the jury by a preponderance of the evidence that he is correct. Above, by allowing a showing that the dangerous condition was continuous or reasonably foreseeable to be sufficient, the court presumed that the store had notice of the condition, which placed the burden on Woolworth (D) to show otherwise.

Quicknotes

DIRECTED VERDICT A verdict ordered by the court in a jury trial.

PREPONDERANCE OF THE EVIDENCE A standard of proof requiring the trier of fact to determine whether the fact sought to be established is more probable than not.

REASONABLE FORESEEABILITY A reasonable expectation that an act or omission would result in injury.

H.E. Butt Groc. Co. v. Resendez

Grocery store (D) v. Customer (P)

Tex. Sup. Ct., 988 S.W.2d 218 (1999)

NATURE OF CASE: Action for injuries sustained in a slip-and-fall.

FACT SUMMARY: A grocery-store customer slipped and fell near a grape display that permitted customer sampling. The customer sued the store for her injuries, claiming that merely displaying the produce for customer sampling created an unreasonable risk of harm.

RULE OF LAW

Merely displaying produce for customer sampling in a grocery store, without more, does not create an unreasonable risk of harm.

FACTS: The H.E. Butt Grocery Co. (HEB) (D) put up two grape displays in one of its stores. One of the displays had loose grapes in a bowl on a table for customer sampling; the bowl sat on ice about five inches below the top of the table. A three-inch rail surrounded the table's edge. The floor was a non-skid floor, floor mats had been placed around the tables, and warning cones also sat near the displays. Resendez (P) slipped near the displays and fell. At trial the jury returned a verdict for Resendez (P), and Texas's intermediate appellate court affirmed.

ISSUE: Does merely displaying produce for customer sampling in a grocery store, without more, create an unreasonable risk of harm?

HOLDING AND DECISION: (Per curiam) No. Merely displaying produce for customer sampling in a grocery store, without more, does not create an unreasonable risk of harm. Contrary to the court of appeals' reasoning, the law requires plaintiffs to show more than merely displaying produce for customer sampling to demonstrate an unreasonable risk of harm. Resendez's (P) burden required her to show (1) actual or constructive knowledge of the store's condition, (2) the existence of an unreasonable risk of harm in the condition, (3) HEB's (D) failure to exercise reasonable care to remove the risk, and (4) the failure to exercise care caused Resendez's (P) injuries. Unlike the plaintiff in *Corbin v. Safeway Stores*, 648 S.W.2d 292 (Tex. 1983), Resendez (P) failed to prove an unreasonable risk of harm. The plaintiff in *Corbin* proved more than the mere existence of a grape display; the determinative fact in *Corbin* was the slanted angle of the display in which the store offered its grapes without any floor mats around the display for further protection. Such additional evidence is not present in this case. Reversed.

ANALYSIS

The store owners in *H.E. Butt* took several affirmative steps to ensure its customers' safety around a potentially dangerous produce display. Those facts further distinguish this case from the cited precedent, *Corbin*, where the defendant not only failed to take such steps but also admitted full prior awareness of the circumstances that caused the plaintiff's injuries in that case. *See* 648 S.W.2d 292, 296 (Tex. 1983). Also worth noting is that *H.E. Butt* does not address the issue of actual or constructive notice at all. Is it possible that the store's affirmative exercises of caution had the effect of both admitting notice and turning that issue to the store's persuasive advantage by showing a diligent effort to discharge its duty of care?

Quicknotes

ACTUAL NOTICE The direct communication of information to a person.

CONSTRUCTIVE NOTICE Knowledge of a fact that is imputed to an individual who was under a duty to inquire and who could have learned of the fact through the exercise of reasonable prudence.

DUTY OF CARE A principle of negligence requiring an individual to act in such a manner as to avoid injury to a person to whom he or she owes a duty.

Byrne v. Boadle

Injured passerby (P) v. Shop owner (D)

Ex., 2 H&C 722, 159 Eng. Rep. 299 (1863)

NATURE OF CASE: Action to recover damages for negligence.

FACT SUMMARY: While Byrne (P) was walking along the street, passing Boadle's (D) shop, a barrel fell from the shop window and struck Byrne (P), injuring him.

RULE OF LAW

When it is highly probable that an injury is due to the negligence of the defendant, and the defendant has better access to the evidence concerning the injury, the doctrine of res ipsa loquitur creates an inference that the defendant was negligent, and puts the burden on defendant to introduce contrary evidence.

FACTS: Byrne (P) was walking in a public street past Boadle's (D) flour shop, when a barrel of flour rolled out of the window above Byrne (P), striking and injuring him. The trial court nonsuited Byrne (P), ruling that there was no evidence of any negligence.

ISSUE: When it is highly probable that an injury is due to the negligence of the defendant, and the defendant has better access to the evidence concerning the injury, does the doctrine of res ipsa loquitur create an inference that the defendant was negligent, and put the burden on defendant to introduce contrary evidence?

HOLDING AND DECISION: (Pollock, C.B.) Yes. When it is highly probable that an injury is due to the negligence of the defendant, and the defendant has better access to the evidence concerning the injury, the doctrine of res ipsa loquitur creates an inference that the defendant was negligent, and puts the burden on defendant to introduce contrary evidence. According to the ancient doctrine of res ipsa loquitur, "the thing speaks for itself." The mere fact that a barrel of flour fell on a passer-by outside of Boadle's (D) flour shop is prima facie evidence of the latter's negligence, and Byrne (P) cannot be expected to prove that it could not have happened without some negligence. If there are any facts inconsistent with a finding of negligence, it is for Boadle (D) to prove them.

ANALYSIS

This is one of the earliest cases applying the doctrine of res ipsa loquitur. In a later English case, the rule was stated as follows: "There must be reasonable evidence of negligence; but where the thing is shown to be under the management of the defendant or his servants, and the accident is such as in the ordinary course of things does not happen if those who have the management use proper care, it affords reasonable evidence, in the absence of explanation by the defendants, that the accident arose from want of care." To invoke the doctrine, the plaintiff need not explain away all possibilities, as long as he shows that such accidents do not occur without negligence; the burden of proof is then shifted to the defendant.

Quicknotes

NEGLIGENCE Conduct falling below the standard of care that a reasonable person would demonstrate under similar conditions.

NONSUIT Judgment against a party who fails to make out a case.

RES IPSA LOQUITUR A rule of law giving rise to an inference of negligence where the instrument inflicting the injury is in the exclusive control of the defendant and where such harm could not ordinarily result in the absence of negligence.

RULE NISI Motion by one party to make a final ruling against the opponent, unless the opponent can show cause as to why such ruling should not be ordered.

Larson v. St. Francis Hotel

Accident victim (P) v. Hotel (D)

Cal. Dist. Ct. App., 83 Cal. App. 2d 210, 188 P.2d 513 (1948)

NATURE OF CASE: Action to recover damages for personal injuries due to negligence.

FACT SUMMARY: Larson (P), walking on the sidewalk near the St. Francis Hotel (D), on V-J Day, was hit on the head by a falling overstuffed armchair.

RULE OF LAW

The doctrine of res ipsa loquitur applies only where the cause of the injury is shown to be under the exclusive control and management of the defendant.

FACTS: Amidst the celebrations of V-J Day, August 14, 1945, Larson (P) was walking on the sidewalk near the St. Francis Hotel ("the Hotel") (D) in San Francisco. Just after she stepped out from under the marquee, Larson (P) was hit on the head by a heavy, overstuffed armchair, knocked unconscious, and injured. No one saw where the chair came from. At the trial, Larson (P) relied on res ipsa loquitur and the judge granted a nonsuit against her. She appealed.

ISSUE: Does the doctrine of res ipsa loquitur apply only where the cause of the injury is shown to be under the exclusive control and management of the defendant?

HOLDING AND DECISION: (Bray, J.) Yes. The doctrine of res ipsa loquitur applies only where the cause of the injury is shown to be under the exclusive control and management of the defendant. It does not apply to a case where an unexplained event may have been attributable to one of several causes, for some of which the defendant is not responsible. In this case, the Hotel (D) did not have exclusive control of its furniture. The Hotel's (D) guests had partial control over the furniture. The injury to Larson (P) is as likely due to the fault of a guest or other person as to the Hotel (D). The most logical inference is that some such person threw the chair from a window. It thus appears that this occurrence is not such as ordinarily does not happen without the negligence of the party charged, but, rather, one in which the accident ordinarily might happen despite the fact that the defendants used reasonable care and were totally free from negligence. Affirmed.

ANALYSIS

Note the difference between this case and *Byrne v. Boadle*, Ex., 2 H&C 722, 159 Eng. Rep. 299 (1863), where a flour barrel fell on plaintiff. The nature of the hotel business is such that there are likely to be guests or visitors on the premises who may negligently throw furniture, whereas the nature of the flour warehousing business is such that no one except employees are likely to be on the premises who may negligently drop a flour barrel. The "exclusive control" rule is not always as literally or rigidly applied as this case might seem to indicate. Its purpose is basically to make sure that it is reasonable to pin the negligence on the defendant. Accordingly, where other causes for an event besides defendant's negligence (such as acts of third parties) are in the first instance equally probable, evidence which permits the jury to eliminate such causes will serve to make res ipsa loquitur applicable. It has been suggested that it would avoid confusion if this rule were not stated on terms of "control" at all, but rather were stated as a requirement that the apparent cause of the accident must be such that the defendant would be responsible for any negligence connected with it.

Quicknotes

EXCLUSIVE CONTROL RULE Necessary element of res ipsa loquitur doctrine that the defendant have total control of the instrument that inflicted the injury.

NEGLIGENCE Conduct falling below the standard of care that a reasonable person would demonstrate under similar conditions.

NONSUIT Judgment against a party who fails to make out a case.

RES IPSA LOQUITUR A rule of law giving rise to an inference of negligence where the instrument inflicting the injury is in the exclusive control of the defendant and where such harm could not ordinarily result in the absence of negligence.

Cruz v. DaimlerChrysler Motors Corp.

Vehicle owner (P) v. Manufacturer (D)

R.I. Sup. Ct., 66 A.3d 446 (2013)

NATURE OF CASE: Appeal from summary judgment for defendant in action for negligence asserting, inter alia, res ipsa loquitur.

FACT SUMMARY: Nelson Cruz (P), who was injured when the airbags of his minivan deployed while he was cleaning it out, asserted the doctrine of res ipsa loquitur against Ricky Smith Pontiac GMC, Inc. (Ricky Smith) (D), the dealership that sold him the vehicle three years earlier, in an effort to establish a prima facie case of negligence by Ricky Smith (D).

RULE OF LAW

A plaintiff cannot use the doctrine of res ipsa loquitur to raise an inference of the defendant's negligence where, although the injury-causing event at issue ordinarily does not occur in the absence of negligence, the plaintiff cannot present evidence that points the negligence to the defendant.

FACTS: Nelson Cruz (P) was injured when he was cleaning out his minivan and the front airbags deployed. Cruz (P) brought suit against manufacturer DaimlerChrysler Motors Corp. (DaimlerChrysler) (D) and Ricky Smith Pontiac GMC, Inc. (Ricky Smith) (D), the car dealership that had sold him the minivan three years earlier. Because Daimler-Chrysler (D) had declared bankruptcy, Cruz (P) dropped the claims against it, and pursued claims for negligence and negligent misrepresentation against Ricky Smith (D). Cruz (P) asserted the doctrine of res ipsa loquitur in an effort to establish a prima facie case of negligence. The trial court, finding that Cruz (P) produced no evidence that Ricky Smith (D) negligently caused harm to Cruz (P), and that Cruz's (P) res ipsa loquitur claim and other claims failed, granted summary judgment to Ricky Smith (D). Cruz (P) appealed, and the state's highest court granted review.

ISSUE: Can a plaintiff use the doctrine of res ipsa loquitur to raise an inference of the defendant's negligence where, although the injury-causing event at issue ordinarily does not occur in the absence of negligence, the plaintiff cannot present evidence that points the negligence to the defendant?

HOLDING AND DECISION: (Indeglia, J.) No. A plaintiff cannot use the doctrine of res ipsa loquitur to raise an inference of the defendant's negligence where, although the injury-causing event at issue ordinarily does not occur in the absence of negligence, the plaintiff cannot present evidence that points the negligence to the defendant. The res ipsa loquitur doctrine is used to establish inferential evidence of a defendant's negligence where a plaintiff—like Cruz (P) here—lacks direct proof of a defendant's negligence. As set forth in § 328(D) of the Restatement (Second) of Torts, a plaintiff may avail itself of the doctrine where: (a) the event is of a kind that ordinarily does not occur in the absence of negligence; (b) other responsible causes, including the conduct of the plaintiff and third persons, are sufficiently eliminated by the evidence; and (c) the indicated negligence is within the scope of the defendant's duty to the plaintiff. Here, the first element is satisfied, since, absent negligence, airbags ordinarily do not spontaneously deploy while a car is being cleaned. However, three years have elapsed since the vehicle was sold. Although Ricky Smith (D) had a duty to discover any defects that were extant at the time of sale that would have caused the spontaneous airbag deployment, no evidence has been presented that the vehicle was defective when it was sold. Thus, Cruz (P) has failed to point the negligence to Ricky Smith (D). Here, other responsible causes have not been sufficiently eliminated by the evidence. Affirmed.

ANALYSIS

As this case illustrates, the availability of the res ipsa loquitur doctrine is fact dependent. For example, in this case, had the airbags deployed shortly after Cruz (P) purchased the vehicle, res ipsa loquitur might have permitted the inference that Ricky Smith (D) was negligent in failing to inspect and detect the defect. However, here the three years between the sale of the vehicle and the deployment of the bags raised the specter of too many possible other responsible causes, so that such an inference was not supported, and the doctrine was unavailable.

Quicknotes

RES IPSA LOQUITUR A rule of law giving rise to an inference of negligence where the instrument inflicting the injury is in the exclusive control of the defendant and where such harm could not ordinarily result in the absence of negligence.

James v. Wormuth

Patient (P) v. Physician (D)

N.Y. Ct. App., 21 N.Y.3d 540, 997 N.E.2d 133 (2013)

NATURE OF CASE: Appeal from affirmance of directed verdict to defendant in medical malpractice action.

FACT SUMMARY: James (P) claimed Wormuth (D) committed medical malpractice after Wormuth (D) intentionally left a dislodged guide wire in James's (P) body upon ending a surgical procedure, as Wormuth (D) was unable to manually find the wire and determined that completing the procedure was in James's (P) best interest. The wire was removed during a second operation.

RULE OF LAW

In a medical malpractice action based on a foreign object being left in a patient's body, the theory of res ipsa loquitur may not be used to establish a physician's negligence where the physician intentionally left the foreign object in the patient's body based on the physician's judgment that doing so would be in the patient's best interest.

FACTS: During a surgical operation conducted by Dr. Wormuth (D) on James (P), Wormuth (D) discovered that a guide wire had dislodged. Wormuth (D) could not find the wire after manually searching for it for 20 minutes, and determined that concluding the procedure was in James's (P) best interest, so as not to extend the period of time James (P) was anaesthetized nor to enlarge the incision. Although Wormuth (D) was in charge of the procedure, there were other medical personnel involved in the process of inserting the wire and transporting James (P) prior to Wormuth's (D) discovery that the wire had dislodged. He informed James (P) of these facts and his decisions after the procedure. Several weeks later, after James (P) complained of pain, Wormuth (D) performed a second operation to remove the wire. James (P) then sued Wormuth (D) for medical malpractice, claiming she had post-operative pain that impacted her work. Wormuth (D) moved to dismiss, asserting that James (P) failed to establish that Wormuth (D) had deviated from accepted standards of medical practice, or that such deviation was the proximate cause of James's (P) injuries. Wormuth (D) argued that res ipsa loquitur was inapplicable because there was no expert evidence that Wormuth (D) had not adhered to acceptable standards of medical practice or of any error by Wormuth (D) that caused the wire to become dislodged. James (P) objected, arguing that expert testimony was unnecessary because Wormuth (D) had admitted he intentionally left the wire, so a jury could infer negligence given there was no medical reason to leave the wire, as a special X-ray device could have been used to located and remove the wire, as it was during the second procedure. The trial court granted Wormuth (D) a directed verdict, and the state's intermediate appellate court affirmed. The state's highest court granted review.

ISSUE: In a medical malpractice action based on a foreign object being left in a patient's body, may the theory of res ipsa loquitur be used to establish a physician's negligence where the physician intentionally left the foreign object in the patient's body based on the physician's judgment that doing so would be in the patient's best interest?

HOLDING AND DECISION: (Rivera, J.) No. In a medical malpractice action based on a foreign object being left in a patient's body, the theory of res ipsa loquitur may not be used to establish a physician's negligence where the physician intentionally left the foreign object in the patient's body based on the physician's judgment that doing so would be in the patient's best interest. To establish a prima facie case of negligence in support of a res ipsa loquitur charge, a plaintiff must establish three elements: (1) the event must be of a kind that ordinarily does not occur in the absence of someone's negligence; (2) it must be caused by an agency or instrumentality within the exclusive control of the defendant; and (3) it must not have been due to any voluntary action or contribution on the part of the plaintiff. Further, where a foreign object has been left in the patient's body, res ipsa loquitur is applicable where the object is unintentionally left in the patient following an operative procedure. Here, however, James's (P) case focused on Wormuth's (D) intentional decision to leave the wire inside James's (P) body. Therefore, James (P) had to establish that Wormuth's (D) judgment deviated from acceptable standards of medical practice, and that such deviation proximately caused her injuries. A jury could not assess such judgment based on its common lay knowledge, and, therefore, expert evidence was necessary to aid the jury's understanding of whether Wormuth's (D) judgment was negligent. James (P) failed to present any such evidence of the standards of practice, and, therefore, her complaint was properly dismissed. The argument that Wormuth (D) had exclusive control of the wire must be rejected, as there was evidence that other personnel were involved in the wire's placement. Given that James (P) failed to produce any evidence that Wormuth (D) had exclusive control of the wire, or sufficient proof that eliminated within reason all explanations for the injury other than the Wormuth's (D) negligence, the control element

Continued on next page.

has not been satisfied. Finally, the wire should not, contrary to James's (P) argument, be treated as a foreign object for res ipsa loquitur purposes, since here James (P) was contending that Wormuth (D) negligently decided to leave the wire, not that the wire was unintentionally left. Affirmed.

ANALYSIS

Because James (P) was effectively placing Wormuth's (D) professional judgment in issue, she had the burden of proof as to whether his judgment deviated from accepted community standards of practice. Although the res ipsa loquitur doctrine helps plaintiffs who are unable to adduce direct evidence of negligence, the doctrine does not relieve a plaintiff of the burden of proof. Here, to address that burden, James's (P) counsel should have presented expert testimony as to whether Wormuth's (D) decision came within accepted standards of practice.

Quicknotes

DIRECTED VERDICT A verdict ordered by the court in a jury trial.

RES IPSA LOQUITUR A rule of law giving rise to an inference of negligence where the instrument inflicting the injury is in the exclusive control of the defendant and where such harm could not ordinarily result in the absence of negligence.

Sullivan v. Crabtree

Parents of deceased passenger (P) v. Truck driver (D)

Tenn. Ct. App., 36 Tenn. App. 469, 258 S.W.2d 782 (1953)

NATURE OF CASE: Action for damages resulting from a car accident.

FACT SUMMARY: Sullivan was killed while a guest in a truck driven by Crabtree (D), who swerved into an embankment.

RULE OF LAW

The doctrine of res ipsa loquitur merely affords reasonable evidence, in the absence of an explanation that injury was caused by negligence. Even if the facts are unexplained in a res ipsa loquitur situation, the jury may still refuse to make a finding of negligence.

FACTS: Sullivan was a guest in a motor truck driven by Crabtree (D). When Crabtree (D) was driving down a mountain, he suddenly swerved from his right side over to his left, ran off the left shoulder, overturned down a steep embankment, and crushed Sullivan to death. Sullivan's parents (P) sued Crabtree (D) and the owner (D) of the truck. The case went to trial against Crabtree (D) alone. Crabtree (D) testified that gravel on the road or the broken pavement might have caused him to lose control of the truck but he could not say definitely that the gravel or the pavement was the cause of the accident. The jury ruled for Crabtree (D), and the parents (P) appealed.

ISSUE: Even if the facts are unexplained in a res ipsa loquitur situation, may the jury still refuse to make a finding of negligence?

HOLDING AND DECISION: (Felts, J.) No. The doctrine of res ipsa loquitur merely affords reasonable evidence, in the absence of an explanation that the injury was caused by negligence. Even if the facts are unexplained in a res ipsa loquitur situation, the jury may still refuse to make a finding of negligence. Here, the facts make up a case of res ipsa loquitur. This means that the facts of the accident show some evidence of negligence. Here, the jury refused to find that Crabtree (D) was negligent because it thought that it was more probable that Crabtree (D) was not negligent. The jury may find a defendant not to be negligent in a case of res ipsa loquitur, even if the defendant cannot explain what caused the accident, if it thinks that a finding of no negligence is more reasonable. Therefore, the court will uphold the jury's finding, in this case, that Crabtree (D) was not negligent, even though Crabtree (D) could not explain what caused the accident. Affirmed.

ANALYSIS

The courts are in disagreement as to the precise effect that a finding of res ipsa loquitur has on the defendant's burden of proof. A finding of res ipsa loquitur in a case shifts the burden of proof to the defendant. Some courts have ruled that a finding of res ipsa loquitur warrants an inference that the defendant is negligent, which the jury may or may not agree with, as in this case. Other courts rule that it raises a presumption of negligence which requires the jury to find negligence if the defendant does not produce evidence sufficient to rebut the presumption. Other courts rule that it not only raises a presumption of negligence, but also shifts the ultimate burden of proof to the defendant and requires him to prove by a preponderance of all the evidence that the injury was not caused by his negligence. This case is in accord with the majority of the courts which hold that res ipsa loquitur still allows the jury to draw its own inference from the facts.

Quicknotes

INFERENCE A deduction from established facts.

NEGLIGENCE Conduct falling below the standard of care that a reasonable person would demonstrate under similar conditions.

PRESUMPTION A rule of law requiring the court to presume certain facts to be true based on the existence of other facts, thereby shifting the burden of proof to the party against whom the presumption is asserted to rebut.

RES IPSA LOQUITUR A rule of law giving rise to an inference of negligence where the instrument inflicting the injury is in the exclusive control of the defendant and where such harm could not ordinarily result in the absence of negligence.

CHAPTER 5

Causation in Fact

Quick Reference Rules of Law

Perkins v. Texas and New Orleans R. Co.

Deceased widow (P) v. Railroad (D)

La. Sup. Ct., 243 La. 829, 147 So. 2d 646 (1962)

NATURE OF CASE: Appeal of award of damages for wrongful death.

FACT SUMMARY: A locomotive travelling at an excessive speed was involved in an accident that would have occurred even if the train had not been speeding.

RULE OF LAW

Negligence will not give rise to liability if the injury would have happened even if the negligence had not occurred.

FACTS: Texas and New Orleans Railway Co. ("the Railway") (D) operated a line through Vinton, Louisiana. The legal train speed limit was 25 mph. At a blind intersection an accident occurred wherein the speed of the train was 37 mph and the speed of the automobile, which contained Perkins's (P) decedent, could not be determined. Evidence showed that even at 25 mph the train could not possibly have stopped before the crossing in the period after the auto became visible. A jury awarded Perkins (P) damages for wrongful death, and the court of appeals affirmed. The Railway (D) appealed.

ISSUE: Will negligence give rise to liability if the injury would have happened even if the negligence had not occurred?

HOLDING AND DECISION: (Sanders, J.) No. Negligence will not give rise to liability if the injury would have happened even if the negligence had not occurred. It is fundamental that negligence will lead to liability only if it is the sole or a substantial factor in bringing about the injury. Where the injury would have occurred even in the absence of negligence, the negligence cannot be said to be a substantial factor. Here, the engineer was negligent. However, even if he had been travelling 25 mph, a non-negligent speed, the train would have reached the crossing. Since no reliable evidence of the auto's speed exists, it is impossible to know whether the auto could have avoided the collision had the train been travelling slower. This being so, it has not been established that the engineer's negligence was a substantial factor in the injury. Reversed.

ANALYSIS

The question of causation is often reduced to a "but for" test. The question is whether, but for the negligence, would no accident have occurred? If the answer is in the affirmative, then legal causation will exist.

Quicknotes

CAUSE IN FACT The event without which an injury would not have been incurred.

NEGLIGENCE Conduct falling below the standard of care that a reasonable person would demonstrate under similar conditions.

Reynolds v. Texas & Pac. Ry. Co.

Obese woman (P) v. Railroad (D)

La. Ct. App., 37 La. Ann. 694 (1885)

NATURE OF CASE: Action for damages caused by unlit stairs.

FACT SUMMARY: Mrs. Reynolds (P), who was heavy, fell down unlit stairs at a train depot owned by Texas & Pacific Ry. Co. (D).

RULE OF LAW

Although an injury might possibly have occurred even in the absence of another's negligence, if the negligence greatly multiplies the chances of accident to the injured person and is of a character naturally leading to the accident's occurrence, the mere possibility that the accident might have happened without the negligence is not sufficient to break the chain of cause and effect between the negligence and the injury.

FACTS: Mrs. Reynolds (P) weighed two hundred and fifty pounds. She emerged from the sitting room of a train depot, which was brightly lit, and went down unlit stairs. During her descent, she fell and was thrown beyond the narrow platform and the slope beyond, sustaining serious injuries. She was awarded $2,000 in damages, and Texas Ry. (D) appealed.

ISSUE: Although an injury might possibly have occurred even in the absence of another's negligence, if the negligence greatly multiplies the chances of accident to the injured person and is of a character naturally leading to the accident's occurrence, is the mere possibility that the accident might have happened without the negligence sufficient to break the chain of cause and effect between the negligence and the injury?

HOLDING AND DECISION: (Fenner, J.) No. Although an injury might possibly have occurred even in the absence of another's negligence, if the negligence greatly multiplies the chances of accident to the injured person and is of a character naturally leading to the accident's occurrence, the mere possibility that the accident might have happened without the negligence is not sufficient to break the chain of cause and effect between the negligence and the injury. The fact that a defendant can show a possibility that an accident might have occurred without his negligence is insufficient proof that his negligence was not the "cause in fact" of the plaintiff's injuries, especially if his negligence greatly multiplied the plaintiff's chances of having an accident and is the type of negligence that usually causes the accident to occur. Here, there is a possibility that Mrs. Reynolds (P) might have fallen even if the stairs were well lit because she is heavy. But Texas Ry.'s (D) failure to light the stairs greatly increased the chances that she would fall. Unlit stairs often cause falls. Therefore, Texas Ry. (D) has not shown that its negligence did not cause her injuries. The court will look at what naturally happens, and not at remote speculations that there was a possibility that the accident was not connected with the negligence. Affirmed.

ANALYSIS

This case illuminates the majority rule that a plaintiff is not required to prove his case beyond a reasonable doubt in order to recover. The plaintiff must prove that the defendant's negligence probably caused his injuries. The defendant cannot prove that his negligence was not a "cause in fact" merely by showing that there is a possibility that the plaintiff's injuries would have occurred without his negligence.

Quicknotes

NEGLIGENCE Conduct falling below the standard of care that a reasonable person would demonstrate under similar conditions.

POST HOC After this moment.

POST HOC ERGO PROPTER HOC The doctrine that because an occurrence followed a prior occurrence, it must have been the result of that prior occurrence.

Gentry v. Douglas Hereford Ranch, Inc.

Widower (P) v. Ranch company (D)

Mont. Sup. Ct., 290 Mont. 126, 962 P.2d 1205 (1998)

NATURE OF CASE: Wrongful death and survival suit.

FACT SUMMARY: Gentry (P) brought a wrongful death and survival suit against Bacon (D), a ranch company (D) and a cattle company (D), when his wife died as a result of Bacon's (D) rifle accidentally discharging when he allegedly stumbled on the deck steps.

RULE OF LAW

Cause in fact is established when a plaintiff can demonstrate that an event would not have occurred but for the defendant's conduct.

FACTS: Bacon (D) was preparing to hunt deer while his wife and their friend, Barbara Gentry, painted the inside of a house owned by Bacon's (D) wife's grandmother. He stumbled on the stairs and accidentally discharged the rifle, shooting Barbara in the head. She died several weeks later. Her husband (P) brought wrongful death and survival actions against Bacon (D), the ranch company (D) owned by the grandmother, and a cattle company (D) that owned part of the ranch, alleging Bacon (D) was negligent in handling the rifle and the ranch (D) and cattle companies (D) had been negligent in maintaining the stairs. Bacon (D) declared bankruptcy and was dismissed and the court entered summary judgment in favor of the ranch company.

ISSUE: Is cause in fact established when a plaintiff can demonstrate that an event would not have occurred but for the defendant's conduct?

HOLDING AND DECISION: (Trieweiler, J.) Yes. Cause in fact is established when a plaintiff can demonstrate that an event would not have occurred but for the defendant's conduct. In order to establish negligence, plaintiff must show that a duty existed, breach of that duty, causation and damages. If the plaintiff fails to establish any of these elements, then summary judgment for the defendant is proper. Proof of causation requires a showing of proof of both cause in fact and proximate cause. Cause in fact is established if the plaintiff can prove that the event would not have occurred but for the defendant's conduct. Here Gentry (P) claimed the ranch company (D) was negligent in failing to maintain the steps on which Bacon (D) tripped in a reasonably safe condition. He argued that the step was unstable and cluttered by debris. Bacon (D) testified, however, that his fall was not attributable to any of those circumstances. Rather, he could not remember what caused to him to stumble on the steps. A suspicion or speculation is not sufficient to raise a genuine issue of material fact so as to defeat a motion for summary judgment. Affirmed.

ANALYSIS

In *Krone v. McCann*, 196 Mont. 260 (1982), plaintiff sought damages for an injury sustained when she tripped and fell over an object on defendant's property. The court affirmed summary judgment for the defendant on the basis that the plaintiff did not know what caused her to fall. The court stated that a plaintiff must show evidence leading the court to reasonably infer that the defendant's negligent conduct caused the injury.

Quicknotes

CAUSE IN FACT The event without which an injury would not have been incurred.

NEGLIGENCE Conduct falling below the standard of care that a reasonable person would demonstrate under similar conditions.

PROXIMATE CAUSE The natural sequence of events without which an injury would not have been sustained.

SUMMARY JUDGMENT Judgment rendered by a court in response to a motion by one of the parties, claiming that the lack of a question of material fact in respect to an issue warrants disposition of the issue without consideration by the jury.

WRONGFUL DEATH An action brought by the beneficiaries of a deceased person, claiming that the deceased's death was the result of wrongful conduct by the defendant.

Kramer Service Inc. v. Wilkins

Hotel (D) v. Hotel guest (P)

Miss. Sup. Ct., 184 Miss. 483, 186 So. 625 (1939)

NATURE OF CASE: Action for damages resulting from a defective door.

FACT SUMMARY: Plaintiff cut his forehead on a piece of glass that fell from a broken transom when plaintiff opened the door in defendant's hotel. Two years later, plaintiff discovered that skin cancer had developed at the point of the glass injury.

RULE OF LAW

One cannot recover for an injury if one shows just a possibility that the injury was caused by another's negligence.

FACTS: Plaintiff was a guest in defendant's hotel. Plaintiff was cut on his forehead when a piece of glass fell from a broken transom as he was opening a door. There was evidence that the hotel's disrepair had existed long enough so that defendant should have known about it. Plaintiff's wound did not heal and two years after the injury plaintiff went to a specialist in skin diseases, who found that at the point of the injury a skin cancer had developed.

ISSUE: Can one recover for an injury if one shows just a possibility that the injury was caused by another's negligence?

HOLDING AND DECISION: (Griffith, J.) No. One cannot recover for an injury if one shows just a possibility that the injury was caused by another's negligence. Laymen have no experience with skin cancer, so the court must accept the undisputed testimony of specialists that there was, at most, a remote possibility that plaintiff's cancer resulted from the original forehead cut. The jury should not be allowed to speculate when they have no experience with a disease and the medical experts are undisputed. This is an exception to the advisory. The mere possibility that plaintiff's cancer might have been caused by his forehead cut is insufficient proof of causation and, therefore, will not sustain a verdict for plaintiff. While plaintiff may recover for the forehead cut, plaintiff may not recover for the cancer. Affirmed as to liability; reversed and remanded as to damages.

ANALYSIS

This case accords with the majority view that a mere possibility that negligence caused an injury is insufficient proof of "cause in fact." Accordingly, the court will direct a verdict for the defendant when the only proof of a causal connection is based on speculation.

Quicknotes

POST HOC ERGO PROPTER HOC The doctrine that because an occurrence followed a prior occurrence, it must have been the result of that prior occurrence.

Smith v. Providence Health & Services

Patient (P) v. Hospital (D)

Or. Sup. Ct., 361 Or. 456, 393 P.3d 1106 (2017)

NATURE OF CASE: Appeal from affirmance of dismissal, for failure to state a claim, of medical negligence action brought on the theory that hospital negligently caused a loss of plaintiff's chance at recovery.

FACT SUMMARY: Smith (P), who suffered permanent brain damage, brought a medical negligence action, alleging that, because doctors (D) and the hospital (D) at which they practiced had not taken proper steps to follow up on his complaints of stroke symptoms, he lost a chance for treatment that, in one-third of cases, provides a patient with no or reduced complications following the stroke. The doctors (D) and hospital (D) contended that Smith (P) failed to state a claim under state law, which, they contended, did not recognize the loss-of-chance theory.

RULE OF LAW

A limited loss-of-chance theory of injury is cognizable in common-law negligence claims of medical malpractice where reliable scientific evidence about the statistical probability of the outcome involved in the case is available and the plaintiff can demonstrate the loss of a substantial chance of recovery or a better medical outcome.

FACTS: Smith (P) went to doctors (D) complaining of symptoms of stroke. Allegedly, because the doctors (D) did not take proper steps to follow up on Smith's (P) complaints, he suffered permanent brain damage from a stroke. Smith (P) sued the doctors (D) and the hospital (D) at which they practiced for common-law medical negligence, contending that because of the doctors' (D) alleged negligence, he lost a chance for treatment that, in one-third of cases, or around 33 percent, provides a patient with no or reduced complications following the stroke. The trial court dismissed for failure to state a claim, determining that state law did not recognize Smith's (P) loss-of-chance theory of negligence. The state's intermediate appellate court affirmed, and the state's highest court granted review.

ISSUE: Is a limited loss-of-chance theory of injury cognizable in common-law negligence claims of medical malpractice where reliable scientific evidence about the statistical probability of the outcome involved in the case is available and the plaintiff can demonstrate the loss of a substantial chance of recovery or a better medical outcome?

HOLDING AND DECISION: (Nakamoto, J.) Yes. A limited loss-of-chance theory of injury is cognizable in common-law negligence claims of medical malpractice where reliable scientific evidence about the statistical probability of the outcome involved in the case is available and the plaintiff can demonstrate the loss of a substantial chance of recovery or a better medical outcome. Ordinarily, the plaintiff in a negligence action must prove causation by a "reasonable probability." Here, the defendants (D) argued that Smith (P) had failed to allege that it was more likely than not that the delay in treatment, rather than the underlying condition itself, caused his permanent disability. Smith (P), however, argued that loss of chance is not an aspect of causation, but rather is a distinct type of injury or harm. Such a theory of medical malpractice has gained traction in courts in about half the states, and would be responsive to a case such as Smith's (P), where the doctors (D) undertook his care when he presented with symptoms of stroke, they breached the duty to him by performing below the standard of care, and Smith (P) suffered brain damage, and the doctors (D) demonstrably caused him to lose a 33 percent chance at recovering from the stroke, i.e., where a plaintiff does not allege (and cannot prove) that defendants caused the medical outcome given that the plaintiff's chance of recovery with proper treatment was not greater than 50 percent. The courts that have recognized this theory have observed that traditional notions of "more likely than not" causation pose a problematic barrier to recovery by patients who have experienced poor medical outcomes as a result of a doctor's failure to diagnose and that other theories of recovery may be viable in that context. The majority of those courts have found that the loss of chance of achieving a favorable outcome should be compensable and should be valued appropriately, rather than treated as an all-or-nothing proposition dependent on proof of a greater-than-50-percent chance of a better outcome absent the alleged malpractice. Thus, under this theory, in a medical malpractice situation in which a patient presents with symptoms of a condition and a physician negligently fails to diagnose and treat that condition, the preexisting medical condition (which clearly was not caused by the negligence) is merely something that is taken into account when valuing the harm that actually was caused by the negligent failure to diagnose, and the defendant is subject to liability only to the extent that the defendant tortiously contributed to the harm by allowing a preexisting condition to progress. Here, for example, Smith (P) could show by a preponderance of the evidence that he was deprived of a 33 percent chance of a cure or a better medical outcome. However, Smith (P) could do so, in part, because there is ample reliable scientific evidence about the statistical probability of outcomes

Continued on next page.

in situations of delay of diagnosis. That is, the plaintiff can demonstrate, through use of expert testimony, the statistical likelihood of a better medical outcome but for the negligent conduct. In some jurisdictions that have recognized the loss-of-chance theory, plaintiffs are required to demonstrate that they lost a "substantial" chance of improved outcome. Here, as a matter of law, a 33 percent chance of improved outcome is "substantial." Also, in applying the theory, in fairness to defendants, a plaintiff must plead with specificity the lost chance of a better medical outcome. In practical terms, that means that a plaintiff must plead the percentage and quality of the loss of chance, which in turn must be based on the plaintiff's experts and relevant scientific evidence that meets the standard of reasonable medical probability. Also, the plaintiff must have suffered the physical harm that the plaintiff might well have avoided if non-negligent medical care had been provided. That present adverse medical outcome is an essential element of a common-law medical malpractice claim and provides the foundation for a calculation of plaintiff's damages. Finally, damages must be calculated in accordance with the diminished chance of recovery. Accordingly, Smith (P) would be able to recover damages only to the possible extent of 33 percent of the damages resulting from the adverse medical outcome. Reversed and remanded.

ANALYSIS

A small minority of courts have characterized loss-of-chance theories of recovery in the medical malpractice context as involving a relaxation of the causation standard. Those jurisdictions use a test for the causal connection between the patient's ultimate physical harm and the doctor's negligence that substitutes "substantial factor" or "substantial probability" for "preponderance of the evidence," that is, more-likely-than-not or greater-than-50-percent causation. To the contrary, the majority of courts, including the Oregon Supreme Court in this decision, have adopted an approach that has been favored by commentators and that recognizes the lost chance at recovery or an improved medical outcome, as an injury in itself.

Quicknotes

CAUSATION The aggregate effect of preceding events that bring about a tortious result; the causal connection between the actions of a tortfeasor and the injury that follows.

COMMON LAW A body of law developed through the judicial decisions of the courts as opposed to the legislative process.

Daubert v. Merrell Dow Pharmaceuticals, Inc.

Injured (P) v. Pharmaceutical company (D)

43 F.3d 1311 (9th Cir. 1995)

NATURE OF CASE: Products liability suit.

FACT SUMMARY: Two minors (P) brought suit against Merrell Dow Pharmaceuticals, Inc. (D) claiming they suffered limb reduction birth defects because their mothers had taken Benedictin, a drug prescribed to treat morning sickness.

RULE OF LAW

Expert scientific testimony is admissible if it reflects "scientific knowledge," if the findings are "derived by the scientific method," if the work product amounts to "good science," and if it logically advances a material aspect of the proposing party's case.

FACTS: Two minors (P) brought suit against Merrell Dow Pharmaceuticals, Inc. (D) claiming they suffered limb reduction birth defects because their mothers had taken Benedictin, a drug prescribed to treat morning sickness. Expert testimony to establish that Benedictin had caused their injuries was admitted that was counter to the consensus within the scientific community. The district court granted summary judgment on this basis under the test set forth in *Frye*, which allows the admission of scientific evidence if based on a scientific technique generally accepted as reliable within the scientific community. This court affirmed. The United States Supreme Court reversed, holding that the *Frye* test, *Frye v. United States*, 293 F. 1013 (D.C. Cir. 1923), was superseded by Fed. R. Evid. 702, and remanded, 125 L. Ed. 2d 469, 113 S. Ct. 2786 (1993).

ISSUE: Is expert scientific testimony admissible if it reflects "scientific knowledge," if the findings are "derived by the scientific method," if the work product amounts to "good science," and if it logically advances a material aspect of the proposing party's case?

HOLDING AND DECISION: (Kozinski, J.) Yes. Expert scientific testimony is admissible if it reflects "scientific knowledge," if the findings are "derived by the scientific method," if the work product amounts to "good science," and if it logically advances a material aspect of the proposing party's case. Establishing that an expert's proffered testimony grows out of prelitigation research or that the expert's research has been subjected to peer review are the two ways the proponent of the proffered testimony can satisfy the first prong of Fed. R. Evid. 702. Here none of the experts based his testimony on pre-existing or independent research. None claims to have studied the effect of Benedictin on limb reduction defects. The proponent of the testimony may also satisfy its burden through the testimony of its experts, who must explain precisely how they came to their conclusions and point to an objective source to show they have followed a scientific method as followed by at least a recognized minority of scientists in their field. Plaintiffs here have made no such showing. The second prong of Fed. R. Evid. 702 requires a valid scientific connection to the pertinent inquiry as a precondition to admissibility. Here the pertinent inquiry is causation. California tort law requires plaintiffs to show not merely that Benedictin increased the likelihood of injury, but that it more likely than not caused their injuries. The strongest inference to be drawn from the testimony is that Benedictin could have possibly caused the plaintiff's injuries. District court affirmed.

ANALYSIS

The relatively simple *Frye* test required the proponent of the expert testimony to show that it was based on the method generally accepted in the scientific community. The test set forth in *Daubert* focuses on the reliability of the expert's methodology; thus, it need not be the view espoused by the majority. However, the expert must explain his methodology and demonstrate its reliability in an objectively verifiable manner.

Quicknotes

CAUSATION The aggregate effect of preceding events that bring about a tortious result; the causal connection between the actions of a tortfeasor and the injury that follows.

EXPERT TESTIMONY Testimonial evidence about a complex area of subject matter relevant to trial presented by a person competent to inform the trier of fact due to specialized knowledge or training.

Hill v. Edmonds

Injured passenger (P) v. Driver (D) and truck owner (D)

N.Y. App. Div., 26 A.D.2d 554, 270 N.Y.S.2d 1020 (1966)

NATURE OF CASE: Appeal from dismissal of action for damages for negligence.

FACT SUMMARY: Although Edmonds (D), the driver of the car in which Hill (P) was a passenger, had acted negligently in running into a truck, the owner of the truck, Bragoli (D), also acted questionably in leaving it parked without lights in the middle of the road on a stormy night.

RULE OF LAW

When separate acts of negligence combine to produce directly a single injury, each tortfeasor is responsible for the entire result, even though his act alone might not have caused it.

FACTS: Bragoli (D) had left the truck he owned parked without lights in the middle of the road on a stormy night. Hill (P) suffered injuries when the car in which she was a passenger collided with the truck. She sued both parties for damages for personal injury. The testimony was that Edmonds (D), the driver of the car, had seen the truck when it was four lengths ahead of her and that she saw it in time to turn. However, Edmonds (D) also indicated that she did not know just what happened, that she swerved to avoid the truck, and the next thing she knew she was unconscious. The trial court concluded that Edmonds (D) was guilty of negligence and was solely responsible for the collision. It dismissed the complaint against Bragoli (D), and Hill (P) appealed.

ISSUE: When separate acts of negligence combine to produce directly a single injury, is each tortfeasor responsible for the entire result, even though his act alone might not have caused it?

HOLDING AND DECISION: [Memorandum] Yes. When separate acts of negligence combine to produce directly a single injury, each tortfeasor is responsible for the entire result, even though his act alone might not have caused it. Assuming arguendo that Edmonds (D) was negligent, the fact remains that the accident could not have happened had not Bragoli (D) allowed his unlighted truck to stand in the middle of the roadway. Thus, the complaint against him must be reinstated and a new trial had.

ANALYSIS

The rule of this case is known commonly as the "substantial factor" test. Ordinarily, the test arises in cases where it is uncertain which of two persons caused a third person's injury. In one well-known case, a man riding in a horse drawn wagon was injured when two motorcycles passed simultaneously and frightened his horses. Both motorcyclists were held liable (*Corey v. Havender*, 65 N.E. 69 [Mass. 1902]).

Quicknotes

ARGUENDO Hypothetical argument.

NEGLIGENCE Conduct falling below the standard of care that a reasonable person would demonstrate under similar conditions.

SUBSTANTIAL FACTOR TEST In determining whether one of several joint acts was the proximate cause of an injury for purposes of tort liability, the inquiry is whether the act or omission was a substantial factor in causing the damage and whether the damage was the direct or probable result of the act or omission.

Anderson v. Minneapolis, St. P. & S. St. M. Ry. Co.

Burned-property owner (P) v. Railroad (D)

Minn. Sup. Ct., 146 Minn. 430, 179 N.W. 45 (1920)

NATURE OF CASE: Action for damages resulting from a fire that was negligently set.

FACT SUMMARY: A forest fire, caused by Minneapolis, St. P. & S. St. M. Ry. Co.'s (D) negligence, merged with another fire of uncertain origin and both fires burned over Anderson's (P) property.

RULE OF LAW

If one negligently sets a fire that combines with another fire of no responsible origin, he is liable if his fire would have caused the damage independent of the other fire, or if his fire materially caused the damage. In other words, if one's negligence would have caused the damage complained of, he is liable and it is irrelevant whether, in fact, another force combined to cause the damage.

FACTS: Minneapolis, St. P. & S. St. M. Ry. Co. (Minneapolis Ry.) (D) negligently started a forest fire. Before this fire reached Anderson's (P) property, it merged with another fire of independent and uncertain origins. The combined fires burned over Anderson's (P) property. Minneapolis Ry. (D) claimed that it should not be liable because the other fire alone could have caused the damage. It claimed that the jury instructions in the lower court were incorrect.

ISSUE: If one negligently sets a fire that combines with another fire of no responsible origin, is he liable if his fire would have caused the damage independent of the other fire, or if his fire materially caused the damage?

HOLDING AND DECISION: (Lees, Commr.) Yes. If one negligently sets a fire that combines with another fire of no responsible origin, he is liable if his fire would have caused the damage independent of the other fire, or if his fire materially caused the damage. Even if the fire of unknown origins could have alone produced the damage, if the fire of known origins is a material element in causing the damage, the negligent originator of the known fire is liable. Here, Minneapolis Ry. (D) negligently set off a fire which combined with a fire of unknown origins and then did damage to Anderson's (P) property. Although the unknown fire alone could have destroyed the property, Minneapolis Ry. (D) is still liable because its fire was a material element in causing damage to Anderson's (P) property. This finding of liability is logical because if two known fires combine and cause damage, there is joint and several liability, even though either fire alone could have destroyed the property. Moreover, a statute compels the court to find liability under the facts at bar, although there would be liability even without this statute. Affirmed.

ANALYSIS

This case illustrates the principle of concurrent liability. If a negligent party alone could cause injury, the fact that another party was concurrently causing the same injury does not exculpate the first party, unless he can show that his negligence was not a material element in causing the injury. If the rule were otherwise, it would be easy for a negligent party to escape liability by pointing to the other negligent party; the other party would in turn escape liability in the same manner.

Quicknotes

JOINT AND SEVERAL LIABILITY Liability amongst tortfeasors allowing the injured party to bring suit against any of the defendants, individually or collectively, and to recover from each up to the total amount of damages awarded.

JUDGMENT NOTWITHSTANDING THE VERDICT (JUDGMENT N.O.V.) A judgment entered by the trial judge reversing a jury verdict if the jury's determination has no basis in law or fact.

Summers v. Tice

Shooting victim (P) v. Hunters (D)

Cal. Sup. Ct., 33 Cal. 2d 80, 199 P.2d 1 (1948)

NATURE OF CASE: Action for damages resulting from the negligent shooting of Summers (P).

FACT SUMMARY: Summers (P) was struck in the eye by a shot from one gun although the two defendants had both fired.

RULE OF LAW

When two defendants are both negligent, but only one of them could have caused the plaintiff's injury, the court will hold them both liable when it cannot determine which of the defendants caused the damage.

FACTS: Summers (P) and the two defendants were members of a hunting party. Both defendants, Tice (D) and Simonson (D), negligently fired, simultaneously, at a quail and in Summers's (P) direction. He was struck in the eye by a shot from one gun. There was no evidence from which to determine which gun had caused the injury.

ISSUE: When two defendants are both negligent, but only one of them could have caused the plaintiff's injury, will they be held jointly liable if there is no evidence proving which defendant caused the damage?

HOLDING AND DECISION: (Carter, J.) Yes. When two defendants are both negligent, but only one of them could have caused the plaintiff's injury, the court will hold them both liable when it cannot determine which of the defendants caused the damage. The judgment against both defendants may stand. Although the defendants were not acting in concert and there is insufficient evidence to determine which defendant was guilty of the negligence that caused the injuries, they are jointly liable because otherwise Summers (P) could not recover. It is logical that the defendants have the burden of proving that the other person was the sole cause of harm. It would be unfair to deny the injured person recovery simply because he cannot prove who did the damage when it is certain that between them they did all the damage. Therefore, the court shifts the burden of proof to the wrongdoers such that they must absolve themselves of the wrongdoing. Further, the defendants are in a better position to offer evidence to determine which one caused the injury. Affirmed.

ANALYSIS

This case is in the majority. The doctrine of holding two negligent parties jointly liable when only one of the parties could have caused the damage is analogous to the doctrine of res ipsa loquitur, in the sense that it is the defendant who must come forward with evidence to absolve himself. This case shifts the burden of proof to the defendants, just as the burden of proof is shifted in res ipsa loquitur cases. Were the rule otherwise, the plaintiff would hardly ever be able to prove who caused his injury.

Quicknotes

JOINT LIABILITY Liability owed to an injured party by two or more parties where each party has the right to insist that the other tortfeasors be joined to the matter.

JOINT TORTFEASORS Two or more parties that either act in concert, or whose individual acts combine to cause a single injury, rendering them jointly and severally liable for damages incurred.

RES IPSA LOQUITUR A rule of law giving rise to an inference of negligence where the instrument inflicting the injury is in the exclusive control of the defendant and where such harm could not ordinarily result in the absence of negligence.

Sindell v. Abbott Laboratories

Child of drug user (P) v. Drug manufacturers (D)

Cal. Sup. Ct., 26 Cal. 3d 588, 607 P.2d 924, *cert. denied,* 449 U.S. 912 (1980)

NATURE OF CASE: Damages for product liability.

FACT SUMMARY: Sindell (P) was injured as a result of her mother taking diethylstilbestrol (DES), a prescription drug designed to prevent miscarriages, while pregnant with Sindell (P). Abbott Laboratories (Abbott) (D) and several other drug manufacturers sold DES, but Sindell (P) did not know which drug manufacturer produced the DES that her mother took. Sindell (P) brought this action against Abbott (D) and four other producers of DES (D) but not against any other drug manufacturers.

RULE OF LAW

Where multiple manufacturers produce and distribute a dangerously defective product, an injured party can recover from one or several of them, even if she cannot identify which manufacturer(s) produced the drug that caused the injury.

FACTS: Sindell's (P) mother took the prescription drug diethylstilbestrol (DES) while pregnant with Sindell (P). The drug was designed to prevent miscarriages. Many years after Sindell (P) was born, it was discovered that the drug was inadequately tested by all of its manufacturers and that it caused cancer of female human reproductive organs in the children of DES users. Sindell (P) became a victim of this cancer, and brought this action against five of the manufacturers of DES (D). DES prescriptions were filled from multiple manufacturers, and many pharmacies did not keep track of which manufacturer's drug filled which prescription. Therefore, Sindell (P) could not prove that Abbott Laboratories (D) or the other four defendants (D) manufactured the drug taken by her mother. The trial court dismissed the action and Sindell (P) appealed.

ISSUE: Where multiple manufacturers produce and distribute a dangerously defective drug, can an injured party recover from just one or several of them, even if she cannot identify which manufacturer(s) actually produced the drug that injured her?

HOLDING AND DECISION: (Mosk, J.) Yes. Where multiple manufacturers produce and distribute a dangerously defective product, an injured party can recover from one or several of them, even if she cannot identify which manufacturer(s) produced the drug that caused the injury. At least 200 manufacturers produced DES. Since in our heavily industrialized society there are so many fungible goods that may hurt a party but cannot be traced to a particular manufacturer, the courts must fashion a remedy to address the situation of Sindell (P) and others similarly injured. Sindell (P) alleges that 90 percent of DES was produced by the five companies (D) who she joined in the action. Assuming that Sindell's (P) allegation is true, the five companies (D) should bear the burden of liability since there is such a small chance that they did *not* produce the DES that caused Sindell's (P) injury. Because between an innocent plaintiff and negligent defendants the defendants are in a better position to bear the cost of injury, liability rests with them. Although neither Sindell (P) nor the drug producers (D) can prove causation, the drug producers (D) participated in the unavailability of proof by marketing a drug whose side effects were unknown at the time. In addition, holding the drug producers (D) liable provides an incentive for them to produce safer products. Reversed.

ANALYSIS

The states are split as to whether or not to recognize "substantial share" liability. Courts that have adopted one of the alternative liability theories have had to decide how many of the defendants must be before the court. Most of the courts that do follow substantial share theory or a variation have declined to extend the theory beyond DES cases. The substantial share theory is not available where each manufacturer is engaged in different activities or where the plaintiff is unable to identify the particular market that she seeks to hold liable. With substantial share liability, the question is always raised as to what particular market is to be used in allocating liability. The stronger position is to narrow the market as much as possible. Those who do not recognize the substantial share theory (or some variation thereof) follow traditional common-law requirements that the plaintiff prove the identity of the tortfeasor in order to recover.

Quicknotes

FUNGIBLE GOODS Interchangeable or substitutable goods.

SUBSTANTIAL SHARE LIABILITY The apportionment of liability between each participant in an industry equal to the participant's market share.

CHAPTER 6

Proximate or Legal Cause

Quick Reference Rules of Law

	PAGE
1. *Atlantic Coast Line R. Co. v. Daniels.* The law will look to see whether the wrongful act was the proximate cause of the injury complained of in determining liability.	*100*
2. *Ryan v. New York Central R.R. Co.* Damages can be awarded only when the injury is immediate and not the remote result of defendant's negligence.	*101*
3. *Bartolone v. Jeckovich.* A tortfeasor bears responsibility for all damages proximately caused by tortious conduct, even if the damages appear disproportionate to the tortious conduct.	*102*
4. *In re Arbitration between Polemis and Furness, Withy & Co., Ltd.* The fact that the kind of damage which an act might probably cause was not the damage anticipated is immaterial so long as the resulting damage is directly traceable to the negligent act, and not due to independent cause having no connection with the negligent act.	*103*
5. *Overseas Tankship (U.K.) Ltd. v. Morts Dock & Engineering Co., Ltd. "Wagon Mound No. 1".* Even though injury may result from a negligent act, liability for that injury is limited to the risk reasonably to be foreseen.	*104*
6. *Overseas Tankship (U.K.) Ltd. v. Miller Steamship Co. "Wagon Mound No. 2".* One who is knowledgeable of a risk and can reasonably prevent it is liable for damages resulting from his failure to do so.	*105*
7. *Palsgraf v. Long Island R.R. Co.* The risk reasonably to be perceived defines the duty to be obeyed.	*106*
8. *Yun v. Ford Motor Co.* A claim of strict liability may be defeated if the defendant can show that an intervening superseding event or another sole proximate cause resulted in the plaintiff's injury.	*108*
9. *Derdiarian v. Felix Contracting Corp.* An intervening act will not serve as a superseding cause, relieving the defendant of liability, where the risk of the intervening act occurring is the very same risk which rendered the defendant negligent.	*110*
10. *Watson v. Kentucky & Indiana Bridge & R.R. Co.* The mere fact that an intervening act was unforeseen will not relieve the defendant guilty of primary negligence from liability unless the intervening act is something so unexpected or extraordinary as that it could not or ought not to be anticipated.	*111*
11. *Fuller v. Preis.* As a matter of law, an act of suicide is not a superseding cause in negligence law precluding liability.	*112*
12. *McCoy v. American Suzuki Motor Corp.* The rescue doctrine may be invoked in products liability cases, requiring the rescuer-plaintiff to prove that the defendant's conduct was the proximate cause of his injuries.	*113*
13. *Kelly v. Gwinnell.* A social host may be liable for furnishing alcohol to an intoxicated guest.	*114*
14. *Enright v. Eli Lilly & Co.* An injury to a mother that results in injuries to a later-conceived child does not establish a cause of action in favor of the child against the original tortfeasor.	*115*

Atlantic Coast Line R. Co. v. Daniels

[Parties not identified.]

Ga. Ct. App., 8 Ga. App. 775, 70 S.E. 203 (1911)

NATURE OF CASE: [Facts not stated in casebook excerpt.]

FACT SUMMARY: [Facts not stated in casebook excerpt.]

RULE OF LAW

The law will look to see whether the wrongful act was the proximate cause of the injury complained of in determining liability.

FACTS: [Facts not stated in casebook excerpt.]

ISSUE: Do courts use arbitrary limitations in establishing cause and effect?

HOLDING AND DECISION: (Powell, J.) Yes. The law will look to see whether the wrongful act was the proximate cause of the injury complained of in determining liability. Courts cannot deal with cause and effect in any absolute degree. It must be practically and arbitrarily limited. Words such as "proximate" and "natural" have been used to describe limits for the courts beyond which they will not attempt to find a connection between a cause and effect. The courts must determine whether the wrongful act that allegedly caused an injury was the proximate cause of that injury.

ANALYSIS

Once it is established that the defendant's act was one of the causes of the injury suffered by plaintiff, the question as to whether defendant should be held responsible for it legally arises. Prosser says it is sometimes "a question of whether the conduct has been so significant and important a cause that the defendant should be legally responsible." This can be restated as whether defendant had been under any duty to the plaintiff. Or it can be considered whether any duty defendant had included protecting the plaintiff against the consequences of the harmful act.

Quicknotes

PROXIMATE CAUSE The natural sequence of events without which an injury would not have been sustained.

REDUCTIO AD ABSURDUM The refuting of a legal argument by demonstrating its absurdity.

Ryan v. New York Central R.R. Co.

Owner of burned house (P) v. Railroad (D)

N.Y. Ct. App., 35 N.Y. 210, 91 Am. Dec. 49 (1866)

NATURE OF CASE: Action for damages for injury due to negligence.

FACT SUMMARY: Ryan's (P) house was destroyed by a fire started when a spark from New York Central R.R. Co.'s (D) train engine ignited a wood shed. The fire spread through several houses before reaching Ryan's house (P).

RULE OF LAW

Damages can be awarded only when the injury is immediate and not the remote result of defendant's negligence.

FACTS: Ryan's (P) home in Syracuse was destroyed by a fire that spread from New York Central R.R. Co.'s (Central's) (D) woodshed, which had been ignited by a spark from Central's (D) train engine either through careless management or insufficient condition. Ryan's (P) house was 130 feet from the shed. Several other houses were destroyed. The court found in favor of Central (D), and Ryan (P) appealed.

ISSUE: Can damages be awarded only when the injury is immediate and not the remote result of defendant's negligence?

HOLDING AND DECISION: (Hunt, J.) Yes. Damages can be awarded only when the injury is immediate and not the remote result of defendant's negligence. Liability would extend only to the owner of the first structure, that is, the structure upon which the spark lands. The result to be anticipated is that the structure upon which the spark lands will be damaged or destroyed. But the spread of the fire to other structures is not the necessary or usual result. The defendant has no control over that and cannot be responsible. The immediate result of the negligence was destruction of Central's (D) own woodshed. All other damage was remote. To hold defendant liable for all resulting damage would be to create a liability too great for any individual; all persons run some risk as to their neighbor's conduct. Affirmed.

ANALYSIS

Supposedly, a defendant is liable for damage that is the natural and probable consequence of his act. In New York, there has been created an arbitrary rule that the wrongdoer is liable for fire only to the first, adjoining property, as illustrated above. Here, as the first structure to be struck by sparks belonged to Central (D), it was not liable to anyone. Thus, it would not make any difference whether the adjoining structure was one large building or thirty small stores. Only the owner of the first, adjoining property could recover. Even if the fire covered the entire block, burning a series of small stores, the ones after the first on the block to be ignited would not be covered. The court touched but did not rest its decision upon whether one should be liable for all damage from an intentionally set fire as opposed to a negligently set fire where liability may be limited to the first, adjoining property.

Quicknotes

NONSUIT Judgment against a party who fails to make out a case.

SUBROGATION The substitution of one party for another in assuming the first party's rights or obligations.

Bartolone v. Jeckovich

Car accident victim (P) v. Tortfeasors (D)

N.Y. App. Div., 103 A.D.2d 632, 481 N.Y.S.2d 545 (1984)

NATURE OF CASE: Appeal of judgment n.o.v. in action seeking damages for personal injury.

FACT SUMMARY: Bartolone (P) suffered a total psychological breakdown following a seemingly minor accident.

RULE OF LAW

A tortfeasor bears responsibility for all damages proximately caused by tortious conduct, even if the damages appear disproportionate to the tortious conduct.

FACTS: Bartolone (P) was a bodybuilder involved in an accident caused by the negligence of Jeckovich (D). Bartolone's (P) physical injuries were minor, but he suffered an apparently total psychological breakdown, becoming psychotic. At trial, several mental health professionals opined that Bartolone (P), who had a traumatic childhood, had used bodybuilding as a coping mechanism, and when his routine was disturbed, he fell apart. A jury awarded $500,000. The trial court granted judgment n.o.v., holding that the evidence could not support the verdict. Bartolone (P) appealed.

ISSUE: Does a tortfeasor bear responsibility for all damages proximately caused by tortious conduct, even if the damages appear disproportionate to the tortious conduct?

HOLDING AND DECISION: (Denman, J.) Yes. A tortfeasor bears responsibility for all damages proximately caused by tortious conduct, even if the damages appear disproportionate to the tortious conduct. It is very well settled that a defendant takes a plaintiff as he finds him, and injuries seemingly excessive in comparison to the cause of harm will be compensable, if proven. Here, competent testimony that Bartolone (P) had a latent psychological weakness was believed by a jury, and it was well within its power to award damages as it did. Reversed.

ANALYSIS

This case is a textbook example of what is popularly called the "eggshell plaintiff" rule. A particularly sensitive plaintiff will be permitted to recover for seemingly disproportionate injuries. However, it is still required of a plaintiff he convince a jury that the claimed damages are legitimate.

Quicknotes

EGGSHELL PLAINTIFF RULE Doctrine the defendant is liable in tort for the aggravation of a plaintiff's existing injury or condition, regardless of whether the magnitude of the injury was foreseeable.

JUDGMENT NOTWITHSTANDING THE VERDICT (JUDGMENT N.O.V.) A judgment entered by the trial judge reversing a jury verdict if the jury's determination has no basis in law or fact.

TORTFEASOR Party that commits a tort or wrongful act.

In re Arbitration between Polemis and Furness, Withy & Co., Ltd.

Shipowner (Polemis) v. Ship charterer (Furness)

C.A., 3 K.B. 560 (1921)

NATURE OF CASE: Arbitration for damages for injury due to negligence.

FACT SUMMARY: The ship Polemis, while being unloaded, was destroyed by fire when Furness, Withy & Co., Ltd.'s servant negligently dropped a plank setting off a spark in the hold that exploded vapor seeping from the cargo of petrol and benzine.

RULE OF LAW

The fact that the kind of damage which an act might probably cause was not the damage anticipated is immaterial so long as the resulting damage is directly traceable to the negligent act, and not due to independent cause having no connection with the negligent act.

FACTS: Furness, Withy & Co., Ltd. (Furness) chartered the ship, Polemis, from its owners. It carried a cargo of petrol and benzine. While unloading in Casablanca, a heavy plank fell into the hold setting off a spark which ignited petrol vapor. The resulting explosion completely destroyed the Polemis. Arbitrators found that while a spark resulting from the dropping of the plank would not be reasonably foreseen, the dropping of the plank was due to negligence of Furness's servants. Also found was that some damage could be reasonably anticipated from the dropping of the plank. Damages were stated at £196 1s. 11d.

ISSUE: Is the fact that the kind of damage which an act might probably cause was not the damage anticipated immaterial so long as the resulting damage is directly traceable to the negligent act, and not due to independent cause having no connection with the negligent act?

HOLDING: (Lord Bankes, J.) Yes. The fact that the kind of damage which an act might probably cause was not the damage anticipated is immaterial so long as the resulting damage is directly traceable to the negligent act, and not due to independent cause having no connection with the negligent act. The arbiters are affirmed. It is immaterial that the spark could not be reasonably anticipated; the act of dropping the plank itself was negligent. If the act would or might probably cause damage, the fact that the damage it in fact causes is not the exact kind of damage one would expect is immaterial, so long as the damage is in fact directly traceable to the negligent act, and not due to the operation of independent causes having no connection with the negligent act, except that they could not avoid its results. Appeal dismissed.

HOLDING: (Lord Scrutton, J.) When damage is directly traceable to a negligent act, and no independent cause separates the damage from the negligent act, the unexpectedness of the specific kind of damage is irrelevant. In this case, the fact that some foreseeable damage would result from knocking down the planks makes the act negligent. That the resulting spark was unexpected is irrelevant because the negligent act directly caused the damage. Appeal dismissed.

ANALYSIS

This case follows the rule set out in *Christianson v. Chicago, St. P., M.G.O. Ry. Co.*, 69 N.W. 640 (1896), a minority rule in the United States. The rule is rather mechanical. Basically, if X can be foreseen to result in Y, but instead results in Z, the wrongdoer is still liable for Z even though it may be totally out of proportion to X. Z is proximate to X and, hence, there is liability. Prosser, among others, has called this decision "absurd." Basically, the criticism is that damages are usually just too high, with the rule being "artificial." This case remained a controversy for forty years until it was overruled in 1961.

Quicknotes

FORESEEABILITY A reasonable expectation that an act or omission would result in injury.

Overseas Tankship (U.K.) Ltd. v. Morts Dock & Engineering Co., Ltd. "Wagon Mound No. 1"

Workmen's employer (D) v. Wharf owner (P)

Privy Council 1961, A.C. 388 (1961)

NATURE OF CASE: Action for damages for injury due to negligence.

FACT SUMMARY: A wharf operated by Morts Dock & Engineering Co., Ltd (Dock) (P) was seriously damaged when oil negligently discharged from Overseas Tankship (U.K.) Ltd.'s (D) ship, the Wagon Mound, spread across the water and later caught fire when molten metal dropped by Dock's (P) workmen ignited cotton waste floating on the surface.

RULE OF LAW

Even though injury may result from a negligent act, liability for that injury is limited to the risk reasonably to be foreseen.

FACTS: Morts Dock & Engineering Co., Ltd (Dock) (P) operated a wharf in Port of Sydney, Australia. The ship, Wagon Mound, owned by Overseas Tankship (U.K.) Ltd. (Overseas) (D) and moored about 600 feet away, carelessly discharged a large quantity of furnace oil. The oil spread across the surface of the water and washed against Dock's (P) wharf. Damage was so minor that no claim was made. Cotton waste floating on the surface was ignited by molten metal dropped by Dock's (P) workmen. This set the oil afire, seriously damaging Dock's (P) wharf. The trial court found that Overseas (D) did not know and could not reasonably know that the oil with a flashpoint of 170° could be set afire when spread on water. Dock's (P) was awarded judgment and Overseas (D) appealed to the Privy Council (the appeals court for all Commonwealth Nations except England).

ISSUE: Even though injury may result from a negligent act, is liability for that injury limited to the risk reasonably to be foreseen?

HOLDING AND DECISION: (Viscount Simonds, J.) Yes. Even though injury may result from a negligent act, liability for that injury is limited to the risk reasonably to be foreseen. It is not "consonant with current ideas of justice and morality that for an act of negligence, however slight or venial, which results in some trivial foreseeable damage, the actor should be liable for all consequences, however unforeseeable and however grave, so long as they can be said to be 'direct.'" One should be responsible only for the probable consequences of his act, not the improbable. This keeps the rule from being too harsh while requiring all persons to observe a minimum standard of behavior. There should be some limitation on the consequences of a negligent act for which the wrongdoer will be held responsible and it seems unreasonable to substitute the reasonable foreseeability test with a direct causation test which leads to nothing but "insolvable problems of causation." Action dismissed and case remanded.

ANALYSIS

This case overruled *In re Polemis*, Ct. of Appeals, 3 K.B. 560 (1921). One is responsible for the reasonably foreseeable or probable consequence of his negligent acts. The old rule of responsibility for all damage, foreseeable or not as long as some damage was reasonably foreseeable, was found unjust and harsh. This rule does not apply to the "eggshell skull" doctrine, as that deals with the inherent weakness of plaintiff while foreseeable consequences deals with extent of damages done.

Quicknotes

EGGSHELL SKULL DOCTRINE Doctrine the defendant is liable in tort for the aggravation of a plaintiff's existing injury or condition, regardless of whether the magnitude of the injury was foreseeable.

FORESEEABILITY A reasonable expectation that an act or omission would result in injury.

NEGLIGENCE Conduct falling below the standard of care that a reasonable person would demonstrate under similar conditions.

Overseas Tankship (U.K.) Ltd. v. Miller Steamship Co. "Wagon Mound No. 2"

Ship owner (D) v. Steamship owner (P)

Privy Council 1966, 1 A.C. 617 (1967)

NATURE OF CASE: Action for damages for injury due to negligence.

FACT SUMMARY: Miller Steamship Co.'s (P) two ships were damaged when oil negligently discharged from Overseas Tankship (U.K.) Ltd.'s (D) ship, the Wagon Mound, spread across the water and later caught fire.

RULE OF LAW

One who is knowledgeable of a risk and can reasonably prevent it is liable for damages resulting from his failure to do so.

FACTS: Miller Steamship Co.'s (Miller's) (P) two ships were damaged when oil negligently discharged from Overseas Tankship (U.K.) Ltd.'s (Overseas') (D) ship, the Wagon Mound, spread across the water and later caught fire. The trial court made findings on foreseeability as follows: (1) reasonable people in the position of Wagon Mound officers would consider the furnace oil very difficult to ignite; (2) their personal experience would be that this probably occurred rarely; (3) risk of fire would have been regarded as a possibility but occurred only in exceptional circumstances; (4) the chances of fire would be considered remote; (5) damage to Miller's (P) ships would not be reasonably foreseeable, and, accordingly, damages could not be awarded.

ISSUE: Is one who is knowledgeable of a risk and can reasonably prevent it liable for damages resulting from his failure to do so?

HOLDING AND DECISION: (Lord Reid, J.) Yes. One who is knowledgeable of a risk and can reasonably prevent it is liable for damages resulting from his failure to do so. Findings of the trial court show that the chief engineer should have known that it was possible to ignite the oil on the water. It does not follow that no matter what the circumstances may be that it is justifiable to neglect a risk of such small magnitude. The risk must be weighed against the difficulty of removing it. A reasonable man should not dismiss a small risk when it is so easy to remove it. There was no justification for discharging the oil into the water. In balancing the advantages and disadvantages it was the chief engineer's duty to stop the discharge immediately. Judgment was reversed.

ANALYSIS

Here, the court is balancing what a reasonable man would foresee against the burden of obviating the risk. Overseas (D) should have known that despite the small chance of fire, a risk did exist, and as it was relatively easy to obviate that risk, it should have done so. This is not a throwback to *In re Polemis*, 3 K.B. 560 (1921) exactly, but more of an extension of *Wagon Mound No. 1*, Privy Council 1961, A.C. 388 (1961), which was distinguished on the facts. Here, the trial court made findings of fact that Overseas (D) should have known of the risk. Because the risk was known, the damage was foreseeable. Overseas (D) failed in its duty to remove the risk.

Quicknotes

NEGLIGENCE Conduct falling below the standard of care that a reasonable person would demonstrate under similar conditions.

REASONABLE PERSON STANDARD The standard of care exercised by a hypothetical person who possesses the intelligence, education, knowledge, attention, and judgment required by society of its members when governing behavior; the standard applies to a person's judgment when determining breach of a duty under the theory of negligence.

Palsgraf v. Long Island R.R. Co.

Injured bystander (P) v. Railroad company (D)

N.Y. Ct. App., 248 N.Y. 339, 162 N.E. 99 (1928)

NATURE OF CASE: Action for damages for personal injury due to negligence.

FACT SUMMARY: Mrs. Palsgraf (P) was injured on Long Island R.R. Co.'s (LIRR) (D) train platform when LIRR's (D) servant helped a passenger aboard a moving train, jostling his package, causing it to fall to the tracks. The package, containing fireworks, exploded, creating a shock that tipped a scale onto Mrs. Palsgraf (P).

RULE OF LAW

The risk reasonably to be perceived defines the duty to be obeyed.

FACTS: Mrs. Palsgraf (P) purchased a ticket to Rockaway Beach from Long Island R.R. Co. (LIRR) (D) and was waiting on the train platform. While standing there, two men ran to catch a train that was pulling out from the platform. The first man jumped aboard, but the second man, who appeared as if he might fall, was helped aboard by the guard who had kept the door open so they could jump aboard while a guard on the platform also helped by pushing him into the train. The man was carrying a package wrapped in newspaper. In the process, the man dropped his innocent-looking package, which fell to the tracks. The package contained fireworks, which exploded. The shock of the explosion was apparently of enough strength to tip over scales at the other end of the platform. The scales fell on Mrs. Palsgraf (P) and injured her. She was awarded damages and LIRR (D) appealed.

ISSUE: Does the risk reasonably to be perceived define the duty to be obeyed?

HOLDING AND DECISION: (Cardozo, C.J.) Yes. The risk reasonably to be perceived defines the duty to be obeyed. If there was no foreseeable hazard as the result of a seemingly innocent act with reference to the injured party, the act did not become a tort because it happened to be a wrong, though not to the injured party. Negligence is not enough upon which to base liability—there must be a duty to the injured party which could have been averted or avoided by observance of the duty. There can be no duty owed to an injured party when the wrong was committed towards someone else. The range of the duty is limited by the range of danger. There was nothing to suggest that the parcel from its appearance contained fireworks. Had the guard purposefully thrown down the package, he would have had no warning of a threat of harm to Mrs. Palsgraf (P). Just because the act was inadvertent does not impose liability. In the abstract, negligence itself is not a tort. To be a tort, it must result in the commission of a wrong. A wrong imports the violation of a right. If the wrong was not willful, it must be shown by the plaintiff that the act as to him had such great possibilities of danger, so many and so apparent, as to entitle him to protection against it though the harm was unintentional. Had there been liability for the negligence towards Mrs. Palsgraf (P), she would recover for all injury "however novel or extraordinary." Accordingly, the judgment is reversed in favor of LIRR (D).

ANALYSIS

Cardozo states that negligence is a matter of relationship between the parties. That relationship must be based upon the foreseeability of harm to the person who is, in fact, injured. Just because defendant's act was negligent, it is not necessarily wrong to the injured party. The act must be negligent and wrong to the injured party to enable him to sue in his own right. If there is no duty to the injured party, there was no violation of a right, so even if an act was negligent it could not have violated a wrong to the injured party. The dissent, on the other hand, states that each person owes a duty of due care to society at large. Each person must refrain from any act that unreasonably threatens the safety of others. Accordingly, any party injured by a negligent act would suffer a wrong as the duty owed to each member of society at large would have been violated. A right of action must then arise despite the unforeseeability of the injury. The Restatement has accepted the view of this case that without any duty there can be no negligence, hence, never any liability to the unforeseeable injured party. Note that the determination of any question of duty is a question of law and never one for the jury. Cardozo, on the question of duty, went even further by suggesting that the defendant could owe a duty to one particular interest of the injured party but not to a different interest of the same party. That is to say that there could be a duty to the injured party's property interest but not to his person. So, if defendant negligently set a fire in plaintiff's unoccupied building, and the plaintiff is injured extinguishing the blaze, damages only to the building are recoverable, or vice versa depending upon the original duty. This theory advanced in the dictum of *Palsgraf* was approved by the Restatement's § 281, but it has been widely opposed by most other courts. In fact, there is much authority against it and even Prosser has called this aspect of Cardozo's view "artificial." There are, of course, interests which, as a matter of public policy, should

Continued on next page.

not be protected against certain types of wrongful conduct, but it does not follow from this that protection should always be limited to the interest which is threatened in advance.

Quicknotes

FORESEEABILITY The reasonable anticipation that damage is a likely result from certain acts or omissions.

NEGLIGENCE Failure to exercise that degree of care a person of ordinary prudence would exercise under similar circumstances.

PROXIMATE CAUSE Something which in natural and continuous sequence, unbroken by any new intervening cause, produces an event and without that the injury would not have occurred.

UNFORESEEABLE A result that was not likely to occur from a particular act or failure to act.

Yun v. Ford Motor Co.

Estate representative (P) v. Automobile manufacturer (D)

N.J. Super. Ct. App. Div., 276 N.J. Super. 142, 647 A.2d 841 (1994)

NATURE OF CASE: Products liability suit.

FACT SUMMARY: Yun (P) brought suit on behalf of her deceased father's estate against Ford Motor Co. (D) and other defendants for injuries sustained by the father when he ran across the freeway in an attempt to retrieve an allegedly defective tire assembly that fell off the back of her van.

RULE OF LAW

A claim of strict liability may be defeated if the defendant can show that an intervening superseding event or another sole proximate cause resulted in the plaintiff's injury.

FACTS: Chang was a passenger in a 1987 Ford van owned and driven by his daughter Yun (P). Yun (P) heard a rattling noise coming from the rear of the van. The spare tire and plastic cover screwed to the rear of the van landed directly behind the van and rolled across both lanes of traffic resting against the wooden guard rail. Yun (P) drove the van to the right side of the highway and stopped. Chang ran across the freeway to get the spare tire and was struck by a vehicle driven by Linderman (D). Yun (P) sued Ford Motor Co. (D), Miller (D), Universal (D), Castle (D), the Lindermans (D) and Kim's Automobile Center (D). Summary judgment was granted to defendant and Yun (P) appealed.

ISSUE: May a claim of strict liability be defeated if the defendant can show that an intervening superseding event or another sole proximate cause resulted in the plaintiff's injury?

HOLDING AND DECISION: (Villanueva, J.) Yes. A claim of strict liability may be defeated if the defendant can show that an intervening superseding event or another sole proximate cause resulted in the plaintiff's injury. This action falls within the Products Liability Act. Yun (P) must show the alleged defect in the spare tire bracket proximately caused Chang's injuries. Proximate cause is defined as any cause in the natural sequence of events, unbroken by a sufficient intervening cause, which results in the injury and without which the injury would not have occurred. This refers to conduct setting off a foreseeable sequence of events that is a substantial factor in bringing about the injury and that is not superseded by another event. Here the question is whether Chang's conduct was reasonably foreseeable or highly extraordinary. Here the circumstances were highly extraordinary. Chang's attempt to retrieve the tire by running across the freeway was extraordinarily dangerous and does not conform to the standard of conduct of normal persons. Furthermore, the alleged defect in the tire was not the cause of Chang's injury. A tortfeasor is responsible for negligent conduct if it constitutes a substantial factor in bringing about the plaintiff's injuries. If concurrent events are involved, the manufacturer of a product may defeat a claim of strict liability by showing an intervening, superseding cause or another sole proximate cause that resulted in the injury. Even if the defective tire was a proximate cause of Chang's injuries, his conduct in running across the freeway constituted an intervening, superseding cause. In addition, Yun (P) and Chang's joint decision not to fix the allegedly defective assembly 30 days earlier constituted an intervening superseding cause as well. Affirmed.

CONCURRENCE AND DISSENT: (Baime, J.) The judgments in favor of Ford Motor Co. (D) and Kim's Automobile Center (D) should be affirmed since the record fails to demonstrate facts sufficient for a finding of negligence. However, Yun's (P) evidence with respect to proximate cause on the part of the remaining defendants was sufficient to present an issue of material fact for the jury.

ANALYSIS

Typically the issue of proximate cause is a question for the jury. However, where the issue of proximate cause is a policy question then the court will resolve the issue. This occurs when the consequences of the conduct are highly extraordinary so that the imposition of liability would not be equitable.

Quicknotes

INTERVENING ACT An event whose occurrence breaks the causal chain between the tortfeasor's acts and the resulting injury.

NEGLIGENCE Conduct falling below the standard of care that a reasonable person would demonstrate under similar conditions.

PROXIMATE CAUSE The natural sequence of events without which an injury would not have been sustained.

STRICT LIABILITY Liability for all injuries proximately caused by a party's conducting of certain inherently dangerous activities without regard to negligence or fault.

Continued on next page.

SUMMARY JUDGMENT Judgment rendered by a court in response to a motion by one of the parties, claiming that the lack of a question of material fact in respect to an issue warrants disposition of the issue without consideration by the jury.

Derdiarian v. Felix Contracting Corp.

Injured workman (P) v. Contractor (D)

N.Y. Ct. App., 51 N.Y.2d 308, 414 N.E.2d 666 (1980)

NATURE OF CASE: Action for damages for negligence.

FACT SUMMARY: Derdiarian (P) was severely injured while working at an excavation site constructed by Felix Contracting Corp. (D), when an automobile driven by Dickens (D), an epileptic, careened onto the site.

RULE OF LAW

An intervening act will not serve as a superseding cause, relieving the defendant of liability, where the risk of the intervening act occurring is the very same risk that rendered the defendant negligent.

FACTS: Derdiarian (P), an employee of a subcontractor, was working at an excavation site constructed by Felix Contracting Corp. (Felix) (D), a general contractor, when a car came careening onto the site. Derdiarian (P) was struck by the car and seriously injured. The driver of the car, Dickens (D), had neglected to take his regular medicine and had suffered an epileptic seizure immediately prior to the accident. Derdiarian (P) alleged that Felix's (D) negligence stemmed from its failure to provide adequate protection around the excavation site. Felix (D) contended that even if it had been negligent, the intervening act of Dickens's (D) negligence severed any proximate causation connecting Felix's (D) conduct and the injuries suffered by Derdiarian (P). A verdict against Felix (D) was returned. It appealed.

ISSUE: Will an intervening act serve as a superseding cause, relieving the defendant of liability, where the risk of the intervening act occurring is the very same risk that rendered the defendant negligent?

HOLDING AND DECISION: (Cooke, C.J.) No. Occasionally the difficult question of proximate causation can be decided as a matter of law where an intervening act by a third party is involved. Thus, it has been held that where the intervening act was unforeseeable and where the resulting injuries were different in kind than those normally associated with the defendant's negligence, the defendant, as a matter of law, will not be held to be a proximate cause of the plaintiff's injuries. However, the situation presented here is different. In the instant case, the very reason that Felix's (D) conduct was negligent was that it created a risk of injury due to automobile accidents. Thus, the fact that the risk materialized in a somewhat different fashion than anticipated or that the intervening actor was also negligent cannot serve to absolve Felix (D) of liability as the proximate cause of Derdiarian's (P) injuries. Affirmed.

ANALYSIS

For another case decided on similar grounds, see *Weirum v. RKO General, Inc.*, 15 Cal. 3d 40 (1975). In that case, a radio station conducted a contest whereby its generally young listeners were instructed to locate a personality through clues broadcast periodically. In the course of the contest, a car driven by a teenager at high speed collided with another car and killed the driver. The radio station was held liable, despite the intervening negligence of the teenage driver, since the risk created by its actions was precisely the risk that resulted—an accident resulting from dangerous driving.

Quicknotes

FORESEEABILITY A reasonable expectation that an act or omission would result in injury.

INTERVENING ACT An event whose occurrence breaks the causal chain between the tortfeasor's acts and the resulting injury.

NEGLIGENCE Conduct falling below the standard of care that a reasonable person would demonstrate under similar conditions.

PROXIMATE CAUSE The natural sequence of events without which an injury would not have been sustained.

Watson v. Kentucky & Indiana Bridge & R.R. Co.

Burn victim (P) v. Railroad (D)

Ky. Ct. App., 137 Ky. 619, 126 S.W. 146 (1910)

NATURE OF CASE: Action for damages for injury due to negligence.

FACT SUMMARY: Through Kentucky & Indiana Bridge R.R. Co.'s (D) negligence, a tank car full of gasoline derailed and began leaking. Duerr then struck a match, causing the vapor to explode and injure Watson (P).

RULE OF LAW

The mere fact that an intervening act was unforeseen will not relieve the defendant guilty of primary negligence from liability unless the intervening act is something so unexpected or extraordinary as that it could not or ought not to be anticipated.

FACTS: Through Kentucky & Indiana Bridge & R.R. Co.'s (R.R.'s) (D) negligence, a tank car full of gasoline derailed and its valve broke, allowing gasoline to run into the street. Duerr then struck a match, igniting the vapor and causing an explosion that injured Watson (P). There was conflicting evidence as to whether Duerr lit the match deliberately to cause a fire or innocently to light his cigar. The trial court directed a verdict for R.R. (D).

ISSUE: Will the mere fact that an intervening act was unforeseen relieve the defendant guilty of primary negligence from liability unless the intervening act is something so unexpected or extraordinary as that it could not or ought not to be anticipated?

HOLDING AND DECISION: (Settle, J.) No. The mere fact that an intervening act was unforeseen will not relieve the defendant guilty of primary negligence from liability unless the intervening act is something so unexpected or extraordinary as that it could not or ought not to be anticipated. Here, however, as it is not clear whether Duerr's act was deliberate, the issue cannot be decided; judgment must be reversed, and a new trial ordered. As the lighting of the match resulted in the explosion, the question arose as to whether the act was merely a contributing cause or the proximate cause of injury. There was conflicting evidence on the point but the trial court erroneously directed a verdict and did not permit the jury to determine the fact. It was probable that a match would be lit after the accident and in such case not be the proximate cause of the explosion as the explosion could not have occurred at all without the original negligence of R.R. (D). However, if the lighting of the match was deliberate or malicious, it could not or ought not to have been foreseen that such a thing would be done for such evil purpose. If so, the R.R. (D) could not have reasonably anticipated or guarded against a malicious act and would not be liable. That issue remains to be decided in a new trial. Reversed and remanded.

ANALYSIS

For an intervening cause to be one that will not relieve the original negligent party from liability, it must be one which in ordinary human experience can be reasonably anticipated under the circumstances. Generally, malicious and wanton acts and criminal acts are not foreseeable and will relieve the original negligent party of liability. The procedural error by the court took the issue away from the jury when the jury was supposed to determine all questions of fact, one of which was the deliberateness of Duerr's act.

Quicknotes

CONTRIBUTORY CAUSE Any factor that contributes to the happening of an event.

DIRECTED VERDICT A verdict ordered by the court in a jury trial.

INTERVENING ACT An event whose occurrence breaks the causal chain between the tortfeasor's acts and the resulting injury.

NEGLIGENCE Conduct falling below the standard of care that a reasonable person would demonstrate under similar conditions.

PROXIMATE CAUSE The natural sequence of events without which an injury would not have been sustained.

Fuller v. Preis

Executor of deceased estate (P) v. Car driver (D)

N.Y. Ct. App., 35 N.Y.2d 425, 322 N.E.2d 263, 363 N.Y.S.2d 568 (1974)

NATURE OF CASE: Wrongful death.

FACT SUMMARY: Fuller's (P) decedent committed suicide, allegedly the irresistible impulse of head injuries suffered in a car accident.

RULE OF LAW

As a matter of law, an act of suicide is not a superseding cause in negligence law precluding liability.

FACTS: Dr. Lewis, Fuller's (P) decedent, was injured in an auto accident seven months before he committed suicide. He suffered head injuries, which damaged the part of the brain controlling emotion and motor control. Epileptic seizures occurred 38 times, including three times on the day of the suicide. Dr. Lewis was physically and emotionally healthy prior to the accident. The seizures could not be controlled by drugs and became progressively more severe. He became depressed, unsteady on his feet, and irritable, and he experienced headaches. A neurologist testified that on the day of death, Dr. Lewis was in post-convulsive psychosis, which placed his conduct beyond his control. Suicide notes were left in which Dr. Lewis stated he was sane. Fuller (P) sought damages for wrongful death against Preis (D), who allegedly caused the accident that Fuller (P) argued was the proximate cause of the suicide. A jury verdict for $200,000 was reversed on appeal and the complaint dismissed as contrary to the weight of credible evidence.

ISSUE: As a matter of law, is an act of suicide a superseding cause in negligence law precluding liability?

HOLDING AND DECISION: (Breitel, C.J.) No. As a matter of law, an act of suicide is not a superseding cause in negligence law precluding liability. A tortfeasor may be liable for the wrongful acts of a third party if foreseeable, e.g., a doctor's malpractice. The same applies when death results from an "involuntary" suicidal act of the victim as a direct consequence of the wrongful conduct. There is neither public policy nor precedent barring recovery for suicide of a tortiously injured person driven "insane" by the consequence of the tortious act. The issue at trial was whether the suicide was the result of an "irresistible impulse" caused by traumatic organic brain damage. Medical testimony showed that such result was more likely than not. Even though the decedent believed he was sane, sanity is never established by self-serving certification. Insane persons often are unable to accept or recognize their mental state. In tort law, it is recognized that one may retain the power to intend, to know, and yet to act from involuntary and irresistible impulse. The jury only had to find that Preis's (D) negligence substantially contributed to the suicide. Reversed.

ANALYSIS

The early view did not allow recovery when the suicide retained even the slightest awareness of what he was doing. The suicide was thus a superseding cause, a view strongly influenced by ecclesiastical law which held that one who knowingly committed suicide was a culpable wrongdoer. This case gives a broad interpretation to the irresistible impulse test. Many courts will find an irresistible impulse only when the decedent takes his life in a sudden frenzy.

Quicknotes

IRRESISTIBLE IMPULSE RULE A defense to a criminal prosecution that the defendant, due to some mental disease or defect, was unable to resist the impulse to commit the crime due to his inability to control his actions.

NEGLIGENCE Conduct falling below the standard of care that a reasonable person would demonstrate under similar conditions.

McCoy v. American Suzuki Motor Corp.

Injured rescuer (P) v. Automobile manufacturer (D)

Wash. Sup. Ct., 136 Wash. 2d 350, 961 P.2d 952 (1998)

NATURE OF CASE: Products liability action.

FACT SUMMARY: McCoy (P) sued American Suzuki Motor Corp. (D) claiming that the injuries he sustained while rescuing two individuals from a Suzuki Samurai were proximately caused by a defective condition in the automobile.

RULE OF LAW

The rescue doctrine may be invoked in products liability cases, requiring the rescuer-plaintiff to prove that the defendant's conduct was the proximate cause of his injuries.

FACTS: McCoy (P) was driving on the interstate when the car in front of him, a Suzuki, swerved off the road and rolled. He stopped to render assistance and found the driver of the car badly injured. A state trooper stopped and asked McCoy (P) to place flares along the road. After the accident was cleared, McCoy (P) was walking along the roadway back to his car when he was struck by a hit-and-run driver. He and his wife (P) brought suit against the driver and passenger of the Suzuki for negligence, the State for the trooper's negligence, and American Suzuki Motor Corp. (Suzuki) (D) for its allegedly defective car. Suzuki (D) moved for summary judgment on the basis that the rescue doctrine does not apply to products liability actions and even if it does, McCoy (P) cannot prove Suzuki (D) proximately caused his injuries. Summary judgment was granted for Suzuki (D) and McCoy (P) appealed. The court of appeals reversed, holding that the rescue doctrine applies to products liability cases but that the injured rescuer need not prove that the defendant proximately caused the rescuer's injuries, only that defendant proximately caused the danger and that the rescuer was injured while rescuing.

ISSUE: May the rescue doctrine may be invoked in products liability cases, requiring the rescuer-plaintiff to prove that the defendant's conduct was the proximate cause of his injuries?

HOLDING AND DECISION: (Sanders, J.) Yes. The rescue doctrine may be invoked in products liability cases, requiring the rescuer-plaintiff to prove that the defendant's conduct was the proximate cause of his injuries. The rescue doctrine allows an injured rescuer to sue a party causing the danger that required the rescue. The rescue doctrine imposes a duty on the tortfeasor towards the rescuer on the basis that it is foreseeable that a person will come to the rescue of a person placed in danger by the tortfeasor's conduct. The doctrine also negates the presumption that the rescuer assumed the risk of injury by undertaking the rescue as long as he did not act rashly or recklessly. McCoy (P) argued that the rescue doctrine relieved him of demonstrating that Suzuki's (D) wrongdoing proximately caused his injuries. He argued that a rescuer may prevail if he shows the defendant proximately caused the dangerous condition and that plaintiff was injured while rescuing. The court of appeals erred. The rescuer must still demonstrate the defendant proximately caused his injuries. Thus the issue is whether McCoy (P) has shown that Suzuki (D) proximately caused his injuries. Suzuki (D) argued that it was totally unforeseeable that a rescuer would be injured by a third car under the circumstances of this case and that the court should rule in its favor as a matter of law. The court concludes the issue of foreseeability of the intervening cause is sufficiently close that it should be determined by the jury, not the court. The court may dismiss an action without trial for lack of legal cause where the defendant's actions are too remote so as to be a cause of the plaintiff's injuries. Here Suzuki's (D) alleged fault is not so remote to conclude as a matter of law that its actions were too remote to be the cause of McCoy's (P) injuries. Remanded.

ANALYSIS

In order to demonstrate rescuer status, a rescuer must show: (1) the defendant was negligent to the rescued person and such negligence gave rise to the danger; (2) the danger was imminent; (3) a reasonably prudent person would have concluded the danger existed; and (4) the rescuer acted with reasonable care. Here McCoy (P) introduced sufficient evidence to obtain rescuer status.

Quicknotes

PRODUCT LIABILITY The legal liability of manufacturers and sellers for damages and injuries suffered by buyers, users, and even bystanders because of defects in goods purchased.

PROXIMATE CAUSE The natural sequence of events without which an injury would not have been sustained.

REASONABLY PRUDENT PERSON A hypothetical person whose judgment represents the standard to which society requires its members to act in their private affairs and in their dealings with others.

RESCUE DOCTRINE One whose conduct places a person in danger is liable to a third party for any injuries incurred in effecting a reasonable rescue attempt.

Kelly v. Gwinnell

Injured party (P) v. Driver (D) and host (D)

N.J. Sup. Ct., 96 N.J. 538, 476 A.2d 1219 (1984)

NATURE OF CASE: Appeal of summary judgment dismissing action for damages for personal injury.

FACT SUMMARY: Kelly (P), involved in an accident with Gwinnell (D), who was intoxicated, sued Zak (D), Gwinnell's (D) host.

RULE OF LAW

A social host may be liable for furnishing alcohol to an intoxicated guest.

FACTS: Gwinnell (D) was a guest at Zak's (D) home. Zak (D) furnished alcohol to Gwinnell (D) beyond the point of intoxication. Gwinnell (D) later was in an accident with Kelly (P), who sued both Gwinnell (D) and Zak (D). The trial court granted summary judgment dismissing Zak (D), and the appellate court affirmed. Kelly (P) appealed.

ISSUE: May a social host be liable for furnishing alcohol to an intoxicated guest?

HOLDING AND DECISION: (Wilentz, C.J.) Yes. A social host may be liable for furnishing alcohol to an intoxicated guest. In terms of duty, the law already imposes a duty not to serve an intoxicated minor, and for a business not to serve an intoxicated patron. This, along with a strong social policy against drunk driving, makes the next step of holding hosts liable for serving alcohol to intoxicated guests a logical one. In terms of causation, it is quite foreseeable that serving alcohol to an intoxicated guest may cause an accident. Here, the allegation was that Zak (D) served alcohol to an intoxicated Gwinnell (D), and this court believes liability should be possible in this situation. Reversed and remanded.

DISSENT: (Garibaldi, J.) Before imposing such a high duty on social hosts, many factors and interests need to be weighed. The legislature is in a better position to do this. This decision is improper judicial legislation, and the result is therefore also improper.

ANALYSIS

Social host liability is the minority rule. Historically, some states have had "dram shop acts" which imposed liability on establishments, but such liability on social hosts has been uncommon. California, one of the first states to judicially impose host liability, changed this by statute in 1978.

Quicknotes

CAUSATION The aggregate effect of preceding events that bring about a tortious result; the causal connection between the actions of a tortfeasor and the injury that follows.

FORESEEABILITY A reasonable expectation that an act or omission would result in injury.

SOCIAL HOST LIABILITY Responsibility imposed upon a person who offers alcoholic beverages to a third party for injuries resulting from the intoxication of the individual.

SUMMARY JUDGMENT Judgment rendered by a court in response to a motion by one of the parties, claiming that the lack of a question of material fact in respect to an issue warrants disposition of the issue without consideration by the jury.

Enright v. Eli Lilly & Co.

Granddaughter of DES user (P) v. DES manufacturer (D)

N.Y. Ct. App., 77 N.Y.2d 377, 570 N.E.2d 198 (1991)

NATURE OF CASE: Review of dismissal of personal injury action.

FACT SUMMARY: Enright (P) sought damages for injuries allegedly resulting from her grandmother's ingestion of the drug diethylstilbestrol (DES).

RULE OF LAW

An injury to a mother that results in injuries to a later-conceived child does not establish a cause of action in favor of the child against the original tortfeasor.

FACTS: Enright's (P) grandmother ingested the drug diethylstilbestrol (DES) while pregnant with Enright's (P) mother, Patricia, in 1960. Allegedly, this ingestion led to latent damage to Patricia's reproductive system while being formed in utero. Patricia's injuries, in turn, resulted in congenital defects suffered by Enright (P), who was born prematurely. Enright (P) brought a personal injury action against Eli Lilly (D), the drug's manufacturer. The trial court dismissed, refusing to recognize a cause of action in favor of a child for injuries suffered as a result of a preconception tort committed against the mother. The appellate division affirmed, and the court of appeals (New York's highest court) granted review.

ISSUE: Does an injury to a mother that results in injuries to a later-conceived child establish a cause of action in favor of the child against the original tortfeasor?

HOLDING AND DECISION: (Wachtler, C.J.) No. An injury to a mother that results in injuries to a later-conceived child does not establish a cause of action in favor of the child. To recognize such a cause of action would pose vexing questions with staggering implications in terms of unlimited liability for drug manufacturers. While products liability (as well as negligence liability, for that matter) exists in part to deter unsafe conduct, limiting liability to those who either ingested the drug, like Enright's (P) grandmother, or who were exposed to it in utero, like Patricia, still serves this purpose. On the other hand, to extend liability to those who were never exposed to a dangerous product would lead to such uncertainty in the pharmaceutical industry that the negative impacts on the development of new and much needed drugs would be significant. Consequently, the policy decision must be that the occasional tragedy of individual injury is outweighed by society's need to avoid over-deterrence in the drug industry. Here, Enright (P) was injured as a consequence of injuries to her mother's reproductive system; she was not herself exposed to DES. Therefore, she has no cause of action against Eli Lilly (D). Affirmed.

ANALYSIS

This case provides an excellent example of the difference between cause in fact and proximate (or legal) cause. Cause in fact is just that—a certain act or omission resulting in a certain consequence. Proximate cause is a policy decision, a recognition that at some point cause in fact becomes so attenuated that liability should not be recognized, either because of unforeseeability, the intervention of other acts, or the conduct of a third party.

Quicknotes

LOSS OF CONSORTIUM An action brought based on willful interference with the marital relationship.

MARKET SHARE LIABILITY The apportionment of liability between each participant in an industry equal to the participant's market share.

STRICT LIABILITY Liability for all injuries proximately caused by a party's conducting of certain inherently dangerous activities without regard to negligence or fault.

CHAPTER 7

Joint Tortfeasors

Quick Reference Rules of Law

Bierczynski v. Rogers

Drag racers (D) v. Accident victims (P)

Del. Sup. Ct., 239 A.2d 218 (1968)

NATURE OF CASE: Action to recover damages for negligence.

FACT SUMMARY: Race (D) and Bierczynski (D) were drag racing on a public highway and during the fact hit a car in which C. and S. Rogers (P) were riding.

RULE OF LAW

Individuals who are party to a motor vehicle race on a highway are tortfeasors acting in concert and each participant is liable for harm to a third person arising from tortious conduct because he has engaged in and induced the wrong.

FACTS: Race (D) and Bierczynski (D) were participants in a drag race on a highway. As the two cars involved in the race were coming over a hill, the Rogers's (P) car came into sight. Race (D) attempted to swing his car back into the proper lane but he lost control of the car and it hit the Rogers's (P) car at about 70 miles per hour. The trial court awarded substantial damages in favor of the Rogers (P), holding both Race (D) and Bierczynski (D) jointly liable. Bierczynski's (D) car never actually hit the Rogers's (P) vehicle; thus, he appealed claiming he was not liable for any of the damage.

ISSUE: Are individuals who are party to a motor vehicle race on a highway tortfeasors acting in concert, making each participant liable for harm to a third person arising from tortious conduct because he has engaged in and induced the wrong?

HOLDING AND DECISION: (Herrmann, J.) Yes. A defendant who engages in a motor vehicle race on a public street is liable for the injury caused by the other participant and each participant is liable for harm to a third person arising from tortious conduct because he has engaged in and induced the wrong. In this instance even though Bierczynski (D) never came in contact with the Rogers's (P) car, he was engaged in the race and thus acted in concert to cause the injury to the Rogers (P). The reason for the rule is that it would be unfair to hold only one party liable if both caused the accident, for presumably the defendant who actually contacted the plaintiff might be insolvent. Further, it seems unfair to the defendant who actually collided to make him bear the entire brunt of the damages when the other individual was also responsible for the injuries. Affirmed.

ANALYSIS

The case conforms to the mainstream of opinion that there need not be actual harm done by the party if that party is engaged in the activity which causes the harm. All that is necessary to be a joint tortfeasor is to have encouraged or aided in the harm-producing activity. Further, a tacit understanding, as in this case where two automobiles are in a speed competition, is enough to establish liability. However, the defendant must take some active part in the activity which causes the harm. Mere presence or knowledge of the conduct of another person which may cause harm is not enough to establish liability, for there is no duty for observers to take affirmative action to prevent a tort.

Quicknotes

JOINT LIABILITY Liability owed to an injured party by two or more parties where each party has the right to insist that the other tortfeasors be joined to the matter.

JOINT TORTFEASORS Two or more parties that either act in concert, or whose individual acts combine to cause a single injury, rendering them jointly and severally liable for damages incurred.

NEGLIGENCE Conduct falling below the standard of care that a reasonable person would demonstrate under similar conditions.

Coney v. J.L.G. Industries, Inc.

Decedent's administrator (P) v. Manufacturing company (D)

Ill. Sup. Ct., 97 Ill. 2d 104, 454 N.E.2d 197 (1983)

NATURE OF CASE: Hearing on issue of law certified to the state supreme court in wrongful death action.

FACT SUMMARY: J.L.G. Industries (D) contended that joint and several liability no longer was applicable in a comparative negligence situation.

RULE OF LAW

The adoption of comparative negligence does not require the abolition of joint and several liability.

FACTS: Jasper was killed while using a product made by J.L.G. Industries (J.L.G.) (D). J.L.G. (D) contended that Jasper's employer was partially negligent, and that since Illinois had adopted comparative negligence, the doctrine of joint and several liability had also been abolished, and any judgment against it should be reduced by the percentage of fault attributable to the employer. This issue was certified for decision by the state supreme court.

ISSUE: Does the adoption of comparative negligence require the abolition of joint and several liability?

HOLDING AND DECISION: (Moran, J.) No. The adoption of comparative negligence does not require the abolition of joint and several liability. The effect of comparative negligence is to reduce a plaintiff's verdict by the amount of fault attributable to him. It has nothing to do with the relative faults of two or more defendants. The policy behind joint and several was, and still is, that a plaintiff should not bear the consequences of a judgment-proof defendant. Rather, it is the tortfeasor who should. To abolish joint and several liability would have the effect of reducing a plaintiff's recovery beyond the amount of fault attributable to him, and the adoption of comparative negligence did not contemplate this. Affirmed and remanded.

ANALYSIS

The typical situation these days is for a plaintiff to sue all potential defendants and for the defendants to cross- or third-party complain against each other. If for some reason a plaintiff elects not to proceed against all defendants, the potential defendants will probably be brought in by the existing defendants. As the case states, contributory or comparative negligence as a doctrine has little to do with this.

Quicknotes

COMPARATIVE NEGLIGENCE Doctrine whereby the court in assessing the appropriate measure of damages compares the relative fault of the parties and reduces the amount of damages to be collected by the plaintiff in proportion to his degree of fault.

JOINT AND SEVERAL LIABILITY Liability amongst tortfeasors allowing the injured party to bring suit against any of the defendants, individually or collectively, and to recover from each up to the total amount of damages awarded.

Bartlett v. New Mexico Welding Supply, Inc.

Accident victim (P) v. Other car's owner (D)

N.M. Ct. App., 98 N.M. 152, 646 P.2d 579, *cert. denied*, 98 N.M. 336, 648 P.2d 794 (1982)

NATURE OF CASE: Appeal of new trial order in action for damages for personal injury.

FACT SUMMARY: Bartlett (P) argued that joint and several liability should be applied in a pure comparative negligence jurisdiction.

RULE OF LAW
Joint and several liability will not be applied when pure comparative negligence is adopted.

FACTS: Bartlett (P) was injured in an accident with a vehicle under the control of New Mexico Welding Supply, Inc. (New Mexico Welding) (D). A third, unidentified vehicle was also involved. Bartlett (P) sued New Mexico Welding (D). The jury found Bartlett (P) nonnegligent and New Mexico Welding (D) 30 percent responsible. New Mexico was a pure comparative negligence state. Bartlett (P) argued that under joint and several liability, New Mexico Welding (D) should pay all damages. The trial court refused to enter judgment, but ordered a new trial. New Mexico Welding (D) sought an interlocutory appeal.

ISSUE: Will joint and several liability be applied when pure comparative negligence is adopted?

HOLDING AND DECISION: (Wood, J.) No. Joint and several liability will not be applied when pure comparative negligence is adopted. Pure comparative negligence is based on the notion that blame should be apportioned as it is found to exist. Joint and several liability is that the plaintiff should not bear the burden of an insolvent defendant. However, where there is only one defendant, the plaintiff bears this burden, and the court does not see why an additional defendant should change this. Here, the unidentified tortfeasor was 70 percent responsible, so New Mexico Welding should bear 30 percent of the damages. Reversed and remanded.

ANALYSIS

Joint and several liability has been, in recent years, in the forefront of tort reform debate. Many have argued that it has constituted a strain on municipalities and the insurance industry. Proposals to abolish or modify the rule have been hotly debated in the public arena. Probably the best known attempt at reform was California's 1986 Proposition 51, a compromise which abolished joint and several liability for general damages only.

Quicknotes

INTERLOCUTORY APPEAL The appeal of an issue that does not resolve the disposition of the case, but is essential to a determination of the parties' legal rights.

Bundt v. Embro

Car passengers (P) v. Car owner/drivers (D)

N.Y. Sup. Ct., Queens Co., 48 Misc. 2d 802, 265 N.Y.S.2d 872 (1965)

NATURE OF CASE: Motion for leave to file amended answers in action for damages for personal injuries.

FACT SUMMARY: Bundt (P) and other plaintiffs had recovered against the State of New York for injuries resulting from an auto accident before suing Embro (D) and other defendants.

RULE OF LAW

When individuals are joint tortfeasors with the state, satisfaction from the state discharges the individuals.

FACTS: Two autos were involved in an accident. Various passengers sued the various owners and operators. Some of the defendants moved to amend their answers to include the defense of discharge and satisfaction when they learned that the plaintiffs had sued and recovered on the same accident against the state in the state court of claims.

ISSUE: When individuals are joint tortfeasors with the state, does satisfaction from the state discharge the individuals?

HOLDING AND DECISION: (Groat, J.) Yes. When individuals are joint tortfeasors with the state, satisfaction from the state discharges the individuals. While there can be many perpetrators of a wrongful act, there remains but one act, and there can be but one recovery therefor. Once a plaintiff has been fully compensated for the wrong, all other possible tortfeasors are discharged. The fact that it is the state that compensated for the wrong is of no consequence; in this situation, the state will be treated as would any tortfeasor. Motion granted.

ANALYSIS

The general rule discussed here, almost universally followed, is not an all-or-nothing proposition. It will sometimes happen that one of two or more joint tortfeasors will be able to pay only part of a judgment. When this occurs, the other joint tortfeasor will only be obligated to pay what the other did not. Also, where one party settles out of court before judgment, the settlement monies are credited against the judgment.

Quicknotes

JOINT TORTFEASORS Two or more parties that either act in concert, or whose individual acts combine to cause a single injury, rendering them jointly and severally liable for damages incurred.

PERSONAL INJURY Harm to an individual's person or body.

Cox v. Pearl Investment Co.

Injured party (P) v. Site's owner (D)

Colo. Sup. Ct., 168 Colo. 67, 450 P.2d 60 (1969)

NATURE OF CASE: Action to recover damages for negligence.

FACT SUMMARY: Cox (P) sought recovery against Pearl Investment Co. (Pearl) (D) which owned the property upon which she was injured. Pearl (D) sought to be released from liability on the basis of the fact that Cox (P) had released from liability Goodwill Industries, the tenant of the property.

RULE OF LAW

Plaintiff does not relinquish his cause of action against a tortfeasor by releasing a joint tortfeasor, if the plaintiff expressly reserves the right to sue others who may be liable.

FACTS: Cox (P) was injured on property owned by Pearl Investment Co. (Pearl) (D) and leased by Goodwill Industries (Goodwill). Cox (P) had covenanted with Goodwill to release it from liability beyond $2,500. In the covenant, Cox (P) expressly reserved the right to sue any other persons who might be liable for the damage. Indeed, Cox (P) sued Pearl (D). At trial, Pearl (D) moved for summary judgment on the basis of the common-law rule that a release of one tortfeasor releases all others who may have liability. The motion was granted by the trial court.

ISSUE: Does plaintiff relinquish his cause of action against a tortfeasor by releasing a joint tortfeasor, if the plaintiff expressly reserves the right to sue others who may be liable?

HOLDING AND DECISION: (Hodges, J.) No. A plaintiff who expressly reserves the right to recover against the remaining tortfeasors does not relinquish the right to pursue an action against the nonreleased parties. In this case, the covenant between Goodwill and Cox (P) contained a clause expressing Cox's (P) desire to maintain her right to hold Pearl (D), the other tortfeasor, liable for the injuries. The reasons the court does not allow the covenant made with Goodwill to foreclose Cox's (P) cause of action against Pearl (D) are these: (1) the principle of contract law is that the intentions manifested by the parties shall govern the situation; here the intention of Cox (P) was not to release her cause of action against Pearl (D); (2) there is no danger of double compensation for the court can credit the judgment debtor, Pearl (D), with the amount Cox (P) received from the party released; and (3) the non-settling tortfeasor is not prejudiced by this rule, but rather benefitted, since he is entitled to have the judgment against him reduced by the amount paid by his co-tortfeasor. Reversed and remanded.

ANALYSIS

The case is within the majority faction; until recently, most jurisdictions followed the common-law rule that if one tortfeasor were released, all stood released from liability. This rule was justly condemned and changed by all U.S. jurisdictions except two. The reason for this shift as discussed by Prosser is that the common-law rule placed the plaintiff in the untenable position of either forfeiting the partial compensation he could derive through settlement without suit or forgoing his entire claim against the other without full compensation. Although the release of one tortfeasor had no relation to the breach of the other's duty, the law nevertheless released him from liability.

Quicknotes

COVENANT A written promise to do, or to refrain from doing, a particular activity.

NEGLIGENCE Conduct falling below the standard of care that a reasonable person would demonstrate under similar conditions.

RELEASE The relinquishment of a claim against another party.

SUMMARY JUDGMENT Judgment rendered by a court in response to a motion by one of the parties, claiming that the lack of a question of material fact in respect to an issue warrants disposition of the issue without consideration by the jury.

TORTFEASOR Party that commits a tort or wrongful act.

Elbaor v. Smith

Physician (D) v. Malpractice victim (P)

Tex. Sup. Ct., 845 S.W.2d 240 (1992)

NATURE OF CASE: Appeal from verdict awarding damages for personal injury.

FACT SUMMARY: Smith (P) obtained a large judgment against Elbaor (D) after the other defendants had entered into a "Mary Carter" agreement with Smith (P).

RULE OF LAW

"Mary Carter" settlement agreements, whereby the settling defendant agrees to testify against any remaining defendants in exchange for an offset, are void as against public policy.

FACTS: Smith (P) sued doctors Elbaor (D), Syrquin (D), and Stephens (D) for medical malpractice. Syrquin (D) and Stephens (D) entered into a particular type of settlement agreement with Smith (P) known as the "Mary Carter" arrangement. In the agreement, Syrquin (D) and Stephens (D) guaranteed Smith (P) at least $425,010 if she did not recover that amount from Elbaor (D). Smith (P) agreed to pay them back the $425,010 out of any excess judgment recovered at trial from Elbaor (D). The case proceeded to trial, and Stephens (D) and Syrquin (D) "ganged up" on Elbaor (D). The jury found Elbaor (D) 88 percent responsible and returned a verdict against him of $1,872,848. Elbaor (D) appealed.

ISSUE: Are "Mary Carter" settlement agreements, whereby the settling defendant agrees to testify against any remaining defendants in exchange for an offset, void as against public policy?

HOLDING AND DECISION: (Gonzalez, J.) Yes. "Mary Carter" settlement agreements, whereby the settling defendant agrees to testify against any remaining defendants in exchange for an offset, are void as against public policy. It is the policy of the law to promote settlements, because doing so promotes judicial economy. However, the "Mary Carter" agreement does just the opposite; it virtually guarantees a trial. Beyond this, it is antithetical to the quest for truth embodied by a trial because it fosters collusion between ostensibly opposing parties. Consequently, these sorts of arrangements shall be deemed void as contrary to public policy. Reversed and remanded.

DISSENT: (Doggett, J.) The trial court correctly disclosed the existence of the "Mary Carter" agreements to the jury and otherwise took great care to safeguard the adversarial nature and fairness of the proceedings. So long as at least two parties with antagonistic interests remain—here, Smith (P) and Elbaor (D)—the search for truth is not diminished.

ANALYSIS

The "Mary Carter" agreement is often used when a "deep pocket," such as a governmental entity or large corporation, is a defendant. It depends, for its utility, on joint and several liability. Some states, like California, have either modified or done away with joint and several liability, which has resulted in less frequent use of "Mary Carter" agreements.

Quicknotes

COLLUSION An agreement between two or more parties to engage in unlawful conduct or in other activities with an unlawful goal, typically involving fraud.

JOINT AND SEVERAL LIABILITY Liability amongst tortfeasors allowing the injured party to bring suit against any of the defendants, individually or collectively, and to recover from each up to the total amount of damages awarded.

"MARY CARTER" AGREEMENT Agreement between plaintiff and defendants in multiparty litigation to pay a specified amount regardless of the jury's determination.

MEDICAL MALPRACTICE Conduct on the part of a doctor falling below that demonstrated by other doctors of ordinary skill and competency under the circumstances, resulting in damages.

Knell v. Feltman

Other car's driver (D) v. Cab driver (P)

174 F.2d 662 (D.C. Cir. 1949)

NATURE OF CASE: Action to recover damages for negligence and for contribution.

FACT SUMMARY: A guest passenger in Knell's (D) car was injured because of the negligence of Knell (D) and Feltman (P); Feltman (P) attempted to convince the court to make Knell (D) contribute to the payment of damages caused by his and Knell's (D) negligence.

RULE OF LAW

When a tort is committed by the concurrent negligence of two or more individuals who did not intentionally inflict injury, contribution should be required of the co-tortfeasor even though no joint judgment was obtained by the plaintiff.

FACTS: While riding as a passenger in Knell's (D) car, Langland was injured when it collided with Feltman's (P) taxi. Langland was a personal friend of Knell (D), and so she did not sue him; however, she did sue Feltman (P), who filed a third-party complaint against Knell (D) (making him a defendant and himself a plaintiff for purposes of this case) in an action to determine if Knell's (D) negligence was a sole or contributing factor in the causation of Langland's injuries.

ISSUE: If a tort is committed by the concurrent negligence of two or more individuals who did not intentionally inflict injury, should contribution be required of the co-tortfeasor even though no joint judgment was obtained by the plaintiff?

HOLDING AND DECISION: (Miller, J.) Yes. When a tort is committed due to the concurrent negligence of two persons, contribution should be demanded of the co-tortfeasor even though no judgment was obtained by the plaintiff. In the present case, the injured party, Langland, did not file a complaint against Knell (D) because she was a personal acquaintance; thus, Langland did not obtain a joint judgment against both Knell (D) and Feltman (P). However, Feltman (P) brought Knell (D) into the action through means of a third-party complaint so that the jury was able to determine that his negligence was one source of Langland's injuries. Hence, it is clear that Knell (D) is liable for the injuries. To allow the injured party (Langland) to select who should foot the bill would be unfair to the defendant who is burdened with the total payment. To allow this situation the law would be a party to collusion between the plaintiff and a tortfeasor. Affirmed.

ANALYSIS

There is a split among state jurisdictions on this question of whether to allow contribution among joint tortfeasors. The common-law rule does not allow contribution. Twenty-two states currently adhere to the common-law rule. Seven states allow contribution only between those defendants against whom a joint judgment has been obtained. Sixteen permit contribution from a joint tortfeasor whether joined as a defendant or not and apportion the damages equally. Five permit contribution from a joint tortfeasor whether joined or not and divide damages according to relative degrees of fault.

Quicknotes

CONCURRENT NEGLIGENCE Where the negligence of two independent actors results in a single injury.

CONTRIBUTION The right of a person or party who has compensated a victim for his injury to seek reimbursement from others who are equally responsible for the injury in proportional amounts.

JOINT TORTFEASORS Two or more parties that either act in concert, or whose individual acts combine to cause a single injury, rendering them jointly and severally liable for damages incurred.

Yellow Cab Co. of D.C., Inc. v. Dreslin

Cab company (D) v. Other car driver and passengers (P)

181 F.2d 626 (D.C. Cir. 1950)

NATURE OF CASE: Action to recover damages for negligence and for contribution.

FACT SUMMARY: Mrs. Dreslin (P) was injured in a crash of two motor vehicles caused by the negligence of her husband (D) and Yellow Cab Co. of D.C., Inc. (D).

RULE OF LAW

Since neither husband nor wife is liable for the torts perpetrated against the other, the spouse cannot be held on contribution theory to pay damages for injury to the other spouse because, in order for a right of contribution to exist, there must be coexistent liability.

FACTS: Mrs. Dreslin (P) was injured as a result of the negligence of both her husband (D) and the Yellow Cab Co. of D.C., Inc. (Yellow Cab) (D in relation to Mrs. Dreslin and P in relation to Mr. Dreslin). Mrs. Dreslin (P) sued Yellow Cab (D); and Yellow Cab (as P) cross-claimed against Mr. Dreslin (D) for contribution for any sums recovered by the plaintiffs against it.

ISSUE: Since neither husband nor wife is liable for the torts perpetrated against the other, can the spouse be held on contribution theory to pay damages for injury to the other spouse?

HOLDING AND DECISION: (Proctor, J.) No. Due to the application of the doctrine of interspousal tort immunity, there is no liability on the part of the spouse-tortfeasor; hence, because there is no liability, there can be no right of contribution. The purpose of the immunity doctrine is to preserve the domestic peace; if the co-tortfeasor could extract damages indirectly through the contribution doctrine, the purpose of shielding spouses from liability for torts committed against the other spouse would be destroyed. Affirmed.

ANALYSIS

The case falls within the prevailing view that the contribution defendant must be liable for the plaintiff's injuries. If there was never any liability, as in a case of interfamilial immunity, assumption of the risk, contributory negligence, guest statute, or some other doctrine that nullifies the contribution defendant's liability to the plaintiff, then defendant is not liable for contribution. The statutes dealing with contribution also follow this principle. The case conforms to the modern view of contribution that many states have codified in statutes. The statutes generally allow contribution in cases of negligence but not in cases of intentional injury. Generally, liability is divided among tortfeasors on a pro rata share; however, some jurisdictions apportion liability on the basis of comparative fault. In the situation where a plaintiff gives a release or covenant not to sue to one defendant, that defendant is usually required to contribute his or her pro rata share later.

Quicknotes

ASSUMPTION OF RISK DOCTRINE An affirmative defense to a negligence suit contending that the plaintiff knowingly and voluntarily subjected himself to a hazardous condition absolving the defendant of liability for injuries incurred.

CONTRIBUTION The right of a person or party who has compensated a victim for his injury to seek reimbursement from others who are equally responsible for the injury in proportional amounts.

CONTRIBUTORY NEGLIGENCE Behavior on the part of an injured plaintiff that combines with the defendant's negligence, resulting in injury to the plaintiff.

GUEST STATUTE A state statute requiring a specified level of culpability, usually more than mere negligence, on the part of the driver of an automobile in order for the owner/driver to be liable for injuries resulting to a gratuitous passenger.

INTERSPOUSAL IMMUNITY A common-law doctrine precluding spouses from commencing actions against one another. Some states have abolished the doctrine.

NEGLIGENCE Conduct falling below the standard of care that a reasonable person would demonstrate under similar conditions.

PRO RATA In proportion.

TORTFEASOR Party that commits a tort or wrongful act.

Slocum v. Donahue

Parents (P) v. Driver (D)

Mass. App. Ct., 44 Mass. App. Ct. 937, 693 N.E.2d 179 (1998)

NATURE OF CASE: Vehicular homicide proceeding.

FACT SUMMARY: Donahue (D) sought indemnity and contribution from Ford Motor Company (Ford), claiming Ford was negligent and in breach of the warranties of merchantability and fitness for a particular purpose, causing his automobile to accelerate and resulting in the death of the Slocum's (P) 18-month-old son.

RULE OF LAW

When a release is given in good faith to one of two or more persons liable in tort for the same injury, it discharges the tortfeasor to whom it is granted from all liability for contribution to the other tortfeasor.

FACTS: Donahue (D) pled guilty to a motor vehicle homicide in which he killed the Slocum's (P) 18-month-old son. The Slocums (P) filed suit against Donahue (D) alleging negligence and gross negligence. Donahue (D) filed a third-party complaint against Ford Motor Company (Ford) denying negligence and seeking contribution and indemnity, alleging Ford was negligent and in breach of its warranties of merchantability and fitness for a particular use. Donahue (D) claimed that when he started to back the car out of the driveway, the engine raced and the car continued to accelerate even though he stepped on the brakes. The car's rear wheels hit the curb across the street, causing the car to become airborne, hitting a fence. When Donahue (D) got out of the car he found Todd Slocum lying on the lawn. Donahue's (D) expert testified the floor mat of the car was defective, causing it to interfere with the operation of the brakes. Prior to trial the Slocums (P) and Ford entered a settlement agreement providing Ford would pay them $150,000 in exchange for release of any claim. Ford moved for summary judgment as to Donahue's (D) claims stating that there was no basis for Donahue's (D) indemnity claims. Donahue (D) appealed from a final judgment dismissing his claims against Ford.

ISSUE: When a release is given in good faith to one of two or more persons liable in tort for the same injury, does it discharge the tortfeasor to whom it is granted from all liability for contribution to the other tortfeasor?

HOLDING AND DECISION: [Judge not stated in casebook excerpt.] Yes. When a release is given in good faith to one of two or more persons liable in tort for the same injury, it discharges the tortfeasor to whom it is granted from all liability for contribution to the other tortfeasor. The Donahues (D) argued that the settlement was not made in good faith and was collusive because the settlement amount was far less than the value of the case and Ford offered the Slocums (P) the use of their experts. Facts were introduced showing the settlement was fair and reasonable. Here there was a high likelihood that a jury would find Donahue (D) liable due to his admission of liability and in light of the fact that he was drinking from a bottle of vodka in a brown paper bag under the driver's seat. Here there was no indication of bad faith or collusion in the settlement negotiations. Nor is there evidence that the Slocums' (P) use of experts originally retained by Ford was collusive. Nor did the trial court err on the issue of indemnification. Indemnity allows a party without fault to recover from the tortfeasor the amount of his loss, with reasonable attorney's fees. Indemnity is allowed only when the party seeking indemnity is not responsible for the negligent conduct and where the indemnitee is held vicariously liable for the acts of the tortfeasor. Here indemnity would not have been appropriate since the jury found Donahue (D) solely negligent and his liability was not vicarious. The motion for summary judgment was properly allowed. Affirmed.

ANALYSIS

In addition to its substantive rulings on contribution and indemnity, *Slocum* illustrates a cardinal principle for all practicing attorneys and their clients: Settlement gives parties an opportunity to control their own destinies in litigation without incurring the extraordinary risk of allowing other persons to impose outcomes upon the parties. Here, the court politely understates the obvious by finding it "reasonably predictable" that the criminally liable Donahue (D) would be found civilly liable if the case proceeded to trial. The trial, of course, bore out that predictability, with the jury returning a verdict against Donahue (D). Based on the casebook excerpt, Donahue (D) proceeded to trial because he saw no way to make a $25,000 payment for his share of a proposed settlement. After trial, with third-party defendant Ford now out of the case after making a $150,000 payment to the Slocums (P), Donahue (D) himself presumably would have been liable for a verdict for much more than the $25,000 portion he originally thought he could not pay; even if the jury awarded the Slocums (P) only the amount of their original settlement offer ($400,000), Donahue (D) himself would have had to pay $275,000 to the Slocums (P) after applying his insurance provider's maximum benefit of $125,000. Much of the time,

Continued on next page.

as here, stubbornness actually does not advance a client's best interests.

Quicknotes

BAD FAITH Conduct that is intentionally misleading or deceptive.

COLLUSION An agreement between two or more parties to engage in unlawful conduct or in other activities with an unlawful goal, typically involving fraud.

CONTRIBUTION The right of a person or party who has compensated a victim for his injury to seek reimbursement from others who are equally responsible for the injury in proportional amounts.

IMPLIED WARRANTY OF FITNESS An implied promise made by a merchant in a contract for the sale of goods that such goods are suitable for the purpose for which they are purchased.

INDEMNITY The duty of a party to compensate another for damages sustained.

WARRANTY OF MERCHANTABILITY An implied promise made by a merchant in a contract for the sale of goods that such goods are suitable for the purpose for which they are purchased.

Bruckman v. Pena

Truck driver (D) and owner (D) v. Auto accident victim (P)

Colo. Ct. App., 29 Colo. App. 357, 487 P.2d 566 (1971)

NATURE OF CASE: Action for personal injuries.

FACT SUMMARY: Pena (P) was first injured in an auto accident with Bruckman (D) and then later had his injuries aggravated in another accident with another party.

RULE OF LAW

It is error for a court to instruct the jury that a plaintiff may recover damages for injuries received subsequent to any act of negligence by the defendant and from causes for which the defendant is in no way responsible.

FACTS: Pena (P) was injured on July 21, 1964, in an auto accident as a result of Bruckman's (D) negligence. Armored (D) owned the truck driven by Bruckman (D). On June 11, 1965, his injuries were aggravated in another accident in which Bruckman (D) was in no way involved. Pena (P) filed this action against Bruckman (D) and Armored (D). At the close of evidence, the court instructed the jury that it was their duty to apportion the damages caused to Pena (P) between Bruckman (D), Armored (D), and the subsequent tortfeasor. In addition, the court further instructed the jury "if you find the evidence does not permit such an apportionment, then the defendants are liable for the entire disability." The jury returned judgment for Pena (P) in the amount of $50,000. Bruckman (D) and Armored (D) challenged the quoted instruction on appeal.

ISSUE: Is it error for a court to instruct the jury that a plaintiff may recover damages for injuries received subsequent to any act of negligence by the defendant and from causes for which the defendant is in no way responsible?

HOLDING AND DECISION: (Dwyer, J.) Yes. As a general rule, the burden of proof is on the plaintiff in a personal injury case to establish that the damages he seeks were proximately caused by the negligence of the defendant; and, as such, it is error for a court to instruct that a plaintiff may recover any damages for injuries received subsequent to the act of negligence by the defendant and from causes for which the defendant is in no way responsible—regardless of the difficulty of apportioning the plaintiff's total damages between the defendant's acts and the acts of any subsequent tortfeasor who may have aggravated plaintiff's original injuries. It is true that where subsequent trauma aggravates a preexisting diseased condition, the tortfeasor causing the trauma will be liable for the total injuries caused. The reverse is not true, however, as Pena (P) would have us believe here, since no causation link between prior negligence and subsequent injuries can be established. Reversed and remanded.

ANALYSIS

This case points out the connection between the rules of causation and the apportionment of tort damages. Only damages proximately caused by a tortfeasor may be assigned to him. Note that it has been held that a jury apportionment will be upheld as long as there is "some evidence to sustain the apportionment made, even though, due to circumstances of the particular case, the proofs do not attain the degree of precision which would make possible an exact dividing line between the injuries." *McAllister v. Pennsylvania*, 324 Pa. 65 (1936).

Quicknotes

APPORTIONMENT OF DAMAGES The allocation of damages between two parties typically in ratio to their respective fault or risk.

CAUSATION The aggregate effect of preceding events that brings about a tortious result; the causal connection between the actions of a tortfeasor and the injury that follows.

NEGLIGENCE Conduct falling below the standard of care that a reasonable person would demonstrate under similar conditions.

PERSONAL INJURY Harm to an individual's person or body.

CHAPTER 8

Duty of Care

Quick Reference Rules of Law

		PAGE
1.	*Winterbottom v. Wright.* A contracting party, unless he has undertaken a public duty, has no liability to third parties who are injured as a result of a breach of the contract.	*130*
2.	*MacPherson v. Buick Motor Co.* A manufacturer breaches a duty of care to a foreseeable user of its product if the product was likely to cause an injury if negligently made and it places the product on the market without conducting a reasonable inspection.	*131*
3.	*H.R. Moch Co. v. Rensselaer Water Co.* A water company that contracts with a city to supply water is not liable to a citizen whose house burns when water service fails.	*132*
4.	*Clagett v. Dacy.* In the absence of an underlying contractual attorney-client relationship, an attorney owes no duty of care to a third party.	*133*
5.	*Commonwealth v. Peterson.* Even assuming a special relationship exists between a state university and its students, the university does not have a duty to warn students of the potential for third-party criminal acts where the university does not know, or cannot reasonably foresee, that students will fall victim to third-party criminal harm.	*134*
6.	*Hegel v. Langsam.* Colleges and universities are under no affirmative duty to regulate the private lives of their students.	*136*
7.	*L.S. Ayres & Co. v. Hicks.* The invitor or one who has control of an instrumentality has the legal obligation to aid a helpless person, even if he did not cause the original situation in which the helpless person finds himself.	*137*
8.	*J.S. and M.S. v. R.T.H.* When a spouse has actual knowledge or special reason to know of the likelihood that his or her spouse is engaging in sexually abusive behavior against a particular person, the spouse has a duty of care to take reasonable steps to prevent or warn of the harm and a breach of that duty constitutes a proximate cause of the resultant sexual abuse of the victim.	*138*
9.	*Tarasoff v. Regents of University of California.* A doctor bears a duty to exercise reasonable care and warn potential victims about known violent tendencies or intentions of a patient.	*139*
10.	*Southern California Gas Co. v. Superior Court of Los Angeles County.* A public utility does not have a duty to local businesses to guard against purely economic losses.	*140*
11.	*Daley v. LaCroix.* Whenever a definite and objective physical injury is produced as a result of emotional distress proximately caused by a tortfeasor's negligent conduct, the injured party may recover damages for such physical consequences to himself notwithstanding the absence of any physical impact upon him at the time of the emotional shock.	*142*
12.	*Thing v. La Chusa.* One may recover emotional distress damages for an injury to a relative only if he observes the injury-producing event.	*143*
13.	*Endresz v. Friedberg.* The parents of an unborn fetus whose birth was prevented by negligent conduct may not bring a wrongful death action to redress the wrong that was done.	*144*
14.	*Procanik by Procanik v. Cillo.* An infant plaintiff may recover special damages for "wrongful life" but may not recover general damages therefor.	*145*

Winterbottom v. Wright

Mail coach driver (P) v. Breaching coach repairer (D)

Ex. P., 10 M. & W. 109, 152 Eng. Rep. 402 (1842)

NATURE OF CASE: Action for damages based on negligence.

FACT SUMMARY: Winterbottom (P) was injured while driving a defective mail coach that the government had bought from Wright (D) pursuant to a supply-maintenance contract.

RULE OF LAW

A contracting party, unless he has undertaken a public duty, has no liability to third parties who are injured as a result of a breach of the contract.

FACTS: Wright (D) agreed to supply and maintain mail coaches for the use of the Postmaster General. Atkinson also had a contract with the Postmaster General to supply horses and coachmen to operate the mail coaches. Winterbottom (P), one of Atkinson's coachmen, was injured when one of the coaches supplied by Wright (D) broke down. Winterbottom (P) brought suit against Wright (D), contending that his injuries were the result of Wright's (D) negligent performance of the contract with the Postmaster General.

ISSUE: Does a contracting party, unless he has undertaken a public duty, have liability to third parties who are injured as a result of a breach of the contract?

HOLDING AND DECISION: (Lord Abinger, C. B.) No. Parties to a contract are liable only to each other for breaches of the contract, unless the duty undertaken was to the public. Third parties have no privity with respect to the contract and, therefore, may not sue either party to the contract. If such an action were permitted, contracting parties would be exposed to a potentially unlimited number of suits by strangers to the contract, even in the situation where the breach has been excused or waived. Winterbottom (P) was not privy to the contract between the Postmaster General and Wright (D), and, therefore, may not maintain an action against him. Judgment for the defendant.

CONCURRENCE: (Alderson, B.) If we were to hold that the plaintiff could sue in this case, there is no point at which such actions would stop. The only safe rule is to confine the right to recover to those who enter into the contract.

CONCURRENCE: (Rolfe, B.) This is one of those unfortunate cases in which there has been damnum [wrong], but it is damnum absque [without] injuria [injury]; it is, no doubt, a hardship upon the plaintiff to be without a remedy, but by that consideration we ought not to be influenced.

ANALYSIS

The harsh *Winterbottom* decision was followed by the majority of courts in the United States during the second half of the 19th century, but a number of exceptions developed. The New York court in *Thomas v. Winchester*, 6 N.Y. 397 (1852), allowed a negligence action, by a woman who was poisoned, against a chemist who had sold the falsely labeled poison to her druggist. The court's rationale was that the poison was an "imminently dangerous" article, while the defective mail coach in *Winterbottom* was not. Other applications of the "imminently dangerous" exception proved difficult, however, and the New York court in *MacPherson v. Buick Motor Co.*, 217 N.Y. 382 (1916), finally formulated a general rule of liability of remote manufacturers which eliminated privity as a requirement.

Quicknotes

BREACH OF CONTRACT Unlawful failure by a party to perform its obligations pursuant to contract.

DAMNUM ABSQUI INJURIA When an injury is sustained but the law affords no means of recovery.

NEGLIGENCE Conduct falling below the standard of care that a reasonable person would demonstrate under similar conditions.

PRIVITY OF CONTRACT A relationship between the parties to a contract that is required in order to bring an action for breach.

MacPherson v. Buick Motor Co.

Injured automobile owner (P) v. Car manufacturer (D)

N.Y. Ct. App., 217 N.Y. 382, 111 N.E. 1050 (1916)

NATURE OF CASE: Negligence action.

FACT SUMMARY: MacPherson (P) sued Buick (D) for injuries sustained when a defective wheel on the automobile he purchased collapsed.

RULE OF LAW

A manufacturer breaches a duty of care to a foreseeable user of its product if the product was likely to cause an injury if negligently made and it places the product on the market without conducting a reasonable inspection.

FACTS: Buick (D), an automobile manufacturer, sold a car to a retail dealer who in turn sold it to MacPherson (P). While MacPherson (P) was in the car it suddenly collapsed due to the wheel being made out of defective wood. Although the wheel was not manufactured by Buick (D), there was evidence that a reasonable inspection would have revealed the defects. The supreme court held in favor of MacPherson and the appellate division affirmed. Buick (D) appealed.

ISSUE: Does a manufacturer breach a duty of care to a foreseeable user of its product if the product was likely to cause an injury if negligently made and it places the product on the market without conducting a reasonable inspection?

HOLDING AND DECISION: (Cardozo, J.) Yes. A manufacturer breaches a duty of care to a foreseeable user of its product if the product was likely to cause an injury if negligently made and it places the product on the market without conducting a reasonable inspection. A product is dangerous if it is reasonably certain to place life and limb in peril when negligently made. If the manufacturer knows the item will be used by a person other than the purchaser, the manufacturer is under a duty to manufacture the item carefully. There must be knowledge of a probable danger and that the danger will be borne by others in addition to the buyer in the normal course of events. The proximity or remoteness of the transaction is also to be considered. If the manufacturer of a finished product places it on the market without inspection, then mobility will attach. Buick (D) was not relieved from its duty to inspect because it bought the wheels from a reputable manufacturer. Buick (D) had a duty to inspect the component parts of its automobiles before placing them on the market. Affirmed.

ANALYSIS

There was a traditional distinction between cases involving nonfeasance and misfeasance. Nonfeasance was actionable under contract law and resulted where there was a promise and a subsequent breach of that promise. Misfeasance was actionable in tort and existed when the defendant attempted to perform a contract and did so in error.

Quicknotes

DUTY OF CARE A principle of negligence requiring an individual to act in such a manner as to avoid injury to a person to whom he or she owes an obligatory duty.

MISFEASANCE The commission of a lawful act in a wrongful manner.

NEGLIGENCE Conduct falling below the standard of care that a reasonable person would demonstrate under similar conditions.

NONFEASANCE The omission, or failure to perform, an obligation.

H.R. Moch Co. v. Rensselaer Water Co.

Warehouse owner (P) v. Waterworks company (D)

N.Y. Ct. App., 247 N.Y. 160, 159 N.E. 896 (1928)

NATURE OF CASE: Action to recover damages for negligence.

FACT SUMMARY: Rensselaer Water Co. (D) made a contract with a city to supply water. H.R. Moch Co.'s (P) building caught fire. Water was not supplied, and the building burned.

RULE OF LAW

A water company that contracts with a city to supply water is not liable to a citizen whose house burns when water service fails.

FACTS: Rensselaer Water Co. (D) made a contract with a city to supply water. Water service to fire hydrants and private citizens was included in the contract. During the term of this contract a fire from a nearby building spread to H.R. Moch Co.'s (Moch's) (P) warehouse, destroying the warehouse and its contents. Moch (P) alleged that Rensselaer Water Co. (D) was promptly notified of the fire, but failed to supply water and as a result of this failure, Moch's (P) building was destroyed.

ISSUE: Is a water company that contracts with a city to supply water liable to a citizen whose house burns when water service fails?

HOLDING AND DECISION: (Cardozo, C.J.) No. A water company that contracts with a city to supply water is not liable to a citizen whose house burns when water service fails. Rensselaer Water Co.'s (D) performance on the contract did not bring it into such relation with each citizen that its failure to continue performance without reasonable notice was a tort. The court defined nonfeasance as inaction at the stage of a contract when the inaction is merely the withholding of a benefit. Misfeasance can be inaction also, but the conduct must have gone so far that inaction would result in injury. If inaction is found to be misfeasance, there exists a relation out of which arises a duty to go forward. The court decided here that Rensselaer Water Co.'s (D) failure to supply the water was nonfeasance. Hence, there was no relation, no duty, and no liability. To support its decision the court cites a parade of horribles that would occur if liability were allowed. Coal dealers and manufacturers would be liable if their supply ran low, and anyone making a contract would be held to have a duty to an indefinite number of potential beneficiaries once performance had begun. Affirmed.

ANALYSIS

This case represents the prevailing rule that has been criticized but is followed in all but a few states. The rationale for the rule is that to hold Rensselaer Water Co. (D) liable would place an undue burden on the company. Professor Prosser states that the following three arguments demolish the decisions. First, the water company has commenced performance and supplied water, so its failure to continue to supply is misfeasance, not nonfeasance. Second, its performance gives it the status of a public utility and a relation with individual members of the public. This relation imposes a duty. Third, by commencing performance it has induced the city and its citizens to rely upon it and to forgo other protection.

Quicknotes

MISFEASANCE The commission of a lawful act in a wrongful manner.

NEGLIGENCE Conduct falling below the standard of care that a reasonable person would demonstrate under similar conditions.

NONFEASANCE The omission, or failure to perform, an obligation.

PUBLIC UTILITY A private business that provides a service to the public which is of need.

RELIANCE Dependence on a fact that causes a party to act or refrain from acting.

Clagett v. Dacy

High bidder (P) v. Attorney (D)

Md. Ct. Spec. App., 47 Md. App. 23, 420 A.2d 1285 (1980)

NATURE OF CASE: Appeal from grant of demurrer in malpractice action.

FACT SUMMARY: Dacy (D), an attorney conducting a foreclosure sale, was sued for malpractice by the high bidder at the sale.

RULE OF LAW

In the absence of an underlying contractual attorney-client relationship, an attorney owes no duty of care to a third party.

FACTS: Dacy (D), an attorney, was employed by a mortgagee of land to conduct a foreclosure sale. Because he failed to follow the proper procedures, the sale was set aside on two separate occasions. The resulting delay permitted the mortgage debtor to discharge the loan and thus redeem the property. Clagett (P), the high bidder at the invalidated sales, sued Dacy (D) for malpractice, alleging that his incompetence deprived Clagett (P) of the opportunity to purchase the land and realize a profit on resale. Dacy (D) demurred on the ground that he owed no duty of care toward Clagett (P) and thus could not be negligent. The trial court granted the demurrer. Clagett (P) appealed.

ISSUE: In the absence of an underlying contractual attorney-client relationship, does an attorney owe duty of care to a third party?

HOLDING AND DECISION: (Wilner, J.) No. In the absence of an underlying contractual attorney-client relationship, an attorney owes no duty of care to a third party. The rule requiring strict privity between the parties in an attorney malpractice action has been relaxed to a modest degree. It is now possible for a third party, not privy to the contract between the attorney and client, to sue for malpractice, where that party is a third-party beneficiary to the employment contract. Thus, the beneficiary of a will may sue an attorney, employed by the testator, who negligently drafted the instrument. However, some underlying contractual attorney-client relationship is still required before a duty of care will be imposed as regards a third party. In the instant case, Clagett (P), as a bidder on the foreclosed property, can hardly be deemed a third-party beneficiary to the contract between Dacy (D) and the mortgagee. Dacy (D) was not charged with looking after Clagett's (P) interests. In fact, the opposite was true. As an attorney for the mortgagee, Dacy (D) was seeking the highest price possible for the land. Clagett (P) was interested in obtaining the lowest possible price. Obviously, their interests were antagonistic, rather than mutually dependent. Affirmed.

ANALYSIS

The case of *Donald v. Garry*, 19 Cal. App. 3d 769 (1971), cited by the *Clagett* court, held that "an attorney may be liable for damages caused by his negligence to a person intended to be benefitted by his performance irrespective of any lack of privity of contract between the attorney and the party to be benefitted." The *Clagett* court declined to interpret the case as advocating a broad right to sue for attorney malpractice and instead read it as merely requiring the elements of a third-party beneficiary to be shown.

Quicknotes

DEMURRER The assertion that the opposing party's pleadings are insufficient and that the demurring party should not be made to answer.

DUTY OF CARE A principle of negligence requiring an individual to act in such a manner as to avoid injury to a person to whom he or she owes an obligatory duty.

FORECLOSURE An action to recover the amount due on a mortgage of real property where the owner has failed to pay their debt, terminating the owner's interest in the property which must then be sold to satisfy the debt.

PRIVITY OF CONTRACT A relationship between the parties to a contract that is required in order to bring an action for breach.

Commonwealth v. Peterson

State (D) v. Estate administrator (P)

Va. Sup. Ct., 286 Va. 349, 749 S.E.2d 307 (2013)

NATURE OF CASE: Appeal from judgment for plaintiffs in wrongful death action.

FACT SUMMARY: Based on a shooting incident on one of its state university campuses where two students were shot, which was followed by a mass shooting, the Commonwealth of Virginia ("the Commonwealth") (D) contended that it did not have a duty to warn state university students of the potential for third-party criminal acts where, even assuming there was a special relationship between the Commonwealth (D) and its student, the Commonwealth (D) did not know, or could not have reasonably foreseen, that students would fall victim to third-party criminal harm.

RULE OF LAW

Even assuming a special relationship exists between a state university and its students, the university does not have a duty to warn students of the potential for third-party criminal acts where the university does not know, or cannot reasonably foresee, that students will fall victim to third-party criminal harm.

FACTS: On the morning of April 16, 2007, at approximately 7:30 a.m., police were made aware that two students of Virginia Polytechnic Institute and State University ("Virginia Tech") had been shot in the West Ambler Johnston dormitory, one fatally. University, state, and local police investigated and determined the shootings had been part of a targeted, domestic homicide. They believed this was an isolated incident that posed no danger to others and that the shooter had fled the area. They did not believe that a campus lockdown was necessary, and they started to pursue finding a person of interest (the boyfriend of one of the victims). At around 8 a.m., Virginia Tech's President learned of the shootings and convened a meeting of university administrators tasked with campus safety. After conferring with police, the administrators sent a "blast email" to all students around 9:26 a.m. The notice stated that a shooting incident had occurred at the West Ambler Johnston dormitory earlier in the morning, and that police were investigating. The email advised students to be alert for anything suspicious. By around 9:45 a.m., police had located their person of interest and were investigating him. Around the same time, at a different dormitory (Norris Hall), a mass shooting began. At 9:50 a.m., a second blast email warned students that there was a gunman loose on campus and instructed students to stay in buildings, away from windows, until further notice. Several students were killed. The police subsequently determined that Cho was the shooter, and that the gun he had used in Norris Hall was the same gun that had been used at the West Ambler Johnston dormitory shooting. Administrators (P) of the estates of some of the shooting victims brought wrongful death claims against the Commonwealth of Virginia ("the Commonwealth") (D). The administrators (P) alleged that a special relationship existed between the Commonwealth's (D) employees at Virginia Tech and the slain students, which gave rise to the Commonwealth's (D) duty to warn the students of third-party criminal acts, and that the Commonwealth's (D) failure to warn them was the proximate cause of their deaths. A jury returned verdicts for the administrators (P), and the Commonwealth (D) appealed, arguing that, even assuming a special relationship existed between it and the students, the facts of the case did not give rise, as a matter of law, to a duty to warn of third-party criminal acts, since under the facts and circumstances, the Commonwealth (D) did not know of, or could not have reasonably foreseen, the danger of harm to the students. The state's highest court granted review.

ISSUE: Even assuming a special relationship exists between a state university and its students, does the university have a duty to warn students of the potential for third-party criminal acts where the university does not know, or cannot reasonably foresee, that students will fall victim to third-party criminal harm?

HOLDING AND DECISION: (Powell, J.) No. Even assuming a special relationship exists between a state university and its students, the university does not have a duty to warn students of the potential for third-party criminal acts where the university does not know, or cannot reasonably foresee, that students will fall victim to third-party criminal harm. As a general rule, a person does not have a duty to warn or protect another from the criminal acts of a third person. However, there are narrow exceptions to this rule, but such exceptions are all fact-specific. Before an exception comes into play, the facts must establish the existence of a special relationship, either between the plaintiff and the defendant or between the third-party criminal actor and the defendant. Here, it is assumed, without deciding, that a special relationship existed between the Commonwealth (D) and its students. Thus, the question becomes whether, as a matter of law, under the facts and circumstances of the case, the Commonwealth (D) had a duty to warn students about the potential for third-party criminal acts. To establish a duty, the plaintiff must establish a degree of foreseeability

Continued on next page.

of harm. That degree depends on the nature of the special relationship. One degree of foreseeability is "imminent probability of harm;" a less stringent degree is "known or reasonably foreseeable harm." Here, even applying the less stringent standard, the facts of the case did not give rise, as a matter of law, to the Commonwealth's (D) duty to protect students against third-party criminal acts. In this case, the Commonwealth (D) knew that there had been a shooting in a dormitory in which one student was critically wounded and one was murdered. The Commonwealth (D) also knew that the shooter had not been apprehended. At that time, the Commonwealth (D) did not know who the shooter was, as law enforcement was in the early stages of its investigation of the crime. However, based on representations from three different police departments, Virginia Tech officials believed that the shooting was a domestic incident and that the shooter may have been the boyfriend of one of the victims. Most importantly, based on the information available at that time, the Commonwealth (D) believed that the shooter had fled the area and posed no danger to others. Based on the limited information available to the Commonwealth (D) prior to the shootings in Norris Hall, it cannot be said that it was known or reasonably foreseeable that students in Norris Hall would fall victim to criminal harm. Thus, as a matter of law, the Commonwealth (D) did not have a duty to protect students against third-party criminal acts. Reversed.

ANALYSIS

As this case demonstrates, because acts of assaultive criminal behavior by third parties usually cannot be reasonably foreseen, it is quite rare that courts, as a matter of law, will impose a duty to warn on defendants, notwithstanding the existence of a special relationship. Typically, if such a duty is imposed, it is imposed where the relationship is one of common carrier/passenger, innkeeper/guest, or employer/employee and where the danger of third-party criminal acts is known or reasonably foreseeable. Some courts impose the duty where the relationship is one of business owner/invitee or landlord/tenant and there is an imminent probability of injury from a third-party criminal act.

Quicknotes

DUTY TO WARN An obligation owed by an owner or occupier of land to persons who come onto the premises to inform them of defects or active operations that may cause injury.

REASONABLE FORESEEABILITY A reasonable expectation that an act or omission would result in injury.

SPECIAL RELATIONSHIP A relationship between two persons that imposes a fiduciary responsibility to act where one is threatened with injury, such as the relationship between a parent and child.

WRONGFUL DEATH An action brought by the beneficiaries of a deceased person, claiming that the deceased's death was the result of wrongful conduct by the defendant.

Hegel v. Langsam

Student's parents (P) v. University (D)

Ohio Com. Pl., 55 Ohio Ops. 2d 476, 273 N.E.2d 351 (1971)

NATURE OF CASE: Action for negligence damages.

FACT SUMMARY: Hegel's (P) daughter became a drug user and associated with criminals while a student at college.

RULE OF LAW

Colleges and universities are under no affirmative duty to regulate the private lives of their students.

FACTS: Hegel's (P) 17-year-old daughter was enrolled as a freshman in college and assigned to a dormitory. During her freshman year, the University exercised no control over her comings and goings at the dormitory. She began staying away from it, soon became associated with criminals, was seduced, and became a drug user. Her parents demanded that the University return her to them but school officials could not. This action was soon thereafter filed against the University (D) by the Hegels (P) alleging that the school's negligent failure to perform supervisory duties had resulted in the damage to the Hegels' (P) daughter. The University (D) thereupon made a motion for judgment (in their favor) on the pleadings.

ISSUE: Are colleges and universities under any affirmative duty to control the activities of their students?

HOLDING AND DECISION: (Bettman, J.) No. Colleges and universities are under no affirmative duty to regulate the private lives of their students. A university is an institution of learning—nothing more. It is neither a nursery school, boarding school, nor prison. No one is required to attend and the school is under no duty to require attendance. It is presumed that anyone enrolled in such an institution will have the necessary maturity to take care of himself or herself without the school being forced to supervise them. As such, no duty to do so is imposed upon the school. Since there can be no negligence recovery without some duty, the motion for judgment against Hegel (P) on the pleadings is affirmed.

ANALYSIS

This case recognizes the demise of the "in loco parentis" principle for the administration of institutions of higher education. Indeed, the current trend of authority is to wholly absolve such schools of any actionable duty to their students as students (e.g., no duty to supervise private affairs, provide courses of true educational value, etc.). As such, it appears that the court has adopted a virtual "hands-off" policy on university responsibility questions.

Quicknotes

AFFIRMATIVE DUTY An obligation to undertake an affirmative action for the benefit of another.

IN LOCO PARENTIS A situation in which a person has assumed the responsibilities and obligations of a lawful parent without undergoing the legal adoption process.

JUDGMENT ON THE PLEADINGS Motion for judgment after the pleadings are closed.

NEGLIGENCE Conduct falling below the standard of care that a reasonable person would demonstrate under similar conditions.

L.S. Ayres & Co. v. Hicks

Store (D) v. Escalator victim (P)

Ind. Sup. Ct., 220 Ind. 86, 40 N.E.2d 334 (1942)

NATURE OF CASE: Motion for new trial in action for damages.

FACT SUMMARY: Hicks (P) fell and got his fingers caught in an escalator; L.S. Ayres & Co. (D) unreasonably delayed in stopping the escalator.

RULE OF LAW

The invitor or one who has control of an instrumentality that causes harm to another has the legal obligation to aid a helpless person, even if he did not cause the original situation in which the helpless person finds himself.

FACTS: Hicks (P), a six-year-old boy, went with his mother to go shopping at the L.S. Ayres & Co. (Ayres) (D) department store. Hicks (P) fell on the escalator in the store and as a result, he got his fingers caught in the escalator. Ayres (D) did not immediately stop the escalator but kept it running and as a result Hicks (P) was hurt severely. After an unreasonable time, Ayres (D) did stop the escalator. Ayres (D) was found liable and moved for a new trial.

ISSUE: Does the invitor or one who has control of an instrumentality that causes harm to another have the legal obligation to aid a helpless person, even if he did not cause the original situation in which the helpless person finds himself?

HOLDING AND DECISION: (Shake, C.J.) Yes. An invitor or one who has control of an instrumentality that causes harm to another has the legal obligation to aid a helpless person, even if he did not cause the original situation in which the helpless person finds himself. The mere occurrence of this type of accident creates a relation that gives rise to a legal duty to aid the injured person. Thus, it is irrelevant whether the injured person was contributorily negligent or whether his potential rescuer was negligent or legally responsible for the original injury. Here Ayres (D) was an invitor and had control of the instrumentality causing harm; it had a duty to affirmatively act and to exercise reasonable care to avoid aggravation of the injury. However, Hicks (P) is entitled to recover only for the injuries that resulted when Ayres (D) had the duty to act but failed to do so for an unreasonable time. Reversed. Motion for new trial granted.

ANALYSIS

This case is an exception to the general rule that one has no duty to rescue another unless he caused the predicament. Other exceptions to the rule, accepted in some jurisdictions, include the following situations: where a seaman falls overboard; where an employer can save a helpless employee; carrier and passenger; innkeeper and guest; jailer and prisoner; where one assumes the care of another, e.g., schoolteacher and pupil; and landowner and business visitor, on premises open to the public as in this case.

Quicknotes

CONTRIBUTORY NEGLIGENCE Behavior on the part of an injured plaintiff falling below the standard of ordinary care that contributes to the defendant's negligence, resulting in the plaintiff's injury.

DUTY TO RESCUE The duty to take some action to assist another in danger; such a duty is only imposed under certain circumstances.

INVITOR An individual that induces another to enter upon his property.

REASONABLE CARE The degree of care observed by a reasonably prudent person under similar circumstances; synonymous with due care or ordinary care.

J.S. and M.S. v. R.T.H.

Parents (P) v. Abuser (D)

N.J. Sup. Ct., 155 N.J. 330, 714 A.2d 924 (1998)

NATURE OF CASE: Suit for damages resulting from child abuse.

FACT SUMMARY: The parents of two girls brought suit against their neighbor and his wife, seeking damages based on his sexual abuse of their daughters.

RULE OF LAW

When a spouse has actual knowledge or special reason to know of the likelihood that his or her spouse is engaging in sexually abusive behavior against a particular person, the spouse has a duty of care to take reasonable steps to prevent or warn of the harm and a breach of that duty constitutes a proximate cause of the resultant sexual abuse of the victim.

FACTS: Two young girls spent a substantial period of time with their neighbor at his horse barn. The man, R.T.H. (D), sexually abused the girls. The girls' parents (P) brought suit against the man and his wife (D) for damages, arguing that the wife's (D) negligence rendered her liable for their injuries as well. In an amended answer, the wife (D) argued that she owed no duty of care to the plaintiffs, that any alleged negligence on her part was not the proximate cause of the injuries and that any damages were the result of a third party whose actions were beyond her control. The trial court entered summary judgment for the wife (D) and the appellate division reversed and remanded. The wife (D) appealed.

ISSUE: When a spouse has actual knowledge or special reason to know of the likelihood that his or her spouse is engaging in sexually abusive behavior against a particular person, does the spouse have a duty of care to take reasonable steps to prevent or warn of the harm and does a breach of that duty constitute a proximate cause of the resultant sexual abuse of the victim?

HOLDING AND DECISION: (Handler, J.) Yes. When a spouse has actual knowledge or special reason to know of the likelihood that his or her spouse is engaging in sexually abusive behavior against a particular person, the spouse has a duty of care to take reasonable steps to prevent or warn of the harm and a breach of that duty constitutes a proximate cause of the resultant sexual abuse of the victim. In determining whether to impose a duty, the court must weigh several factors including the nature of the underlying risk of harm, its foreseeabilty and severity, the opportunity and ability to exercise care to prevent the harm, the comparative interests or relationships between the parties, and the societal interests in the proposed solution based on public policy and fairness. The fundamental element in determining whether a duty of care is owed is foreseeability. This is based on the defendant's knowledge of the risk of injury as determined from an objective standard. Such knowledge may be actual or constructive. Where the type of harm is difficult to ascertain, the court may require that the defendant have special reason to know that a particular plaintiff or class of plaintiffs would suffer from the particular type of injury. Moreover, where the risk of harm is that posed by third persons, the plaintiff may be required to show that the defendant knew or had reason to know from past experience that such conduct was likely. Whether a legal duty may be imposed requires a balancing of the conflicting interests of the parties. This requires an assessment of the defendant's responsibility for conditions creating a risk of harm and an analysis of whether the defendant had sufficient control, opportunity and ability to avoid the harm. The question of whether to impose a duty also depends upon public policy and fairness. The court must also consider the scope or boundaries of the duty under the totality of the circumstances and such scope must be reasonable. This includes a consideration of the risk of harm involved and the practicality of preventing it as determined by an objective standard on the particular facts of the case. It is highly foreseeable that a wife's failure to prevent or warn of her husband's sexual abuse or propensity for sexual abuse would result in the occurrence or continuation of such abuse. The wife's (D) negligence was the proximate cause of their injuries. Affirmed.

ANALYSIS

The court engages in a balancing of the competing interests of the parties. On the one hand is the strong public interest in protecting society from the threat of potential sexual abuse. On the other are the defendant's interests in marital privacy. The court concluded that the protection against potential abuse outweighs the interests in marital privacy.

Quicknotes

ACTUAL KNOWLEDGE Knowledge that presently and objectively exists.

CHILD ABUSE Conduct that is harmful to a child's physical or mental health.

CONSTRUCTIVE KNOWLEDGE Knowledge imputed to an individual as a result of its being either in the public record or discoverable through the exercise of reasonable care.

Tarasoff v. Regents of University of California

Murder victim's parents (P) v. Psychiatrists (D) and their employer (D)

Cal. Sup. Ct., 17 Cal. 3d 425, 551 P.2d 334 (1976)

NATURE OF CASE: Action for wrongful death.

FACT SUMMARY: Doctors from the University of California (D) were aware that one of their outpatients intended to kill Tatiana Tarasoff but neglected to warn her of it.

RULE OF LAW

A doctor bears a duty to exercise reasonable care and warn potential victims about known violent tendencies or intentions of a patient.

FACTS: While a mental outpatient at a University of California (U.C.) (D) Hospital, Poddar disclosed his intention to kill Tatiana Tarasoff because she had spurned his romantic advances. The psychologist who learned of this intention, Dr. Moore, notified both the campus police and three staff psychiatrists; but, after a cursory investigation, it was decided that no action to confine Poddar was necessary. Tatiana was not warned of Poddar's intentions. Two months later, Poddar shot and killed Tatiana. At his trial, it was learned that Poddar had discontinued his treatment at the U.C. (D) hospital after the incident two months earlier. Tatiana's parents (P) thereupon filed this action against U.C. (D) alleging that the hospital's negligent failure to warn Tatiana of Poddar's intention had caused her wrongful death. This appeal followed.

ISSUE: Does a doctor bear a duty to exercise reasonable care and warn potential victims about known violent tendencies and intentions of their patients?

HOLDING AND DECISION: (Tobriner, J.) Yes. A doctor bears a duty to exercise reasonable care and warn potential victims about known violent tendencies or intentions of a patient. There is no reason why the rule requiring doctors to take such action to prevent harm from physical illness should not be extended to mental illness situations as well. U.C. (D) contends that the burden of deciding which of the many threats doctors hear should be taken seriously is too great; but there is nothing improper in the law requiring a professional to exercise his professional judgment. U.C. further (D) contends that requiring disclosure of such threats will destroy the confidentiality necessary to effective psychotherapy; but the interest of society in protecting itself from physical violence must take precedence. The action may proceed.

ANALYSIS

This case marks a diversion from the traditional attitude of the courts regarding the duty of a doctor to warn about threats made by a patient in confidence. As Justice Clark in his dissent [not included in the casebook] pointed out here, there is nothing unusual in holding a psychotherapist liable for harm that results from the "negligent discontinuance" of psychotherapy. Pre-*Tarasoff*, however, there was no precedent for predicating liability on a mere failure to disclose dangerous intentions. Note that this new rule is consistent with the psychotherapist-patient privilege since such privilege is expressly inapplicable in situations in which the safety or welfare of any individual is threatened.

Quicknotes

AMICUS BRIEF A brief submitted by a third party, not a party to the action, that contains information for the court's consideration in conformity with its position.

Southern California Gas Co. v. Superior Court of Los Angeles County

Natural gas utility (D) v. Court (P)

Cal. Sup. Ct., 7 Cal. 5th 391, 441 P.3d 881 (2019)

NATURE OF CASE: Appeal from reversal of judgment permitting to go forward a putative class action for purely economic losses arising from negligence.

FACT SUMMARY: After Southern California Gas Co.'s (SoCalGas's) (D) natural gas storage facility developed a leak, requiring the relocation of thousands of nearby residents from the Porter Ranch neighborhood, Porter Ranch area businesses brought a putative class action seeking recovery of purely economic losses that resulted from the relocations and reduction in property values. SoCalGas (D) demurred, arguing that the negligence claims failed as a matter of law because the businesses (P) were seeking to recover for purely economic losses.

RULE OF LAW

A public utility does not have a duty to local businesses to guard against purely economic losses.

FACTS: Southern California Gas Co. (SoCalGas) (D), a natural gas utility, stored vast amounts of natural gas in an underground facility (Aliso Facility) in the hills surrounding the Los Angeles suburb of Porter Ranch, a community of around 30,000 residents. In October 2015, the Aliso Facility developed a large leak that, at its peak, caused the release of 55 tons of natural gas every hour. Porter Ranch residents developed a variety of physical symptoms as a result, and around 15,000 residents within a five-mile radius of the leak had to be relocated, sometimes hundreds of miles away. The leak and resulting relocations devastated the local economy and cost local businesses the loss of considerable earnings. Some Porter Ranch area businesses (P) within the five-mile radius of the leak sought to bring a negligence class action against SoCalGas (D) to recover for these purely economic losses. SoCalGas (D) demurred, arguing that the claims were barred as a matter of law on the grounds that it did not have a tort duty to the businesses (P) to prevent purely economic losses. The trial court overruled the demurrer, explaining that companies "must face the full cost of accidents" they create, or else "they will underinvest in precautions." The trial court acknowledged that economic losses not flowing from conventional injury to person or property, such as physical damage, are ordinarily not recoverable in tort, but questioned the wisdom of that rule. The state's intermediate appellate court reversed, and the state's highest court granted review.

ISSUE: Does a public utility have a duty to local businesses to guard against purely economic losses?

HOLDING AND DECISION: (Cuellar, J.) No. A public utility does not have a duty to local businesses to guard against purely economic losses. Liability in negligence for purely economic losses is the exception, not the rule, when it comes to the tort duty of care. The primary exception to the general rule of no-recovery for negligently inflicted purely economic losses—which is shorthand for pecuniary or commercial loss that does not arise from actionable physical, emotional or reputational injury to persons or physical injury to property—is where the plaintiff and the defendant have a "special relationship," which means that the plaintiff was an intended beneficiary of a particular transaction but was harmed by the defendant's negligence in carrying it out. Concerned about line-drawing problems and potentially overwhelming liability, courts across the country have rejected recovery for purely economic losses stemming from man-made calamity, and have limited liability of the scope of defendants' duty to those who have suffered personal injury or property damage that results from such calamities. In addition to line-drawing difficulties they face, courts are also concerned about safeguarding the efficacy of tort law by setting meaningful limits on liability, so although exposure to liability often provides an important incentive for parties to internalize the social costs of their actions, permitting vast numbers of suits and limitless financial exposure could ultimately deter socially beneficial behavior. The Restatement (Third) of Torts takes a similar view, stating that there is no general duty to avoid the unintentional infliction of economic loss on another. The Restatement's position rests on concerns that purely economic losses threaten liabilities that are indeterminate and out of proportion to a defendant's culpability, and with them exaggerated pressure to avoid an activity altogether. For centuries, in fact, similar concerns have justified strict limits on private recovery for a public nuisance. This case underscores the ineluctable difficulty associated with imposing a duty to guard against purely economic losses in industrial calamity negligence cases, as well as the difficulty of line-drawing, since the claims at bar lack any clear spatial bounds, and there is no viable way to impose temporal limits on recovery. Here, too, the local area businesses (P) did not have a special relationship with SoCalGas (D); their only relevant ties to SoCalGas (D) were having the misfortune of operating near the Aliso Facility. Although the businesses (P) seek to limit membership in the action to businesses operating within a five-mile radius of the leak, i.e., the area from which

Continued on next page.

residents were initially evacuated, this geographic limitation is, effectively, random: there is no compelling basis to let a business operating 4.9 miles away recover its lost profits but deny such recovery to other businesses operating 5.1 miles away, or 6 miles away, or even 10 miles away, if the leak impacted their incomes. Moreover, as the businesses (P) acknowledge, the initial evacuation line was extended beyond five miles. Using the boundary of an evacuation zone as a liability line might not just lack predictability, but, in certain circumstances, it could also inject a dangerous incentive into disaster response efforts by having companies pressure public officials to roll back evacuation lines, or, worse, by keeping officials in the dark about the extent of industrial accidents. In cases such as the one at bar, there is no workable way to limit geographically who may recover purely economic losses. Without one, the dangers of indeterminate liability, over-deterrence, and endless litigation are at their apex. Similarly, there is no way to limit temporally what purely economic losses could be recovered, since such losses from the leak are ongoing to the extent that the entire community has been altered and economic demand lessened, so that such claims would be without end. This does not, however, mean that denying recovery for those who did not suffer injury to person or property is a perfect solution in negligence cases like this one. It is only the least-worst rule out there. Denying recovery for purely economic losses under circumstances like these has the vice of creating results in cases at its edge that are unjust or unfair—or even seemingly perverse—for example, by opening the courthouse doors for people who experience slight physical injury while closing those doors to others who suffer devastating purely economic losses. The problem faced by the courts is that the ripple effects of industrial catastrophe in an interconnected economy defy judicial creation of more finely tuned rule. The legislature may be better suited to create such rules, and, in some instances, the legislature has been able to craft such rules. A partial solution might also be achieved by leveraging the insurance market. Although denying economic losses arguably could result in companies like SoCalGas (D) not taking sufficient precautions, it must be noted that SoCalGas (D) is not getting off scot-free. Around 50,000 claimants have alleged in other litigation that they suffered property damage caused by the leak, and the company has spent some $450 million on remedial measures and agreed to pay another $120 million as part of a settlement with local authorities. SoCalGas (D), which operates in a heavily regulated domain, also remains under investigation, and may face further consequences in the future. Although tort law seeks to compensate those injured from industrial accidents, and to deter industries from causing injury in the first place, society is not necessarily best served by extending tort liability indefinitely. Meaningful limits on tort liability, along with the incentives they set, are crucial to the functioning of society's economy and of the courts. Where such limits leave gaps in the social fabric, tort does not stand alone: insurance also compensates, regulation also deters. And, where gaps persist, the legislature can act. Although the prevailing rule of no recovery for purely economic losses is imperfect, it is one that should be followed. Affirmed.

ANALYSIS

An example of the kind of special relationship needed to recover in negligence for purely economic losses is the relationship between an intended beneficiary of a will and a notary public preparing the decedent's documents. Where the notary was negligent in preparing the documents, the intended beneficiary could recover assets the decedent had intended the beneficiary to receive, and that the beneficiary would have received but for the notary's negligence. A special relationship existed between the intended beneficiary and the notary because the end and aim of the transaction between the nonparty decedent and the notary was to ensure that the decedent's estate passed to the intended beneficiary. See *Biakanja v. Irving,* 49 Cal.2d 647, 320 P.2d 16 (1958). Some courts apply a multifactor test to determine whether there is a special relationship justifying liability of this sort, that analyzes (1) the extent to which the transaction was intended to affect the plaintiff; (2) the foreseeability of harm to the plaintiff; (3) the degree of certainty that the plaintiff suffered injury; (4) the closeness of the connection between the defendant's conduct and the injury suffered; (5) the moral blame attached to the defendant's conduct; and (6) the policy of preventing future harm. However, as the California Supreme Court emphasized in this case, deciding whether to impose a duty of care turns on a careful consideration of the sum total of the policy considerations at play, not a mere tallying of some finite, one-size-fits-all set of factors.

Quicknotes

CLASS ACTION A suit commenced by a representative on behalf of an ascertainable group that is too large to appear in court, who shares a commonality of interests and who will benefit from a successful result.

DEMURRER The assertion that the opposing party's pleadings are insufficient and that the demurring party should not be made to answer.

ECONOMIC LOSS RULE In products liability cases, economic losses can include repair and replacement costs, as well as lost profits and the commercial value lost.

Daley v. LaCroix

Mother (P) and son (P) v. Driver of car (D)

Mich. Sup. Ct., 384 Mich. 4, 179 N.W.2d 390 (1970)

NATURE OF CASE: Action for negligent infliction of emotional distress.

FACT SUMMARY: The Daleys (P) suffered emotional distress after LaCroix's (D) car crashed into a utility pole, which caused damage to their house.

RULE OF LAW

Whenever a definite and objective physical injury is produced as a result of emotional distress proximately caused by a tortfeasor's negligent conduct, the injured party may recover damages for such physical consequences to himself notwithstanding the absence of any physical impact upon him at the time of the emotional shock.

FACTS: In July 1963, a car driven negligently by LaCroix (D) careened off the road and sheared off a utility pole, causing an electrical explosion that damaged the Daleys' (P) house. Though there was no physical impact on either Estelle Daley (P) or her son Timothy (P), both suffered extensive emotional distress, which manifested itself in severe nervousness. As a result, Estelle (P) and Timothy (P) filed this action against LaCroix (D) for negligent infliction of emotional distress. Because such an action is not traditionally permissible absent proof of some "physical impact" (absent here) on the injured party, the trial court directed a verdict for LaCroix (D). This appeal followed.

ISSUE: Whenever a definite and objective physical injury is produced as a result of emotional distress proximately caused by a tortfeasor's negligent conduct, may the injured party recover damages for such physical consequences to himself notwithstanding the absence of any physical impact upon him at the time of the emotional shock?

HOLDING AND DECISION: (Kavanagh, J.) Yes. Whenever a definite and objective physical injury is produced as a result of emotional distress proximately caused by a tortfeasor's negligent conduct, the injured party may recover damages for such physical consequences to himself, notwithstanding the absence of any physical impact upon him at the time of the emotional shock. It is true that damage awards for physical reactions (e.g., nervousness) to emotional distress have traditionally only been recoverable when the emotional distress was accompanied by some immediate "physical impact" on the victim (e.g., blow to the head), from and as a part of the tortfeasor's act. This court's examination of this rule, in light of the increasing sophistication of both the scientific and legal communities regarding it, indicates that it is time to change it. As such, since testimony below was sufficient to raise a jury question of fact as to whether the nervous condition of the Daleys (P) was caused by LaCroix (D), the directed verdict must be reversed. Reversed and remanded.

DISSENT: (Brennan, C.J.) Traumatic neuroses, nervous upsets, etc., must be subjected to a "physical impact" requirement if spurious claims are to be avoided.

ANALYSIS

This case points out the clear trend of modern authority toward rejecting the "physical impact" requirement for negligent infliction of emotional distress. Traditionally, only such outrageous conduct as the negligent mishandling of corpses had been insulated from the "physical impact" requirement for recovery of mental disturbance damages. Several objections have traditionally been made to such recovery. It has been said that mental disturbance is too difficult to measure in terms of money. It has been contended that such "injuries" are too "remote."

Quicknotes

DIRECTED VERDICT A verdict ordered by the court in a jury trial.

NEGLIGENT INFLICTION OF EMOTIONAL DISTRESS Violation of the duty of care owed to another that occurs when an individual creates a foreseeable risk of injury to the other person, which causes emotional distress resulting in some physical harm to that person.

PROXIMATE CAUSE The natural sequence of events without which an injury would not have been sustained.

SUI GENERIS Peculiar to its own type or class.

THE "IMPACT RULE" Doctrine that in order to recover damages for negligent infliction of emotional distress an external impact is required.

Thing v. La Chusa

Injured son's mother (P) v. Driver (D)

Cal. Sup. Ct., 48 Cal. 3d 644, 771 P.2d 814 (1989) (en banc)

NATURE OF CASE: Review of order reversing dismissal of action seeking damages for emotional distress.

FACT SUMMARY: Thing (P) sought emotional distress damages for injuries to her son which she did not contemporaneously observe.

RULE OF LAW

One may recover emotional distress damages for an injury to a relative only if he observes the injury-producing event.

FACTS: Thing's (P) son was injured when an automobile driven by La Chusa (D) struck him. Informed of the accident by her daughter, Thing (P) ran to the scene and saw her son lying bloody and unconscious in the road. Thing (P) sued La Chusa (D) for emotional distress. The trial court granted La Chusa's (D) motion for summary judgment, dismissing the action because Thing (P) had not actually observed the accident. The court of appeals reversed, and the California Supreme Court granted review.

ISSUE: May one recover emotional distress damages for an injury to a relative only if he observes the injury-producing event?

HOLDING AND DECISION: (Eagleson, J.) Yes. One may recover emotional distress damages for an injury to a relative only if he observes the injury-producing event. Emotional distress is part of the human condition and can be inflicted by an unlimited number of traumatic events. On a societal level, it is unacceptable to impose tort liability on a defendant whenever he causes another such distress partly because of the deleterious effects of unlimited liability and because injury is often out of proportion to the level of negligence. A bright-line outer limit of liability for emotional distress caused by trauma to another must be drawn. The most logical point to draw this line is to limit recovery to (1) close relatives, by blood or marriage who, (2) contemporaneously observe the event that causes the injury and the injury itself, and who (3) suffer a serious emotional reaction. Here, Thing (P) did not actually observe her son's accident, so she may not recover. The judgment of the court of appeal is reversed.

CONCURRENCE AND DISSENT: (Kaufman, J.) Liability for emotional distress caused by injuries to third parties should be confined to those in the zone of danger put in fear of their own safety.

ANALYSIS

The common law originally recognized the "impact rule," which requires physical injury for emotional trauma damages. The California Supreme Court jettisoned this requirement in *Dillon v. Legg*, 68 Cal. 2d 728 (1968), which allowed recovery for observing injury to another. In the years between 1968 and 1988, liability in this area had been gradually expanding. The present case closed the door on such growth.

Quicknotes

EMOTIONAL DISTRESS Extreme personal suffering that results from another's conduct and for which damages may be sought.

IMPACT RULE Doctrine that in order to recover damages for negligent infliction of emotional distress an external impact is required.

SUMMARY JUDGMENT Judgment rendered by a court in response to a motion made by one of the parties, claiming that the lack of a question of material fact in respect to an issue warrants disposition of the issue without consideration by the jury.

Endresz v. Friedberg

Stillborn twins' parents (P) v. Driver (D)

N.Y. Ct. App., 24 N.Y.2d 478, 248 N.E.2d 901 (1969)

NATURE OF CASE: Action for wrongful death.

FACT SUMMARY: Endresz's (P) seven-months-pregnant wife (P) delivered stillborn twins after being injured in an auto accident with Friedberg (D).

RULE OF LAW

The parents of an unborn fetus whose birth was prevented by negligent conduct may not bring a wrongful death action to redress the wrong that was done.

FACTS: Janice Endresz (P) was seven months pregnant when she was involved in an auto accident negligently caused by Friedberg (D). As a result of the accident, her twins were stillborn two days later. The Endreszes (P) thereupon filed wrongful death actions on behalf of the twins alleging $100,000 in damages for "loss of anticipated care, comfort, and support" and a personal injury action on behalf of Janice (P). The trial court, however, dismissed the wrongful death actions on the ground that such were not maintainable on behalf of an unborn fetus. The Endreszes (P) appealed, contending that since the court had recently recognized the right of a child to sue for prenatal injuries, it must logically extend such rights to the child's survivors in a wrongful death action.

ISSUE: May the parents of an unborn fetus whose birth was prevented by negligent conduct bring a wrongful death action to redress the wrong that was done?

HOLDING AND DECISION: (Fuld, C.J.) No. The parents of an unborn fetus whose birth was prevented by negligent conduct may not bring a wrongful death action to redress the wrong that was done. The rationale for allowing a child, in his own right, to recover damages for prenatal injuries is that it is unfair to force the child to go through life "bearing the seal of another's fault." Where the child dies, however, no such injustice arises. Since the parents may recover for their suffering, loss of consortium, etc., in a simple personal injury action, the basic underlying policy of the law to compensate for loss is fully served without permitting wrongful death recovery. Affirmed.

DISSENT: (Burke, J.) It is elementary that every wrong must have a remedy. The decision today leaves the wrong done to the unborn twins here without redress.

ANALYSIS

This case reaffirms the traditional rule regarding the rights of parents to recover for the wrongful death of their unborn children. In essence, of course, the logical import of this decision is that society owes no duty of care to the unborn child. Note, however, that this rule changes when the fetus may be classified as "viable"—i.e., capable of surviving outside of the mother. The definition of "viability," of course, varies greatly from jurisdiction to jurisdiction. Some permit recovery only if the child is capable of independent respiration prior to its death. Others permit recovery if respiration is maintainable only by a respirator.

Quicknotes

DUTY OF CARE A principle of negligence requiring an individual to act in such a manner as to avoid injury to a person to whom he or she owes a duty.

LOSS OF CONSORTIUM An action bright based on willful interference with the marital relationship.

PAIN AND SUFFERING A type of recovery in tort for both physical and mental injuries.

PERSONAL INJURY Harm to an individual's person or body.

WRONGFUL DEATH An action brought by the beneficiaries of a deceased person, claiming that the deceased's death was the result of wrongful conduct by the defendant.

Procanik by Procanik v. Cillo

Birth-defective child (P) v. Doctors (D)

N.J. Sup. Ct., 97 N.J. 339, 478 A.2d 755 (1984)

NATURE OF CASE: Appeal of summary adjudication dismissing causes of action seeking special and general damages for "wrongful life."

FACT SUMMARY: An allegedly negligent diagnosis by Cillo (D) prevented Procanik's (P) mother from knowing that he would be born with serious handicaps, which had she known might have caused her to terminate the pregnancy.

RULE OF LAW

An infant plaintiff may recover special damages for "wrongful life" but may not recover general damages therefor.

FACTS: Procanik's (P) mother contracted rubella during the first trimester of her pregnancy. Such an infection causes a great risk of serious birth defects, a danger that proved true in Procanik's (P) case. He was born with serious handicaps. Cillo (D) and other medical personnel had failed to diagnose rubella in the mother. Procanik (P) brought an action seeking, among other things, special damages for extra expenses he would incur throughout his life as a result of the alleged malpractice, on the theory that his mother might have terminated the pregnancy had she been diagnosed and informed of such diagnosis. He also sought general damages for an impaired life. No allegation was made that any defendant had brought about Procanik's (P) handicaps. The trial court dismissed the "wrongful life" causes of action. The appellate court affirmed. Procanik (P) appealed.

ISSUE: May an infant plaintiff recover special and general damages for "wrongful life"?

HOLDING AND DECISION: (Pollock, J.) No. An infant plaintiff may recover special damages for "wrongful life," but may not recover general damages therefor. Earlier decisions held that neither parents nor children could recover special damages for negligent diagnosis that prevented a mother from making an informed choice regarding termination. This was largely due to a judicial reluctance to recognize the legitimacy of abortion. However, in the intervening years, the United States Supreme Court has legitimized abortion, and this court has permitted parents to recover special damages from negligent doctors when the negligence prevented them from properly considering termination. There is no logical reason to deny the same rights to the infant itself, as the expenses will prove just as real through the lifetime of the child. General damages for diminished value of life, however, present an entirely different issue. Beyond the weighty philosophical issue of whether no life can be preferable to impaired life, the damages in such a situation cannot be measured in any rational way. Since such damages would be pure speculation, they cannot be permitted. Here, Procanik (P) may proceed on special damages, but not general ones. Affirmed in part; reversed in part; and remanded.

ANALYSIS

The issues raised here go to the outer edge of judicial competence, being more fit for religious or moral debate than judicial decision. Not surprisingly, the jurisdictions that have spoken on this matter have come down in different directions. Some deny specials and generals; others allow both.

Quicknotes

GUARDIAN AD LITEM Person designated by the court to represent an infant or ward in a particular legal proceeding.

WRONGFUL BIRTH A cause of action brought by the parents of a child born with severe birth defects against a doctor for negligent treatment or advice.

WRONGFUL LIFE A medical malpractice action brought by the parents of a child born with severe birth defects against a doctor, claiming that but for the doctor's negligent treatment or advice they would not have given birth to the child.

CHAPTER 9

Owners and Occupiers of Land

Quick Reference Rules of Law

Taylor v. Olsen

Injured driver (P) v. Tree owner (D)

Or. Sup. Ct., 282 Or. 343, 578 P.2d 779 (1978)

NATURE OF CASE: Appeal from denial of damages for negligence.

FACT SUMMARY: Taylor (P) injured herself when she crashed into a tree, which had fallen onto a highway from Olsen's (D) property.

RULE OF LAW

It is generally a question of fact as to whether a landowner has taken reasonable care in protecting people outside his land from dangerous conditions existing upon the land.

FACTS: Taylor (P) suffered injuries when her car, on a dark and windy January evening, struck a tree, which had fallen across the highway from Olsen's (D) adjacent property. The trial court, noting that there was no evidence suggesting Olsen (D) could have reasonably known about the tree's hazardous condition before it fell, directed verdict for Olsen (D). Taylor (P) appealed.

ISSUE: Is the question of whether a landowner has taken reasonable care in protecting people outside his land from dangerous conditions existing upon the land generally one of fact?

HOLDING AND DECISION: (Linde, J.) Yes. It is generally a question of fact as to whether a landowner has taken reasonable care in protecting people outside his land from dangerous conditions existing upon the land. Usually such a question would be presented to the jury. However, in cases where no evidence has been introduced from which a reasonable jury could impute liability, a directed verdict is proper. The instant action is such a case. Although Taylor (P) testified that an examination of the tree after the accident revealed that the center had decayed, there was no evidence that Olsen (D) could have, through reasonable inspection, determined that fact beforehand. Furthermore, no evidence was adduced suggesting that drilling to the center of a tree to look for decay is a common method of examining trees, absent any external indications that the tree was not structurally sound. As such, Olsen (D) could not be held liable for Taylor's (P) injuries. Affirmed.

ANALYSIS

The general American rule is that a landowner has no duty to protect persons outside his property from natural conditions existing on the property. However, liability has been assessed where the landowner knew of the structural defects of a tree and failed to take reasonable precautions against resulting damage. *Turner v. Ridley*, 144 A.2d 269 (D.C. 1958). There is also a line of cases which distinguish between the care which must be exercised by a rural landowner, and one residing in an urban area. However, this distinction is rejected in *Taylor*.

Quicknotes

DIRECTED VERDICT A verdict ordered by the court in a jury trial.

Salevan v. Wilmington Park, Inc.

Foul ball victim (P) v. Ballpark owner (D)

Del. Super. Ct., 45 Del. (6 Terry) 290, 72 A.2d 239 (1950)

NATURE OF CASE: Action for personal injuries.

FACT SUMMARY: Salevan (P) was injured by a foul ball while walking on a public street adjacent to Wilmington's (D) ballpark.

RULE OF LAW

Landowners whose property is adjacent to public sidewalks or highways owe a duty of care to take reasonable precautions for the protection of the traveling public.

FACTS: Wilmington Park (D) was engaged in the operation of a baseball park located adjacent to East Thirtieth Street in the City of Wilmington. One day, while walking on East Thirtieth Street, Salevan (P) was struck with a foul ball emanating from this park. Salevan (P) thereupon filed this action for personal injuries. At trial, it was adduced that in the course of the average game, some two to three foul balls normally got out of the park, landing on East Thirtieth Street. Though Wilmington Park (D) was aware of this, it took few precautions to protect pedestrians there during any of 68 games played during the season.

ISSUE: Do landowners whose property is adjacent to public sidewalks or highways owe a duty of care to take reasonable precautions for the protection of the traveling public?

HOLDING AND DECISION: (Wolcott, J.) Yes. Landowners whose property is adjacent to public sidewalks or highways owe a duty of care to take reasonable precautions for the protection of the traveling public. Breach of the duty to not interfere with such rights is clearly actionable. The inherent nature of the game of baseball is such as to require a landowner to take reasonable effective precautions to protect the traveling public nearby. While Wilmington Park (D) evidently undertook some cursory precautions here, the fact that two or three balls normally endanger pedestrians on East Thirtieth Street every game anyway should have put them, as landowners, on notice that the precautions they took were inadequate. Judgment for Salevan (P); $2,500 awarded.

ANALYSIS

This case points out the general duty (due of care) assignable to landowners regarding people outside of their land when some dangerous activity is going on the land. Note that, as a general rule, landowners owe no duty to people outside their land for natural conditions on the land. Furthermore, a duty of due care arises even for artificial conditions (e.g., a ditch) on a landowner's land only if the artificial condition abuts adjacent public land (e.g., excavation next to a road). These general duties, of course, arise out of the common law. Note that some jurisdictions (e.g., California) have done away with them.

Quicknotes

DANGEROUS CONDITION A condition of property that poses a reasonably foreseeable substantial risk of injury giving rise to liability for a public entity.

DUTY OF CARE A principle of negligence requiring an individual to act in such a manner as to avoid injury to a person to whom he or she owes an obligatory duty.

FORESEEABILITY A reasonable expectation that an act or omission would result in injury.

Sheehan v. St. Paul & Duluth Ry. Co.

Rail walker (P) v. Railroad (D)

76 F. 201 (7th Cir. 1896)

NATURE OF CASE: Action to recover damages for personal injury.

FACT SUMMARY: While Sheehan (P) was walking on St. Paul & Duluth Ry. Co.'s (D) railroad track, his foot got caught and was run over by St. Paul & Duluth's (D) train.

RULE OF LAW

A landowner owes a duty of care to a trespasser only after he or she has discovered the presence of the trespasser.

FACTS: While Sheehan (P) was walking on St. Paul & Duluth Ry. Co.'s (St. Paul & Duluth) (D) railroad track, his foot slipped and became stuck in the rail. He was unable to get it out before the train ran over his foot. The train crew did not see Sheehan (P) until the train was almost upon him and it was too late to stop. Sheehan (P) filed suit, but the court directed a verdict for St. Paul & Duluth (D). Sheehan (P) appealed.

ISSUE: Does a landowner have a duty of care to a trespasser only after he or she has discovered the presence of the trespasser?

HOLDING AND DECISION: (Seaman, J.) Yes. A landowner does not have a duty of care to a trespasser whose presence the landlord was not aware of, but the landowner does owe a duty of reasonable care after discovering the presence of a trespasser. In this case, the railroad did not have a duty to foresee that a reasonable person would trespass on the track at a place not open to travel. Hence, the St. Paul & Duluth (D) railroad owed no duty of care to trespasser Sheehan (P), since it had no notice of his presence. "The trespasser who ventures to enter upon a track for any purpose of (her or) his own assumes all risks of the conditions which may be found there, including the operation of engines and cars." At public crossings, the railroad does owe a duty of care to the public. The determinative factor is not that the public's passage at these crossings is lawful, but that the crossings by their existence give notice to the railroad. Such notice gives rise to a duty of care. Since there was no notice of Sheehan's (P) presence in this case, St. Paul & Duluth's (D) duty of care did not arise until the train crew discovered his predicament. The only question of liability would be whether after discovering Sheehan's (P) peril, St. Paul & Duluth's (D) train crew was negligent in averting injury to him. Affirmed.

ANALYSIS

This case follows the general rule that the landowner owes no duty of care to the unknown trespasser. Reasons given to support the rule are: that the trespasser is contributorily negligent or a wrongdoer, or that the trespasser's presence is unanticipated and so a reasonable person would not take steps to protect him/her. The latter rationale was used in this case. Prosser feels that the true explanation is that in a society based on private ownership, it is not socially desirable to interfere with a landowner's use of his/her land by imposing the burden of watching for and protecting trespassers. The landowner's immunity has been criticized, and the courts have created exceptions to it. The exceptions are as follows: once the landowner knows of the trespasser's presence, reasonable care is required (as mentioned in this case); where it is known to the landowner that a substantial number of persons frequently trespass in a limited area, a duty is owed; and where the landowner anticipates the presence of trespassers and carries on activity that might be highly dangerous to them, liability may be found. Each of the exceptions is based on the landowner's notice or anticipation of trespassers' presence.

Quicknotes

DUTY OF CARE A principle of negligence requiring an individual to act in such a manner as to avoid injury to a person to whom he or she owes an obligatory duty.

IMMUNITY Exemption from a legal obligation.

PERSONAL INJURY Harm to an individual's person or body.

TRESPASSERS Persons present on the land of another without the knowledge or express permission of the owner, and to whom only a minimum duty of care is owed for injuries incurred while on the premises.

Barmore v. Elmore

Assaulted guest (P) v. Assailant's father (D)

Ill. App. Ct., 83 Ill. App. 3d 1056, 403 N.E.2d 1355 (1980)

NATURE OF CASE: Appeal from denial of damages for negligence.

FACT SUMMARY: Barmore (P) sued Elmore (D) for injuries received from an attack by Elmore's (D) disturbed adult son during a business visit to Elmore's (D) home.

RULE OF LAW

As to a licensee, the owner of premises is only required to warn his guest of any hidden dangers of which the owner has knowledge.

FACTS: Barmore (P) and Elmore (D) were officers and members of a Masonic Lodge. In August 1977, Barmore (P) visited Elmore (D) at his house for the purpose of discussing Lodge business. While he was there, Barmore (P) was attacked by Elmore's (D) disturbed adult son and injured. He brought suit against the elder Elmore (D) alleging that as a landowner, he was negligent in failing to protect Barmore (P) from a dangerous condition upon the premises, namely his son, who had a history of mental illness. The trial court, holding that Barmore (P) was a licensee, rather than an invitee, held that Elmore (D) had not breached any duty toward his guest. Accordingly, he directed a verdict for Elmore (D). Barmore (P) appealed.

ISSUE: As to a licensee, is the owner of premises only required to warn his guest of any hidden dangers of which the owner has knowledge?

HOLDING AND DECISION: (Lindberg, J.) Yes. As to a licensee, the owner of premises is only required to warn his guest of any hidden dangers of which the owner has knowledge. Initially, Barmore's (P) contention that he was an invitee must be dismissed. The primary benefit of Barmore's (P) visit ran not to Elmore (D) but to the lodge of which both parties were members. As such, Barmore (P) must be classified as a licensee. Accordingly, Elmore's (D) duty to Barmore (P) extended only to warning him of any hidden dangers on the premises of which Elmore (D) was aware. It cannot be said that he breached this duty. Although his son had a history of mental illness, there is no evidence suggesting that Elmore (D) knew or could have known that Barmore's (P) visit that night would result in an attack. Therefore, a directed verdict in his favor was properly granted. Affirmed.

ANALYSIS

Some courts have abolished the distinction between a landowner's duty toward a business invitee and that owed to a guest or licensee. In such jurisdictions, a general duty of reasonable care is invoked. See *Rowland v. Christian*, 69 Cal. 2d 108 (1968). The destruction of the business invitee/licensee distinction was accomplished statutorily in at least one jurisdiction. See Conn. Gen. Stat. § 5255.7(a). However, the rule applied in *Barmore*, i.e., that a greater duty is owed to business invitees than to licensees, is still the rule in the majority of American jurisdictions.

Quicknotes

BUSINESS INVITEE A party invited onto another's property in order to conduct business to whom the owner owes a duty of care to protect against known dangers and those capable of discovery through reasonable care.

INVITEE A person who enters upon another's property by an express or implied invitation and to whom the owner of the property owes a duty of care to guard against injury from those hazards which are discoverable through the exercise of reasonable care.

LICENSEE A person who enters upon the land of another by the land owner's express or implied consent to whom the land owner owes a duty of reasonable care to protect against reasonably discoverable hazards; the recipient of a license.

Campbell v. Weathers

Customer (P) v. Lessee (D)

Kan. Sup. Ct., 153 Kan. 316, 111 P.2d 72 (1941)

NATURE OF CASE: Action to recover damages for negligence.

FACT SUMMARY: On his way to the toilet in Weather's (D) place of business, Campbell (P) stepped into a trap door and was injured.

RULE OF LAW

A regular customer of a business establishment who enters the establishment but does not buy anything is considered to be an invitee.

FACTS: Weathers (D) operated a cigar stand and lunch counter at which Campbell (P) was a regular customer. Campbell (P) entered the cigar stand, loitered there for about 15 minutes without making a purchase and then went to use the toilet. On his way to the toilet, Campbell (P) stepped into an open trap door and was injured. The toilet was open to the public. Weathers's (D) demurrer was sustained, and Campbell (P) appealed.

ISSUE: Is a regular customer of a business establishment who enters the establishment but does not buy anything an invitee?

HOLDING AND DECISION: (Wedell, J.) Yes. A regular or prospective customer of a place of business does not have to make a purchase on a particular occasion to be considered an invitee. Here, since Campbell (P) was a regular customer, the fact that he did not make a purchase on the day of his injury does not affect his status as an invitee. However, if it appears that a person had no intention of presently or in the future becoming a customer he could not be held to be an invitee. Reversed.

ANALYSIS

This case follows the mutual benefit rationale for distinguishing between invitees and licensees. The landowner has no financial interest in the entry of a licensee. Therefore, the licensee is entitled to nothing more than an honest disclosure of the dangers that are known to the landowner. But the visit of an invitee (or business visitor) may be financially beneficial to the landowner or possessor. Such visitor is entitled to expect that the possessor will take reasonable care to discover dangerous conditions and either make them safe or warn invitees. The theory is that the duty of affirmative care to make the premises safe is the price the occupier must pay for the present or prospective benefit to be derived from the visitor. The alternative theory, which is accepted by the majority of courts, is that the basis of liability is the representation implied when a possessor encourages others to enter: that reasonable care has been taken to make the place safe. It is not just the invitation but also an implied assurance accompanying the invitation that the place will be safe (which is not found to be present in the case of social guests).

Quicknotes

DANGEROUS CONDITION A condition of property that poses a reasonably foreseeable substantial risk of injury giving rise to liability for a public entity.

DUTY OF CARE A principle of negligence requiring an individual to act in such a manner as to avoid injury to a person to whom he or she owes an obligatory duty.

Whelan v. Van Natta

Customer (P) v. Shopkeeper (D)

Ky. Ct. App., 382 S.W.2d 205 (1964)

NATURE OF CASE: Action to recover damages for personal injury.

FACT SUMMARY: Whelan (P) was injured in a back room of Van Natta's (D) grocery store while looking for a box he'd (P) requested.

RULE OF LAW

An invitee retains the status of an invitee only as long as he remains on that part of the premises to which the land occupier's invitation extends.

FACTS: Whelan (P) entered Van Natta's (D) grocery store and made a purchase. Whelan (P) then asked about a box and was told to go to the back room. While looking for the box in the back room, which was dark, Whelan (P) fell through an unseen stairwell and was injured. Following a court judgment for Van Natta (D), Whelan (P) appealed.

ISSUE: Does an invitee retain the status of an invitee only as long as he remains on that part of the premises to which the land occupier's invitation extends?

HOLDING AND DECISION: (Montgomery, J.) Yes. The land occupier is subject to liability to another as an invitee only for harm sustained while he is on the land within the scope of the land occupier's invitation. The invitation extends to the part of the land upon which the land possessor gives the visitor reason to believe that his presence is desired for the purpose for which he has come. If the invitee goes outside the area of the invitation, he becomes a trespasser or a licensee depending upon whether he goes there with or without the possessor's consent. In this case, Whelan (P) requested a box for his own purpose. He was not invited into the back room as part of his business in the grocery store. He went there to get the box he requested. In going to the back room he left the area of invitation, that is, the area in which Van Natta (D) gave him reason to believe that his presence was desired for the purpose of doing business in the grocery store. Hence, Whelan (P) lost his status as an invitee and became a licensee (since he did have permission to go to the back room). Affirmed.

ANALYSIS

An invitee will also cease to be an invitee if he stays on the land after the expiration of a reasonable time within which to accomplish the purpose for which he is invited. These cases are decided upon and uphold the "invitation" test rather than the "mutual" or "economic" benefit test. The benefit to the land occupier is the same, whether the invitee stays within the area of invitation or not. As in this case, the benefit to Van Natta (D) did not diminish when Whelan (P) went into the back room.

Quicknotes

BUSINESS INVITEE A party invited onto another's property in order to conduct business to whom the owner owes a duty of care to protect against known dangers and those capable of discovery through reasonable care.

INVITEE A person who enters upon another's property by an express or implied invitation and to whom the owner of the property owes a duty of care to guard against injury from those hazards which are discoverable through the exercise of reasonable care.

Rowland v. Christian

Injured guest (P) v. Apartment renter (D)

Cal. Sup. Ct., 69 Cal. 2d 108, 443 P.2d 561 (1968)

NATURE OF CASE: Appeal from summary judgment for the defense in action to recover damages for personal injury.

FACT SUMMARY: While a guest in Christian's (D) house, Rowland (P) was injured by a defective faucet in the bathroom.

RULE OF LAW

An injured person's status as a trespasser, licensee, or invitee will not be determinate as to liability, although the status may have some bearing on the question of liability.

FACTS: Rowland (P) was a social guest in Christian's (D) home. He asked to use the bathroom, and, while there, was injured when a cracked faucet handle broke. Christian (D) had known that the handle was cracked and had complained to the building manager, but did not warn Rowland (P) of its condition. Rowland (P) filed a personal injury action, but the trial court, concluding that Rowland (P), as a social guest, must take the premises as he found them, entered summary judgment for Christian (D). Rowland (P) appealed.

ISSUE: Will an injured person's status as a trespasser, licensee, or invitee will be determinate as to liability, although the status may have some bearing on the question of liability?

HOLDING AND DECISION: (Peters, J.) No. An injured person's status as a trespasser, licensee, or invitee will not be determinate as to liability, although the status may have some bearing on the question of liability. The proper test to determine the possessor's liability is whether in the management of his property, he has acted as a reasonable person in view of the probability of injury to others. Liability is determined by balancing the following factors: foreseeability of harm to the plaintiff, the closeness of the connection between the possessor's conduct and the injury, the moral blame attached to the possessor's conduct, the policy of preventing future harm, the extent of the burden to the possessor, the consequences to the community of imposing a duty of care, and the availability and prevalence of insurance. A plaintiff's status may have a bearing in some cases on some of these factors. In this case Christian (D) was aware of the dangerous condition, that the defect was not obvious, and that Rowland (P) was about to come into contact with it. She neither remedied the condition, nor warned Rowland (P). A guest should reasonably be entitled to a warning of a dangerous concealed condition. Christians's failure to warn constituted negligence. The court feels that the distinctions and immunities attached to trespasser, licensee, and invitee are not justified in light of modern society and the attempt to use the categories in a just manner has given rise to a confused and complex system. "The common law rules obscure rather than illuminate the proper considerations which should govern determination of the question of duty." Reversed.

DISSENT: (Burke, J.) The distinctions among trespassers, licensees and invitees have been developed and applied by the courts over a period of many years. Tort law should be modified by the legislature, not by the courts.

ANALYSIS

In rejecting the categories the court follows a position adopted by an English statute in 1957. The statute declares that the possessor owes the same duty of care to invitees and licensees, with the matter of entry bearing only on the issue of reasonable care. The U.S. Supreme Court has refused to apply the categories to a guest on a ship. The position followed here, that the plaintiff's status is irrelevant as to the duty of reasonable care owed, but may be relevant to the question whether the possessor acted reasonably, is a minority position, followed so far only in California and Hawaii.

Quicknotes

DUTY OF REASONABLE CARE Duty to exercise the degree of care as would a reasonably prudent person under like circumstances.

INVITEE A person who enters upon another's property by an express or implied invitation and to whom the owner of the property owes a duty of care to guard against injury from those hazards which are discoverable through the exercise of reasonable care.

LICENSEES Persons known to an owner or occupier of land, who come onto the premises voluntarily and for a specific purpose although not necessarily with the consent of the owner.

PERSONAL INJURY Harm to an individual's person or body.

SUMMARY JUDGMENT Judgment rendered by a court in response to a motion by one of the parties, claiming that the lack of a question of material fact in respect to an

Continued on next page.

issue warrants disposition of the issue without consideration by the jury.

TRESPASSERS Persons present on the land of another without the knowledge or express permission of the owner, and to whom only a minimum duty of care is owed for injuries incurred while on the premises.

Borders v. Roseberry

Injured guest (P) v. Landlord (D)

Kan. Sup. Ct., 216 Kan. 486, 532 P.2d 1366 (1975)

NATURE OF CASE: Action for personal injuries.

FACT SUMMARY: Borders (P) slipped and fell on the icy steps of the house in which Roseberry (D) was landlord, while visiting as a social guest.

RULE OF LAW

Landlords are liable for defective conditions existing at the time of leasing to a tenant only in regard to: (1) undisclosed dangerous conditions known to lessor and unknown to lessee; (2) conditions dangerous to persons outside of the premises; (3) premises leased for admission of the public; (4) parts of land retained in lessor's control which lessee is entitled to use; (5) situations in which lessor contracts to repair; and/or (6) negligence by lessor in making repairs.

FACTS: Borders (P) went to premises over which Roseberry (D) was a landlord as a social guest of the tenants. While there, he slipped and fell on the front steps of the premises, injuring himself. Water had dripped from the roof on to the steps and frozen, creating the slippery condition which occasioned the fall. Though Roseberry (D) had promised to repair the roof and install guttering, no such work had been done at the time of the fall. Borders (P) filed this personal injury action against Roseberry (D), but the trial court concluded, as a matter of law, that Roseberry (D) was under no duty to anyone to make the proposed repairs or maintain the premises in a safe condition. Borders (P) appealed.

ISSUE: Is a landlord under a general duty of care to social guests of his tenants to remedy defective conditions on his land?

HOLDING AND DECISION: (Prager, J.) No. Landlords are liable for defective conditions existing at the time of leasing to a tenant in regard to: (1) undisclosed dangerous conditions known to lessor and unknown to lessee; (2) conditions dangerous to persons outside of the premises; (3) premises leased for admission of the public; (4) parts of land retained in lessor's control which lessee is entitled to use; (5) situations in which lessor contracts to repair; and/or (6) negligence by lessor in making repairs. There is no general duty, only the above-mentioned six exceptions. Exceptions 1 through 4 are clearly inapplicable. Exception 5 is also inapplicable since Roseberry's (D) mere promise to repair hardly constitutes a contract to do so. Finally, exception 6 is also inapplicable since the lessee here obviously knew of the dangerous condition of the steps—thereby neutralizing the risk for Roseberry (D). Affirmed.

ANALYSIS

This case points out the generally recognized rule and exceptions governing the duties of landlords (i.e., lessors) to their lessees and their lessees' guests. At common law, a lease was considered a sale of property for a term. For such term, the lessee assumed all risks of liability normally associated with ownership except where unusual circumstances (i.e., the six exceptions above) gave rise to a special duty for the landlord. Note, of course, that this rule is subject to challenge and revision in many jurisdictions in which statutory duties to repair and court-implied warranties of habitability have been imposed upon landlords.

Quicknotes

DUTY OF CARE A principle of negligence requiring an individual to act in such a manner as to avoid injury to a person to whom he or she owes an obligatory duty.

PERSONAL INJURY Harm to an individual's person or body.

Pagelsdorf v. Safeco Ins. Co. of America

Injured guest (P) v. Landlord (D) and his insurer (D)

Wis. Sup. Ct., 91 Wis. 2d 734, 284 N.W.2d 55 (1979)

NATURE OF CASE: Appeal from denial of damages for negligence.

FACT SUMMARY: Pagelsdorf (P), an invitee of a tenant in Mahnke's (D) building, was injured due to a structural defect in the building, the failure of a balcony railing.

RULE OF LAW

A landlord must exercise ordinary care toward his tenants and toward others on the premises with the tenants' permission.

FACTS: Pagelsdorf (P) was assisting Blattner, a tenant in Mahnke's (D) building, in moving some furniture. He was injured when a balcony railing upon which he was leaning collapsed. The railing had dry rot and should have been replaced. At trial, Pagelsdorf (P) was termed a licensee of Mahnke (D). Accordingly, the jury returned a verdict for Mahnke (D), finding that he had no knowledge that the railing was defective. Pagelsdorf (P) appealed, contending that Mahnke (D) should have been held to a higher standard of care.

ISSUE: Must a landlord exercise ordinary care toward his tenants and toward others on the premises with the tenants' permission?

HOLDING AND DECISION: (Callow, J.) Yes. Traditionally a landlord, with certain exceptions, has been held not liable for injuries to his tenants and their visitors resulting from defects in the premises. However, this rule is grounded in outdated concepts of a lease as a property conveyance. The modern lease is recognized as a contract for land and services. Thus, an implied warranty of habitability in residential leases has been found in many modern jurisdictions, including Wisconsin. Using the same logic, the ancient cloak of immunity enjoyed by landlords toward their tenants and visitors must be abolished. A landlord must now exercise reasonable ordinary care toward both his tenants and their guests, or be liable for the consequences. Reversed and remanded.

ANALYSIS

As mentioned in the principal case, the traditional landlord's "cloak of immunity" was riddled with exceptions. One such exception is described in § 379 of the Restatement (Second) of Torts: "A lessor of land who transfers its possession in a condition which he realizes or should realize will involve unreasonable risk of physical harm to others outside of the land, is subject to the same liability for physical harm subsequently caused to them by the condition as though he had remained in possession." A similar provision, contained in § 358, made the landlord liable for injuries to tenants in certain situations.

Quicknotes

IMPLIED WARRANTY OF HABITABILITY A warranty implied by a landlord that the premises are suitable, and will remain suitable, for habitation.

LEASE An agreement or contract that creates a relationship between a landlord and tenant (real property) or lessor and lessee (real or personal property).

NEGLIGENCE Conduct falling below the standard of care that a reasonable person would demonstrate under similar conditions.

ORDINARY CARE The degree of care exercised by a reasonable person when conducting everyday activities or under similar circumstances; synonymous with due care.

Kline v. 1500 Massachusetts Ave. Apartment Corp.

Assault victim (P) v. Lessor (D)

439 F.2d 477 (D.C. Cir. 1970)

NATURE OF CASE: Action for personal injuries.

FACT SUMMARY: Kline (P) was assaulted in a common area of her apartment building, owned by Apt. Corp. (D).

RULE OF LAW

A landlord is under a duty to take precautions to protect tenants from foreseeable criminal acts committed by third parties.

FACTS: Sarah Kline (P) was a tenant of Apt. Corp. (D) residing in a 585-unit combination office-apartment building at 1500 Massachusetts Ave. in Washington, D.C. At approximately 10:15 p.m. one evening, she was criminally assaulted and robbed in the common hallway of the complex. Though the building had been the scene of several such crimes in the past, Apt. Corp. (D) had discontinued the posting of a doorman and had not installed any electronic security devices in the building. Alleging that this failure breached a duty to her, Kline (P) filed this personal injury action against Apt. Corp. (D). The district court dismissed her complaint and this appeal followed on the question of whether an urban landlord owes any such duty to his tenant.

ISSUE: Is a landlord under a duty to take precautions to protect tenants from foreseeable criminal acts committed by third parties?

HOLDING AND DECISION: (Wilkey, J.) Yes. A landlord is under a duty to take precautions to protect tenants from foreseeable criminal acts committed by third parties. A landlord must take reasonable care to minimize the predictable risk of crime to his tenants where: (1) he has notice of repeated crimes in the past; (2) he has notice that these crimes occurred in "common areas" retained in his control; (3) he has every reason to expect reoccurrence of such crimes; and (4) he has the exclusive power to take preventive action. Though he is not an insurer of his tenants, a landlord is the only one who is in a position to make the building, as a whole, safe. Though he is not a policeman, he is the only one who can take protective measures in hallways, garages, etc., that policemen cannot be expected to patrol. Finally, though the exact measures necessary will vary from building to building, it is fair to say here that Apt. Corp. (D) should be held to a duty to provide roughly the same protection today as it promised Kline (D), by contract, in 1959 when she moved in. Reversed and remanded.

ANALYSIS

Though this case points up the decidedly minority rule, it does reflect an increasing judicial sensitivity to the rights of crime victims. Note that the duty imposed by the courts is analogous to that which an innkeeper is held to owe to his patrons (as well as third parties in dram-shop act jurisdictions), as a result of the innkeeper's control of his premises. Similar duties are imposed upon common carriers, hospitals, landowners regarding invitees and other businessmen regarding the (invitee) patrons. Note, of course, that the question of what precautions are necessary is a difficult question of fact, to be resolved in each case by the trier of fact.

Quicknotes

COMMON CARRIER An entity whose business is the transport of persons or property.

DRAM SHOP ACT Law that imposes liability upon the seller of alcoholic beverages for injuries to a third party resulting from the intoxication of the buyer.

DUTY TO PROTECT/AID A moral duty and not one imposed by law; no liability attaches to those persons who fail to undertake a rescue or otherwise aid a person in need absent a special relationship between them.

FORESEEABILITY A reasonable expectation that an act or omission would result in injury.

PERSONAL INJURY Harm to an individual's person or body.

CHAPTER 10

Damages

Quick Reference Rules of Law

Anderson v. Sears, Roebuck & Co.

Burn victim's guardian (P) v. Heater manufacturer (D)

377 F. Supp. 136 (E.D. La. 1974)

NATURE OF CASE: Motion for remittitur in action for personal injuries.

FACT SUMMARY: A small child was severely burned in a fire caused by a heater which had been defectively manufactured by Sears (D).

RULE OF LAW

In determining whether a damage award is excessive in a personal injury case, the court must individually examine each of the five cardinal elements of damages: (1) past physical and mental pain; (2) future physical and mental pain; (3) future medical expenses; (4) loss of earning capacity; and (5) permanent disability and disfigurement.

FACTS: Anderson (P) filed this action on behalf of Helen Britain, a young child, who was severely burned in a fire that destroyed her home. The blaze was ignited by a defective heater that had been manufactured by Sears, Roebuck & Co. (Sears) (D). At trial it was proved, inter alia, that Helen Britain suffered burns to over 40 percent of her body, causing extreme scarring, the adhesion of her fingers, and a permanent bend in her elbow, that she had had and would for the rest of her life require several operations of enormous cost, that her future earning capacity would be severely limited, and that she would be permanently disfigured. The jury returned a $2,000,000 judgment. Sears (D) thereupon moved for remittitur (lowering of the award as legally excessive).

ISSUE: Should a motion for remittitur (i.e., lowering of a damage award as legally excessive) be granted on the mere ground that the aggregate award is enormous?

HOLDING AND DECISION: (Cassibry, J.) No. In determining whether a damage award is excessive in a personal injury case, the court must individually examine each of the five cardinal elements of damages: (1) past physical and mental pain (here arising from the grotesque and deforming pain, fever, vomiting, infection, etc., associated with such injuries); (2) future physical and mental pain (here, arising from the future operations that will be necessary to restore any semblance of normalcy to Helen Britain's life); (3) future medical expenses (here, arising from 27 projected operations, psychiatric counseling, etc.); (4) loss of earning capacity (here, arising from the probability that Helen will never be self-supporting); and (5) permanent disability and disfigurement (including loss of speech, hair, skin, and use of legs and fingers). Viewed in such a context, the award was not legally excessive. Motion denied.

ANALYSIS

This case catalogues the major personal injury damage elements. While some elements are easily computed, most require complex economic calculations involving inflation, discounting future losses, etc. Note that large awards are regularly reported in various legal journals so as to permit comparisons by attorneys in similar cases. Indeed, services are available which inform attorneys of the going rate for arms, legs, etc., within a jurisdiction. Note also that "remittitur" is the motion by which a defendant may have a jury award reduced. Though it is permitted in many jurisdictions, "additur" (adding to insufficient award) is considered unconstitutional unless defendant consents.

Quicknotes

INTER ALIA Among other things.

REMITTITUR The authority of the court to reduce the amount of damages awarded by the jury.

Richardson v. Chapman

Injured (P) v. Driver (D)

Ill. Sup. Ct., 175 Ill. 2d 98, 676 N.E.2d 621 (1997)

NATURE OF CASE: Suit for damages in a personal injury suit.

FACT SUMMARY: Chapman (D) challenged the award of damages for injuries sustained by Richardson (P) when Chapman (D) drove a semi-trailer into Richardson's (P) car while it was stopped at a traffic light.

RULE OF LAW

An award of damages may be deemed excessive if it exceeds the range of fair and reasonable compensation, is the result of passion or prejudice, or is so large that it shocks the conscience.

FACTS: Richardson (P) was driving a car in which McGregor (P) was a passenger when the car was hit from behind by a semi-trailer driven by Chapman (D). The trial judge directed a verdict in favor of Richardson (P) and against Chapman (D) and Chapman's employer on the issue of liability. The jury returned verdicts in favor of Richardson (P) and McGregor (P) in the respective amounts of $22,358,814 and $102,215. The defendants challenged these verdicts stating that Richardson's (P) expert witness used an incorrect calculation concerning the present value of Richardson's (P) future economic losses and that the award of damages was excessive.

ISSUE: May an award of damages be deemed excessive if it exceeds the range of fair and reasonable compensation, is the result of passion or prejudice, or is so large that it shocks the conscience?

HOLDING AND DECISION: (Miller, J.) Yes. An award of damages may be deemed excessive if it exceeds the range of fair and reasonable compensation, is the result of passion or prejudice, or is so large that it shocks the conscience. Richardson (P) argued that the larger damages award was attributable to the jury's decision to award her expenses that were likely to occur in the future but were not specifically included in the expert's calculations. While the trier of fact enjoys some leeway in awarding medical costs that are likely to arise in the future but are not specifically itemized in the testimony, here the award was $1.5 million more than the higher of the two figures presented at trial. Such a difference cannot be attributable simple to miscellaneous costs. Thus it is proper for the court by remittitur to reduce by $1 million that differential. The remainder of the damages award is not excessive as claimed by Chapman (D). The issue of damages is a question for the trier of fact. Such an award of damages is excessive if it falls outside the range of fair and reasonable compensation or results from passion or prejudice, or is so large that it shocks the conscience. When reviewing the amount of compensatory damages award for a nonfatal injury, the court may consider the permanency of the plaintiff's condition, the possibility of future deterioration, the extent of the medical expenses, and the restrictions imposed on the plaintiff by the injuries. Richardson (P) suffered devastating injuries as a result of the accident and thus it cannot be found that the damages award shocks the conscience or lacks evidentiary support. Affirmed in part, reversed in part and vacated in part.

CONCURRENCE AND DISSENT: (McMorrow, J.) The majority erred by reducing the plaintiffs' jury awards. The evidence showed that Richardson's (P) award of $1.5 million for present cash value of future medical expenses was based on a minimum estimate of her expected medical-care needs. Reducing that portion of her award by two-thirds of the amount the jury found reasonable is an improper, arbitrary invasion of the jury's function. Furthermore, the reduction of the other plaintiff's award for pain and suffering, from $100,000 to $50,000, suffers the same fundamental flaw. On this second award, too, the majority has merely substituted its own subjective assessment of the evidence for that of the jury.

ANALYSIS

In personal injury cases such as this, a plaintiff may be compensated for both present and future medical expenses. Present medical expenses are easily ascertainable by introducing into evidence bills reflecting services rendered or testimony. Future medical expenses, however, must be demonstrated through expert testimony of the predicted costs. When the injury results in the plaintiff being permanently removed from the workplace, she may also recover for loss or impairment of future earning capacity. This requires expert testimony in order to establish what the plaintiff would have earned in her lifetime had she not sustained the injuries.

Quicknotes

COMPENSATORY DAMAGES Measure of damages necessary to compensate victim for actual injuries suffered.

DIRECTED VERDICT A verdict ordered by the court in a jury trial.

Continued on next page.

PERSONAL INJURY Harm to an individual's person or body.

REMITTITUR The authority of the court to reduce the amount of damages awarded by the jury.

Montgomery Ward & Co., Inc. v. Anderson

Retail store (D) v. Customer (P)

Ark. Sup. Ct., 334 Ark. 561, 976 S.W.2d 382 (1998)

NATURE OF CASE: Personal injury suit seeking damages for medical expenses.

FACT SUMMARY: After Anderson (P) fell in its Little Rock store, Montgomery Ward (D) sought to exclude evidence of her total medical expenses, and it tried to admit evidence of a negotiated discount that Anderson (P) obtained from the hospital.

RULE OF LAW

Gratuitous or discounted medical services are a collateral source and are not to be considered in assessing the damages owed by a tortfeasor to a plaintiff in a personal injury suit.

FACTS: Anderson (P) was injured when she fell in Montgomery Ward's (D) Little Rock store. Montgomery Ward (D) sent her to the hospital to be treated. Anderson (P) underwent surgical and other medical procedures incurring expenses of approximately $25,000. Montgomery Ward (D) moved in limine to prohibit Anderson (P) from introducing the total amount billed by the hospital as proof of her medical expenses and asked that her evidence be limited to actual expenses for which she was responsible to pay. Anderson's (P) attorney had agreed with the hospital that her expenses would be discounted 50 percent. Anderson (P) argued that the collateral source rule prohibited Montgomery Ward (D) from introducing evidence of the discount. The trial court denied the motion in limine, ruled that the discount was a collateral source and allowed evidence to be introduced of the total amount of expenses. Montgomery Ward (D) appealed from the ruling and the denial of its motion for a new trial.

ISSUE: Are gratuitous or discounted medical services a collateral source, not to be considered in assessing the damages owed by a tortfeasor to a plaintiff in a personal injury suit?

HOLDING AND DECISION: (Newbern, J.) Yes. Gratuitous or discounted medical services are a collateral source and are not to be considered in assessing the damages owed by a tortfeasor to a plaintiff in a personal injury suit. The collateral source rule applies unless evidence of the benefits from the collateral source is relevant for a purpose other than mitigation of damages. Here the issue is whether the forgiveness of a debt for medical services is a collateral source to be protected by the rule. The collateral source rule requires the trial court to exclude evidence of payments received by an injured party from sources collateral to the tortfeasor. Such recoveries are not to inure to the benefit of the wrongdoer, even if they result in multiple recoveries. There are four circumstances under which the rule does not apply: (1) to rebut testimony of the plaintiff that he returned to work prematurely or did not receive additional medical care because of financial need; (2) the plaintiff's condition was attributable to some other cause; (3) for impeachment purposes of plaintiff's testimony that he paid the medical expenses himself; or (4) to show plaintiff continued to work if he claimed to be out of work. None of the exceptions apply here. Both the Restatement (Second) of Torts § 920A and case law have also held that gratuitous medical services fall under the collateral source rule. Affirmed.

ANALYSIS

The Restatement (Second) of Torts § 920A provides that payments or benefits received by an injured party from a collateral source are not credited against the tortfeasor's liability, although they cover all or a part of the harm for which the tortfeasor is liable. The comments also provide that plaintiff is allowed to keep any benefits received. Moreover, if the plaintiff receives gratuities of cash or services those sources are not to be deducted from the tortfeasor's liability, since the tortfeasor must compensate the injured party for the total harm sustained, not just his or her net loss.

Quicknotes

COLLATERAL SOURCE RULE The doctrine that compensation given to an injured party from a third party should not be considered in assessing the damages to be paid by the party who inflicted the injury.

MOTION IN LIMINE Motion by one party brought prior to trial to exclude the potential introduction of highly prejudicial evidence.

PERSONAL INJURY Harm to an individual's person or body.

Cheatham v. Pohle

Ex-wife (P) v. Ex-husband (D)

Ind. Sup. Ct., 789 N.E.2d 467 (2003)

NATURE OF CASE: Appeal from a punitive-damages award in a suit for invasion of privacy and intentional infliction of emotional distress.

FACT SUMMARY: After the parties divorced, the ex-husband publicly displayed copies of nude photos of his former wife, as well as photos of the couple performing a consensual sexual act. A jury awarded the ex-wife punitive damages, but Indiana's punitive-damages statute required 75 percent of her punitive-damages award to be deposited into a state fund for public benefit.

RULE OF LAW

The Takings Clauses of the federal and Indiana Constitutions do not prohibit the Indiana state legislature from requiring 75 percent of punitive-damages awards to be deposited into state-operated funds for public benefit.

FACTS: Doris Cheatham (P) and Michael Pohle (D) divorced. Four years later, Pohle (D) distributed at least 60 copies of nude photos of Cheatham (P), as well as photos of Cheatham (P) and Pohle (D) performing a consensual sexual act. The recipients of the copies of the photos were all in the small Indiana community where both Cheatham (P) and Pohle (D) still lived and worked. Cheatham (P) sued Pohle (D) for invasion of privacy and intentional infliction of emotional distress. The jury agreed with Cheatham (P), awarding her $100,000 in compensatory damages and $100,000 in punitive damages. Cheatham (P) based an appeal on her punitive-damages award, arguing that Indiana's punitive-damages statutory scheme reduced the punitive-damages award she actually collected by violating the Takings Clauses of the federal and Indiana Constitutions. Indiana's punitive-damages statutes provided that a recipient of a punitive-damages award shall actually collect only 25 percent of such an award; under the statute, the remaining 75 percent of the award went to Indiana's Violent Crimes Victims Compensation Fund.

ISSUE: Do the Takings Clauses of the federal and Indiana Constitutions prohibit the Indiana state legislature from requiring 75 percent of punitive-damages awards to be deposited into state-operated funds for public benefit?

HOLDING AND DECISION: (Boehm, J.) No. The Takings Clauses of the federal and Indiana Constitutions do not prohibit the Indiana state legislature from requiring 75 percent of punitive-damages awards to be deposited into state-operated funds for public benefit. Punitive damages are quasi-criminal awards and have no basis in traditional compensatory notions of making the plaintiff whole or otherwise valuing the plaintiff's injuries. There is therefore no right to punitive damages because such awards do nothing to compensate an injured party. Based in the common law as they are, punitive damages are completely subject to the legislative will; under the federal Constitution, no rights vest in anyone in any common-law rule. Legislatures thus may abolish punitive damages altogether or, as in Indiana, they may impose an intermediate approach to punitive damages, punishing the defendant with a punitive-damages award but limiting a plaintiff's recovery under the award. Because any interest a plaintiff holds in a punitive-damages award derives entirely from state law, it also follows that the plaintiff has no property interest in a punitive-damages award, which in turn means that no property of Cheatham's (P) is taken and deposited into Indiana's Violent Crimes Victims Compensation Fund. It is of no consequence that a punitive-damages award must be supported by a compensatory award: requiring a basis in an award to which plaintiffs do have a right does not change the nature of any subsequent award of punitive damages. Affirmed.

ANALYSIS

Cheatham was a 3-2 decision, a fact that puts the confidence of Justice Boehm's discussion in the majority opinion in perspective. The casebook excerpt does not address the disturbing, more general question of whether requiring deposit of part of a money judgment does constitute a taking of "property." Justice Dickson, writing in dissent, argued that such a requirement is a taking of property because, regardless of the quasi-criminal nature of punitive damages, "[a] judgment for money is property," 789 N.E.2d at 477 (quoting *Wilson v. Berkshire*, 126 Ind. 497, 506, 25 N.E. 131, 134 (1890)), and because "[i]t is not within the power of a legislature to take away rights [that] [*sic*] have been once vested by a judgment." *Id.* at 478 (quoting *McCullough v. Virginia*, 172 U.S. 102, 123–124 (1898)). Defendants still would be punished under Justice Dickson's analysis. The only difference would be that plaintiffs would get to keep all of the punitive damages that they are awarded as, Justice Dickson argued, the federal and Indiana Constitutions require.

Quicknotes

COMPENSATORY DAMAGES Measure of damages necessary to compensate victim for actual injuries suffered.

State Farm Mutual Automobile Ins. Co. v. Campbell

Insurer (D) v. Insured (P)

538 U.S. 408 (2003)

NATURE OF CASE: Certiorari review of damages awarded in a bad faith, fraud, and intentional infliction of emotional distress action.

FACT SUMMARY: Campbell (P) sued State Farm Mutual Automobile Insurance Co. (State Farm) (D), his automobile insurer, for bad faith, fraud, and intentional infliction of emotional distress when State Farm (D) refused to settle a claim brought against Campbell (P) by Ospital's estate and by Slusher.

RULE OF LAW

In determining the validity of a punitive damages award, consideration is given to the degree of reprehensibility of the defendant's misconduct, the disparity between the actual or potential harm suffered by the plaintiff and the punitive damages award, and the difference between the punitive damages award by the jury and the civil penalties authorized or imposed in comparable cases.

FACTS: Campbell (P) caused a collision that killed Ospital and left Slusher permanently disabled. Ospital's estate and Slusher sued Campbell (P) for wrongful death and in tort. Campbell's (P) insurance company, State Farm Mutual Automobile Insurance Co. (State Farm) (D) refused to settle with Ospital and Slusher even though Ospital and Slusher agreed to settle for the policy limit of $25,000 each. State Farm (D) assured Campbell (P) that State Farm (D) would represent Campbell's (P) interests, that Campbell's (P) assets were safe, and that Campbell (P) did not need to procure separate counsel. A jury found Campbell (P) to be at fault and awarded $185,849 to Ospital and Slusher. Initially, State Farm (D) refused to cover the $135,849 in excess liability and refused to post a bond so Campbell (P) could appeal. State Farm (D) told Campbell (P) that he may as well put a "For Sale" sign on his house. Campbell (P) obtained his own attorney, filed his appeal and, in the meantime, agreed to let Slusher and Ospital's attorney represent him (P) in a case against State Farm (D) for bad faith, fraud, and intentional infliction of emotional distress. In exchange, Slusher and Ospital agreed not to seek satisfaction from Campbell (P), but would play a central role in the bad faith action, including receiving 90 percent of any verdict against State Farm (D). The appeals court denied Campbell's (P) appeal in the wrongful death and tort actions and State Farm (D) paid the entire judgment, including the amounts in excess of the policy limits. Despite State Farm's (D) payment, Campbell (P) filed suit against State Farm (D) alleging bad faith, fraud, and intentional infliction of emotional distress. The trial court found in favor of Campbell (P) and awarded him $2.6 million in compensatory damages and $145 million in punitive damages. The award was subsequently reduced to $1 million and $25 million, respectively. The appeals court affirmed the $1 million and reinstated the $145 million in punitive damages. The United States Supreme Court granted certiorari.

ISSUE: Is an award of $145 million in punitive damages, where full compensatory damages are $1 million, excessive and in violation of the Due Process Clause?

HOLDING AND DECISION: (Kennedy, J.) Yes. An award of $145 million in punitive damages, where full compensatory damages are $1 million, is excessive and in violation of the Due Process Clause because the reprehensibility of State Farm's (D) misconduct could have been punished in a more modest way and still have satisfied state objectives. The disparity between the actual or potential harm suffered by Campbell (P) and the punitive damages awarded was significant, and the difference between the punitive damages award by the jury and the civil penalties authorized or imposed in comparable cases was great. Although states have discretion over the amount of punitive damages allowed, there are constitutional limitations on these awards. The imposition of grossly excessive or arbitrary punishments on a tortfeasor is prohibited because of fundamental notions of fairness. Moreover, because defendants subjected to punitive damages in civil cases do not have the same protections applicable in criminal proceedings, such awards pose an acute danger of arbitrary deprivation of property. In the present case, it was erroneous for the $145 million to be reinstated. Although State Farm's (D) handling of the claims against Campbell (P) was reprehensible, in that they would probably get a judgment over the policy limits, but still went to trial and then told Campbell (D) to sell his house, a more modest punishment for these actions could have satisfied the state's legitimate objectives. Instead, this case was used to expose State Farm's (D) perceived nationwide deficiencies, and a state does not have a legitimate concern in imposing punitive damages to punish a defendant for unlawful acts committed outside the state's jurisdiction. A state cannot punish a defendant for conduct that may have been lawful where it occurred. Lawful out-of-state conduct may be probative when it demonstrates the deliberateness and culpability of the defendant's action in the state where it is tortuous, but that conduct must have a nexus to the specific harm suffered by the plaintiff. More-

Continued on next page.

over, the courts erred in awarding punitive damages to punish and deter conduct that bore no relation to Campbell's (P) harm. Due process does not permit courts to adjudicate the merits of other parties' hypothetical claims against a defendant. Furthermore, the disparity between the actual or potential harm suffered by Campbell (P) and the punitive damages award is much too large to be valid. Few awards exceeding a single-digit ratio between punitive and compensatory damages will satisfy due process. Usually an award of no more than four times the amount of compensatory damages is the maximum. The ratio in the present case is 145 to 1. The measure of punishment in this case was neither reasonable nor proportionate to the amount of harm to Campbell (P) and to the general damages recovered. The harm Campbell (P) suffered was minor economic damage and not physical, and the excess verdict was paid before the complaint was filed. Lastly, the disparity between the punitive damages award and the civil penalties authorized or imposed in comparable cases is great. The civil sanction is a $10,000 fine for an act of fraud. Reversed and remanded.

ANALYSIS

There is much analysis in legal literature concerning the theoretical basis and practical operation of punitive damages in tort cases.

Quicknotes

BAD FAITH Conduct that is intentionally misleading or deceptive.

DUE PROCESS CLAUSE Clauses, found in the Fifth and Fourteenth Amendments to the United States Constitution, providing that no person shall be deprived of "life, liberty, or property, without due process of law."

FRAUD A false representation of facts with the intent that another will rely on the misrepresentation to his detriment.

INTENTIONAL INFLICTION OF EMOTIONAL DISTRESS Intentional and extreme behavior on the part of the wrongdoer with the intent to cause the victim to suffer from severe emotional distress, or behavior performed with reckless indifference, resulting in the victim's suffering from severe emotional distress.

PUNITIVE DAMAGES Damages exceeding the actual injury suffered for the purposes of punishment, deterrence and comfort to plaintiff.

CHAPTER 11

Wrongful Death and Survival

Quick Reference Rules of Law

PAGE

1. *Moragne v. States Marine Lines, Inc.* Although Congress has not enacted a specific remedy for wrongful death in admiralty, an action for wrongful death does lie under maritime common law for death caused by violation of maritime duties. *168*

2. *Selders v. Armentrout.* The measure of damages recoverable by a parent for the wrongful death of a minor child includes the loss of society, comfort and companionship of the child, as well as any pecuniary loss. *169*

3. *Murphy v. Martin Oil Co.* When an injury caused by tortious conduct results in death, survivors of the decedent can recover from the tortfeasor both under the Illinois Wrongful Death Statute for the decedent's death and under the State Survival Statute for any damages suffered by the decedent during the interval between his injury and death. *170*

Moragne v. States Marine Lines, Inc.

Longshoreman's widow (P) v. Vessel's owner (D)

398 U.S. 375 (1970)

NATURE OF CASE: Appeal from denial of a wrongful death action.

FACT SUMMARY: After Edward Moragne, a longshoreman, was killed aboard a vessel in navigable waters, his widow (P) brought an action against States Marine Lines, Inc. (D), owner of the vessel, to recover damages for wrongful death.

RULE OF LAW

Although Congress has not enacted a specific remedy for wrongful death in admiralty, an action for wrongful death does lie under maritime common law for death caused by violation of maritime duties.

FACTS: Edward Moragne, a longshoreman, was killed in navigable waters while working aboard the vessel Palmetto State. Thereafter, Moragne's widow (P) brought an action against the States Marine Lines, Inc. (D), owner of the Palmetto State. However, the state court held that maritime law (applicable because Edward's death occurred in navigable waters) did not afford a cause of action for wrongful death. Thereupon, Moragne's widow (P) appealed.

ISSUE: Is there a cause of action for wrongful death under general maritime law?

HOLDING AND DECISION: (Harlan, J.) Yes. Although Congress has not enacted a specific remedy for wrongful death in admiralty, an action for wrongful death does lie under maritime common law for death caused by violation of maritime duties. Although *The Harrisburg*, 119 U.S. 199 (1886), held that there is no cause of action for wrongful death under U.S. maritime law, today *The Harrisburg* must be overruled. The fact that every state in the United States has enacted a wrongful death statute makes it clear that there is a general policy today in favor of allowing wrongful death actions. This policy is based upon the reasoning that "where existing law imposes a primary duty, violations of which are compensable if they cause injury, nothing in ordinary notions of justice suggests that a violation would be nonactionable simply because it was serious enough to cause death." Of course, this reasoning is equally applicable to maritime law. As such, whenever a violation of maritime duties causes a death, the appropriate persons, a category to be defined through future litigation, should be allowed to bring an action for wrongful death. Reversed and remanded.

ANALYSIS

This case illustrates the general rejection of the "felony-murder doctrine." Under this English doctrine (generally adopted by American courts before this century), there was no civil recovery for an act that resulted in death—that is, for an act that constituted both a tort and a felony. This doctrine was founded upon the fact that the punishment for a felony was death of the felon and forfeiture of his property to the Crown. As such, nothing remained of the felon or his property on which to base a civil action. As noted in this case, however, every state in the United States now has a wrongful death act which allows for civil recovery.

Quicknotes

ADMIRALTY That area of law pertaining to navigable waters.

MARITIME LAW That area of law pertaining to navigable waters.

WRONGFUL DEATH An action brought by the beneficiaries of a deceased person, claiming that the deceased's death was the result of wrongful conduct by the defendant.

Selders v. Armentrout

Accident victim's parents (P) v. Other driver (D)

Neb. Sup. Ct., 190 Neb. 275, 207 N.W.2d 686 (1973)

NATURE OF CASE: Appeal from damages award for a wrongful death.

FACT SUMMARY: When the Selderses (P) brought an action to recover damages for the wrongful deaths of three of their minor children, a jury only awarded them medical and funeral expenses as damages.

RULE OF LAW

The measure of damages recoverable by a parent for the wrongful death of a minor child includes the loss of society, comfort and companionship of the child, as well as any pecuniary loss.

FACTS: Earl and Ila Selders ("the Selderses") (P) were involved in an automobile accident with the Armentrouts (D). As a result of this accident, three of the Selderses' (P) minor children were killed. The Selderses (P) brought an action against Charles and William Armentrouts ("the Armentrouts") (D) to recover damages for the wrongful deaths of their minor children. Before the jury deliberated on a verdict, the court instructed it that, "except for medical and funeral expenses, the damages should be the monetary value of the contributions and services which the parents could reasonably have expected to receive from the children less the reasonable cost to the parents of supporting the children." The jury found the Armentrouts (D) negligent and returned a verdict for the Selderses (P) in the amount of the medical and funeral expenses of the three children. The Selderses (P) brought this appeal to recover further damages.

ISSUE: Does the measure of damages recoverable by a parent for the wrongful death of a minor child include the loss of society, comfort and companionship of the child, as well as any pecuniary loss?

HOLDING AND DECISION: (McCown, J.) Yes. The measure of damages recoverable by a parent for the wrongful death of a minor child includes the "loss of society, comfort and companionship" of the child, as well as any pecuniary loss. Of course, to limit damages to any pecuniary loss (i.e., to the monetary value of the services which the parent could reasonably have expected to receive from the child less the reasonable cost of supporting the child) would be to "stamp almost all modern children as worthless in the eyes of the law." Since this would be grossly unfair, the Selderses (P) are entitled to recover for loss of "society, comfort and companionship" of their children. Affirmed as to liability; reversed as to damages; and remanded.

DISSENT: (White, C.J.) A jury should not be allowed to translate emotional, conjectural, and speculative sentimental values incapable of having any objective standards applied to them into an award of money.

ANALYSIS

This case illustrates a very recent trend that specifically allows compensation for the "loss of companionship" of a child wrongfully killed. The general rule, however, is still that damages are limited to any pecuniary loss. Note, though, that even those states that limit damages to "pecuniary" loss usually allow substantial damages for the loss of a child, on the theory that the child would have "eventually" made a substantial monetary contribution to his parents.

Quicknotes

LOSS OF COMPANIONSHIP An action brought based on willful interference with the marital relationship.

WRONGFUL DEATH An action brought by the beneficiaries of a deceased person, claiming that the deceased's death was the result of wrongful conduct by the defendant.

Murphy v. Martin Oil Co.

Burn victim's widow (P) v. Property owner (D)

Ill. Sup. Ct., 56 Ill. 2d 423, 308 N.E.2d 583 (1974)

NATURE OF CASE: Action under both a wrongful death statute and a survival statute.

FACT SUMMARY: After Mr. Murphy died from a fire on the Martin Oil Co.'s (D) land, his wife (P) brought an action against Martin Oil Co. (D) to recover for her husband's wrongful death and for the damages he suffered during the interval between his injury and death.

RULE OF LAW

When an injury caused by tortious conduct results in death, survivors of the decedent can recover from the tortfeasor both under the Illinois Wrongful Death Statute for the decedent's death and under the State Survival Statute for any damages suffered by the decedent during the interval between decedent's injury and death.

FACTS: Mr. Murphy died several days after he suffered injuries in a fire on the Martin Oil Co.'s (Martin Oil's) (D) premises. Thereafter, his wife (P) brought a negligence action against Martin Oil (D) in two counts. First, she claimed damages to herself (as a result of her husband's death) under the Illinois Wrongful Death Statute. Second, she claimed damages under the State Survival Statute for Mr. Murphy's mental and physical suffering before his death, for his loss of wages following the injury, and for his loss of clothing worn at the time of the injury. The state court dismissed the wife's (P) claim under the Survival Statute on the ground that Illinois law makes wrongful death recovery the exclusive remedy in such situations. This appeal followed.

ISSUE: Is recovery for wrongful death the exclusive remedy when death results from injuries caused by tortious conduct?

HOLDING AND DECISION: (Ward, J.) No. When an injury caused by tortious conduct results in death, survivors of the decedent can recover from the tortfeasor both under the Illinois Wrongful Death Statute for the decedent's death and under the State Survival Statute for damages suffered by the decedent during the interval between decedent's injury and death. Of course, under the older view, an action for personal injury did not survive death under the Survival Statute if death resulted from the tortious conduct that caused the injury (i.e., wrongful death recovery was the exclusive remedy in such cases). However, such limitation was unfair since it denied full liability for wrongs and full recovery for victims. As such, Murphy's wife (P) is entitled to recovery under the Wrongful Death and Survival Statutes. Affirmed in part and reversed in part.

ANALYSIS

This case illustrates the general rule (in states which have both of the discussed statutes) that recovery may be had under both Wrongful Death and Survival Statutes concurrently. Note that most jurisdictions today have Survival Statutes covering actions for injury to tangible property and for personal injury actions. Very few states, however, provide for the survival of intangible interests in personality (e.g., defamation actions).

Quicknotes

SURVIVAL STATUTE Law providing a cause of action to a deceased person's estate for certain unlawful acts committed upon the deceased person up until the time of his death.

WRONGFUL DEATH An action brought by the beneficiaries of a deceased person, claiming that the deceased's death was the result of wrongful conduct by the defendant.

CHAPTER 12

Defenses

Quick Reference Rules of Law

Butterfield v. Forrester

Injured horseback rider (P) v. Road blocker (D)

K.B., 11 East 59, 103 Eng. Rep. 926 (1809)

NATURE OF CASE: Action to recover damages for personal injury.

FACT SUMMARY: While riding very fast, Butterfield (P) ran into an obstruction Forrester (D) had put in the road and was injured.

RULE OF LAW

A plaintiff will not be able to recover where his lack of due care contributed to the occurrence of the accident.

FACTS: Forrester (D) was making some repairs on his house and put up a pole across a road. However, passage was still possible. Butterfield (P) was riding very fast on the road, did not see the pole, and ran into it. He fell with his horse and was injured. There was no evidence of his being intoxicated. There was evidence that it was possible to see 100 yards away at the time of the accident and that, had Butterfield (P) not been riding so fast, he might have seen and avoided the pole.

ISSUE: Will a plaintiff be able to recover where his lack of due care contributed to the occurrence of the accident?

HOLDING: (Lord Bayley, J. [who also tried the case]) By riding his horse as fast as possible, Butterfield (P) failed to exercise ordinary care. He therefore was entirely responsible for the accident.

HOLDING: (Lord Ellenborough, C.J.) One person's fault does not relieve another from the duty to exercise ordinary care himself. Butterfield (P) thus could have prevailed here only by showing that Forrester (D) wrongly obstructed the road, and that Butterfield (P) himself exercised ordinary care to avoid the obstruction.

DECISION: (Per curiam) Rule refused.

ANALYSIS

This case states the defense of contributory negligence. The following lines of reasoning have been used to support the theory: Plaintiff is denied recovery to punish him for his own misconduct; plaintiff must come into court with "clean hands"; the defense is a deterrent to plaintiffs' negligence; plaintiff's negligence is a superseding cause which makes the defendant's negligence no longer the proximate cause. The same standard is used as to determine negligence: the average reasonable person.

Quicknotes

CONTRIBUTORY NEGLIGENCE Behavior on the part of an injured plaintiff falling below the standard of ordinary care that contributes to the defendant's negligence, resulting in the plaintiff's injury.

NEGLIGENCE Conduct falling below the standard of care that a reasonable person would demonstrate under similar conditions.

REASONABLE PERSON STANDARD The standard of care exercised by a hypothetical person who possesses the intelligence, education, knowledge, attention, and judgment required by society of its members when governing behavior; the standard applies to a person's judgment when determining breach of a duty under the theory of negligence.

Davies v. Mann

Donkey's owner (P) v. Wagon driver (D)

Ex., 10 M. & W. 546, 152 Eng. Rep. 588 (1842)

NATURE OF CASE: Action to recover damages for negligence.

FACT SUMMARY: Davies (P) left his donkey on a public highway, and Mann (D) drove into it, killing it.

RULE OF LAW

Where a plaintiff's negligence has put him in a dangerous position and defendant discovers plaintiff's danger and fails to use due care to avoid injuring plaintiff, plaintiff's negligence will not bar his recovery. This is the last clear chance doctrine

FACTS: Davies (P) fettered the forefeet of his ass and turned it onto a public highway. It was grazing off the side of the road when Mann's (D) wagon, which was coming at a fast pace, knocked it down and killed it.

ISSUE: Where plaintiff's negligence has put him in a dangerous position and defendant discovers plaintiff's danger and fails to use due care to avoid injuring plaintiff, will plaintiff's negligence bar his recovery?

HOLDING: (Lord Abinger, C.B.) No. Where plaintiff's negligence has put him in a dangerous position and defendant discovers plaintiff's danger and fails to use due care to avoid injuring plaintiff, plaintiff's negligence will not bar his recovery. In this case, whether Davies's (P) ass was lawfully or wrongfully on the road makes no difference, since Mann (D) might, by using proper care, have avoided hitting the ass and did not. He is liable for the consequences of his negligence, even though the ass might have been there improperly.

HOLDING: (Parke, B.) Even if Davies (P) wrongfully placed the ass in the highway, Mann (D) still had a duty to drive his wagon at a pace enabling him to avoid the accident.

DECISION: Verdict for the plaintiff.

ANALYSIS

The following reasons have been given for the last clear chance doctrine: (1) If the defendant has the last clear opportunity to avoid the harm, the plaintiff's negligence is no longer a proximate cause of the resulting injury; and (2) the later negligence of the defendant involves a higher degree of fault. The assumption is that he is the more culpable because his opportunity to avoid the injury was later. Prosser feels that the real explanation for the doctrine is the dislike for the defense of contributory negligence. Prosser further states that "as an ultimate, just solution, it is obviously inadequate" since usually it merely transfers from the plaintiff to the defendant an entire loss due to the fault of both.

Quicknotes

CONTRIBUTORY NEGLIGENCE Behavior on the part of an injured plaintiff falling below the standard of ordinary care that contributes to the defendant's negligence, resulting in the plaintiff's injury.

PERSONAL INJURY Harm to an individual's person or body.

REASONABLE CARE The degree of care observed by a reasonably prudent person under similar circumstances; synonymous with due care or ordinary care.

McIntyre v. Balentine

Pickup truck driver (P) v. Tractor driver (D)

Tenn. Sup. Ct., 833 S.W.2d 52 (1992)

NATURE OF CASE: Appeal from jury verdict rejecting claim for personal injury.

FACT SUMMARY: After he and another driver were both found to have been at fault in a car accident, McIntyre's (P) claim for personal injury was rejected based on the defense of contributory negligence.

RULE OF LAW

Contributory negligence is abolished as a defense.

FACTS: McIntyre (P) was involved in an auto accident with Balentine (D). Both were intoxicated. McIntyre (P) sued for personal injury. The jury found both parties equally negligent. Based on a contributory negligence instruction, the jury returned a defense verdict. McIntyre (P) appealed.

ISSUE: Is contributory negligence abolished as a defense?

HOLDING AND DECISION: (Drowota, J.) Yes. Contributory negligence is abolished as a defense. The doctrine was originally based on the notion that a person should not benefit from his own wrongdoing. It may have arisen out of the all-or-nothing nature of issue pleading in common-law England. To vitiate its more egregious characteristics, rather artificial doctrines such as last clear chance and superseding cause have been grafted onto the contributory negligence doctrine. However, it appears that the best approach at this time would simply be to adopt a system of comparative fault. Some states have adopted "pure" comparative fault, where a plaintiff can recover even if he is 90 percent or more at fault. However, a modified comparative fault system, wherein a plaintiff can recover only if he is less than 50 percent at fault, is more consistent with a fault-based compensation system. In this case, the jury would probably not have found McIntyre (P) and Balentine (D) equally at fault if it had considered an instruction based on the rule announced here, so a new trial is necessary. Reversed in part, affirmed in part, and remanded.

ANALYSIS

Almost all states (forty-six, in fact) have jettisoned contributory negligence in favor of comparative fault. As the opinion intimates, two main forms of comparative fault exist: the form adopted here and "pure" comparative negligence. For an example of an opinion that opted for pure comparative fault, see *Li v. Yellow Cab Co.*, 13 Cal. 3d 804, 532 P.2d 1226 (1975).

Quicknotes

COMPARATIVE FAULT Doctrine whereby a plaintiff's damages are reduced by a percentage equal to that of his own causal fault so long as the plaintiff's fault is not the sole proximate cause of the injury.

CONTRIBUTORY NEGLIGENCE Behavior on the part of an injured plaintiff falling below the standard of ordinary care that contributes to the defendant's negligence, resulting in the plaintiff's injury.

MODIFIED COMPARATIVE FAULT Under modified comparative fault, the plaintiff will be barred from all recovery if her fault is as great as (or, in some jurisdictions, greater than) that of the defendant.

PERSONAL INJURY Harm to an individual's person or body.

PURE COMPARATIVE FAULT Under pure comparative fault, the plaintiff can recover as long as her fault is not the sole proximate cause of her injury.

Seigneur v. National Fitness Institute, Inc.

Customer (P) v. Fitness club (D)

Md. Ct. Sp. App., 132 Md. App 271, 752 A.2d 631 (2000)

NATURE OF CASE: Negligence action against a fitness club.

FACT SUMMARY: A fitness-club customer injured her right shoulder during her initial evaluation on the club's weight machines. She and her husband sued the club for negligence. The club moved to dismiss, arguing that she had assumed all risk for any injuries sustained at the club by signing an agreement that contained an express exculpatory clause.

RULE OF LAW

An express exculpatory clause in an agreement can excuse a defendant's negligence.

FACTS: Gerilynne Seigneur (P) signed a written agreement when she started her membership with her fitness club, National Fitness Institute, Inc. (NFI) (D). The agreement contained an express provision in which Seigneur (P) agreed to assume all risk for any injuries she might incur at NFI's (D) facilities. The provision also stated an express waiver of all claims for negligence against NFI (D). Seigneur (P) then injured her right shoulder at her initial evaluation on NFI's (D) weight machines. She and her husband sued NFI (D) for negligence—vicariously for the allegedly negligent conduct of the NFI (D) employee who conducted the evaluation, and directly for allegedly negligently hiring and training the employee. NFI (D) responded with a motion to dismiss, arguing that Seigneur (P) had assumed all risk by entering her agreement with the club, and that the club therefore was entitled to judgment against her. On NFI's motion to dismiss, which the trial court treated as a motion for summary judgment, Seigneur (P) contended that the agreement was an adhesion contract, the agreement's assumption-of-risk provision violated public policy, and the agreement was ambiguous. The trial judge entered summary judgment in favor of NFI (D). Seigneur (P) appealed.

ISSUE: Can an express exculpatory clause in an agreement excuse a defendant's negligence?

HOLDING AND DECISION: (Salmon, J.) Yes. An express exculpatory clause in an agreement can excuse a defendant's negligence. Maryland law requires an exculpatory agreement to be clear and specific in releasing a defendant from liability for his negligence; the agreement here meets that standard, and the agreement did not result from any improper purpose on the part of NFI (D), either. Further, no public policy typically prohibits an exculpatory clause that is clear and freely entered by the parties. There are, however, three exceptions: (1) when the protected party engages in intentionally, recklessly, wantonly harmful conduct, or in grossly negligent harmful conduct, (2) when the bargaining power between the parties is grossly unequal, and (3) when the public has an interest in the transaction. Here, Seigneur (P) bases her appeal on the second and third exceptions; neither ground, however, is persuasive in this case. The agreement was indeed an adhesion contract, but that fact alone does not mean that the parties were grossly unequal in bargaining power. Seigneur (P) was free to go elsewhere for the non-essential services provided by a fitness club. Nor does the transaction implicate the larger public interest. To determine public interest in this context, courts consider the totality of the circumstances, focusing on such concerns as whether the business is publicly regulated, whether the protected party provides a service of great public importance, whether the protected party actively performs the service for any person meeting set requirements or for any member of the public, whether the protected party has a distinctly greater bargaining power against his clients and confronts his public with a standard adhesion contract, and whether the purchaser's person or property becomes subject to the seller's (i.e., the protected party's) control. Under these factors, NFI's (D) exculpatory clause does not patently offend Maryland sensibilities because the club does not perform an essential public service. Affirmed.

ANALYSIS

In this intersection of tort law and contract law, the sanctity of contract prevails. As the court notes, parties generally are free to govern their own destinies by their agreements. That principle applies even when, as in *Seigneur*, the agreement permits one party to avoid potential liability in tort.

Quicknotes

ADHESION CONTRACT A contract, usually in standardized form, that is prepared by one party and offered to another, whose terms are so disproportionately in favor of the drafting party that courts tend to question the equality of bargaining power in reaching the agreement.

ASSUMPTION OF RISK DOCTRINE An affirmative defense to a negligence suit contending that the plaintiff knowingly and voluntarily subjected himself to a hazardous

Continued on next page.

condition absolving the defendant of liability for injuries incurred.

EXCULPATORY CLAUSE A clause in a contract relieving one party from liability for certain unlawful conduct.

NEGLIGENCE Conduct falling below the standard of care that a reasonable person would demonstrate under similar conditions.

SUMMARY JUDGMENT Judgment rendered by a court in response to a motion made by one of the parties, claiming that the lack of a question of material fact in respect to an issue warrants disposition of the issue without consideration by the jury.

WILLFUL AND WANTON MISCONDUCT Unlawful, intentional or reckless conduct without regard to the consequences.

Rush v. Commercial Realty Co.

Injured tenant (P) v. Landlord (D)

N.J. Sup. Ct., 7 N.J. Misc. 337, 145 A. 476 (1929)

NATURE OF CASE: Action to recover damages for personal injury.

FACT SUMMARY: While a tenant of Commercial Realty Co. (D), Rush (P) fell through the outhouse floor and was injured.

RULE OF LAW

The defense of assumption of risk requires that the plaintiff has voluntarily encountered the risk, and the risk is not assumed where the defendant has left the plaintiff no reasonable alternatives.

FACTS: Rush (P) was a tenant of Commercial Realty Co. (D). Commercial Realty Co. (D) provided an outhouse for the use of its tenants. Rush (P) went to use the outhouse and fell through a trap door in the floor, thereby sustaining injuries. Rush (P) testified that the floor was in bad condition. Commercial Realty Co. (D) appealed the denial of its motion for nonsuit and its motion for a directed verdict.

ISSUE: Does the defense of assumption of risk require that the plaintiff has voluntarily encountered the risk, and the risk is not assumed where the defendant has left the plaintiff no reasonable alternatives?

HOLDING AND DECISION: (Per curiam) Yes. The defense of assumption of risk requires that the plaintiff has voluntarily encountered the risk, and the risk is not assumed where the defendant has left the plaintiff no reasonable alternatives. If the defendant has left the plaintiff no reasonable alternatives, it will not be assumed that the plaintiff's choice to assume the risk was a voluntary one. Here, Rush (P) had no choice but to use the facilities provided by Commercial Realty Co. (D). Her use was not assumption of risk. She was not required to leave her home and go elsewhere. The jury might find that her stepping on the floor she knew was in bad repair was contributory negligence, but her use was not assumption of risk. The denial of Commercial Realty Co.'s (D) motion is affirmed.

ANALYSIS

This case represents the general rule that voluntariness cannot be assumed where no reasonable alternative exists. Likewise, those who dash in to save their property or lives or the property of others, from a peril caused by defendant's negligence, do not assume the risk. Of course, the value of plaintiff's interest may not be sufficient to warrant the risk in some situations. Then plaintiff might be charged with contributory negligence, not assumption of risk.

Quicknotes

ASSUMPTION OF RISK DOCTRINE An affirmative defense to a negligence suit by the defendant contending that the plaintiff knowingly and voluntarily subjected himself to the hazardous condition wholly absolving the defendant of liability for injuries incurred.

DIRECTED VERDICT A verdict ordered by the court in a jury trial.

PERSONAL INJURY Harm to an individual's person or body.

Teeters v. Currey

Unsterilized woman (P) v. Doctor (D)

Tenn. Sup. Ct., 518 S.W.2d 512 (1974)

NATURE OF CASE: Malpractice action.

FACT SUMMARY: Over three years after Currey (D), a physician, performed an operation to sterilize Mrs. Teeters (P), she discovered that the operation was a failure.

RULE OF LAW

The statute of limitations for a medical malpractice action for negligently performed surgery runs not from the date of the injury, but from the time that the patient discovers, or should have reasonably been expected to discover, the injury.

FACTS: On June 5, 1970, Mrs. Teeters (P) gave birth to a normal child with Dr. Currey (D) as the attending physician. At that time, because of complications, Dr. Currey (D) performed a bilateral tubal ligation to prevent future pregnancies. However, on December 6, 1972, Mrs. Teeters (P) discovered that she was again pregnant. Thereafter, on March 9, 1973, she delivered a premature child and there were severe complications. On November 15, 1973, Mrs. Teeters (P) instituted a suit against Dr. Currey (D) on the basis that the earlier tubal ligation was negligently and inadequately performed. In response, Dr. Currey (D) alleged that the one-year statute of limitations barred any action against him. After a lower court held for Currey (D), Mrs. Teeters (P) appealed.

ISSUE: Does the statute of limitations for a medical malpractice action for negligently performed surgery run not from the date of the injury, but from the time that the patient discovers, or should have reasonably been expected to discover, the injury?

HOLDING AND DECISION: (Henry, J.) Yes. The statute of limitations for a medical malpractice action for negligently performed surgery runs not from the date of the injury, but from the time that the patient discovers, or should have reasonably been expected to discover, the injury. This rule is based upon the rationale that an injured patient should not be denied recovery (and a doctor allowed to escape liability) merely because the injury is not evident for a long period of time. Here, Mrs. Teeters (P) did not discover Dr. Currey's (D) negligence and her own injury until three years after the operation. However, after discovering her injury, Mrs. Teeters (P) brought an action within the time allowed by the statute of limitations. As such, her action is not barred. Reversed and remanded.

ANALYSIS

This case illustrates the majority rule for medical malpractice actions. However, some courts still use the time-of-damage approach. Others have held that the statute of limitations begins to run when the doctor-patient relationship ends, even if the patient has not discovered the injury. Still others have limited the time-of-discovery rule to negligent surgical practices and applied the time-of-damage rule to cases of negligent diagnosis.

Quicknotes

STATUTE OF LIMITATIONS A law prescribing the period in which a legal action may be commenced.

STATUTE OF REPOSE A law prescribing the period of time in which an action can be commenced that begins to run upon the delivery of goods or the completion of performance.

Freehe v. Freehe

Husband (P) v. Wife (D)

Wash. Sup. Ct., 81 Wash. 2d 183, 500 P.2d 771 (1972)

NATURE OF CASE: Action for negligence damages.

FACT SUMMARY: Clifford Freehe (P) brought an action against his wife, Hazel Freehe (D), to recover for personal injuries caused by negligence.

RULE OF LAW

Interspousal tort immunity in personal injury cases is hereafter abandoned.

FACTS: Clifford Freehe (P) was injured by a tractor owned by Hazel Freehe (D), his wife, as her separate property. This tractor was also located on Hazel Freehe's (D) separate property farm. After his injury, Clifford Freehe (P) brought an action against Hazel Freehe (D) to recover compensation for his injuries. This action was based on Hazel Freehe's (D) negligent maintenance of the tractor and her failure to warn Clifford Freehe (P) of its unsafe condition. In response, Hazel Freehe (D) brought a motion for summary judgment on the basis of interspousal tort immunity. After the trial court granted Hazel's (D) motion, Clifford (P) brought this appeal.

ISSUE: Has the interspousal immunity in personal injury cases been abandoned?

HOLDING AND DECISION: (Neill, J.) Yes. Interspousal tort immunity in personal injury cases is hereafter abandoned, since those reasons previously advanced in support of it are no longer valid. First, husband and wife are no longer considered to be "one person" (i.e., the identity of the wife is not merged with that of the husband). Second, there is no validity to the argument that allowance of tort actions between spouses will destroy marital "peace and tranquility." "If a state of peace and tranquility exists between spouses, then the situation is such that either no action will be commenced or that the spouses . . . will allow the action to continue only so long as their personal harmony is not jeopardized." Finally, criminal and divorce laws do not provide adequate alternatives to tort actions (i.e., neither compensate for damages done nor provide any remedy for nonintentional torts). Here, therefore, Clifford (P) is entitled to maintain an action for negligence against his wife (D). Reversed and remanded.

ANALYSIS

This case illustrates the rule followed in approximately half of the states: i.e., complete abandonment of interspousal tort immunity. Furthermore, many other states have partially abandoned such immunity by creating various exceptions. For example, most states exempt from immunity any intentional tort actions. Note that a majority of the states do still retain intrafamily tort immunity in order to prevent suits between parent and child.

Quicknotes

IMMUNITY Exemption from a legal obligation.

INTERSPOUSAL IMMUNITY A common-law doctrine precluding spouses from commencing actions against one another for their torts.

SUMMARY JUDGMENT Judgment rendered by a court in response to a motion by one of the parties, claiming that the lack of a question of material fact in respect to an issue warrants disposition of the issue without consideration by the jury.

Zellmer v. Zellmer

Parents of deceased child (P) v. Stepfather of deceased stepchild (D)

Wash. Sup. Ct., 164 Wash. 2d 147, 188 P.3d 497 (2008)

NATURE OF CASE: Action for the wrongful death of a child under supervision of her stepfather.

FACT SUMMARY: While under her stepfather's (D) supervision, a three-year-old girl (D) drowned. The parents (P) sued the stepfather (D) for wrongful death. The stepfather (D) claimed that he was shielded from liability under the parental immunity doctrine because he was acting *in loco parentis.* The parents (P) claimed that parental immunity does not extend to a stepparent.

RULE OF LAW

The doctrine of parental immunity, which shields a parent from liability for negligent acts against a child, does not extend to a stepparent or anyone other than a biological or adoptive parent, even if such person is standing *in loco parentis.*

FACTS: A three-year old girl, Ashley McLellan, who lived with her mother, Mrs. Zellmer (P), and her stepfather, Mr. Zellmer (D), drowned in the family pool while under the supervision of Mr. Zellmer (D). According to Mr. Zellmer (D), he started a video for Ashley and then went downstairs to build a fire. About an hour later, he realized that Ashley was no longer in her room, saw that the sliding glass door leading to the backyard was open, and found Ashley floating in the swimming pool. He pulled Ashley out of the pool and called 911; the paramedics resuscitated Ashley, but she died two days later. Ashley's parents (P) sued for wrongful death, and Mr. Zellmer (D) brought a summary judgment motion based upon parental immunity, claiming that by providing emotional and financial support, he was standing *in loco parentis.* The trial court granted summary judgment to Mr. Zellmer (D). The court of appeals affirmed. The parents (P) appealed to the Supreme Court of Washington.

ISSUE: Does the doctrine of parental immunity, which shields a parent from liability for negligent acts against a child, extend to a stepparent or anyone other than a biological or adoptive parent, even if such person is standing *in loco parentis?*

HOLDING AND DECISION: (Madsen, J) No. The doctrine of parental immunity, which shields a parent from liability for negligent acts against a child, does not extend to a stepparent or anyone other than biological or adoptive parent, even if such person is standing *in loco parentis.* In fact, courts in several states have limited or abrogated the parental immunity doctrine altogether, and those that have not abrogated it have limited it to cases of ordinary negligence and not gross negligence or recklessness. While the court affirms the use of the parental immunity defense, it will not extend it to a stepparent. A stepparent does not gain parental rights and does not assume any obligations merely by reason of the relationship. The stepparent is held to an ordinary negligence standard. Reversed and remanded.

ANALYSIS

The doctrine of parental immunity in negligence cases does not apply to anyone other than a biological or adoptive parent. The doctrine must remain a viable defense so that parental control is not undermined and the state does not unduly interfere with child rearing. However, stepparents or other individuals standing *in loco parentis* do not have the parental immunity defense available to them. Anyone other than a biological or adoptive parent must be held to an ordinary negligence standard. A "reasonable parent" standard, which has been adopted by some states instead of the parental immunity defense, does not change anything in any meaningful way because substituting "parent" for "person" is simply semantics—the status of the actor in a negligence case is *always* relevant.

Quicknotes

IN LOCO PARENTIS Standing in the place of a parent.

REASONABLE PARENT STANDARD The standard of care exercised by a hypothetical parent who possesses the intelligence, education, knowledge, attention, and judgment required by society of its members when governing behavior; the standard applies to a person's judgment when determining breach of a duty under the theory of negligence.

Abernathy v. Sisters of St. Mary's

Patient (P) v. Hospital (D)

Mo. Sup. Ct., 446 S.W.2d 599 (1969)

NATURE OF CASE: Personal injury negligence action.

FACT SUMMARY: Abernathy (P) brought an action against the Sisters of St Mary's Hospital ("the Hospital") (D), a charitable institution, for damages for personal injuries allegedly suffered as a result of the Hospital's (D) negligence.

RULE OF LAW

The doctrine of immunity of charitable institutions from liability for torts is hereafter abolished.

FACTS: Abernathy (P) was injured in the Sisters of St. Mary's Hospital ("the Hospital") (D) when an employee of the Hospital (D) negligently failed to assist him as he moved from his bed to the bathroom. Thereafter, Abernathy (P) brought an action against the Hospital (D) to recover damages for his personal injuries. In response, the Hospital (D) moved for summary judgment on the basis it was immune from liability for torts as a charitable institution. After the lower court held for the Hospital (D) Abernathy (P) brought this appeal.

ISSUE: Has the doctrine of immunity of charitable institutions from liability for torts been abolished?

HOLDING AND DECISION: (Henley, C.J.) Yes. The doctrine of immunity of charitable institutions from liability for torts is hereafter abolished. As such, a charitable institution "is liable for its own negligence and for the negligence of its agents and employees acting within the scope of their employment." Such liability is necessary since immunity only "fosters neglect and breeds irresponsibility, while liability promotes care and caution." Furthermore, today charity is "big business" which can afford to pay for its torts. Here, therefore, the Hospital (D) is not immune from liability for its torts. Reversed and remanded for further proceedings.

ANALYSIS

This case does not illustrate the majority view. That is, most jurisdictions have not "completely abolished" charitable immunity. However, most have "partially abolished" it by creating various exceptions (e.g., many have limited immunity to "recipients of the benefits of the charity"). Note that there are two principal arguments that have been used to support charitable immunity. First, there is the theory of "implied waiver." Under this theory, "he who accepts the benefit of charity impliedly agrees he will not assert against the institution any right of recourse for wrong done him." Second, there is the "trust fund" theory. Under this theory, a charitable institution's funds are held in trust for charitable purposes and cannot be used to "pay" judgments resulting from tort claims.

Quicknotes

CHARITABLE IMMUNITY A rule absolving charities from liability for tortious activity.

Clarke v. Oregon Health Sciences University

Injured infant (by his guardian) (P) v. State hospital (D) and employees (D)

Or. Sup. Ct., 343 Or. 581, 175 P.3d 418 (2007)

NATURE OF CASE: Action for personal injury to an infant due to negligence of employees of a public hospital.

FACT SUMMARY: Employees (D) of the Oregon Health Sciences University (D), a state hospital, operated on an infant, Jordaan Clarke (P), to repair a congenital heart defect. During the surgery, Clarke (P) suffered prolonged oxygen deprivation causing him permanent brain damage. Infant (P) seeks over $17,000,000 in damages from the hospital (D) and its employees (D).

RULE OF LAW

Damage limits, coupled with the elimination of a cause of action against individual employees, are not constitutional under Article I, § 10 of the Oregon Constitution.

FACTS: Jordaan Clarke (P), an infant, had surgery at Oregon Health Sciences University (OHSU) (D) to repair a congenital heart defect. After surgery, due to the negligence of OHSU employees (D), Clarke (P) suffered prolonged oxygen deprivation causing permanent brain damage. As a result, Clarke (P) is totally disabled. His guardian (P) sought over $17 million in economic and non-economic damages from OHSU (D) and individual employees involved in the surgery (D). The employees (D) sought dismissal based upon the provision of the Oregon Tort Claims Statute (OTCA) that makes the remedy against the state exclusive. Clarke (P) challenged the constitutionality of the statute in light of the $200,000 damages cap applicable to tort actions against the state. The trial court granted judgment on the pleadings to Clarke (P) against the state for $200,000, and judgment in favor of the individual employees (D) based on the exclusive remedy provision of 30.270(1). The court of appeals affirmed as against the state (D) but reversed for the individual employees (D), finding the exclusive remedy provision in conjunction with the damages cap violated the Oregon Constitution. The parties filed cross-appeals.

ISSUE: Are damage limits, coupled with the elimination of a cause of action against individual employees (D), constitutional under Article I, § 10 of the Oregon Constitution?

HOLDING AND DECISION: (De Muniz, C.J.). No. Damage limits, coupled with the elimination of a cause of action against individual employees, are not constitutional under Article I, § 10 of the Oregon Constitution. The elimination of a cause of action against the public employees (D) violates the remedy clause of Article I, § 1, because the substituted remedy is an "emasculated" version of the remedy available at common law. The pertinent section states in part, "[J]ustice shall be administered, openly and without purchase, completely and without delay, and every man shall have remedy by due course of law for injury done him in his person, property, or reputation." A remedy in the amount of $200,000 is wholly inadequate, considering a lifetime of medical expenses that resulted from the surgery and its complications. Court of appeals affirmed, circuit court judgment reversed, and case remanded.

ANALYSIS

The Oregon Health Sciences University, an instrumentality of the state, enjoys the same degree of sovereign immunity as does the state itself. This is true of all state instrumentalities created before the state adopted tort claim legislation. The degree to which municipal corporations consent to be sued varies so much that there is no real "rule." Beginning in 1957, there have been a number of decisions abrogating municipal immunity, even for governmental functions, some abrogating it completely. More commonly, the immunity has been abrogated by legislation, rather than by case law. Generally, even those states that have waived or limited governmental immunity have retained immunity for the judicial and legislative functions of the government.

Quicknotes

SOVEREIGN IMMUNITY Doctrine precluding an action against the government or an instrumentality thereof, unless it has consented to be sued.

Riss v. New York

Assault victim (P) v. Municipality (D)

N.Y. Ct. App., 22 N.Y.2d 579, 240 N.E.2d 860 (1968)

NATURE OF CASE: Action for personal injuries.

FACT SUMMARY: Despite repeated pleas to the police for protection, Riss (P) was blinded and maimed by a criminal who had openly threatened her for years.

RULE OF LAW

Absent a specific legislative mandate to the contrary, the government is not liable for the negligent failure of police authorities to protect citizens from crime.

FACTS: For over six months in 1959, Linda Riss (P) was terrorized and threatened by a rejected suitor named Burton Pugach, described by the court as a "miscreant masquerading as a respectable attorney." Specifically, he threatened, "If I can't have you, no one else will have you, and when I get through with you, no one else will want you." Though she repeatedly reported such threats to the police, pleading for help, none was given in any significant way. On the day after, at an engagement party for Riss (P), who was to marry another man, a "thug" hired by Pugach threw acid in Riss's (P) face, blinding her in one eye and scarring her for life. Riss (P) filed this action against the City of New York (D) alleging that the negligent failure of NYPD to protect her was the cause of her injuries. She appealed the dismissal of her complaint, contending that the City of New York (D) was under a duty to protect her.

ISSUE: Absent a specific mandate to the contrary, is the government liable for the negligent failure of police authorities to protect citizens from crime?

HOLDING AND DECISION: (Breitel, J.) No. Absent a specific legislative mandate to the contrary, the government is not liable for the negligent failure of police authorities to protect citizens from crime. Such immunity applies even where specific threats have been made known to the authorities by particularly endangered persons. Though such immunity superficially appears harsh, any other holding could only result in interference with the allocation of police manpower by the courts. Such a decision is for the legislature, not the court, to make. The dismissal is affirmed.

DISSENT: (Keating, J.) The court today readopts one of the law's most enduring non sequiturs: "Because we owe a duty to everybody, we owe it to nobody." Examination of the traditional justifications for this rule recommends its demise. First, it is suggested that permitting recovery in cases such as this would subject the city to "limitless liability"—but this rationale has long been discredited by the results of rejection of the general doctrine of sovereign immunity. Second, it is suggested that permitting recovery would invite a suit every time a crime is committed—but this rationale ignores the fact that such litigants would still be forced to prove causation, etc., before they could recover—a clear deterrent to spurious actions. Third, it is suggested that permitting recovery would interfere with police manpower allocation—but what is in fact threatened is merely tort liability for negligent allocation. More fundamentally, liability is necessary here to affect the most important function of tort law: redistribution of the burden of loss arising from crime to society as a whole.

ANALYSIS

Though the court here states the clear majority rule today, Justice Keating's eloquent dissent points out what may develop into a trend of authority. More and more states have adopted statutes providing for the compensation for crime victims (e.g., California) under some circumstances. Furthermore, anti-crime liability insurance is encouraged and available to personal and business customers. Most writers agree, however, that it is highly unlikely that general tort immunity in this area will ever be supplanted.

Quicknotes

MUNICIPAL IMMUNITY Immunity from liability for local government entities.

PERSONAL INJURY Harm to an individual's person or body.

DeLong v. Erie County

Decedent's widower (P) v. County (D) and city (D)

N.Y. App. Div., 89 A.D.2d 376, 455 N.Y.S.2d 887 (1982)

NATURE OF CASE: Appeal of award of damages against a municipality for negligent withholding of police protection.

FACT SUMMARY: After DeLong dialed 911 to report a burglar, the official handling the call mistakenly recorded the address she gave and the police did not follow standard verification procedures.

RULE OF LAW

Liability may arise when standard procedures are not followed in an emergency summons for police help.

FACTS: DeLong, discovering a burglar attempting to force entry, dialed 911. The official receiving the call mistakenly recorded the address she gave. When the police found a non-existent address, they dismissed the call as a prank. Standard procedure was to have the tape of the call reviewed to see if the address was correct. This was not done. DeLong was killed by the burglar, and her survivors (P) sued for wrongful death. A jury awarded damages against the village of Kenmore (D), which had responded to the call. The village appealed.

ISSUE: May liability arise when standard procedures are not followed in an emergency summons for police help?

HOLDING AND DECISION: (Hancock, J.) Yes. Liability may arise when standard procedures are not followed in an emergency summons for police help. The standard rule is that a general failure to provide police protection is not compensable because allocation of police resources is a decision best left to the legislative and executive branches of government. When, however, a special relationship is formed between police and an individual, negligent execution of duties may lead to liability. Common examples of individuals with special relationships include undercover informants and protected witnesses. One placing an emergency call and told help is on the way is in a special relationship, as that individual is now relying on assurances that the police will arrive and may, therefore, not take defensive measures he otherwise might. This appears to have been the case here, as DeLong did not flee the house. Affirmed.

ANALYSIS

Tort immunity regarding municipal and county government may be characterized as a dichotomy. The two elements are discretionary and ministerial functions. Historically, liability may not arise in a situation where an official exercises discretion in some matter, but liability may arise when a ministerial function is negligently performed. Needless to say, there can be much disagreement into which category any situation may fall.

Quicknotes

MUNICIPAL IMMUNITY Immunity from liability for local government entities.

Deuser v. Vecera

Survivors of deceased (P) v. Federal government (D)

139 F.3d 1190 (8th Cir. 1998)

NATURE OF CASE: Wrongful death suit.

FACT SUMMARY: Deuser's survivors (P) brought suit against the United States (D) under the Federal Tort Claims Act based on the alleged negligence of two park rangers (D) resulting in Deuser's death.

RULE OF LAW

The federal government is immune from civil liability under the discretionary function exception if the federal government or its employees' conduct involves an element of judgment or choice of the type that the exception was designed to shield.

FACTS: Deuser attended the Veiled Prophet Fair on the grounds of the Jefferson National Expansion Memorial. The memorial is a national park and under the jurisdiction of the National Park Rangers. Rangers Vecera (D) and Bridges (D) observed Deuser grabbing women on the buttocks and urinating in public. They arrested him and turned him over to local police who decided to release him. Deuser was released in a parking lot with no money or transportation. He wandered onto an interstate highway and was struck and killed. Deuser's survivors (P) brought a wrongful death action against the United States (D) under the Federal Tort Claims Act (FTCA) based on the allegedly negligent acts of the park rangers. The claim was dismissed and the survivors (P) appealed.

ISSUE: Is the federal government immune from civil liability under the discretionary function exception if the federal government or its employees' conduct involves an element of judgment or choice of the type that the exception was designed to shield?

HOLDING AND DECISION: (Bowman, J.) Yes. The federal government is immune from civil liability under the discretionary function exception if the federal government or its employees' conduct involves an element of judgment or choice of the type that the exception was designed to shield. The FTCA waives the federal government's immunity to civil suit for money damages for injury or loss of property or personal injury or death caused by the negligent or wrongful act or omission of any of its employees acting within the scope of their employment. The federal courts have subject matter jurisdiction over such claims where a private party would be liable to the claimant under the law of the particular place where the act or omission occurred. There are, however, exceptions where the federal government is not amenable to suit, such as the discretionary function exception. This exception shields the government from civil liability for claims based on the exercise or performance of a discretionary function or duty on the part of the federal government or its employees, whether or not the discretion involved be abused. The court applies a two-step analysis in determining whether the exception applies. First is whether the conduct was discretionary. This requires there to be an element of judgment or choice. Here the rangers' (D) decision to terminate the arrest requires such element of judgment or choice. The rangers' Standard Operating Procedure for an arrest and the VP Fair Operations Handbook did not set forth a policy for terminating an arrest; however, the court concluded that such a determination is similar to the decision to make the arrest in the first place. Such decisions have been held to be in the discretion and judgment of the arresting officers. Thus the termination of Deuser's arrest was a discretionary function. Second it must be determined whether the judgment is of the kind that the discretionary function exception was designed to shield. To avoid liability, the rangers' (D) conduct must be based on the social, economic or political goals of the Handbook's discretionary enforcement guidelines. Here all three were the basis for the rangers' (D) conduct. Affirmed.

ANALYSIS

Immunity relieves a party from liability under any circumstance within the scope of the immunity. The immunity is conferred because of the position of the tortfeasor. While the underlying conduct still constitutes a tort, the particular person is shielded from liability by virtue of his status.

Quicknotes

GOVERNMENTAL IMMUNITY Implied immunity of state and federal governments from taxation by the other.

WRONGFUL DEATH An action brought by the beneficiaries of a deceased person, claiming that the deceased's death was the result of wrongful conduct by the defendant.

CHAPTER 13

Vicarious Liability

Quick Reference Rules of Law

Bussard v. Minimed, Inc.

Car accident victim (P) v. Negligent driver's employer (D)

Cal. Ct. App., 105 Cal. App. 4th 798, 129 Cal. Rptr. 2d 675 (2003)

NATURE OF CASE: Negligence action against a driver's employer under a theory of respondeat superior.

FACT SUMMARY: A company's employee rear-ended a stopped car while driving home after becoming ill at work and going home early for the day.

RULE OF LAW

An employer can be held liable when an employee leaves work early and foreseeably causes an accident while driving home.

FACTS: Hernandez, an employee of Minimed, Inc. (D), became ill at work after she inhaled fumes from pesticide sprayed at the Minimed (D) facility, at Minimed's (D) request, the night before. Hernandez grew dizzy and left work early, declining the suggestion from one of her supervisors that she see the company doctor. While driving home, Hernandez rear-ended Bussard's (P) car, which was stopped at a red light. Bussard (P) sued Hernandez for negligence and Minimed (D) for vicarious liability as Hernandez's employer, claiming that Hernandez was acting within the scope of her employment when the accident occurred. Minimed (D) eventually responded with a motion for summary judgment based in part on a denial that Hernandez was acting within the scope of her employment when she rear-ended Bussard (P). The trial court granted summary judgment for Minimed (D), and Bussard (P) appealed.

ISSUE: Can an employer be held liable when an employee leaves work early and foreseeably causes an accident while driving home?

HOLDING AND DECISION: (Rubin, J.) Yes. An employer can be held liable when an employee leaves work early and foreseeably causes an accident while driving home. Respondeat superior generally applies to injuries caused by employees who are acting within the scope of their employment because, so the theory goes, a business should be accountable for costs incurred to promote its interests. The definition of "acting within the scope of employment" is broad, but typically not so expansive that it includes an employee's daily commute to and from work. But there is an exception to this going-and-coming rule: When an employee imposes upon others a risk that arose at, or is otherwise related to, work, and the risk was foreseeable, the employer can be held liable for the employee's conduct under the theory of respondeat superior. Foreseeability in this context differs from the foreseeability used in the law of negligence; here the foreseeability analysis asks whether the employee's conduct is so startling that it cannot fairly be attributed to the employer. In this case, Hernandez's unfitness for driving was foreseeable in this manner, and the going-and-coming rule therefore does not preclude judgment against Minimed (D). Hernandez's job at Minimed (D) created a risk that Hernandez then imposed upon Bussard (P). Minimed's (D) diligent inquiries into Hernandez's condition before she left work do nothing to undermine that determinative fact. Whatever weight such arguments might have when the issue is negligence, they are irrelevant when the asserted liability is vicarious. Reversed.

ANALYSIS

Bussard contradicts a key aspect of the casebook's discussion of respondeat superior. The casebook stresses that the "superior" who is held liable "is without any fault of his own." The exception and the foreseeability test applied in *Bussard,* however, are rooted in Minimed's (D) role in both creating the risk and being able to predict its consequences. In this particular case, then, concern for the superior's own fault clearly supports the decision, regardless of whether such a concern fits the hornbook description of respondeat superior.

Quicknotes

FORESEEABLE DANGER A danger that is likely to result from a certain act or failure to act.

NEGLIGENCE Conduct falling below the standard of care that a reasonable person would demonstrate under similar conditions.

RESPONDEAT SUPERIOR Rule that the principal is responsible for tortious acts committed by its agents in the scope of their agency or authority.

SCOPE OF EMPLOYMENT Those duties performed pursuant to a person's occupation or employment.

SUMMARY JUDGMENT Judgment rendered by a court in response to a motion made by one of the parties, claiming that the lack of a question of material fact in respect to an issue warrants disposition of the issue without consideration by the jury.

VICARIOUS LIABILITY The imputed liability of one party for the unlawful acts of another.

O'Shea v. Welch

Car accident victim (P) v. Negligent driver (D) and his employer (D)

350 F.3d 1101 (10th Cir. 2003)

NATURE OF CASE: Suit for negligent driving and for vicarious liability against the driver's employer.

FACT SUMMARY: A store manager drove into another car when, on a whim, he tried to turn his car into a service station to get an estimate on his car. He was en route to his employer's district office to deliver football tickets to other managers when the accident occurred.

RULE OF LAW

A reasonable juror could conclude that driving a personal car to deliver sports tickets to one's fellow employees during working hours, and turning one's personal car into a service station to get a maintenance estimate while delivering the sports tickets during working hours, are actions within the scope of an employee's employment.

FACTS: Welch (D), a store manager for Osco (D), drove from his store toward Osco's (D) district office to deliver Kansas City Chiefs football tickets to other Osco (D) store managers. Welch (D) suddenly decided to turn his car into a service station to get an estimate on his car, and his car then struck O'Shea's (P). O'Shea (P) sued Welch (D) and Osco (D), Welch (D) for negligence and Osco (D) for vicarious liability. The parties filed cross-motions for summary judgment. The trial judge ruled for Osco (D) on the issue of vicarious liability, reasoning that, even if Welch's (D) delivery of the tickets was within the scope of his employment, no reasonable juror could conclude that Welch's (D) attempt to get an estimate on his personal car was within the scope of his employment for Osco (D). O'Shea (P) appealed.

ISSUE: Could a reasonable juror conclude that driving a personal car to deliver sports tickets to one's fellow employees during working hours, and turning one's personal car into a service station to get a maintenance estimate while delivering the sports tickets during working hours, are actions within the scope of an employee's employment?

HOLDING AND DECISION: (McKay, J.) Yes. A reasonable juror could conclude that driving a personal car to deliver sports tickets to one's fellow employees during working hours, and turning one's personal car into a service station to get a maintenance estimate while delivering the sports tickets during working hours, are actions within the scope of an employee's employment. Kansas law, which applies in this case, restricts employer liability to injuries caused within the scope of an employee's employment. That limitation can extend to actions reasonably incidental to that employment, to conduct that an employer can fairly be expected to have foreseen based on the kind of employment and its related duties. Kansas courts probably would determine the boundaries of these principles by reference to the "slight deviation" rule. To determine whether an employee acted within the scope of his employment under that rule, courts ask whether the employee was acting on a frolic or a detour. A detour is within that scope, but a frolic is not. The question is whether the employee entirely leaves the employer's business purpose, even for a moment; if such an abandonment occurs, the act is outside the scope of employment and the employer cannot be held liable for any injuries caused by the employee's actions. Under this analysis, whether Welch's (D) attempted turn into the service station was a frolic or a detour is a fact-question for a jury to decide. Several specific fact-questions inform the "slight deviation" analysis: what the employee intended, when and where the deviation occurred, how long the deviation lasted, what the employee's typical work responsibilities were, what incidental actions the employer reasonably expected from the employee, and how much latitude the employee enjoyed in his work. These factors show that a reasonable juror could return a finding for O'Shea (P) in this case. Welch (D) intended to get an estimate for a car that he used for Osco's (D) benefit. The accident happened only a matter of minutes and feet away from the road Welch (D) was driving on to reach Osco's (D) district office. The accident arguably occurred on the main road, since Welch (D) did not complete his turn into the service station, and it is therefore reasonable to conclude that he was still discharging work-related duties for Osco (D) even if the intended trip to the service station was only a personal errand. Any deviation from the employment purpose lasted a very short time. It is also reasonable to conclude that a person in a managerial position, as Welch (D) was, normally had latitude to tend to personal errands during working hours. Thus, seeing the summary-judgment evidence in the light most favorable to O'Shea (P), a reasonable juror could conclude that Welch (D) was acting within the scope of his employment in trying to turn into the service station. Moreover, as the trial judge correctly noted, genuine issues of material fact are present on whether delivering football tickets to one's fellow employees fell within the scope of Welch's (D) employment in the first instance; summary judgment therefore would not be appropriate on that question either. Trial is necessary on both questions. Remanded for trial.

Continued on next page.

ANALYSIS

Lest this case be seen as offering little more than a dry procedural ruling—on whether a reasonable juror could render a reasonable conclusion on the given questions of fact—consider the next step in this lawsuit. O'Shea (P) has just won the right to proceed to the risky world of trial, where he will have little to lose and everything to gain, and where Osco (D) will have much to lose and nothing to gain. O'Shea's (P) bargaining position in settlement negotiations, in other words, has just increased dramatically. Indeed, O'Shea (P) now *has* a bargaining position, whereas, before the appellate court's decision, he had none. Another key practice point of note in *O'Shea* is the court's use of evidence in deciding the appeal. Note that the court does not decide whether Welch's (D) actions were, in fact, within the scope of his employment; it decides only that a juror can point to record evidence (assuming that the evidence before the appellate court is eventually properly admitted at trial) to conclude that Welch (D) was acting within the scope of his employment. The court can review such evidence before trial solely because O'Shea's (P) counsel put such evidence before the trial court in opposing Osco's (D) motion for summary judgment. The first goal of O'Shea's (P) counsel in opposing summary judgment was to demonstrate genuine issues of material fact, see Fed. R. Civ. P. 56(c), questions whose resolution could go either way and thus require the assistance of a factfinder to determine which side's interpretation of the evidence is more likely true. O'Shea's (P) counsel succeeded in that objective in this case.

Quicknotes

QUESTION OF FACT An issue relating to a factual assertion that is disputed at trial and is properly left to the jury to resolve.

SCOPE OF EMPLOYMENT Those duties performed pursuant to a person's occupation or employment.

SUMMARY JUDGMENT Judgment rendered by a court in response to a motion made by one of the parties, claiming that the lack of a question of material fact in respect to an issue warrants disposition of the issue without consideration by the jury.

VICARIOUS LIABILITY The imputed liability of one party for the unlawful acts of another.

Murrell v. Goertz

Assault victim (P) v. Deliveryman (D) and employer (D)

Okla. Ct. App., 597 P.2d 1223 (1979)

NATURE OF CASE: Appeal from dismissal of action for battery.

FACT SUMMARY: The trial court ruled that Goertz (D), a newspaper deliverer, was an independent contractor and thus Oklahoma Publishing Co. (D) was not vicariously liable for his striking a customer (P) on his delivery route.

RULE OF LAW

An independent contractor is one who performs a service for another, free from control and direction of his employer in all matters connected with the performance of the service, except for the end result.

FACTS: Goertz (D), a newspaper deliverer, got into an argument with Murrell (P), one of his customers. The argument culminated in Goertz (D) striking Murrell (P), allegedly causing her injury. She brought suit for assault and battery against both Goertz (D) and the Oklahoma Publishing Co. (D), publisher of the newspaper that Goertz (D) had been delivering. At trial, the court sustained Oklahoma Publishing's (D) motion for summary judgment, which contended that Goertz (D) was an independent contractor, and thus Oklahoma Publishing (D) could not be charged with vicarious liability for his actions. Murrell (P) appealed the trial court order.

ISSUE: Is one who performs a service for another, free from control and direction of his employer in all matters connected with the performance of the service, except for the end result, an independent contractor?

HOLDING AND DECISION: (Reynolds, J.) Yes. An independent contractor is one who performs a service for another, free from control and direction of his employer in all matters connected with the performance of the service, except for the end result. The evidence adduced at trial shows that Oklahoma Publishing (D) had no connection at all with Goertz (D). Instead, it dealt with an independent distributor who hired Goertz (D). It is true that the company placed certain guidelines on the performance of all its distributors and deliverers, including Goertz (D). However, it in no way exercised the requisite control and direction over Goertz's (D) performance necessary to have him classified as an employee. As he was clearly an independent contractor, Oklahoma Publishing (D) could not be held vicariously liable for his torts. Thus, the action was properly dismissed as to the company (D). Affirmed.

ANALYSIS

Traditionally, in cases of this kind, the court focused on the performance of the independent contractor/servant, and his freedom from control or lack thereof, in determining his status. However, there has been somewhat of a recent trend focusing on the enterprise involved, and determining which of the parties receives the primary benefit from it. When this approach is taken, it is more likely that an employer-employee relationship will be found, and vicarious liability imposed. See *Konick v. Berke, Moore Co., Inc.*, 355 Mass. 463 (1969).

Quicknotes

BATTERY Unlawful contact with the body of another person.

INDEPENDENT CONTRACTOR A party undertaking a particular assignment for another who retains control over the manner in which it is executed.

MOTION FOR SUMMARY JUDGMENT Judgment rendered by a court in response to a motion by one of the parties, claiming that the lack of a question of material fact in respect to an issue warrants disposition of the issue without consideration of the jury.

VICARIOUS LIABILITY The imputed liability of one party for the unlawful acts of another.

Maloney v. Rath

Injured driver (P) v. Other driver (D)

Cal. Sup. Ct., 69 Cal. 2d 442, 445 P.2d 513 (1968)

NATURE OF CASE: Action for personal injuries.

FACT SUMMARY: The brakes on Rath's (D) automobile failed causing his automobile to collide with Maloney's (P) automobile.

RULE OF LAW

An employer who fails to provide specified safeguards or precautions will not be insulated from liability for injuries caused by the negligence of an independent contractor.

FACTS: Maloney (P) was injured when Rath's (D) automobile ran into hers. She (P) thereupon filed this action to recover damages for the personal injuries suffered. At trial, it was proved that the accident had resulted from brake failure on Rath's (D) car, that Rath (D) had no idea of the defective condition of his brakes prior to the accident, that Rath (D) had his brakes overhauled by an independent contractor mechanic, Peter Evanchick, only three months before, and that Evanchick's negligent repair effort had been the cause of the accident. The trial court gave judgment to Rath (D) on the ground that he (D) was not liable for the negligence of his independent contractor mechanic. Maloney (P) appealed on the ground that Rath's (D) duty was nondelegable since it was (1) dangerous and (2) statutorily required by the California Vehicle Code.

ISSUE: Will an employer who fails to provide specified safeguards or precautions be insulated from liability for injuries caused by the negligence of an independent contractor?

HOLDING AND DECISION: (Traynor, J.) No. An employer who fails to provide specified safeguards or precautions will not be insulated from liability for injuries caused by the negligence of an independent contractor. Certain duties are nondelegable and the duty involved in the conduct of a dangerous activity, like driving a car or the satisfaction of a statutory duty, like the one here, are such duties. Such a standard is not strict liability but rather a refusal to shift liability to a third party who may not be able to pay. Reversed and remanded.

ANALYSIS

This case points out the "nondelegable duty" limitation on the independent contractor exception to the doctrine of respondeat superior. Contrast this rule with strict liability since here a tortfeasor may escape liability by showing that he exercised due care in the performance of his "nondelegable" duty. Note, however that the determination of what duties are nondelegable (e.g., compliance with safety codes) is done on an ad hoc basis for largely independent policy reasons in each case.

Quicknotes

INDEPENDENT CONTRACTOR A party undertaking a particular assignment for another who retains control over the manner in which it is executed.

NEGLIGENCE Conduct falling below the standard of care that a reasonable person would demonstrate under similar conditions.

PERSONAL INJURY Harm to an individual's person or body.

RESPONDEAT SUPERIOR Rule that the principal is responsible for tortious acts committed by its agents in the scope of their agency or authority.

STRICT LIABILITY Liability for all injuries proximately caused by a party's conducting of certain inherently dangerous activities without regard to negligence or fault.

Popejoy v. Steinle

Accident victim (P) v. Estate representative (D)

Wyo. Sup. Ct., 820 P.2d 545 (1991)

NATURE OF CASE: Appeal from summary judgment dismissing action seeking damages for personal injury.

FACT SUMMARY: Popejoy (P) sought to hold Steinle (D) vicariously liable when Steinle's (D) wife was involved in a car accident while traveling to buy a family pet.

RULE OF LAW

Vicarious liability will not be imposed on a tortfeasor's spouse for acts arising in a personal context.

FACTS: Steinle's (D) wife, while driving her daughter to buy a calf, was involved in an accident with Popejoy (P). Although the Steinles (D) owned a ranch, the evidence was essentially uncontroverted that the calf was being bought for their daughter to raise as a pet rather than for a commercial purpose. Mrs. Steinle died in the accident. Popejoy (P), whose injuries at first seemed minor, did not make a creditor's claim against Mrs. Steinle's estate. By the time Popejoy (P) filed a suit, the estate had been probated. Popejoy (P) filed a suit against the estate of Mr. Steinle (D), who had since died of unrelated causes, contending that Mr. Steinle (D) had been vicariously liable for his wife's negligence. The trial court granted summary judgment, dismissing the case, and Popejoy (P) appealed.

ISSUE: Will vicarious liability be imposed on a tortfeasor's spouse for acts arising in a personal context?

HOLDING AND DECISION: (Golden, J.) No. Vicarious liability will not be imposed on a tortfeasor's spouse for acts arising in a personal context. Vicarious liability exists among members of a joint enterprise. A joint enterprise involves four elements: (1) an express or implied agreement among members; (2) a common purpose; (3) a common pecuniary interest; and (4) an equal right of control. The third element implies that the enterprise must be for some commercial purpose and that the act giving rise to liability must have been in furtherance of that purpose. A personal act, even if between enterprising members, does not lead to vicarious liability. Here, even though the Steinles owned a commercial ranch, Mrs. Steinle had been on a personal mission at the time of the accident, so Mr. Steinle (D) was not vicariously liable. Affirmed.

ANALYSIS

The imposition of vicarious liability for a joint enterprise is essentially based on notions of fairness. A member of a joint enterprise obtains benefits from other members' acts. Consequently, he should also bear any consequential burdens.

Quicknotes

JOINT ENTERPRISE Venture undertaken based on an express or implied agreement between the members, common purpose and interest, and an equal power of control.

PERSONAL INJURY Harm to an individual's person or body.

SUMMARY JUDGMENT Judgment rendered by a court in response to a motion by one of the parties, claiming that the lack of a question of material fact in respect to an issue warrants disposition of the issue without consideration by the jury.

VICARIOUS LIABILITY The imputed liability of one party for the unlawful acts of another.

Malchose v. Kalfell

Injured driver (P) v. Offending driver (D) and his parents (D)

N.D. Sup. Ct., 664 N.W.2d 508 (2003)

NATURE OF CASE: Suit for negligence arising out of an automobile accident.

FACT SUMMARY: Eric Kalfell (D) struck an automobile driven by Kelly Malchose (P). Malchose (P) sued Eric Kalfell (D) personally for negligence and his parents Lance and Lisa Kalfell (D) for negligence under the family car doctrine as well as negligent entrustment.

RULE OF LAW

In determining whether a member of a family other than the driver is vicariously liable for the negligence of the driver ("family car doctrine"), one must evaluate the "totality of the circumstances."

FACTS: Eric Kalfell (D), an adult living away from home, struck an automobile driven by Kelly Malchose (P). Malchose (P) sued Eric Kalfell (D) and his parents Lance and Lisa Kalfell (D) for negligence, claiming that the parents (D) were owners of the car under the "family car doctrine" and "negligent entrustment." Eric Kalfell (D) claimed that the evidence showed that his parents (D) were the liable parties: the parents (D) were named on the vehicle's certificate of title as owners at the time of the accident; Eric Kalfell (D) listed his parents' ranch as his address on his driver's license; his parents claimed him as a dependent on their tax return; and they financially supported him while he was in college. At the same time, the Kalfell parents (D) claimed that it was their son (D) who was liable because he (D) had used the vehicle as collateral for a loan and he had moved away from home and was no longer a member of the Kalfell family. The trial court found Eric Kalfell (D) at fault for negligence and his parents Lance and Lisa Kalfell (D) at fault under the family car doctrine. All three Kalfell defendants appealed.

ISSUE: In determining whether a member of a family other than the driver is vicariously liable for the negligence of the driver ("family car doctrine"), must one evaluate the "totality of the circumstances?"

HOLDING AND DECISION: (Neumann, J.) Yes. In determining whether a member of a family other than the driver is vicariously liable for the negligence of the driver ("family car doctrine"), one must evaluate the "totality of the circumstances." To be "clearly erroneous," the court's findings must either (1) be based upon an erroneous view of the law; or (2) even if there is some evidence to support the findings of fact, that the record as a whole leaves one with a definite and firm conviction that a mistake has been made. In this case, there were numerous facts proffered that, taken together, would lead to the conclusion that the family car doctrine should be invoked. The family car doctrine places liability on the head of household if he furnishes the vehicle for the use, pleasure or business of another family member. It is not necessary for the head of household to own the car for the doctrine to apply. In order to determine if the family car doctrine applies, one must look to the totality of the circumstances. In this case, the driver's (D) parents were named on the title to the car, he (D) listed his parents' address on his driver's license, he (D) could not have financially maintained the car and attended college without his parents' (D) support, he (D) was listed as a dependent on his parents' (D) tax return, and the parents (D) supported him (D) while he was away at college. Even if the parents (D) had transferred title to the driver (D), they could still incur liability, as this would be but one of the many factors comprising the "totality of the circumstances," and under the "clearly erroneous" standard, that one fact would not negate the conclusion reached by finding that the rest of the facts were true. Judgment affirmed. [Because the Kalfells were liable under the family car doctrine, there was no need to reach the claim for negligent entrustment.]

ANALYSIS

The family car doctrine is a court-created legal fiction where the car's owner is held vicariously liable when the car is negligently driven by a member of the immediate household. The doctrine is predicated on the assumption that the driver is implementing a "family purpose," even if he is only using the automobile for his own pleasure or convenience. The driver must have the owner's permission to drive the car, but this permission can be inferred from very general circumstances. It is generally limited to cars, but a Georgia case extended it to boats. *See Stewart v. Stephens*, 225 Ga. 185 (1969). The family car doctrine is not the only vicarious liability theory that has been accepted. Other theories include liability on owners of private aircraft, on municipalities for acts committed by a mob through "anti-lynching" statutes, and on parents for certain intentional torts committed by their children.

Quicknotes

VICARIOUS LIABILITY The imputed liability of one party for the unlawful acts of another.

Seaborne-Worsley v. Mintiens

Owner-passenger of car hit by truck (P) v. Owner of truck hitting car (D)

Md. Ct. App., 458 Md. 555, 183 A.3d 141 (2018)

NATURE OF CASE: Appeal from affirmance of judgment for defendant in negligence action.

FACT SUMMARY: Seaborne-Worsley (P), who was the passenger in a car that she owned and that was hit by Mintiens (D) when driving his truck, contended that the doctrine of imputed negligence should not be applied to her to preclude any recovery for Mintiens' (D) negligence, even though her husband, the driver of her car, was contributorily negligent in causing the accident.

RULE OF LAW

The presumption, under the doctrine of imputed negligence, that an owner-passenger who is injured in an automobile accident had operational control over a permissive driver of the vehicle, and is therefore responsible for any negligence of the driver, will not be applied in an automobile tort action.

FACTS: Seaborne-Worsley (P) was the passenger in a car that she owned and that was driven by her husband to a restaurant to pick up food. Seaborne-Worsley's (P) husband had stopped the car in a travel lane perpendicular to the parking space in which Mintiens' (D) truck was parked while the husband retrieved the couple's take-out order from the restaurant. Mintiens (D) backed his truck out of the parking space and struck the car in which Seaborne-Worsley (P) was seated. Seaborne-Worsley (P) sued Mintiens (D) in negligence for damages resulting from her personal injuries and damage to her car. Mintiens (D) asserted that Seaborne-Worsley's (P) husband had been contributorily negligent, and that such contributory negligence which in the state would be a complete bar to recovery—should be imputed to Seaborne-Worsley (P) under the doctrine of imputed negligence. Under the doctrine of imputed negligence, the negligence of one individual may be imputed to another who was otherwise without fault. In the realm of automobile torts, the doctrine has been applied to ascribe the negligence of a permissive driver of a car to the owner of the car if the driver operates the car negligently while the owner is a passenger. In that context, the doctrine of imputed negligence is based on the fiction that the owner is able to control the actions of the driver and therefore is responsible for any misstep of the driver. The trial court, which found that Seaborne-Worsley's (P) husband had been contributorily negligent, applied the imputed negligence doctrine, and accordingly entered judgment for Mintiens (D). The state's intermediate appellate court affirmed, and the state's highest court granted review.

ISSUE: Will the presumption, under the doctrine of imputed negligence, that an owner-passenger who is injured in an automobile accident had operational control over a permissive driver of the vehicle, and is therefore responsible for any negligence of the driver, be applied in an automobile tort action?

HOLDING AND DECISION: (McDonald, J.) No. The presumption, under the doctrine of imputed negligence, that an owner-passenger who is injured in an automobile accident had operational control over a permissive driver of the vehicle, and is therefore responsible for any negligence of the driver, will not be applied in an automobile tort action. In the past, the doctrine functioned to ensure that individuals injured in automobile accidents would be able to obtain compensation from the party most likely to be financially responsible—the car's owner. However, developments in the law and in insurance coverage make reliance on the fiction of owner control less compelling. Moreover, in situations where an owner-passenger is injured and innocent of any negligence, application of the doctrine, in conjunction with a defense of contributory negligence, can have the perverse effect of foreclosing compensation to an injured party who was not personally at fault. As a result, courts in many states have abrogated or limited the doctrine of imputed negligence. The doctrine of imputed negligence is not based on any negligence of the owner-passenger. Rather, it is a form of vicarious liability, based on legal fiction. Under what is sometimes called the "both ways" theory, the doctrine of imputed negligence has been applied not only to hold an owner-passenger liable to an injured third party, but also to foreclose a claim by an injured owner-passenger on the ground of contributory negligence—as occurred in the lower courts in this case. Although seemingly logical, experience and changed circumstances, brought about by changes in insurance practices and statutory law, have rendered the "both ways" theory antiquated and unnecessary. Moreover, in dealing with the doctrine of imputed negligence, the state's appellate courts have recognized that its premise—owner control—is entirely fictional in the context of automobile torts, noted that certain applications of the doctrine lead to results at odds with its original purpose, and have circumscribed its reach by creating an exception (does not apply to a co-owner) and enlarging the breadth of that exception (need not be on the title to be a co-owner). Courts in other states have limited or abrogated the doctrine based upon similar criticisms, and the Restatement of Torts has taken a

Continued on next page.

similar view. In sum, the time has come to discard the imputed negligence doctrine in automobile tort cases, which is defensible only on grounds of its antiquity. Accordingly, the courts of this state should no longer indulge the presumption that an owner-passenger who was injured in an automobile accident had operational control over a permissive driver of the vehicle and is therefore responsible for any negligence of the driver. This jettisoning of the presumption, however, does not mean that an owner-passenger can never be contributorily negligent, since there may be any number of ways in which an owner-passenger's own actions or omissions could be a proximate cause of an accident, not the least of which could be wresting control of the steering wheel from the driver. The lower courts in this case faithfully applied existing case-law precedent in this area; however, that precedent has now become obsolete, and it is this court's role to say as much. Vacated and remanded.

ANALYSIS

The doctrine of imputed negligence is distinct from the tort of negligent entrustment, whereby a car's owner permits another to use the car when the owner knows, or reasonably should know, that the other person is likely to use the car in a manner likely to cause injury to others. The tort of negligent entrustment is thus based on the negligent action of the car owner and is a form of direct negligence, rather than a form of vicarious liability. By contrast, the doctrine of imputed negligence is not premised on any negligence of the car owner, but only on the car owner's ownership and presence at the time of the accident. Although the doctrine of imputed negligence has been largely rejected in the area of automobile torts, and in other areas of the law, it still has viability in a few areas of the law, such as where the contributory negligence of an employee will be imputed to a plaintiff employer, or where the contributory negligence of an injured party will be imputed to a plaintiff where the plaintiff's claim is derived from that of the injured party, as in the case of loss of consortium or wrongful death actions.

Quicknotes

CONTRIBUTORY NEGLIGENCE Behavior on the part of an injured plaintiff that combines with the defendant's negligence, resulting in injury to the plaintiff.

IMPUTED NEGLIGENCE The assignment of negligence liability from one person or legal entity to another based on the relationship between the two.

CHAPTER 14

Strict Liability

Quick Reference Rules of Law

Rylands v. Fletcher

Flood victim (P) v. Mill owners (D)

Ex., 3 H&C 774, 159 Eng. Rep. 737 (1865), Ex. Ch., L.R. 1 Ex 265 (1866), H.L., L.R. 3 H.L. 330 (1868)

NATURE OF CASE: Action to recover damages for injury to plaintiff's coal mine.

FACT SUMMARY: Fletcher (D), mill owners, built a reservoir on their land. The water escaped through an abandoned coal mine shaft and flooded an adjoining mine owned by Rylands (P).

RULE OF LAW

A person using his land for a dangerous, non-natural use is strictly liable for any damage to another's property resulting from such non-natural use.

FACTS: Fletcher (D), mill owners, built a water reservoir on their land. The water broke through into an abandoned coal mine shaft and flooded along connecting passages into Ryland's (P) adjoining mine. Fletcher (D) was not negligent in allowing the reservoir to break, although the independent contractors who did the actual construction on the reservoir may have been at fault. There was no trespass by Fletcher (D), since the flooding was not direct or immediate; nor was there a nuisance (as then defined). Rylands (P) was nevertheless allowed to recover upon an analogy of the strict liability for trespassing cattle, dangerous animals, and "absolute" nuisance. The case went to the Exchequer Chamber, where Justice Blackburn used language often erroneously quoted as the rule of the case, to the effect that a person is strictly liable whenever he brings something dangerous on his land and it escapes and does damage. The case then went to the House of Lords, where Blackburn's broad statement was sharply limited, as discussed below.

ISSUE: Is a person using his land for non-natural, dangerous purposes strictly liable for any damage to another's property stemming from such non-natural use?

HOLDING AND DECISION: (Lord Blackburn, J.) Yes. A person using his land for a dangerous, non-natural use is strictly liable for any damage to another's property that results from such non-natural use. A person is strictly liable when he damages another by a thing or activity that is unduly dangerous and inappropriate to character and surroundings of the place where it is maintained. Judgment for plaintiff.

HOLDING AND DECISION: (Lord Cairns, L.C.) The defendants could have used their reservoir for any ordinary purpose, and Rylands (P) could not have complained if the water then had escaped onto, and damaged, his property from natural causes. In such circumstances, Rylands (P) would have been obligated to protect his property from those accidents caused by nature. Court of Exchequer Chamber judgment affirmed.

ANALYSIS

This is the leading case that developed the doctrine of strict liability for abnormally dangerous activities or conditions. In determining whether a certain activity is a non-natural use, the court looks to the place where the activity occurs, the customs of the community, and the natural fitness or adaptation of the premises for the purpose. By and large, the rule is followed in most states. The Restatement had accepted the principle of *Rylands*, but has limited it to "ultrahazardous activities," defined as ones which "necessarily involve a risk of serious harm to ... others which cannot be eliminated by the exercise of the utmost care." Most frequently, in all American courts, the same strict liability is imposed under the name of "nuisance." These nuisance cases generally recognize that the activity's relation to its surroundings is the controlling factor. Thus, "non-natural" use has become "unreasonable" use.

Quicknotes

ABNORMALLY DANGEROUS ACTIVITY An activity, as set forth in Restatement (Second) of Torts § 520, giving rise to strict liability on the part of the actor for damages caused thereby.

NUISANCE An unlawful use of property that interferes with the lawful use of another's property.

STRICT LIABILITY Liability for all injuries proximately caused by a party's conducting of certain inherently dangerous activities without regard to negligence or fault.

Miller v. Civil Constructors, Inc.

Injured (P) v. Gravel pit owners (D)

Ill. Ct. App., 272 Ill. App. 3d 263, 651 N.E.2d 239 (1995)

NATURE OF CASE: Claims sounding in strict liability for injuries sustained during nearby firearms practice.

FACT SUMMARY: A stray bullet injured a man after it ricocheted from a nearby gravel pit during firearms practice by law enforcement officers.

RULE OF LAW

The use of guns or firearms is not an ultrahazardous activity as required for strict liability.

FACTS: Miller (P) was struck and injured by a stray bullet that ricocheted out of a nearby property, a gravel pit, while law enforcement officers took firing practice there. Miller (P) sued the owners of the gravel pit, Civil Constructors, Inc. (D), alleging, among other claims, two counts for strict liability. The trial court dismissed those two counts on grounds that shooting a firearm is not an ultrahazardous activity. Miller (P) appealed.

ISSUE: Is the use of guns or firearms an ultrahazardous activity as required for strict liability?

HOLDING AND DECISION: (Bowman, J.) No. The use of guns or firearms is not an ultrahazardous activity as required for strict liability. The general rule is that the use of guns or firearms is a matter of negligence, not strict liability, and thus the appropriate standard of care in such cases is generally accepted to be that of ordinary care. Miller (P), however, argues that shooting a gun or firearm is an ultrahazardous activity that justifies strict liability. Section 519 of the Restatement of Torts posits six factors to consider in deciding whether an activity is ultrahazardous: a high degree of risk of harm, the likelihood that any harm will be substantial, the futility of exercising reasonable care, the commonness of the activity, the activity's appropriateness for the place where it occurs, and the degree to which the community benefits from the activity outweigh its dangers. Under these factors, the use of a gun or firearm is not an ultrahazardous activity. First, reasonable care will suffice to prevent the dangers. Second, use of guns is common; guns are not inherently dangerous. Third, the court assumes that the location was appropriate because Miller's (P) complaint alleges no facts to the contrary. Fourth, the firearm practice, allegedly performed by law enforcement officers, provides benefits to the community. Miller's (P) allegations on the strict-liability counts are therefore facially insufficient, and those counts were properly dismissed. Affirmed.

ANALYSIS

The key point in the developed rule of *Rylands v. Fletcher*, Ex., 3 H&C 774, 159 Eng. Rep. 737 (1865), Ex. Ch., L.R. 1 Ex 265 (1866), H.L., L.R. 3 H.L. 330 (1868),—the appropriateness of the activity to the place—was assumed by the court in *Miller*. Given the weakness of Miller's (P) claim on the other factors stated in section 519 of the Restatement, though, his argument that guns are ultrahazardous very likely would have failed even if his complaint had alleged that a gravel pit was not an appropriate location for firing practice.

Quicknotes

NEGLIGENCE Conduct falling below the standard of care that a reasonable person would demonstrate under similar conditions.

ORDINARY CARE The degree of care exercised by a reasonable person when conducting everyday activities or under similar circumstances; synonymous with due care.

STANDARD OF CARE A uniform degree of behavior against which a person's conduct can be measured when determining liability in negligence cases.

STRICT LIABILITY Liability for all injuries proximately caused by a party's conducting of certain inherently dangerous activities without regard to negligence or fault.

ULTRAHAZARDOUS ACTIVITIES Dangerous activities that give rise to strict liability by presenting a risk of serious harm to the community that cannot be removed through any exercise of due care.

Indiana Harbor Belt R.R. Co. v. American Cyanamid Co.

Railroad (P) v. Chemical manufacturer (D)

916 F.2d 1174 (7th Cir. 1990)

NATURE OF CASE: Appeal of damages awarded for injury to property.

FACT SUMMARY: American Cyanamid Co. (D), manufacturer of a dangerous chemical, was held strictly liable when a quantity of it spilled during transportation.

RULE OF LAW

Strict liability will not be imposed against the manufacturer of a toxic chemical for accidents occurring during transportation.

FACTS: American Cyanamid Co. (D), a chemical manufacturer, engaged a railroad car to transport 20,000 gallons of liquid acrylonitrile, a toxic substance, to a processing plant in New Jersey. While the car was sitting in a Chicago railroad yard owned by Indiana Harbor Belt R.R. Co. (P), about 5,000 gallons spilled, which necessitated an evacuation of nearby homes and nearly $1 million in cleanup. Indiana Harbor Belt R.R. (P) filed suit against American Cyanamid (D) to recover the cost of cleanup, contending that the transportation of toxic chemicals was an ultrahazardous activity for which the manufacturer should be strictly liable. A district court, sitting in diversity, agreed and so instructed the jury. A verdict for damages was rendered, and American Cyanamid (D) appealed.

ISSUE: Will strict liability be imposed against the manufacturer of a toxic chemical for accidents occurring during transportation?

HOLDING AND DECISION: (Posner, J.) No. Strict liability will not be imposed against the manufacturer of a toxic chemical for accidents occurring during transportation. The Restatement (Second) of Torts, at § 520, lists six factors to be considered in determining whether an activity is ultrahazardous: (1) great probability of harm; (2) potentially serious level of harm; (3) the activity is not a matter of common usage; (4) harm cannot be prevented by utmost care; (5) the activity is inappropriate for the location; and (6) the social value of the activity is not sufficient to offset the risks. The basic purpose behind the ultrahazardous activity doctrine is to encourage the use of alternative methods when possible. In this case, no alternative exists to transport chemicals other than truck transport, which is not inherently safer. It would not be feasible to reroute the shipment of all hazardous materials around Chicago. Moreover, the negligence regime is perfectly adequate for deterring railway spills. Finally, the ultrahazardous activity doctrine concentrates on the activity, not the subject of the activity. American Cyanamid (D) is not considered to be engaged in an abnormally dangerous activity just because a product it manufactures becomes dangerous when handled. It is the transportation, not the manufacture of the chemical, which is under scrutiny. For these reasons, strict liability is inappropriate in this context. Reversed and remanded.

ANALYSIS

The classic case of ultrahazardous activity is dynamite blasting in an urban area. It entails a great risk of harm, and a less dangerous (albeit more expensive) method of building demolition exists—the wrecking ball. The ultrahazardous activity rule will make the demolisher strictly liable if he chooses the more dangerous method.

Quicknotes

STRICT LIABILITY Liability for all injuries proximately caused by a party's conducting of certain inherently dangerous activities without regard to negligence or fault.

Foster v. Preston Mill Co.

Mink farm owner (P) v. Blasters (D)

Wash. Sup. Ct., 44 Wash. 2d 440, 268 P.2d 645 (1954)

NATURE OF CASE: Action to recover for damages due to blasting operations.

FACT SUMMARY: Mother mink, frightened by blasting, killed their own kittens.

RULE OF LAW

Strict liability is only imposed for those injuries resulting as the natural consequence of that which makes an activity ultrahazardous.

FACTS: Foster (P) raised mink, which are by nature very nervous creatures. Blasting operations carried out by Preston Mill Co. (D) frightened the mink mothers and caused them to eat their kittens. Foster (P) informed Preston Mill (D) of the effect their blasting was having on his mink, but they kept on blasting. Foster (P) sought to hold Preston Mill (D) strictly liable for his damages, and was awarded $1,953.

ISSUE: Is strict liability only imposed for those injuries resulting as the natural consequence of that which makes an activity ultrahazardous?

HOLDING AND DECISION: (Hamley, J.) Yes. Strict liability is only imposed for those injuries resulting as the natural consequence of that which makes the activity ultrahazardous. One who carries on an ultrahazardous activity is liable to another whose person, land, or chattels the actor should recognize as likely to be harmed by the unpreventable miscarriage of the activity for harm resulting thereto from that which makes the activity ultrahazardous, although the utmost care is exercised to prevent the harm. The risk that mink may eat their young when frightened by the noise is not one of the things that make blasting ultrahazardous. It is the mink's exceedingly nervous disposition, rather than the normal risks inherent in blasting operations, that must bear the responsibility for the loss sustained. Reversed.

ANALYSIS

The court in this case limits the application of the doctrine of strict liability. The court bases its decision on the same kind of policy considerations that underlie the doctrine of "proximate cause" in the law of negligence. A defendant cannot be held limitlessly responsible for every consequence flowing from his actions. In strict liability law, the line is drawn at those injuries that result from the very things that cause an activity to be classified as ultrahazardous. Had the mink been killed by flying rocks and debris, for example, strict liability may have been imposed. Note that the court accepts the policy that strict liability is not designed to protect against harms incident to a plaintiff's extraordinary or unusual use of his land. The court here is applying the principle that the extent to which one man in lawful conduct of his business is liable for injuries to another is an adjustment of conflicting interests. Here, the plaintiff's interests must yield.

Quicknotes

CHATTEL An article of personal property, as distinguished from real property; a thing personal and moveable.

NEGLIGENCE Conduct falling below the standard of care that a reasonable person would demonstrate under similar conditions.

PROXIMATE CAUSE The natural sequence of events without which an injury would not have been sustained.

STRICT LIABILITY Liability for all injuries proximately caused by a party's conducting of certain inherently dangerous activities without regard to negligence or fault.

ULTRAHAZARDOUS ACTIVITIES Dangerous activities that give rise to strict liability by presenting a risk of serious harm to the community that cannot be removed through any exercise of due care.

Golden v. Amory

Flood victim (P) v. Hydroelectric plant owner (D)

Mass. Sup. Jud. Ct., 329 Mass. 484, 109 N.E.2d 131 (1952)

NATURE OF CASE: Action to recover damages caused by the overflow of a dike.

FACT SUMMARY: A hurricane caused floods, damaging the Golden's land.

RULE OF LAW

The rule of strict liability for the escape of stored water does not apply where the injury results from an act of God, which the owner had no reason to anticipate.

FACTS: Amory (D) owned a hydroelectric plant and built a dike on a river. A hurricane caused the river to overflow, damaging Golden's (P) land. Golden (P) brought an action based on both strict liability and negligence.

ISSUE: Does the rule of strict liability for the escape of stored water apply where the injury results from an act of God, which the owner had no reason to anticipate?

HOLDING AND DECISION: (Lummus, J.) No. The rule of strict liability for the escape of stored water does not apply where the injury results from an act of God, which the owner had no reason to anticipate. In the present case, the flood was plainly beyond the capability of anyone to anticipate, and was clearly an act of God. Exceptions overruled.

ANALYSIS

This case is an example of the decision to limit strict liability when the harm is caused by acts of God unforeseen by the defendant. In negligence law, the defendant is frequently held liable when the risk he has created is realized through unforeseeable intervening causes. But in strict liability law, the strong current of authority—notwithstanding the Restatement, which is contrary—relieves the defendant of liability in such a case. Thus, act of God is used to mean an unforeseeable, intervening force of nature. In the same manner, the defendant has been relieved from liability by the independent act of a third person, which he could not have foreseen or prevented.

Quicknotes

VIS MAJOR Damages incurred as the result of a natural cause and which could not have been prevented.

Sandy v. Bushey

Horse-kick victim (P) v. Horse owner (D)

Me. Sup. Jud. Ct., 124 Me. 320, 128 A. 513 (1925)

NATURE OF CASE: Action to recover damages for injuries sustained when kicked by a horse.

FACT SUMMARY: Sandy (P) was kicked by Bushey's (D) horse when he went into the pasture to feed his own horse.

RULE OF LAW

The keeper of a vicious domestic animal known to be dangerous cannot interpose contributory negligence as a defense to relieve him of his strict liability as an insurer.

FACTS: Sandy (P) turned his horses out in a neighbor's pasture, where Bushey's (D) horse was also pastured. When Sandy (P) was in the pasture feeding his mare, he was seriously injured when kicked by Bushey's (D) horse, which had previously exhibited vicious tendencies, known to Bushey (D). Sandy (P) brought an action in strict liability for the keeping of a vicious domestic animal. Bushey (D) attempted to plead Sandy's (P) contributory negligence as a defense.

ISSUE: Can the keeper of a vicious domestic animal known to be dangerous interpose contributory negligence as a defense to relieve him of his strict liability as an insurer?

HOLDING AND DECISION: (Sturgis, J.) No. The keeper of a vicious domestic animal known to be dangerous cannot interpose contributory negligence as a defense to relieve him of his strict liability as an insurer. In an action for an injury caused by such an animal, the plaintiff has only to allege and prove the keeping, the vicious propensities, and the scienter. Negligence is not the ground of liability; therefore, contributory negligence cannot be a defense. Something more than slight negligence or want of due care on the part of the injured party must be shown in order to relieve the keeper of a vicious domestic animal known to be such from his liability as an insurer. The owner is only relieved of liability if the injured party voluntarily and knowingly put himself in harm's way, or if he incites the animal and brings the attack on himself. Motion overruled.

ANALYSIS

This case illustrates the policy that places the absolute responsibility for preventing harm upon the defendant. A plaintiff who is injured by a defendant's dangerous animal is not barred from recovery by his own lack of ordinary care in failing to discover its presence, or in inadvertently coming in contact with it. He will only be barred from recovery if his own conduct brings the attack on himself.

Quicknotes

CONTRIBUTORY NEGLIGENCE Behavior on the part of an injured plaintiff falling below the standard of ordinary care that contributes to the defendant's negligence, resulting in the plaintiff's injury.

STRICT LIABILITY Liability for all injuries proximately caused by a party's conducting of certain inherently dangerous activities without regard to negligence or fault.

CHAPTER 15

Products Liability

Quick Reference Rules of Law

MacPherson v. Buick Motor Co.

Injured automobile owner (P) v. Automobile manufacturer (D)

N.Y. Ct. App., 217 N.Y. 382, 111 N.E. 1050 (1916)

NATURE OF CASE: Negligence action.

FACT SUMMARY: MacPherson (P) sued Buick Motor Co. (D) for injuries sustained when a defective wheel on the automobile he purchased collapsed.

RULE OF LAW

A manufacturer breaches a duty of care to a foreseeable user of its product if the product was likely to cause an injury if negligently made and the manufacturer places the product on the market without conducting a reasonable inspection.

FACTS: Buick Motor Co. (D), an automobile manufacturer, sold a car to a retail dealer who in turn sold it to MacPherson (P). While MacPherson (P) was in the car it suddenly collapsed due to the wheel being made out of defective wood. While the wheel was not manufactured by Buick (D), there was evidence that a reasonable inspection would have revealed the defects. The state supreme court held in favor of MacPherson (P) and the appellate division affirmed. Buick (D) appealed.

ISSUE: Does a manufacturer breach a duty of care to a foreseeable user of its product if the product was likely to cause an injury if negligently made and the manufacturer places the product on the market without conducting a reasonable inspection?

HOLDING AND DECISION: (Cardozo, J.) Yes. A manufacturer breaches a duty of care to a foreseeable user of its product if the product was likely to cause an injury if negligently made and the manufacturer places the product on the market without conducting a reasonable inspection. A product is dangerous if it is reasonably certain to place life and limb in peril when negligently made. If the manufacturer knows the item will be used by a person other than the purchaser, the manufacturer is under a duty to manufacture the item carefully. There must be knowledge of a probable danger and that the danger will be borne by others in addition to the buyer in the normal course of events. The proximity or remoteness of the transaction is also to be considered. If the manufacturer of a finished product places it on the market without inspection, then mobility will attach. Buick (D) was not relieved from its duty to inspect because it bought the wheels from a reputable manufacturer. Buick (D) had a duty to inspect the component parts of its automobiles before placing them on the market. Affirmed.

ANALYSIS

There was a traditional distinction between cases involving nonfeasance and misfeasance. Nonfeasance was actionable under contract law and resulted where there was a promise and a subsequent breach of that promise. Misfeasance was actionable in tort and existed when the defendant attempted to perform a contract and did so in error.

Quicknotes

DUTY OF CARE A principle of negligence requiring an individual to act in such a manner as to avoid injury to a person to whom he or she owes an obligatory duty.

FORESEEABLE USER A person who is likely to use a certain product or service.

MISFEASANCE The commission of a lawful act in a wrongful manner.

NEGLIGENCE Conduct falling below the standard of care that a reasonable person would demonstrate under similar conditions.

NONFEASANCE The omission, or failure to perform, an obligation.

Baxter v. Ford Motor Co.

Injured car owner (P) v. Car manufacturer (D)

Wash. Sup. Ct., 168 Wash. 456, 12 P.2d 409 (1932)

NATURE OF CASE: Action to recover damages for personal injuries, based on breach of warranty in tort.

FACT SUMMARY: Baxter (P), while driving a car whose windshield, according to representations made by Ford Motor Co. (D), was made of nonshatterable glass, suffered injuries when a pebble struck the windshield, causing small pieces of glass to fly into his eyes.

RULE OF LAW

A manufacturer or retailer of a product is responsible in tort for all representations upon which the consumer must rely, regardless of a contractual relationship between plaintiff and defendant.

FACTS: Baxter (P) purchased a car from a dealer, who acquired it in turn from Ford Motor Co. (Ford) (D). Baxter (P) was injured when a pebble from a passing car struck the windshield of his car, causing small pieces of glass to fly into his eyes, and resulting in loss of his left eye and damage to his right eye. Ford (D) had made misrepresentations through its advertising that the windshields of its automobiles were constructed of nonshatterable glass. Ford (D) contended, however, that there can be no implied or express warranty without privity of contract, and warranties as to personal property do not attach themselves to, and run with, the article sold. The trial court refused to admit into evidence the printed matter containing Ford's (D) misrepresentations, and entered judgment for Ford (D). Baxter (P) appealed.

ISSUE: Is a manufacturer or retailer of a product responsible in tort for all representations upon which the consumer must rely, regardless of a contractual relationship between plaintiff and defendant?

HOLDING AND DECISION: (Herman, J.) Yes. A manufacturer or retailer of a product is responsible in tort for all representations upon which the consumer must rely, regardless of a contractual relationship between plaintiff and defendant. The purchaser has a right to a remedy against the manufacturer because of damages suffered by reason of a failure of goods to comply with the manufacturer's representations as to the existence of qualities which they did not in fact possess, when the absence of such qualities was not readily discoverable, even though there was no privity of contract between the purchaser and the manufacturer. Here, Ford (D) made representations as to the nonshatterability of its windshields, upon which Baxter (P) was forced to rely, as he as a consumer had no means of testing their truthfulness. Ford (D) was therefore under a duty to ascertain that their representations were true, and it is immaterial that they did not in fact know that the representations were false, or that there was in existence no better make of glass. The trial court erred in excluding evidence of the representations from trial and in taking the case from the jury. The rule which long afforded a remedy, independent of contract, to the purchaser of a dangerous article, such as a drug, against the manufacturer who misrepresents its contents is now extended to all consumer goods. It would be unjust, and against public policy, to permit manufacturers of goods to create a demand for their products by representing that they possess qualities which they in fact, do not possess, and then, because there is no privity of contract existing between the consumer and the manufacturer, deny the consumer the right to recover if damages result from the absence of those qualities, when such absence is not readily noticeable. Reversed for a new trial.

ANALYSIS

The action in *Baxter* was based on breach of an express warranty, but the effect of the decision was to hold manufacturers and retailers to strict liability for their misrepresentations. See Restatement (Second) of Torts § 402B, which holds the manufacturer liable for physical harm to a consumer caused by the latter's justifiable reliance upon the former's misrepresentations, regardless of contractual relationship, fraud, or negligence. However, in order for there to be strict liability, the representation must be made with the expectation that it will reach the plaintiff, and he, in turn, must actually rely upon the representation in his use of the product. The above case is the leading decision in this area, and has been followed almost without exception.

Quicknotes

EXPRESS WARRANTY An express promise made by one party to a contract that the other party may rely on a fact, relieving that party from the obligation of determining whether the fact is true and indemnifying the other party from liability if that fact is shown to be false.

IMPLIED WARRANTY An implied promise made by one party to a contract that the other party may rely on a fact, relieving that party from the obligation of determining whether the fact is true and indemnifying the other party from liability if that fact is shown to be false.

Continued on next page.

PRIVITY OF CONTRACT A relationship between the parties to a contract that is required in order to bring an action for breach.

Henningsen v. Bloomfield Motors, Inc.

Injured car owner (P) v. Manufacturer (D) and dealer (D)

N.J. Sup. Ct., 32 N.J. 358, 161 A.2d 69 (1960)

NATURE OF CASE: Action to recover damages for personal injuries based on a theory of implied warranty of merchantability.

FACT SUMMARY: Mrs. Henningsen (P), severely injured when her steering gear malfunctioned and caused her car to crash into a wall, sued the manufacturer, Chrysler Corp. (D), and the dealer, Bloomfield Motors, Inc. (D), from whom her husband purchased the car.

RULE OF LAW

When a manufacturer and a dealer put a new automobile in the stream of trade and promote its purchase by the public, an implied warranty that it is reasonably suitable for use as such accompanies it into the hands of the ultimate purchaser, despite any contractual provisions to the contrary.

FACTS: Mrs. Henningsen (P) was badly injured when the steering gear in her car malfunctioned, causing her to crash into a wall. The car was a gift from her husband, who purchased it from Bloomfield Motors, Inc. (D), who had, in turn, acquired it from Chrysler Corp. (D). Mr. Henningsen signed a contract for sale, the back of which contained a disclaimer of warranties, express or implied, except for a promise to repair or replace any defective parts within 90 days, or 4,000 miles, after delivery to the original purchaser (whichever came first). This form was standard, not only with Chrysler (D), but with the entire automotive industry. Mrs. Henningsen's (P) claim based on negligence was dismissed, the case went to the jury solely on the issues of an implied warranty of merchantability, and a verdict was returned for Mrs. Henningsen (P). Chrysler Corp. (D) and Bloomfield Motors, Inc. (D) appealed.

ISSUE:

(1) Is privity of contract necessary for an implied warranty of merchantability (fitness for use) to run from the manufacturer of a car to the ultimate purchaser?

(2) Can the implied warranty be nullified by an express contractual agreement?

(3) Is the dealer, as well as the manufacturer, bound by this implied warranty of merchantability?

HOLDING AND DECISION: (Francis, J.)

(1) No. Where the buyer of a product, such as an automobile, has neither the opportunity nor the capacity to inspect or determine its fitness for use, and must rely upon the manufacturer, the law will not limit the latter's responsibility to the bare terms of the contract; rather it will imply a warranty that the product is reasonably fit for its intended use, and extend this warranty for the protection of the ultimate consumer. In this way, the burden of losses consequent upon the use of defective articles is borne by the manufacturer, who is in a position both to minimize the danger through care in construction, and to make an equitable distribution (through insurance and price control) of any losses that do occur.

(2) No. Recognizing the gross inequality of bargaining position between Mr. Henningsen, an individual purchaser, and Chrysler Corp. (D), a large corporation whose practices here are mirrored by the rest of the same industry, public policy implies a warranty of merchantability for the protection of the ultimate consumer, in this case, Mrs. Henningsen (P). Consequently, the law will not allow the protection to be nullified through a contract of adhesion which purports to either limit liability or disclaim any implied warranty. Any such terms will be declared unconscionable and void.

(3) Yes. The principles that establish the obligation of the manufacturer apply with equal force to the retailer, even though there may be no agency relationship between the two. The bargaining position of the dealer is stronger than that of the consumer, and even though the dealer may have only a limited opportunity for inspection of the car, he is in a position to make an equitable distribution of any losses through insurance and price control. Affirmed.

ANALYSIS

Under early common-law concepts of contractual liability, only those parties who were parties to the bargain could sue for a breach of it. In this decision, the court took judicial notice of the realities of modern-day mass marketing, particularly of the fact that people do not buy goods strictly for their own consumption or use. The ultimate consumer must therefore be protected. Furthermore, the court, taking notice of the consumer's lack of bargaining power, protected him by implying a warranty and refusing to honor disclaimers to the contrary. However, the value of the "implied warranty of merchantability" as a weapon in the consumer's legal arsenal has been largely superseded by the advent of strict liability in tort.

Quicknotes

IMPLIED WARRANTY OF MERCHANTABILITY An implied promise made by a merchant in a contract for the sale

Continued on next page.

of goods that such goods are suitable for the purpose for which they are purchased.

PRIVITY OF CONTRACT A relationship between the parties to a contract that is required in order to bring an action for breach.

Greenman v. Yuba Power Products, Inc.

Injured tool user (P) v. Manufacturer (D)

Cal. Sup. Ct., 59 Cal. 2d 57, 377 P.2d 897 (1963)

NATURE OF CASE: Action to recover damages for personal breach of warranties and negligence.

FACT SUMMARY: Greenman (P), injured when a piece of wood flew out of a power tool he was using and struck his forehead, sued the manufacturer and retailer of the product.

RULE OF LAW

When an article is placed on the market by a manufacturer that knows that the product will be used without inspection for defects, the manufacturer will be strictly liable in tort for any injury caused by a defect in the product.

FACTS: Greenman (P) was injured when a power tool his wife had given him malfunctioned. Ten-and-a-half months later, Greenman (P) gave the manufacturer, Yuba Power Products, Inc. (Yuba) (D), notice of claimed breaches of the express warranties contained in the latter's brochures. At trial, Greenman (P) introduced substantial evidence that his injuries were caused by the tool's defective design and construction. Yuba (D) contended that Greenman (P) did not give prompt notification of the breach of warranty, as required by state law. After judgment for Greenman (P), Yuba (D) appealed.

ISSUE: When an article is placed on the market by a manufacturer that knows that the product will be used without inspection for defects, will the manufacturer be strictly liable in tort for any injury caused by a defect in the product?

HOLDING AND DECISION: (Traynor, J.) Yes. When an article is placed on the market by a manufacturer that knows that the product will be used without inspection for defects, the manufacturer will be strictly liable in tort for any injury caused by a defect in the product. The liability of the manufacturer is governed not by the law of contract warranties, but by the law of strict liability in tort. Therefore, the manufacturer, in this case Yuba (D), is held strictly liable for all injuries resulting from defects in its products, regardless of negligence, contractual relationship, or warranties (express or implied), as it placed its product on the market knowing it would be used without inspection. The purpose of such liability is to insure that the costs of injuries resulting from defective products are borne by the manufacturers that put such products on the market, rather than the injured persons who are powerless to protect themselves. Sales warranties serve this purpose fitfully at best. Affirmed.

ANALYSIS

In this landmark decision, Justice Traynor reasoned that: (1) since a manufacturer's liability is based on a warranty implied by law, (2) since there need be no privity of contract, and (3) since the law prohibits the manufacturer from limiting his liability disclaimer, the liability has evolved from a contractual basis to that of strict liability. This concept, as stated in § 402A of the Restatement (Second) of Torts, is now accepted and applied by a good majority of American courts. Section 402A applies to damage to the person or property of any user, whether or not the user bought the product from the seller, and it is no longer necessary, of course, to prove negligence on the part of the manufacturer.

Quicknotes

CONTRACT WARRANTY An express promise made by one party to a contract that the other party may rely on a fact, relieving that party from the obligation of determining whether the fact is true and indemnifying the other party from liability if that fact is shown to be false.

NEGLIGENCE Conduct falling below the standard of care that a reasonable person would demonstrate under similar conditions.

STRICT LIABILITY Liability for all injuries proximately caused by a party's conducting of certain inherently dangerous activities without regard to negligence or fault.

Rix v. General Motors Corp.

Accident victim (P) v. Truck manufacturer (D)

Mont. Sup. Ct., 222 Mont. 318, 723 P.2d 195 (1986)

NATURE OF CASE: Appeal from defense verdict in personal injury action.

FACT SUMMARY: Rix (P) contended that General Motors Corp. (D) had manufactured a vehicle with a defective braking system.

RULE OF LAW

A manufacturer will be strictly liable for manufacturing defects.

FACTS: Rix (P) was injured when he was hit from behind by a truck manufactured by General Motors Corp. (GMC) (D) that failed to brake. Rix (P) filed a personal injury action alleging defective brakes. GMC (D) argued that the brakes had been altered after the truck left its assembly line. A jury returned a defense verdict, and Rix (P) appealed, arguing that the jury instructions regarding strict liability under a manufacturing defect theory were incorrect.

ISSUE: Will a manufacturer be strictly liable for manufacturing defects?

HOLDING AND DECISION: (Weber, J.) Yes. A manufacturer will be strictly liable for manufacturing defects. One who sells any product in a defective condition unreasonably dangerous to the consumer is subject to liability for physical harm thereby caused to the consumer if the product reaches the consumer without substantial change in the condition in which it was sold. In this case, the jury was instructed that Rix (P) must establish three elements in order to recover under a strict liability theory: (1) that GMC (D) manufactured and sold a product in a defective condition; (2) that the product reached the ultimate consumer without substantial change in its condition; and (3) that the defective condition caused Rix's (P) injuries. A manufacturing defect is an imperfection of the type that inevitably occurs in products of a given design as a result of the fallibility of the manufacturing process, where the end result does not match the design. The jury instructions given here were an adequate explanation of the applicable law with regard to strict liability under a manufacturing defect theory. [The verdict was reversed and the case remanded on other, unstated grounds.]

ANALYSIS

Defects come in two types, manufacturing and design. True strict liability exists only in manufacturing defects. Defective design issues involve an analysis of possible alternative designs and a cost-benefit analysis and therefore incorporate elements of negligence.

Quicknotes

DESIGN DEFECT A situation product that is manufactured in accordance with a particular design; however, such design is inherently flawed so that it presents an unreasonable risk of injury.

PERSONAL INJURY Harm to an individual's person or body.

STRICT PRODUCT LIABILITY Liability of a manufacturer or seller of a product for injuries sustained as a result of any defects without the necessity of a showing of negligence.

Prentis v. Yale Manufacturing Co.

Forklift operator (P) v. Manufacturer (D)

Mich. Sup. Ct., 421 Mich. 670, 365 N.W.2d 176 (1984)

NATURE OF CASE: Appeal of reversal of denial of damages in products liability action.

FACT SUMMARY: Prentis (P) contended that he had been injured due to a defectively designed forklift manufactured by Yale Manufacturing Co. (D).

RULE OF LAW

Liability for a defectively designed product shall be based on a pure negligence analysis.

FACTS: Prentis (P), operating a forklift manufactured by Yale Manufacturing Co. (Yale) (D), was injured. He brought a products liability action against Yale (D) on a design defect theory. The trial court in defining "design defect" couched the meaning in terms of negligence. The jury found that the forklift was not defectively designed and gave a defense verdict. Prentis (P) appealed, contending that the phrase "design defect" should have been characterized in terms of strict liability. The appellate court reversed. Yale (D) appealed.

ISSUE: Will liability for a defectively designed product be based on a pure negligence analysis?

HOLDING AND DECISION: (Boyle, J.) Yes. Liability for a defectively designed product will be based on a pure negligence analysis. The modern trend in products liability is to focus on the product, not the manufacturer's conduct. When addressing a manufacturing defect, this is proper. However, in a design defect situation, to focus on the product obscures the true inquiry, which is an examination of conscious decisions made by a manufacturer. Incorporated into the analysis are risk-benefit, consumer expectations, and other related concepts. All of these issues come back to the larger question of whether a manufacturer made prudent design choices. For this reason, a design defect analysis is necessarily one of negligence. Moreover, a negligence standard will reward a careful manufacturer, a result to be encouraged. These factors compel the conclusion that the analysis in design defect cases will be negligence. This was the standard used by the trial court, and it was proper. Reversed.

ANALYSIS

Design and manufacturing defects are often lumped under the generic term "products liability." As the present case demonstrates, however, there is much overlap between products liability and general negligence. Several courts besides that writing in this instance have agreed that design defects are properly analyzed in terms of negligence.

Quicknotes

DESIGN DEFECT A defect in a product manufactured according to the intended design, but present because the design of the product itself presents a risk of harm to consumers.

NEGLIGENCE Conduct falling below the standard of care that a reasonable person would demonstrate under similar conditions.

PRODUCTS LIABILITY The legal liability of manufacturers and sellers for damages and injuries suffered by buyers, users, and even bystanders because of defects in goods purchased.

STRICT LIABILITY Liability for all injuries proximately caused by a party's conducting of certain inherently dangerous activities without regard to negligence or fault.

Anderson v. Owens-Corning Fiberglas Corp.

Asbestosis victim (P) v. Manufacturer (D)

Cal. Sup. Ct., 53 Cal. 3d 987, 810 P.2d 549 (1991)

NATURE OF CASE: Appeal from an order allowing state-of-the-art evidence in a products liability action.

FACT SUMMARY: Owens-Corning Fiberglas Corp. (D), an asbestos manufacturer, sought to admit evidence regarding the knowability of the risks of asbestos exposure at the time of the distribution.

RULE OF LAW

Knowability is a required element of strict liability for failure to warn.

FACTS: Anderson (P) alleged that he contracted asbestosis and other lung ailments through exposure to asbestos while working as an electrician from 1941 to 1976. Anderson (P) filed a strict liability action against Owens-Corning Fiberglas Corp. (Owens-Corning) (D), the manufacturer of the asbestos, for failure to warn of the risk of harm. Owens-Corning (D) sought to introduce evidence that the risk was unknowable at the time of the manufacture and distribution of all asbestos products. Anderson (P), asserting that this type of evidence was not relevant in a strict liability action, appealed the decision to allow Owens-Corning (D) to present it at the trial.

ISSUE: Is knowability a required element of strict liability action for failure to warn?

HOLDING AND DECISION: (Panelli, J.) Yes. Knowability is a required element of strict liability for failure to warn. Strict liability was adopted to insure that the costs of injuries resulting from defective products were borne by the manufacturers. The doctrine relieves injured plaintiffs of many of the onerous evidentiary burdens in a negligence action. However, strict liability was not intended to make manufacturers absolutely liable for all injuries. Strict liability seeks to direct the trier of fact's attention to the condition of the product rather than to the conduct of the manufacturer. The admission of state-of-the-art evidence regarding the knowability of risks does infuse negligence concepts into strict liability cases by focusing on the actions of the manufacturer. However, this must be allowed because failure-to-warn actions are significantly different from design defect claims. Strict liability would become absolute liability if manufacturers were required to warn about risks that were unknowable at the time of distribution. Furthermore, the infusion of some negligence features into a strict liability failure-to-warn suit would only require the injured plaintiff to prove that the manufacturer did not warn of a knowable risk rather than to prove that a standard of due care has been breached. Therefore, in a failure-to-warn theory of strict liability, knowability of the risk according to the state-of-the-art evidence at the time of distribution is relevant. Affirmed.

ANALYSIS

In a separate opinion, Justice Mosk advocated that failure-to-warn actions should be maintained only in negligence, given the fact that there was nearly no distinction left after this ruling. This decision is in accord with the majority rule that a fault-based standard is applicable in warnings cases. See *Fibreboard Corp. v. Fenton*, 845 P.2d 1168 (Colo. 1993).

Quicknotes

FAILURE TO WARN The failure of an owner or occupier of land to inform persons present on the property of defects or active operations which may cause injury.

STATE OF THE ART The relevant information available at a particular time.

STRICT LIABILITY Liability for all injuries proximately caused by a party's conducting of certain inherently dangerous activities without regard to negligence or fault.

Friedman v. General Motors Corp.

Runaway-car driver (P) v. Manufacturer (D)

Ohio Sup. Ct., 43 Ohio St. 2d 209, 331 N.E.2d 702 (1975)

NATURE OF CASE: Action to recover damages for personal injuries against car manufacturer.

FACT SUMMARY: Friedman (P) was injured when he started his car and it unexpectedly leapt forward; in an action against the car's manufacturer, Friedman (P) was unable to present direct evidence that the ignition system was defectively designed.

RULE OF LAW

A product defect may be proved by circumstantial evidence, where a preponderance of that evidence establishes that an accident was caused by a defect and not other possibilities, although not all other possibilities need be eliminated.

FACTS: Friedman (P), in his complaint against General Motors Corp. (D) alleged that he turned the ignition on his 17-month-old 1966 Oldsmobile while the gearshift was in the "drive" position, and that unexpectedly, the car "leaped forward, and so startled [him] that he could not regain control before the automobile ran wild," crashing, and thereby injuring him and his family. At trial, testimony by the car's retailer-dealer and Friedman (P) suggested that the linkages and the adjustments existing at the time of the accident were the original factory set. Friedman (P) and his family testified that the car had always been started in Park, thus affording no opportunity for discovering the alleged defect, that the gear shift indicator and transmission had always operated properly, and that prior to impact the Toronado accelerated. There was also evidence that a Toronado starts only in Neutral or Park gear position. However, expert witnesses called by Friedman (P) could only state that the gear shift pointer was probably damaged; they could not point to an identifiable defect. General Motor's (D) expert witness suggested that any damage to the indicator resulted from the accident. The trial court's directed verdict for General Motors (D) was reversed by the intermediate appellate court. General Motors (D) appealed.

ISSUE: May a product defect be proved by circumstantial evidence, where a preponderance of that evidence establishes that an accident was caused by a defect and not other possibilities, although not all other possibilities need be eliminated?

HOLDING AND DECISION: (Brown, J.) Yes. A product defect may be proved by circumstantial evidence, where a preponderance of that evidence establishes that an accident was caused by a defect and not other possibilities, although not all other possibilities need be eliminated. All a plaintiff need present, in terms of evidence, is that the product was defective; that the defect existed at the time the product left the factory; and that the defect was the direct and proximate cause of the accident and injuries. Since Friedman (P) met this burden, the case should have been left to the jury. Affirmed.

DISSENT: (Stern, J.) While evidence may be sufficient to permit an inference that something was wrong with a car, that alone is not sufficient to establish a defect except, perhaps, in cases analogous to res ipsa loquitur, in which ordinary human experience tells us that the event could not happen without a defect. The instant case is not such a case, for driver error, failure of some part, accidental or unwitting damage to the car, and other possibilities do provide other explanations.

ANALYSIS

A design defect has been defined as applying to the situation where the product is as intended by the manufacturer, but is designed in such manner as to pose an inherent danger of injury in ordinary usage. Cases involving design defect may usually be argued either on a strict liability or negligence theory, and fall into three main groups: failure to provide a product with safety features; failure to anticipate emergency situations which are foreseeable; and failure to adequately test a product before placing it in the stream of commerce.

Quicknotes

CIRCUMSTANTIAL EVIDENCE Evidence that, though not directly observed, supports the inference of principal facts.

DESIGN DEFECT A defect in a product manufactured according to the intended design, but present because the design of the product itself presents a risk of harm to consumers.

Daly v. General Motors Corp.

Driver's survivor (P) v. Car manufacturer (D)

Cal. Sup. Ct., 20 Cal. 3d 725, 575 P.2d 1162 (1978)

NATURE OF CASE: Appeal from denial of damages in products liability action.

FACT SUMMARY: Daly (P), whose decedent was killed in an automobile accident, alleged that a defective door latch caused the death, while General Motors Corp. (D) attributed the death to the driver's failure to use a shoulder harness and his intoxication.

RULE OF LAW

A plaintiff's recovery in a strict products liability action may be reduced according to the extent to which his injury resulted from his own lack of reasonable care.

FACTS: Daly's (P) decedent was killed in an automobile accident. Daly (P) alleged that the door latch of the Opel automobile in question was defective, and that the defect caused the accident. General Motors Corp. (D), the manufacturer of the Opel, alleged that the accident and death were caused by the driver's failure to wear a shoulder harness and by his intoxication at the time of the accident. At trial, the jury gave its verdict for General Motors (D). Daly (P) appealed.

ISSUE: May a plaintiff's recovery in a strict products liability action be reduced according to the extent to which his injury resulted from his own lack of reasonable care?

HOLDING AND DECISION: (Richardson, J.) Yes. A plaintiff's recovery in a strict products liability action may be reduced according to the extent to which his injury resulted from his own lack of reasonable care. This case presents the question of whether the principles of comparative negligence now in force in this state should be applicable to actions brought under the theory of strict products liability. This court has already recognized that a plaintiff's negligence in such a case comprises a defense when it reaches the level of assumption of risk. Terms such as "assumption of risk" and "comparative negligence" are not exact measurements, and the judicial posture in applying them must be flexible rather than doctrinaire. The purpose and goal of strict products liability is to eliminate problems of proof of negligence. With the application in these cases of the comparative negligence doctrine, proof of negligence is still obviated, but the defendant may show that its negligence caused the injury only to the extent that the plaintiff's own conduct did not. Thus, a plaintiff's recovery in a strict products liability action may be reduced according to the extent to which his injury resulted from his own lack of reasonable care. This moves the law closer to the goal of the equitable allocation of legal responsibility for personal injuries. Reversed.

ANALYSIS

There is an important distinction between strict products liability and absolute liability. Absolute liability is imposed where a defendant is held as an insurer of the plaintiff's safety as a matter of social policy. The defendant's use of even the utmost care will not relieve him of absolute liability. These cases usually arise in the context of ultra-hazardous activities or the keeping of wild animals and are sometimes referred to as "strict liability" cases, though "absolute liability" is a term better demonstrating the difference between these cases and strict products liability cases. The plaintiff's conduct is irrelevant in absolute liability cases, though some jurisdictions permit assumption of the risk as a defense. In strict products liability cases, however, assumption of risk is always a defense, and under the above case, the comparative negligence of the plaintiff can reduce, if not defeat, his recovery.

Quicknotes

ABSOLUTE LIABILITY Liability for all injuries proximately caused by a party's conducting of certain inherently dangerous activities without regard to negligence or fault.

ASSUMPTION OF RISK DOCTRINE An affirmative defense to a negligence suit by the defendant contending that the plaintiff knowingly and voluntarily subjected himself to the hazardous condition wholly absolving the defendant of liability for injuries incurred.

COMPARATIVE NEGLIGENCE Doctrine whereby the court in assessing the appropriate measure of damages compares the relative fault of the parties and reduces the amount of damages to be collected by the plaintiff in proportion to his degree of fault.

STRICT PRODUCT LIABILITY Liability of a manufacturer or seller of a product for injuries sustained as a result of any defects without the necessity of a showing of negligence.

Ford Motor Co. v. Matthews

Tractor manufacturer (D) v. Estate administrator (P)

Miss. Sup. Ct., 291 So. 2d 169 (1974)

NATURE OF CASE: Action for wrongful death on a theory of strict liability.

FACT SUMMARY: Matthews's Ford (D) tractor was not supposed to start while in gear; while standing alongside it, Matthews turned on the ignition while the tractor was in gear, it started and ran over Matthews, killing him.

RULE OF LAW

Although misuse of a product that causes an injury is normally a bar to strict liability, a manufacturer is liable for injuries resulting from abnormal or unintended use of his product if such use was reasonably foreseeable.

FACTS: Matthews purchased a Ford Motor Co. (Ford) (D) tractor equipped with a starter safety switch that was designed to prevent the tractor from being started in gear. While the tractor was in gear, Matthews, standing alongside it, started the ignition. Matthews was killed as a result of being run over by the tractor. Matthews's estate (P) sued Ford (D) for wrongful death, contending that the plunger connected with the safety switch was defective, thus allowing the tractor to be started in gear. Ford (D) argued that Matthews's act of standing on the ground and starting the tractor while in gear was a misuse of the product and constituted an absolute limitation on its liability. After a judgment for the estate (P), Ford (D) appealed.

ISSUE: Although misuse of a product that causes an injury is normally a bar to strict liability, is a manufacturer liable for injuries resulting from abnormal or unintended use of his product if such use was reasonably foreseeable?

HOLDING AND DECISION: (Rodgers, P.J.) Yes. Although misuse of a product that causes an injury is normally a bar to strict liability, a manufacturer is liable for injuries resulting from abnormal or unintended use of his product if such use was reasonably foreseeable. The Restatement (Second) of Torts § 402A provides: "A product is not in a defective condition when it is safe for normal handling and consumption. If the injury results from abnormal handling . . . the seller is not liable." However, the cases the institute cites in support of its position either involved no defect, or if a defect was present it played no part in the accident. Here, the failure of the safety gear switch was a cause of the accident. Matthews had neither been warned nor knew of the danger. A manufacturer is free from liability for misuse of his product only when such use is not reasonably foreseeable. Ford (D) could certainly foresee that one day a tractor operator might carelessly crank the engine without first making certain that it was not in gear, especially if he were aware of the purpose of the safety switch system. Affirmed.

ANALYSIS

Prosser lists as normal foreseeable uses the following: "standing on a chair, heating coffee, testing heating fixtures, or wearing a cocktail robe in proximity to the kitchen stove. The seller of pork usually has been held to be entitled to expect that it will be cooked to kill trichinae; but where the question has arisen, it has been held that there is a normal use where the pork is cooked to an extent which the buyer erroneously believes to be sufficient." *Law of Torts* (1971 4th ed.), ch. 17, § 96, p. 648. Thus, the manufacturer's duty to warn the consumer of all reasonably foreseeable dangers has been broadly applied by the courts.

Quicknotes

DUTY TO WARN An obligation owed by an owner or occupier of land to persons who come onto the premises, to inform them of defects or active operations which may cause injury.

FORESEEABLE DANGER A danger that is likely to result from a certain act or failure to act.

STRICT LIABILITY Liability for all injuries proximately caused by a party's conducting of certain inherently dangerous activities without regard to negligence or fault.

WRONGFUL DEATH An action brought by the beneficiaries of a deceased person, claiming that the deceased's death was the result of wrongful conduct by the defendant.

Peterson v. Lou Bachrodt Chevrolet Co.

Pedestrians (P) v. Driver (D), car owner (D) and retailer (D)

Ill. Sup. Ct., 61 Ill. 2d 17, 329 N.E.2d 785 (1975)

NATURE OF CASE: Action to recover damages for wrongful death, and for personal injuries on a theory of strict liability.

FACT SUMMARY: Consumer suit sought to impose strict liability on a used-car dealer (D) who had sold a 1965 Chevrolet that had defective brakes.

RULE OF LAW

Strict liability does not extend to the seller of a defective used car.

FACTS: Two minors, Mark (P) and Maradean Peterson, were struck by a used 1965 Chevrolet automobile while on their way home from school. Maradean suffered fatal wounds, and Mark (P) sustained severe injuries. Maradean's estate (P) and Mark (P) brought, respectively, a wrongful death suit and an action for personal injuries against the driver (D) of the used car, its owners (D), and the retailer of the car, Lou Bachrodt Chevrolet Co. (D). The count against Lou Bachrodt (D), which was founded on a theory of strict liability, alleged that at the time the 1965 Chevrolet was sold it was defective and not reasonably safe for driving in that springs in the braking system were missing, a brake shoe was completely worn out, and a part of the cylinder braking system was missing. The trial court dismissed the count against Lou Bachrodt (D), and Maradean's estate (P) and Mark (P) appealed. The appellate court reversed.

ISSUE: Does strict liability extend to the seller of a defective used car?

HOLDING AND DECISION: (Schaefer, J.) No. Strict liability should not be imposed upon a defendant who is outside the original producing and marketing chain. Imposition of liability upon wholesalers and retailers is justified on the ground that their position in the marketing process enables them to exert pressure on the manufacturer to enhance the safety of the product. The manufacturer is liable on the ground that having created the risk and reaped the profit by placing the product in the stream of commerce, it should bear the loss. However, a used-car dealer, who ordinarily does not create the defects, should not become an insurer against defects that had come into existence after the chain of distribution was completed, and while the product was under the control of one or more consumers. Reversed.

DISSENT: (Goldenhersh, J.) Strict liability has been held applicable to the lessor of a motor vehicle. The same reasoning should extend to a used car dealer who can discover a defect upon reasonable inspection.

ANALYSIS

Most courts, and the Restatement (Second) of Torts § 402, have limited the application of strict product liability to only those individuals who are regularly engaged in the business of selling, leasing, or manufacturing. Thus, the occasional bailor or lessor is, as a rule, not strictly liable for defects in the chattel he loans out. The application of this limitation to used car retailers has been criticized as ignoring the fact that used car dealers are in fact engaged in an ongoing business.

Quicknotes

STRICT LIABILITY Liability for all injuries proximately caused by a party's conducting of certain inherently dangerous activities without regard to negligence or fault.

WRONGFUL DEATH An action brought by the beneficiaries of a deceased person, claiming that the deceased's death was the result of wrongful conduct by the defendant.

Erie Ins. Co. v. Amazon.com

Insurance company (P) v. Online commerce company (D)

925 F.3d 135 (4th Cir. 2019)

NATURE OF CASE: Appeal from grant of summary judgment to defendant in action for negligence, breach of warranty and strict liability in tort.

FACT SUMMARY: Erie Insurance Co. (Erie) (P), as the subrogee of donees of a headlamp purchased by the donor through Amazon.com's (Amazon's) (D) website, brought a products liability action against Amazon (D) sounding in negligence, breach of warranty, and strict liability in tort to recover for over $300,000 in damages sustained when the headlamp's batteries malfunctioned and ignited the donees' house, contending that Amazon (D) was, for all intents and purposes, the headlamp's "seller" and could, therefore, be held liable under state law.

RULE OF LAW

An electronic commerce company that provides fulfillment services to purchasers of manufacturers' products is not a "seller" subject to products liability for damages sustained when a product sold by a manufacturer through the company's fulfillment services malfunctions and causes damages, where the manufacturer transfers possession of the product to the company without the company's payment of a purchase price or agreement transferring title to it, and the agreement between company and manufacturer repeatedly specifies and contemplates that the manufacturer retains title to goods it stores in the company's warehouses as part of the company's fulfillment program.

FACTS: Cao purchased a headlamp on Amazon.com (Amazon) (D) and then gave it to friends as a gift. The headlamp's batteries malfunctioned, igniting the friends' house, resulting in over $300,000 in damages. Erie Insurance Company (Erie) (P), which insured the house, paid the loss. As subrogee, Erie (P) sued Amazon (D) in state court, contending it was the "seller" of the headlamp, for negligence, breach of warranty, and strict liability in tort. Amazon (D) removed the action to federal district court. Amazon's (D) website had clearly stated that the headlamp was sold by Dream Light and fulfilled by Amazon (D). Pursuant to the arrangement between Dream Light and Amazon (D), Dream Light could ship its inventory to an Amazon (D) warehouse for storage and, once an order was received online for a product, Amazon (D) would retrieve the product from inventory, box it, and ship it to the purchaser. In this case, Dream Light shipped its headlamps to Amazon's (D) warehouse in Virginia, and, when Cao's order for one came in, Amazon (D) packaged and shipped it to Cao using the third-party shipper, UPS Ground. As part of its fulfillment services, Amazon (D) also collected payment and, after withdrawing its service fee, remitted the balance to Dream Light, which set the price for the headlamp, created the content of the product's description used on the Amazon (D) site, and had the discretion to offer a warranty—which it did not in this case. Erie (P) contended that Amazon (D), like a brick-and-mortar store such as Home Depot, is a seller of products and therefore liable under state law for the defective products that it sells. Although Erie (P) conceded that the document evidencing the transaction in this case indicated that Dream Light was the seller, it argued that Amazon (D), through its fulfillment services program, took so much control over the transaction that it effectively became the seller and therefore became responsible under theories of negligence, breach of warranty, and strict liability in tort. Amazon (D) maintained that it was not the seller, as it never held title to the headlamp. Amazon (D) moved for summary judgment, which the district court granted, finding that Amazon (D) was not the headlamp's "seller" under state law. The court of appeals granted review.

ISSUE: Is an electronic commerce company that provides fulfillment services to purchasers of manufacturers' products a "seller" subject to products liability for damages sustained when a product sold by a manufacturer through the company's fulfillment services malfunctions and causes damages, where the manufacturer transfers possession of the product to the company without the company's payment of a purchase price or agreement transferring title to it, and the agreement between company and manufacturer repeatedly specifies and contemplates that the manufacturer retains title to goods it stores in the company's warehouses as part of the company's fulfillment program?

HOLDING AND DECISION: (Niemeyer, J.) No. An electronic commerce company that provides fulfillment services to purchasers of manufacturers' products is not a "seller" subject to products liability for damages sustained when a product sold by a manufacturer through the company's fulfillment services malfunctions and causes damages, where the manufacturer transfers possession of the product to the company without the company's payment of a purchase price or agreement transferring title to it, and the agreement between company and manufacturer repeatedly specifies and contemplates that the manufacturer retains title to goods it stores in the company's warehouses as part of the company's fulfillment program.

Continued on next page.

Under state substantive law, which federal courts must follow, irrespective of whether the theory of recovery is breach of warranty, negligence or strict liability, a plaintiff must show three product litigation basics—defect, attribution of defect to seller, and a causal relationship between the defect and the injury. The defect must be shown to exist at the time the product left the seller (whether manufacturer, distributor, or retailer) or at the time the sale was made. In each case, state law imposes liability on the seller. The state's courts have repeatedly noted that products liability claims sounding in negligence, breach of warranty, and strict liability in tort overlap, all focusing on the liability of a seller for a defective product. Moreover, there is no indication that the term "seller," as used in the state's products liability law, should be understood in any manner other than its ordinary meaning, which is that a "seller" is one that offers property for sale, with "sale" defined as the transfer of ownership of and the title to property from one person to another for a price. Accordingly, insofar as liability in the state for defective products falls on "sellers" and manufacturers (who are also sellers), it is imposed on owners of personal property who transfer title to purchasers of that property for a price. In this sense, a manufacturer, distributor, dealer, and retailer who own—i.e., have title to—the products during the chain of distribution are sellers, whereas shippers, warehousemen, brokers, marketers, auctioneers, and other bailees or consignees, who do not take title to property during the course of a distribution but rather render services to facilitate that distribution or sale, are not sellers. Although Amazon (D) does in fact sell products that it owns on its website and thus would be considered a seller of those products, in this case it facilitated the sale for Dream Light under its fulfillment program. Therefore, Dream Light was the seller. Although Amazon's (D) services were extensive in facilitating the sale, they are no more meaningful to the analysis than are the services provided by UPS Ground, which delivered the headlamp to Cao. Neither Amazon (D) nor UPS Ground was a seller incurring liability for the defective product in this particular transaction, since neither transferred ownership of the property for a price. When Amazon (D) sells its own goods on its website, it has the responsibility of a "seller," just as any other retailer, such as Home Depot, would have. In contrast, when it provides a website for use by other sellers of products and facilitates those sales under its fulfillment program, it is not a seller, and it does not have the liability of a seller. [Affirmed as to this issue.]

CONCURRENCE: (Motz, J.) The court reaches the correct conclusion under state law that Amazon (D) was not a "seller" of the headlamp at issue in this case. However, technological advances may require that the law change to reflect current realities. Much of the state's product liability law was adopted at a time when the American economy operated much differently than it does now. In a traditional supply chain, manufacturers transfer new goods to consumers through multiple links, with each link in the chain—from manufacturer to distributor to retailer—taking title to, and possession of, the product. Because seller liability extends to manufacturers, distributors, and retailers alike, the consumer at the end of this supply chain almost always has some legal recourse in the event of an injury, for some entity in this linear supply chain is clearly a "seller" and available for service of process within the United States. Amazon (D) disrupts this traditional supply chain. By design, Amazon's (D) business model cuts out the middlemen between manufacturers and consumers, reducing the friction that might keep foreign (or otherwise judgment-proof) manufacturers from putting dangerous products on the market. Although Amazon (D) makes up at least 46 percent of the online retail marketplace, selling more than its next twelve online competitors combined, Amazon's (D) business model shields it from traditional products liability whenever state law strictly requires the exchange of title for seller liability to attach, in many cases forcing consumers to bear the cost of injuries caused by defective products (particularly where the formal "seller" of a product fails even to provide a domestic address for service of process). Looking at the substance of the transaction at issue, Amazon (D) had an outsized role: nearly the only thing Amazon (D) did not do was to hold title to the headlamp. Thus, considerations of public policy may justify changing the law as it currently stands. A federal court sitting in diversity, however, must proceed with caution. A federal court must take state law as it finds it or, if necessary, predict how the state's highest court would rule on an unsettled issue. Given the policy-intensive nature of this inquiry, the lack of on-point state precedent, and Amazon's (D) novel business model, it cannot be confidently predicted that the state's courts would treat Amazon (D) as a seller under state law. Moreover, it would not be appropriate, in the absence of a request from either party, to certify this question to the state's highest court on this court's own initiative. Nonetheless, nothing prevents the state's own courts or legislators from taking up and resolving these difficult, fast-changing, and cutting-edge issues differently. To be sure, Amazon's (D) strategy of removing nearly every products liability case to federal court has complicated this endeavor and arguably stunted the development of state law. But legislative reforms, non-removable lawsuits, and (in appropriate cases) certification remain available to consumers and state leaders who seek to confront these uniquely modern challenges.

ANALYSIS

In a case with a similar factual posture, a Third Circuit three-judge panel, in *Oberdorf v. Amazon.com, Inc.*, 930 F.3d 136 (3d Cir. 2019), relied on policy considerations

Continued on next page.

enumerated in Pennsylvania's state case law to hold that Amazon (D) was a "seller" subject to strict products liability, notwithstanding that it had neither title nor even control over the defective product involved (the product was shipped directly from the vendor to the customer, not to an Amazon (D) warehouse). The court concluded that those factors, taken from *Musser v. Vilsmeier Auction Co.*, *Inc.*, 522 Pa. 367, 562 A.2d 279 (1989), weighed in favor of finding that Amazon (D) was the seller. Those factors are: the operator (Amazon (D)) was the only member of the marketing chain available to the customer for redress; imposition of strict liability upon the operator would serve as an incentive to safety; the operator was in a better position than the customer to prevent the circulation of defective products; and the operator's ability to distribute the cost of compensating for injuries resulting from product defects.

Quicknotes

BREACH OF WARRANTY The breach of a promise made by one party to a contract on which the other party may rely, relieving that party from the obligation of determining whether the fact is true and indemnifying the other party from liability if that fact is shown to be false.

NEGLIGENCE Conduct falling below the standard of care that a reasonable person would demonstrate under similar conditions.

STRICT LIABILITY Liability for all injuries proximately caused by a party's conducting of certain inherently dangerous activities without regard to negligence or fault.

SUBSTANTIVE LAW Law that pertains to the rights and interests of the parties and upon which a cause of action may be based.

SUMMARY JUDGMENT Judgment rendered by a court in response to a motion made by one of the parties, claiming that the lack of a question of material fact in respect to an issue warrants disposition of the issue without consideration by the jury.

T.H. v. Novartis Pharmaceuticals Corp.

Child of woman prescribed medication while pregnant (P) v. Pharmaceutical company (D)

Cal. Sup. Ct., 4 Cal. 5th 145, 407 P.3d 18, 226 Cal. Rptr. 3d 336 (2017)

NATURE OF CASE: Appeal in action for negligent drug labeling. [The procedural posture of the case is not presented in the casebook extract.]

FACT SUMMARY: Minor children of a woman, who while pregnant had been prescribed the generic drug terbutaline, a generic form of the brand-name drug Brethine, brought suit against Novartis Pharmaceuticals Corp. (Novartis) (D), the manufacturer of Brethine, alleging that they had suffered fetal brain injury as a result of their mother having taken terbutaline; that Novartis (D) knew or should have known that the drug posed a serious risk to fetal brain development; and that the drug's label unreasonably failed to include a warning about this risk and falsely represented that the drug was safe for use by pregnant women. The minor children sought to hold Novartis (D) responsible for the alleged warning label deficiencies. Novartis (D) countered that it owed no duty to the minor children (P) to update or maintain an accurate label because (1) it did not manufacture the terbutaline that caused their injuries; and (2) it had divested ownership of Brethine, the brand-name drug, several years before the children's (P) mother had been prescribed terbutaline.

RULE OF LAW

A brand-name drug manufacturer has the duty under state law to warn of the risks about which it knew or reasonably should have known, regardless of whether and when the consumer is prescribed the brand-name drug or its generic bioequivalent.

FACTS: Twin children (P), who suffered from the effects of fetal brain injury after their mother was prescribed terbutaline sulfate (terbutaline) when she was pregnant, brought suit against Novartis Pharmaceuticals Corp. (Novartis) (D), the manufacturer of Brethine, which was the brand-name form of terbutaline, alleging that Novartis (D) knew or should have known that the drug posed a serious risk to fetal brain development, and that the drug's label unreasonably failed to include a warning about this risk and falsely represented that the drug was safe for use by pregnant women. Federal law explicitly conveys to the brand-name manufacturer—and only that manufacturer—the responsibility to provide an adequate warning label for both generic drugs and its own brand-name bioequivalent drugs. Only the brand-name drug manufacturer has unilateral authority to modify a drug's label by adding to or strengthening a warning, and generic drug manufacturers are required to follow the brand-name manufacturer's label to the letter for generic drugs that are the bioequivalent of their brand-name counterparts. Although their mother had not been prescribed Brethine, and although Novartis (D) had stopped manufacturing Brethine and sold all rights to the drug six years before the children's (P) injury, the children (P) claimed that Novartis's (D) control over the Brethine label rendered it responsible for any deficiencies in the terbutaline label, given that generic drug manufacturers are legally obligated to use the label crafted by the brand-name drug manufacturer. Novartis (D) contended that it owed no duty to the children to update or maintain an accurate label because (1) it did not manufacture the terbutaline that caused plaintiffs' injuries; and (2) it had divested ownership of Brethine, several years before plaintiffs' mother was prescribed terbutaline. The state's intermediate appellate court ruled in favor of the children (P), and, upon appeal by Novartis (D), the state's highest court granted review. [The complete procedural posture of the case is not presented in the casebook extract.]

ISSUE: Does a brand-name drug manufacturer have the duty under state law to warn of the risks about which it knew or reasonably should have known, regardless of whether and when the consumer is prescribed the brand-name drug or its generic bioequivalent?

HOLDING AND DECISION: (Cuellar, J.) Yes. A brand-name drug manufacturer has the duty under state law to warn of the risks about which it knew or reasonably should have known, regardless of whether and when the consumer is prescribed the brand-name drug or its generic bioequivalent. Under state law, a brand-name drug manufacturer has a duty to warn of known or reasonably knowable adverse effects arising from an individual's use of its drug. To determine whether Novartis (D) may be held liable for deficiencies in its warning label for its brand-name drug, that then is copied by a generic drug manufacturer, and injuries are caused by the generic drug that is a bioequivalent of the brand-name drug, a number of policy factors must be considered and weighed. If Novartis (D) is to be susceptible to liability, it must be determined that a brand-name manufacturer owes a duty of ordinary care to those who may be injured by deficiencies in its warning label. The factors to be considered are foreseeability, the certainty of the injury, and the closeness of the connection between the plaintiff and the defendant—factors that address the foreseeability of the relevant injury—and the remaining factors—moral blame, the policy of preventing future harm, the burden on the defendant and the general

Continued on next page.

public, and the availability of insurance—focus on the public policy justifications for or against carving out an exception to the general duty of care in this category of cases. The factor that weighs most heavily is the foreseeability of physical harm. Here, Novartis (D) could reasonably have foreseen that deficiencies in its Brethine label could mislead physicians about the safety of terbutaline, which was legally required to bear an identical label. A pharmaceutical company's burden and the consequences to the community of imposing a duty of care must be balanced against the public interest in preventing harm. The burden that matters, though, is not the cost of compensating individuals for injuries that the defendant has actually and foreseeably caused. Shielding tortfeasors from the full magnitude of their liability for past wrongs is not a proper consideration in determining the existence of a duty. Rather, the most relevant burden is the cost to the defendant of upholding, not violating, the duty of ordinary care. Strictly speaking, then, the burden on brand-name drug manufacturers of satisfying a common law duty of care to those who are prescribed the generic version of the drug is zero. Under federal law, brand-name manufacturers already have a continuing duty to warn of potential risks as soon as there is reasonable evidence of an association of a serious hazard with a drug; a causal relationship need not have been proved. A brand-name manufacturer's burden to maintain an adequate warning label persists without regard to the happenstance that a given prescription for a brand-name drug may—because of insurance company cost-savings rules, or a pharmacist's discretion—be filled with a generic bioequivalent. Thus, where the brand-name manufacturer provides an adequate label, it necessarily has also fulfilled its duty with respect to the generic bioequivalent. Rejected is Novartis's (D) argument that unless the ordinary duty of care is narrowed, the brand-name drug manufacturer would end up an insurer for the entire market, even in situations where the brand-name manufacturer may hold only a small fraction of the combined sales of the brand-name drug and its generic bioequivalent. If tort law simply carved out those who were given the generic bioequivalent from obtaining otherwise available compensation for injuries attributable to the brand-name drug manufacturer's defective warning label, then consumers would insist on the brand-name drug over the cheaper bioequivalent, inflating health costs with no corresponding increase in safety and in contradiction to the stated federal policy of making low-cost generic drugs more available. Novartis (D) nonetheless predicts that unless such a carve-out is judicially created for those taking generic drugs, warning label liability will lead to overwarning—i.e., inclusion of a slew of speculative risks in the warning label—that would dilute the effectiveness of any individual warning. However, why this would occur is far from clear. To recognize that the duty of care includes all those who would foreseeably be affected by a deficient brand-name drug label merely preserves the brand-name manufacturer's duty as it existed when its patent excluded all competitors from the market. Nor has Novartis (D) identified any surge in overwarning since warning label liability was first recognized. Moreover, the consequences of any overwarning on physicians' prescription decisions can be solved through the FDA's power to reject a labeling change it deems unnecessary or counterproductive. Equally unpersuasive is Novartis's (D) contention that warning label liability would stifle innovation by substantially raising drug costs and chilling the development and marketing of new drugs. The logic buttressing this argument is far from self-evident. Warnings about a product's efficacy or danger may indeed risk diminishing its value to the manufacturer. Less obvious is the manufacturer's response to this predicament. One might just as easily assert that a drug company, after adding a new warning, will be incentivized to develop new and safer alternatives to the drug so that it can recapture the market for treatment of that disease. For these reasons, in this state, where a brand-name drug manufacturer has a duty to warn of known or reasonably knowable adverse effects arising from an individual's use of its drug, brand-name drug manufacturers have a duty to use ordinary care in warning about the safety risks of their drugs, regardless of whether the injured party (in reliance on the brand-name manufacturer's warning) was dispensed the brand-name or generic version of the drug. Additionally, a brand-name manufacturer's sale of the rights to a drug does not, as a matter of law, terminate its liability for injuries foreseeably and proximately caused by deficiencies present in the warning label prior to the sale. Affirmed.

ANALYSIS

Novartis (D) sought from the California Supreme Court in this decision an unequivocal declaration that California law relieves a manufacturer of any failure-to-warn liability relating to another manufacturer's products. California law ordinarily relieves a manufacturer of the duty to warn consumers about a product's risks where the product is that of another manufacturer, since a product manufacturer ordinarily will have no control over the design or safety of another manufacturer's product, the other manufacturer's use of dangerous materials, or any warnings the other manufacturer might place on the product, and since a manufacturer ordinarily does not have the ability to influence a customer's decision to buy another manufacturer's product. Without such predicate connections between one manufacturer and another, it would be difficult, if not impossible, for a manufacturer to foresee the dangers lurking in the seemingly limitless number of other products that might be used with or in its product. However, as the California Supreme Court explained, the prescription drug markets are different because they present the unusual situation where one entity's misrepresentations about its own product foreseeably

Continued on next page.

and legally will contribute substantially to the harm caused by another entity's product (i.e., the generic drug bearing the warning label drafted by the brand-name manufacturer). That key circumstance distinguishes the situation in the pharmaceuticals market from situations involving the general run of products. The Court thus concluded that the negligence causes of action in this case were potentially viable because of the allegedly deficient representations in Novartis's (D) warning label, since Novartis (D) was not being sued for dangers inherent in the generic terbutaline manufactured by some other entity, nor did the plaintiff children (P) claim that any product manufactured by Novartis (D) caused them harm. They claimed instead that allegedly deficient representations and omissions in Novartis's (D) warning label caused them harm. The tort claims were not based on the manufacturing of the product but instead alleged that the label—drafted by the brand-name manufacturer and required by federal law to be replicated verbatim on the generic version of the medication—failed to warn. For these reasons, the Court effectively ruled that the plaintiffs stated a cause of action against Novartis (D).

Quicknotes

CAUSATION The aggregate effect of preceding events that bring about a tortious result; the causal connection between the actions of a tortfeasor and the injury that follows.

CAUSE OF ACTION A fact or set of facts the occurrence of which entitles a party to seek judicial relief.

DUTY OF CARE A principle of negligence requiring an individual to act in such a manner as to avoid injury to a person to whom he or she owes a duty.

FORESEEABILITY OF HARM An inquiry into the relatedness of events that contributed to the plaintiff's injury; whether the harm was foreseeable determines whether the tortfeasor's conduct was the proximate cause of the injury.

PUBLIC POLICY Policy administered by the state with respect to the health, safety and morals of its people in accordance with common notions of fairness and decency.

Hector v. Cedars-Sinai Medical Center

Patient (P) v. Medical center (D)

Cal. Ct. App., 180 Cal. App. 3d 493, 225 Cal. Rptr. 595 (1986)

NATURE OF CASE: Appeal from dismissal of a personal injury claim.

FACT SUMMARY: Hector (P) sought to bring a strict products liability action against Cedars-Sinai Medical Center (D), the hospital where her defective pacemaker was implanted.

RULE OF LAW

Since the essence of the relationship between hospitals and patients is for the provision of medical services, hospitals are not liable under strict products liability because they are not engaged in the business of selling products.

FACTS: Hector (P) had a pacemaker, manufactured by American Technology, implanted at Cedars-Sinai Medical Center (Cedars-Sinai) (D). Hector (P) filed a complaint against Cedars-Sinai (D), alleging personal injuries from a defective pacemaker. The complaint contained causes of action under negligence, strict liability, and breach of warranty theories. Cedars-Sinai (D) moved for the dismissal of the strict liability action, and the trial court granted the motion. Hector (P) appealed.

ISSUE: May hospitals be held liable under a strict products liability theory?

HOLDING AND DECISION: (Spencer, J.) No. Since the essence of the relationship between hospitals and patients is for the provision of medical services, hospitals are not liable under strict products liability because they are not engaged in the business of selling a product. Originally, strict liability was applied to manufacturers who placed a product on the market. Later, strict liability was extended to retailers because retailers were engaged in the business of distributing goods to the public and were an integral part of the overall enterprise. In other words, every party who plays a vital part in the chain of production and distribution may be held strictly liable. However, strict liability does not apply to a supplier of professional services. Medical personnel furnish services as a healer of illnesses. These services depend upon the skill and judgment derived from specialized training, knowledge, and experience. Doctors who treat patients cannot be construed as selling a product. Similarly, a hospital is not ordinarily engaged in the business of selling any products. The essence of the transaction between a hospital and a patient does not relate essentially to any product. Thus, hospitals may not be held strictly liable for products, such as blood or pacemakers, which it may supply to its patients. Furthermore, the policy considerations behind strict liability, which is based in part on the ability of manufacturers and distributors to protect themselves through testing and promoting safety, would not be served by holding a hospital strictly liable. The hospital is in a poor position to test pacemakers and other medical products. Cedars-Sinai (D) does not ordinarily stock pacemakers and does not recommend, sell, or distribute these devices. In this case, Hector (P) entered the hospital to obtain a course of treatment that included the implantation of the pacemaker. Thus, the essence of the transaction was for the provision of services, and strict liability may not be applied to Cedars-Sinai (D). Affirmed.

ANALYSIS

This court drew a distinction between products and services that is also included in the Uniform Commercial Code and § 402A of the Restatement (Second) of Torts. The rationale behind this distinction is that, in service transactions, there is no mass production, and the risk of loss cannot be easily passed on to consumers. In hybrid transactions, which include both a product and a service, courts usually look to see whether the transaction was predominantly a service or a sale.

Quicknotes

STRICT LIABILITY Liability for all injuries proximately caused by a party's conducting of certain inherently dangerous activities without regard to negligence or fault.

CHAPTER 16

Nuisance

Quick Reference Rules of Law

Philadelphia Electric Co. v. Hercules, Inc.

Polluted-property owner (P) v. Successor (D)

762 F.2d 303 (3d Cir. 1985)

NATURE OF CASE: Appeal from award of damages for nuisance.

FACT SUMMARY: Philadelphia Electric Co. (PECO) (P) contended that Hercules, Inc.'s (D) predecessor created a private nuisance on property purchased by PECO (P), which later had to pay the cost of eliminating the nuisance.

RULE OF LAW

A vendor of real property cannot be held liable in nuisance to the vendee.

FACTS: The Pennsylvania Industrial Chemical Corp. (Pennsylvania Industrial) owned property known as the "Chester" site, on which it operated a hydrocarbon resin plant. The property was sold to Gould, who in turn sold it to Philadelphia Electric Co. (PECO) (P). Hercules, Inc. (D) then took over all debts of Pennsylvania Industrial and assumed all of its liabilities. It was determined that chemicals used by Pennsylvania Industrial were polluting the Delaware River, and PECO (P) was required to pay $400,000 to clean up the pollution. It sued Hercules (D), contending the condition constituted a nuisance. Hercules (D) defended on the basis that no duty was owed to the vendee of land, and thus PECO (P) had no standing to sue. The jury found for PECO (P), and Hercules (D) appealed.

ISSUE: Can a vendor of real property be held liable in nuisance to the vendee?

HOLDING AND DECISION: (Higginbotham, J.) No. A vendor of real property cannot be held liable in nuisance to the vendee. The relationship between buyer and seller is ruled by the maxim "caveat emptor." The duty not to maintain a nuisance on one's property is owed to the owner or occupiers of adjacent land who would be affected by it. No duty is owed to the vendee in this regard. The vendee's remedies arise out of the sales transaction and any breach therein must be remedied within the contractual area. Similarly, no cause of action for public nuisance exists because PECO (P) suffered no injury distinct from that suffered by the public in general. Reversed.

ANALYSIS

This case illustrates the elements necessary to establish a cause of action for private and public nuisance. A private nuisance incurs damage to an individual while a public nuisance impacts on society generally. A private action for public nuisance requires a showing of distinct injury. See Restatement (Second) of Torts § 821 C.

Quicknotes

CAVEAT EMPTOR Let the buyer beware; doctrine that a buyer purchases something at his own risk.

VENDEE Purchaser.

VENDOR Seller.

Morgan v. High Penn Oil Co.

Property owner (P) v. Refinery (D)

N.C. Sup. Ct., 238 N.C. 185, 77 S.E.2d 682 (1953)

NATURE OF CASE: Action to recover temporary damages for a private nuisance, and to enjoin such nuisance.

FACT SUMMARY: Morgan (P) owned land next to High Penn Oil Co.'s (D) refinery, which emitted nauseating gases and odors.

RULE OF LAW

A person who intentionally creates or maintains a private nuisance is liable for the resulting injury to others, regardless of the degree of care or skill exercised by him to avoid such injury.

FACTS: Morgan (P) owned a nine-acre tract of land. High Penn Oil Co. (D) owned an adjoining tract on which it operated an oil refinery 1,000 feet from Morgan's (P) house. A few days each week, the refinery emitted nauseating gases and odors, which invaded Morgan's (P) land and made people sick. High Penn Oil Co. (D) failed to stop the pollution after notice and demand from Morgan (P) to abate it. High Penn Oil Co. (D) contended that the refinery was a modern plant, of a type in general use, and that, since it was not negligent in the plant's operation or maintenance, Morgan (P) could not recover.

ISSUE: Is a person who intentionally creates or maintains a private nuisance liable for the resulting injury to others, regardless of the degree of care or skill exercised by him to avoid such injury?

HOLDING AND DECISION: (Ervin, J.) Yes. A person who intentionally creates or maintains a private nuisance is liable for the resulting damage to others regardless of the degree of care or skill exercised by him to avoid such injury. Nuisances *per accidens* or in fact are those that become nuisances by reason of their location, or by reason of the manner in which they are constructed, maintained, or operated. A private nuisance in fact may be created or maintained without negligence. Nuisance, as a concept of law, has more than one meaning. The primary meaning does not involve the element of negligence as one of its essential factors. One acts sometimes at one's peril. In such circumstances, the duty to desist is absolute whenever conduct, if persisted in, brings damage to another. Defendant's motion is sustainable, but new trial ordered on different basis.

ANALYSIS

This case gives a good discussion of the difference between a nuisance *per se* or at law and a nuisance *per accidens* or in fact. A nuisance *per se* is an act, occupation, or structure that is nuisance at all times under any circumstances, regardless of location or surroundings. Nuisances *per accidens* or in fact are those that become nuisances by reason of their location, or by reason of the manner in which they are constructed, maintained, or operated. An oil refinery is, obviously, not a nuisance *per se* since it is a lawful enterprise, lawfully carried on. But the emission of nauseating gases that invade neighboring property make the refinery a nuisance in fact, even if the refinery is carefully operated. Note that the nuisance is a field of tort liability rather than a type of tortious conduct. It has a reference to the interests invaded, to the damage or harm inflicted, and not to any particular kind of act or omission that has led to the invasion. Negligence is merely one type of conduct that may give rise to a nuisance. Liability for nuisance may rest upon an intentional invasion of the plaintiff's interests, or upon a negligent one, or conduct that is abnormal.

Quicknotes

DICTUM Statement by a judge in a legal opinion that is not necessary for the resolution of the action.

NUISANCE An unlawful use of property that interferes with the lawful use of another's property.

NUISANCE *PER ACCIDENS* An action, occupation or building that becomes a nuisance due to its location or method of operation.

NUISANCE *PER SE* An action, occupation or building that is a nuisance at any time and under any condition.

Carpenter v. The Double R Cattle Company, Inc.

Homeowners (P) v. Feedlot owners (D)

Idaho Sup. Ct., 108 Idaho 602, 701 P.2d 222 (1985)

NATURE OF CASE: Appeal from denial of damages for nuisance.

FACT SUMMARY: The court of appeals held that The Double R Cattle Company, Inc. (D) had maintained a nuisance even though the utility of maintaining the feedlot outweighed the harm caused thereby.

RULE OF LAW

No nuisance may be found where the utility of the activity outweighs the gravity of harm.

FACTS: The Double R Cattle Company, Inc. (Double R) (D) maintained a feedlot for cattle. The lot fed approximately 9,000 cattle. Carpenter (P) and other adjacent homeowners sued in nuisance, contending the accumulation of manure, pollution of the river, odors, and insect infestation caused by the cattle damaged their right to quiet enjoyment of their land. The trial court refused Carpenter's (P) requested jury instructions based on Restatement (Second) of Torts § 826, which provided a nuisance could be found even where the gravity of harm was outweighed by the utility of the act, if damages could be paid. The jury found for Double R (D), and Carpenter (P) appealed. The court of appeals reversed, and Double R (D) appealed.

ISSUE: May nuisance be found where the utility of the activity outweighs the gravity of harm?

HOLDING AND DECISION: (Bakes, J.) No. A nuisance cannot be found where the utility of the activity outweighs the gravity of harm. In modern society, individuals must be willing to accept a certain amount of interference with quiet enjoyment in order to foster coexistence. The balancing test between harm and utility is well suited to this task. As a result, the Restatement does not reflect the law of Idaho, and the trial court did not err in failing to instruct the jury as requested by Carpenter (P) even where the gravity of harm is outweighed by the utility of activity. Reversed.

DISSENT: (Bistline, J.) While community interest is a factor, the blind adherence to ancient antiquated precedent serves to deny a remedy to a clear wrong. Such must be changed due to changes in modern lifestyle.

ANALYSIS

The court relied heavily on the specific factual circumstances in this case in arriving at its decision. It indicated that Idaho is sparsely populated and its economy is based on agribusiness. Thus, because the feedlot promotes this type of economy, it will be sanctioned only if the harm outweighs its utility. It is likely that if this case arose in a nonagricultural state, the utility of the act would be viewed differently, and the result would differ.

Quicknotes

NUISANCE An unlawful use of property that interferes with the lawful use of another's property.

Boomer v. Atlantic Cement Co., Inc.

Property owners (P) v. Cement plant (D)

N.Y. Ct. App., 26 N.Y.2d 219, 257 N.E.2d 870 (1970)

NATURE OF CASE: Action for an injunction to enjoin maintenance of a nuisance, and for damages.

FACT SUMMARY: Property owners (P) sued a cement plant (D) alleging that pollution emanating from the plant had injured their lands; while the trial court refused an injunction, it did authorize successive actions for damages.

RULE OF LAW

Although a nuisance will be enjoined even when a marked disparity is shown in economic consequence between the effect of the injunction and the effect of the nuisance, if the practical effect of the injunction will be to close a production plant, a court will condition on equitable grounds the continuance of the injunction on the payment of permanent damages.

FACTS: The Atlantic Cement Co., Inc. (Atlantic) (D) operated a large cement plant near Albany, New York in which it had invested $45,000,000, and employed over 300 workers. A group of neighboring landowners (P) brought actions for injunction and damages against Atlantic (D) alleging injury to their property from dirt, smoke, and vibration emanating from the plant. The trial court held that a nuisance existed, but denied the issuance of an injunction. Rather, it awarded the landowners (P) damages up to the time of trial, thus permitting them to maintain successive actions at law for damages thereafter as further injury was incurred. Atlantic (D) appealed.

ISSUE: Where the issuance of an injunction to enjoin the maintenance of a manufacturing operation as a nuisance would have the effect of closing the plant, will a court award permanent damages as an alternative?

HOLDING AND DECISION: (Bergan, J.) Yes. Although a nuisance will be enjoined even when a marked disparity is shown in economic consequence between the effect of the injunction and the effect of the nuisance, if the practical effect of the injunction will be to close a production plant, a court will condition on equitable grounds the continuance of the injunction on the payment of permanent damages. Courts should be wary of using a decision in private litigation as a purposeful mechanism to achieve direct public objectives greatly beyond the rights and interests before the court. The judicial establishment is neither equipped in the limited nature of any judgment it can pronounce nor prepared to lay down and implement an effective policy for the elimination of air pollution. This is a problem government alone is to resolve. Although an injunction should not be denied because the damage to a plaintiff is slight as compared to the defendant's expense of abating a nuisance, to follow this rule literally in this case would have the immediately drastic effect of closing the plant. One alternative would be to grant the injunction but postpone its effect to a specified future date to give opportunity for technical advances to permit Atlantic (D) to eliminate the nuisance. However, it is unlikely that Atlantic (D) by itself will be able to eliminate its pollution in the near future. The rate of the research is simply beyond its control. A better alternative would be to grant the injunction unless Atlantic (D) pays the landowners (P) permanent damages as may be fixed by the court. An amount of $185,000 would fairly compensate the landowners (P) for all past and future injury they have and will suffer. Reversed and remanded.

DISSENT: (Jasen, J.) The majority has in effect licensed a continuing wrong. Furthermore, once permanent damages are assessed and paid, the incentive to alleviate the wrong would be eliminated. Moreover, Atlantic (D) should not be allowed, as a private party, inverse condemnation; the public is not being benefitted. Finally, the landowners (P) are being forced to accept servitude on their land for the benefit of a private party.

ANALYSIS

In determining whether or not to enjoin a nuisance, a court "may take into consideration the relative economic hardship which will result to the parties from the granting or denial of the injunction, the good faith or intentional misconduct of each, and the interest of the general public in the continuation of the defendant's enterprise." Prosser, *Law of Torts* (1971 4th ed.) ch. 15, § 90 to p. 604. Another factor, as this case illustrates, is the financial investment each party has made in his land.

Quicknotes

INJUNCTION A court order requiring a person to do, or prohibiting that person from doing, a specific act.

INVERSE CONDEMNATION Taking of private property for public use so as to impair or decrease the value of property near or adjacent to, but not a part of, the property taken.

NUISANCE An unlawful use of property that interferes with the lawful use of another's property.

Spur Industries, Inc. v. Del E. Webb Development Co.

Feedlot operator (D) v. Retirement community (P)

Ariz. Sup. Ct., 108 Ariz. 178, 494 P.2d 700 (1972)

NATURE OF CASE: Action by developer to enjoin operation of a business as a public nuisance.

FACT SUMMARY: Del E. Webb Development Co. (P), developer of Sun City, a residential community that sprang up in a rural area near Spur Industries Inc.'s (Spur's) (D) cattle feedlot, sought an injunction against Spur (D) on the ground that as a breeder of flies the feedlot constituted a public nuisance.

RULE OF LAW

Although the operation of a business, lawful in the first instance, which becomes a nuisance by reason of a nearby residential area, may be enjoined in an action brought by the developer of the residential area, the developer must indemnify the business for a reasonable amount of the cost of moving or shutting down.

FACTS: Spur Industries, Inc. (Spur) (D) maintained a cattle feedlot in an area that had long been devoted to farming. Del E. Webb Development Co. (Del Webb) (P) began to develop Sun City, a retirement community, originally some distance from Spur (D). However, the development progressed rapidly and expanded, coming within 500 feet of Spur (D). Complaining that the Spur (D) feeding operation was a public nuisance because of the flies and the odor being blown over Sun City, Del Webb (P) sought a permanent injunction against Spur's (D) continued operations. State law defined a public nuisance as including "any condition or place in populous areas which constitutes a breeding place" for disease-carrying "flies, rodents, mosquitoes, and other insects. . . ." The trial court, finding that some of the citizens of Sun City were unable to enjoy the outdoor living Del Webb (P) had advertised, and that prospective purchasers were being discouraged, issued the injunction, but denied any compensatory relief for Spur (D) who appealed.

ISSUE:

(1) May a residential tract bring an action to abate a business as a public nuisance if the business was in the area first?

(2) If an injunction is issued, must the developer of the tract indemnify the business?

HOLDING AND DECISION: (Cameron, V.C.J.)

(1) Yes. Under the doctrine of "coming to the nuisance," courts of equity held that a residential landowner may not have relief if he knowingly came into a neighborhood reserved for industrial or agricultural endeavors and has been damaged thereby. The reasoning behind this rule is that a party cannot justly call upon the law to make the place suitable for his residence which was not so when he selected it. However, under our state statute, a business which is not per se a public nuisance may become such by being carried on at a place where the health, comfort, or convenience of a populous neighborhood is affected. Were Del Webb (P) the only injured party, "coming to the nuisance" would be a bar to the relief sought by it. However, since the residents of Sun City are being injured as well, Spur (D) must move, not because of any wrongdoing on its part, but because of the court's concern for the health and safety of the public.

(2) Yes. It does not seem harsh to require a developer, who has taken advantage of the lesser land values in a rural area, as well as the availability of large tracts of land on which to build and develop a new town or city in the area, to indemnify those who are forced to leave as a result. Del Webb (P) must therefore compensate Spur (D) for a reasonable amount of the cost of moving or shutting down. Affirmed in part; reversed in part; and remanded.

ANALYSIS

Most courts have held that ordinarily a plaintiff who purchases land next to a nuisance is not barred from bringing an action by the "coming to the nuisance" doctrine. However, where the equities between the two parties are fairly evenly balanced, the doctrine may be invoked and given controlling weight. The instant case perhaps represents a new trend in balancing the equities by looking to the compensation accorded the defendant were the plaintiff to prevail, and discarding the "coming to the nuisance" doctrine. Note, however, that "public nuisance" is specifically defined by statute in Arizona.

Quicknotes

COMING TO THE NUISANCE A claim may be weakened when a plaintiff moves to the defendant's established locale.

INDEMNIFY Securing against potential injury; compensation for injury suffered.

PUBLIC NUISANCE An activity that unreasonably interferes with a right common to the overall public.

CHAPTER 17

Defamation

Quick Reference Rules of Law

Belli v. Orlando Daily Newspapers, Inc.

Libeled attorney (P) v. Newspaper (D)

389 F.2d 579 (5th Cir. 1967), *cert. denied* 393 U.S. 825 (1968)

NATURE OF CASE: Action for damages for libel and slander.

FACT SUMMARY: A newspaper (D) printed a false story that Belli (P) had charged clothing to his hotel bill and that this had to be paid for by the local bar association.

RULE OF LAW

If a statement may be interpreted in both a defamatory and nondefamatory manner, it is the province of the jury to determine which one the general public would have taken.

FACTS: Belli (P), a well-known attorney, agreed to aid a local bar association in exchange for his hotel bills. Nine years later, this story was relayed to a local gossip columnist. It was embellished to include allegations that Belli (P) had charged numerous items of clothing to his hotel bill. This was false, but was published by Orlando Daily Newspapers, Inc. (D), which failed to verify the story. Belli (P) sued for libel and slander. The court dismissed on the basis that the story had not diminished Belli's (P) reputation and was not defamatory. The court apparently felt that the story would be viewed by the general public in a nondefamatory light and refused to submit the issue to the jury. Belli (P) appealed on the basis that the story had a defamatory connotation in that it held him up to ridicule, hatred, etc.

ISSUE: If a statement may be interpreted in both a defamatory and nondefamatory manner, is it the province of the jury to determine which one the general public would have taken?

HOLDING AND DECISION: (Wisdom, J.) Yes. The court makes the initial decision as to whether a statement is defamatory. If it is legally nondefamatory, the court removes it from the jury. If it is susceptible to two meanings, one defamatory and the other not, the jury must decide the issue. Here, the story might be viewed as a cute tale of how Belli (P) conned the local bar association. It might also be viewed as defamatory in that it exposed Belli (P) to hate, ridicule, etc., and lowered his reputation in the eyes of the community. It should have been submitted to the jury. Reversed and remanded.

ANALYSIS

Defamation has tended to broaden in scope in recent years. It is a communication that damages reputation, i.e., diminishes the respect, goodwill, confidence or esteem in which a party is held. It may also excite adverse or unpleasant feelings about a party. It may even include situations where decent citizens would regard a party only with pity. Alternative or companion causes of action include intentional infliction of emotional distress and invasion of privacy.

Quicknotes

ACTIONABLE PER SE Language of such an extreme nature that the law will presume that the person who is the subject of the communication has suffered injury and for which proof of damages is not required.

DEFAMATORY Subjecting to hatred, ridicule or injuring one in his occupation or business.

LIBEL A false or malicious publication that subjects a person to scorn, hatred or ridicule, or that injures him in relation to his occupation or business.

SLANDER Defamatory statement communicated orally.

Grant v. Reader's Digest Association

Libeled attorney (P) v. Publisher (D)

151 F.2d 733 (2d Cir. 1945)

NATURE OF CASE: Action to recover damages for libel.

FACT SUMMARY: Reader's Digest Association (D) printed in its publication an article that made reference to the fact that Grant (P) had been a legislative representative for the Massachusetts Communist Party. Grant (P) brought a suit for libel.

RULE OF LAW

Libel consists of utterances that arouse hatred, contempt, scorn, obloquy, or shame in the minds of people whether or not those persons are "right thinking" people.

FACTS: Reader's Digest Association (D) published in a periodical of general circulation (read by lawyers, judges, and the general public) an article that made reference to a Massachusetts lawyer, Sidney S. Grant (P), as having been hired by the Massachusetts Communist party to act as its legislative agent. Sidney S. Grant (P) brought this action against Reader's Digest Association (D) for libel. The complaint in libel was dismissed for insufficiency in law upon its face and Grant (P) appeals.

ISSUE: Does libel consist of utterances that arouse hatred, contempt, scorn, obloquy, or shame in the minds of people whether or not those persons are "right thinking" people?

HOLDING AND DECISION: (Hand, J.) Yes. The interest at stake in all defamation actions is the reputation of the person assailed. The New York decisions define libel as consisting of utterances which arouse "hatred, contempt, scorn, obloquy or shame" and the like. However, the opinions at the time seem to make it an additional condition that to bring an action for libel, the words must be such as would cause "right thinking" people to be aroused to hatred, contempt, etc., toward the plaintiff. This limitation has been recognized in England, and there is no doubt that there must come a point when words claimed to be defamatory must be defamatory to "right thinking" people. It is argued that "right thinking" people would not have such feelings toward a person who is a member of the Communist party. This court, however, does not believe that it is necessary to say whether "right thinking" people harbor such feelings toward a lawyer who was an agent for the Communist Party. It is enough if there are some persons who feel hatred, contempt, scorn, obloquy, or shame towards the plaintiff even though they would be "wrong thinking" people if they felt that way. Reversed and remanded.

ANALYSIS

It has been held in England that communications must tend to defame the plaintiff in the eyes of the community in general, or at least of a reasonable man, rather than in the opinion of any particular group or class. The American courts have taken a more realistic view, recognizing that the plaintiff may suffer real damage if he is lowered in the esteem of any substantial and respectable group, even though it may be quite a small minority. It has sometimes been said that these must be "right thinking" people, but this seems clearly wrong, since the court cannot be called upon to make a definitive pronouncement upon whether the views of different segments of the community are right or wrong, sound, or morally justifiable.

Quicknotes

DEFAMATION An intentional false publication, communicated publicly in either oral or written form, subjecting a person to scorn, hatred or ridicule, or injuring him or her in relation to his or her occupation or business.

LIBEL A false or malicious publication subjecting a person to scorn, hatred or ridicule, or injuring him or her in relation to his or her occupation or business.

MORAL OBLOQUY Blame; reproach; censure.

Kilian v. Doubleday & Co., Inc.

Libeled officer (P) v. Publisher (D)

Pa. Sup. Ct., 367 Pa. 117, 79 A.2d 657 (1951)

NATURE OF CASE: Action for damages based on libel.

FACT SUMMARY: A book published by Doubleday & Co., Inc.(D) contained an article that claimed that Kilian (P), as commander of an army camp and hospital, had mistreated patients.

RULE OF LAW

To claim truth as a defense, it must be shown that the statements in the article were substantially true, not that other acts of a different nature occurred.

FACTS: Wolfe held a creative writing course for disabled veterans. Wolfe decided to publish the articles of his students in book form. Doubleday & Co., Inc. (Doubleday) (D) agreed to publish it. One article contained an allegedly first-hand account of mistreatment of patients and staff at an army hospital by Kilian (P), the hospital commander. At the end of the article, the editors added a note that Kilian (P) had been reprimanded and fined for his actions. Kilian (P) brought suit for libel. At trial, it was shown that the author of the article had never been at the hospital but was merely relating stories he had heard. Kilian's (P) reprimand had been for neglect of duty in allowing certain punishments to be inflicted on prisoners by his men. Doubleday (D) had three witnesses testify as to actions they had observed at the hospital that showed cruel punishments being inflicted. There was no showing that the lashing recounted in the article had ever occurred or that Kilian (P) had been personally present at any of the incidents. The jury found that Doubleday (D) had shown that similar but different incidents had occurred and found for Doubleday (D).

ISSUE: To claim truth as a defense, must it be shown that the statements in the article were substantially true, not that other acts of a different nature occurred?

HOLDING AND DECISION: (Stern, J.) Yes. To claim truth as a defense, it must be shown that the statements in the article were substantially true, not that other acts of a different nature occurred. Here, there was no such showing. While misconduct was shown, it was of a different nature. The events were not the same and there was no showing that Kilian (P) was ever present at these "punishments." None of the witnesses testified as to any lashings administered to staff members. It is not enough to show that different offenses occurred, even if they were more serious. Where specific incidents are alleged, they must be proven. The court erred in submitting the case to the jury. Reversed and remanded.

ANALYSIS

While this holding might seem unfair, it must be borne in mind that the author was reporting hearsay that could have as easily been false. Where a person's reputation is at stake, it seems fair to require a reasonable attempt to verify such facts. Defendant must establish that the statement is substantially true. This means that the basic accusations must be true in a majority of the facts.

Quicknotes

HEARSAY An out-of-court statement made by a person other than the witness testifying at trial that is offered in order to prove the truth of the matter asserted.

LIBEL A false or malicious publication subjecting a person to scorn, hatred or ridicule, or injuring him or her in relation to his or her occupation or business.

Neiman-Marcus v. Lait

Department store owner (P) v. Author (D)

13 F.R.D. 311 (S.D.N.Y. 1952)

NATURE OF CASE: Action to recover damages for libel.

FACT SUMMARY: Lait (D) published a book in which he referred to Neiman-Marcus (P) models (P) and saleswomen (P) as being call girls and which referred to Neiman-Marcus (P) dress and millinery designers (P) as fairies. Working at Nieman-Marcus were 382 saleswomen (P), 25 salesmen (P), and nine models (P).

RULE OF LAW

Where a group or class disparaged is a large one, absent circumstances pointing to a particular plaintiff as the person defamed, no individual member of the group or class has a cause of action. However, where the group or class libeled is small, and each and every member of the group or class is referred to, then any individual member can sue.

FACTS: In their book entitled *U.S.A. Confidential*, the authors (D) stated that some Neiman-Marcus models (P) are call girls. It further stated that Neiman-Marcus salesgirls (P) are also call girls. The authors further state that "the nucleus of the Dallas Fairy Colony" is composed of Neiman-Marcus dress and millinery designers (P). At the time of the publication of the book, there were nine models (P) working at Neiman-Marcus (P). There were 15 individual salesmen, of a total of 25 salesmen, who worked for Neiman-Marcus (P) at the time of publication and who brought this suit on behalf of themselves and the other salesmen. Also, 30 individual saleswomen (P) of a total of 382 saleswomen sued for libel. Lait (D) requested a motion to dismiss all causes of action for failure to state a cause of action.

ISSUE: Where a group or class disparaged is a large one, absent circumstances pointing to a particular plaintiff as the person defamed, does any individual member of the group or class have a cause of action?

HOLDING AND DECISION: (Kaufman, J.) It depends on the size of the group. Where the group or class libeled is large, none can sue even though the language used is inclusive. However, where the group or class libeled is small, and each and every member of the class or group is referred to, then any individual member can sue. Where the group or class libeled is small and the publication complained of libels some or less than all of the group, the Restatement of Torts § 564 indicates that each member of the group has a cause of action. The court finds that the plaintiff salesmen, of whom it is alleged that "most . . . are fairies" have a cause of action. However, the saleswomen do not have a cause of action because their group is too large and no reasonable reader of the libelous statement could believe that 382 saleswomen were all call girls. Nonetheless, if any individual plaintiff saleswoman can prove that some particular circumstances point to her as the person defamed then she may recover. Amended complaint dismissed.

ANALYSIS

This plaintiff must sustain the burden of proof, by way of "colloquium," that the defamatory meaning attached to him. Reference to the plaintiff may, of course, be an indirect one, with the identification depending upon circumstances known to the hearers. When a group is defamed the plaintiff must first of all show that he is in fact a member of the class defamed. Beyond this, he must establish some reasonable personal application of the words to himself.

Quicknotes

COLLOQUIUM The connection between the libelous statements of the defendant and the plaintiff in a defamation action.

DEFAMATION An intentional false publication, communicated publicly in either oral or written form, subjecting a person to scorn, hatred or ridicule, or injuring him or her in relation to his or her occupation or business.

LIBEL A false or malicious publication subjecting a person to scorn, hatred or ridicule, or injuring him or her in relation to his or her occupation or business.

Bindrim v. Mitchell

Group therapist (P) v. Author (D)

Cal. Ct. App., 92 Cal. App. 3d 61, 155 Cal. Rptr. 29 (1979), *cert. denied* 444 U.S. 984 (1979), *reh. denied* 444 U.S. 1040 (1980)

NATURE OF CASE: Appeal from award of damages for libel.

FACT SUMMARY: Bindrim (P) alleged that he was defamed in a book written by Mitchell (D).

RULE OF LAW

The test of identification in a libel action is whether a reasonable person, viewing the work, would identify the "fictional" character described therein as the plaintiff.

FACTS: Gwen Davis Mitchell (D), a novelist, enrolled in a nude therapy group, run by Bindrim (P). She claimed to have enrolled for therapeutic reasons only and warranted that she would not write for publication regarding her experiences in the group. Shortly after undergoing the therapy, Mitchell (D) contracted with Doubleday Publishing Co. (D) to write a book based on the nude therapy group. The book, entitled *Touching*, went on to become a bestseller. Bindrim (P) brought suit for libel, alleging that certain false representations were made regarding the character in the novel, which was based on him. A jury returned a verdict in Bindrim's (P) favor. The court issued a remittitur. Mitchell (D) appealed, alleging that Bindrim (P) was not readily identifiable as the character in her book. Bindrim (P) also appealed.

ISSUE: Is the test of identification in a libel action whether a reasonable person, viewing the work, would identify the "fictional" character described therein as the plaintiff?

HOLDING AND DECISION: (Kingsley, J.) Yes. Mitchell (D) seems to base her defense on the fact that there were several major distinctions between the character in her novel and Bindrim (P); namely the physical appearance and the professional degree held. Thus, Mitchell (D) seeks a ruling that as a matter of law, Bindrim (P) cannot claim to be defamed by her book. However, such a ruling can only be made in certain extreme cases, of which this is not one. The test of identification in a case of this kind is whether a reasonable person, viewing the work, would identify the fictional character described therein as being the plaintiff. Given the factual circumstances presented here, it appears there were many similarities between Mitchell's (D) character and Bindrim (P). As such, the jury's finding that Bindrim (P) was identifiable as the character in *Touching* will not be disturbed on appeal. Affirmed.

CONCURRENCE: (Jefferson, J.) The fictional setting does not insure immunity when a reasonable person would understand that the fictional character is a portrayal of the plaintiff. The First Amendment right to comment does not include a right to commit libel.

DISSENT: (Files, P.J.) In the first instance, Mitchell's (D) book is not defamatory. In the second instance, the leading character cannot be readily identified, except through tortured logic, as Bindrim (P). Accordingly, an action for libel should not lie.

ANALYSIS

The *Bindrim* decision relies upon a long list of cases that hold that a reference to a libel plaintiff need not expressly name him to be actionable. It is enough that it is reasonably understood as referring to him. See, e.g., *Youssopoff v. M.G.M. Pictures*, 99 A.L.R. 864 (1934). Conversely, there will be no defamation if the plaintiff cannot prove that the statement may be reasonably understood as referring to him.

Quicknotes

DEFAMATION An intentional false publication, communicated publicly in either oral or written form, subjecting a person to scorn, hatred or ridicule, or injuring him or her in relation to his or her occupation or business.

LIBEL A false or malicious publication subjecting a person to scorn, hatred or ridicule, or injuring him or her in relation to his or her occupation or business.

REASONABLE PERSON STANDARD The standard of care exercised by a hypothetical person who possesses the intelligence, education, knowledge, attention, and judgment required by society of its members when governing behavior; the standard applies to a person's judgment when determining breach of a duty under the theory of negligence.

REMITTITUR The authority of the court to reduce the amount of damages awarded by the jury.

Terwilliger v. Wands

Slandered party (P) v. Slanderer (D)

N.Y. Ct. App., 17 N.Y. 54, 72 Am. Dec. 420 (1858)

NATURE OF CASE: Action to recover damages for slander.

FACT SUMMARY: Wands (D) said that Terwilliger (P) was having sexual intercourse with Mrs. Fuller, a married woman.

RULE OF LAW

Words that claim a man is having extra-marital intercourse are not actionable without a demonstration of special damages, since they do not disparage the man's character or reputation.

FACTS: Wands (D) told a third person that Terwilliger (P) was visiting Mrs. Fuller regularly for the purpose of having sexual intercourse with her, and that Terwilliger (P) would do all he could to keep Mrs. Fuller's husband in the penitentiary so that he could have access to her. The damages alleged were that Terwilliger (P) became ill and was unable to work after hearing of the reports circulated by Wands (D). Wands's motion for a nonsuit was sustained.

ISSUE: Are words that claim a man is having extra-marital intercourse actionable without a demonstration of special damages, since they do not disparage the man's character or reputation?

HOLDING AND DECISION: (Strong, J.) No. Words that have a natural and immediate tendency to produce injury are actionable per se and are adjudged to be injurious, though no special loss or damage can be proved. However, words that do not apparently and upon their face impart such defamation as will, of course, be injurious are not actionable per se and special damages must be shown. The kind of special damages that must be shown to have resulted from the words are damages produced by, or through, impairing the reputation. The words must be defamatory in nature, and must, in fact, disparage the character, and this disparagement must be evidenced by some positive loss arising therefrom. Hence, words that do not degrade the character do not injure and cannot occasion loss. In this case, Wands's (D) words were defamatory, and it may be assumed that Terwilliger's (P) illness was a result of the words. However, this result does not prove that Terwilliger's (P) character was injured, and so Terwilliger (P) cannot recover for slander. Affirmed.

ANALYSIS

This case demonstrates the difficulty of recovering if the slanderous words do not fall into one of the four categories that do not require the showing of special damages (pecuniary loss). Prosser states that since a plaintiff is seldom able to prove any specific pecuniary loss as a result of slander, the effect of the rule requiring a demonstration of such loss has been to deny recovery unless slander fits into one of the four categories. The fourth category added was words which accuse a woman of unchastity. Such words are actionable per se, without a showing of special damages, because of their harmfulness to a woman's reputation. As this case demonstrates, the law reflects society's double standard, and this rule is not applied to men, since such accusations are not as damaging to their reputation.

Quicknotes

ACTIONABLE PER SE Language of such an extreme nature that the law will presume that the person who is the subject of the communication has suffered injury and for which proof of damages is not required.

NONSUIT Judgment against a party who fails to make out a case.

SLANDER Defamatory statement communicated orally.

SPECIAL DAMAGES Damages caused by a specific act that are not the usual consequence of that act and which must be specifically pled and proven.

Economopoulos v. A.G. Pollard Co.

Defamed party (P) v. Clerk's employer (D)

Mass. Sup. Jud. Ct., 218 Mass. 294, 105 N.E. 896 (1914)

NATURE OF CASE: Action to recover damages for defamation.

FACT SUMMARY: Economopoulos (P) was told by agents of A.G. Pollard Co. (D) that he had stolen a handkerchief. Economopoulos (P) was told this by a clerk in English and it was later repeated to Economopoulos (P) in Greek. There was no evidence that a third party heard the English conversation or understood the Greek conversation.

RULE OF LAW

For a cause of defamation to lie there must be publication to third parties of the defamatory statement in such a manner so as to be understood by those hearing the statement.

FACTS: Economopoulos (P) was told by the agent of A.G. Pollard Co. (D) that he had stolen a handkerchief. Economopoulos (P) was told this by a clerk who spoke to him in English. At the time the statement was made in English no one else was present to overhear the statement. The statement was later repeated to Economopoulos (P) in Greek by a Greek clerk of A.G. Pollard Co. (D) and, although there were others present who could have overheard the statement at that time, it was not shown that anyone other than the clerk and Economopoulos (P) could understand Greek.

ISSUE: For a cause of defamation to lie must there be publication to third parties of the defamatory statement in such a manner so as to be understood by those hearing the statement?

HOLDING AND DECISION: (Loring, J.) Yes. For a cause of defamation to lie there must be publication to third parties of the defamatory statement in such a manner so as to be understood by those hearing the statement. The statement to Economopoulos (P) was not published. No one but Economopoulos (P) heard the clerk's statement to Economopoulos (P) in English. The evidence also failed to show that anyone besides Economopoulos (P) who heard the statements in Greek understood those statements. Exceptions overruled.

ANALYSIS

The student up to this time has been exposed to the general categories of defamation, slander, and libel. This case is an extension of all of those categories in that it discusses publication of the defamatory statement. "Publication" is a word of art in defamation cases. It does not mean printing, writing, or even publicity, but merely communication of the defamatory words to someone other than the person defamed. It is never enough that the words are spoken to the plaintiff himself, even in the presence of others, if no one overhears them. Therefore, in this case, the crucial point was made that although a potentially defamatory statement was made to the plaintiff, no one else overheard the statement, and that they did not understand it, which is just as effective as if they had not heard the statement to begin with.

Quicknotes

DEFAMATION An intentional false publication, communicated publicly in either oral or written form, subjecting a person to scorn, hatred or ridicule, or injuring him or her in relation to his or her occupation or business.

PUBLICATION The communicating of a defamatory statement to a third party.

Carafano v. Metrosplash.com, Inc.

Established actress (P) v. Online dating service (D)

339 F.3d 1119 (9th Cir. 2003)

NATURE OF CASE: Appeal from a ruling on summary judgment relieving an online dating service from liability for publishing false or defamatory information.

FACT SUMMARY: An unknown person pretended to be an established actress and, without the actress's consent, posted sexually suggestive information to an online dating service under the actress's identity.

RULE OF LAW

The immunity provision of the Communications Decency Act (CDA), 47 U.S.C. 230(c)(1), immunizes an interactive computer service (ICS) from liability for publishing false or defamatory material if another party besides the ICS provides the objectionable material.

FACTS: Matchmaker.com, Inc. (D), an online dating service, allowed its members to post profiles that included their pictures and written descriptions of themselves. Much of the descriptive information was posted in response to a questionnaire provided by Matchmaker.com (D). The service's policies forbade members from posting their last names and personal contact information in their profiles. Matchmaker.com (D), however, did not review its members' posted written information to ensure compliance with the company's policies. An unknown person purporting to be Carafano (P) posted a free trial profile, under the name of "Chase529," in Matchmaker.com's (D) Los Angeles section. At the time, Carafano (P) was an established film and TV actress, whose stage name was Chase Masterson. Pictures of her were readily available on the Internet, and the fake profile contained several of those readily available photos. Her purported responses to the questionnaire included several sexually suggestive comments, mention of two of her films, her home address, and an email address. When people tried to contact Carafano (P) at the listed email address, an automatic reply provided them her home address and telephone number. Carafano (P) herself knew nothing of the posting when it happened and did not consent to it. Within two weeks after the posting, Carafano (P) received sexually explicit voice mail on her home telephone and a threatening, sexually explicit fax whose threats also applied to Carafano's (P) son. Carafano (P) soon took her son and lived away from her home for months. Within two days of Carafano's (P) request, Matchmaker.com (D) deleted her fake profile. Carafano (P) sued Matchmaker.com (D) in several counts in tort in a California state court, but Matchmaker.com (D) had the case removed to federal court. There, the trial judge granted Matchmaker.com's (D) motion for summary judgment, reaching the merits of Carafano's (P) allegations after ruling that the immunity provisions of the Communications Decency Act, 47 U.S.C. 230(c)(1), did not shield Matchmaker.com (D) from liability. Carafano (P) appealed.

ISSUE: Does the immunity provision of the CDA, 47 U.S.C. 230(c)(1), immunize an interactive computer service (ICS) from liability for publishing false or defamatory material if another party besides the ICS provides the objectionable material?

HOLDING AND DECISION: (Thomas, J.) Yes. The immunity provision of the CDA, 47 U.S.C. 230(c)(1), immunizes an interactive computer service (ICS) from liability for publishing false or defamatory material if another party besides the ICS provides the objectionable material. The broad immunity granted to an ICS by the CDA serves two policy objectives: the unfettered dissemination of ideas online and voluntary control of online content. Courts of appeals are reaching a consensus that such immunity shields an ICS from liability when a third party is the primary provider of the objectionable content. Matchmaker.com's (D) questionnaire in this case does not mean that the company provided the objectionable content, and the company therefore is not an "information content provider" under the CDA. Matchmaker.com's (D) questionnaire is similar to the system of customer responses at issue in *Gentry v. eBay, Inc.*, 99 Cal. App. 4th 816 (2002), in which an online service invited users to rate their satisfaction with persons who used the service to sell products via the Internet. Just as in *Gentry*, here too the ICS was not an "information content provider" as required by the CDA: Neither the collecting nor the classifying of information from the third party in this case makes Matchmaker.com (D) the actual provider of the information. Moreover, Matchmaker.com's (D) transmission of the fake profile did not mean that the service provided the specific personal information about Carafano (P). Matchmaker.com (D) is therefore immune from Carafano's (P) suit. Affirmed.

ANALYSIS

Carafano illustrates the different standard of liability applied to Internet providers as opposed to that used for traditional media. Embedded within the casebook excerpt, though, is a further key point about the law of defamation. Matchmaker.com (D) removed the fake profile promptly after Carafano (P) complained to the company about the

Continued on next page.

material. At a minimum, counsel for Matchmaker.com (D) could have reasoned that leaving the material online, after the company had reason to doubt its accuracy, could have made Matchmaker.com (D) an "information content provider" no longer shielded from liability by 47 U.S.C. 230(c)(1).

Quicknotes

DEFAMATION An intentional false publication, communicated publicly in either oral or written form, subjecting a person to scorn, hatred or ridicule, or injuring him or her in relation to his or her occupation or business.

Ogden v. Association of the United States Army

Libeled party (P) v. Publisher (D)

177 F. Supp. 498 (D.D.C. 1959)

NATURE OF CASE: Action to recover damages for libel.

FACT SUMMARY: The Association of the United States Army (D) published a book on the Korean War in which it criticized the handling of a platoon it said Ogden (P) commanded during certain engagements in Korea. Ogden (P) claimed that every individual sale of a book gives rise to a new cause of action at the time of sale and, therefore, Ogden (P) claimed his action is not barred by the statute of limitations.

RULE OF LAW

The publication of a book, periodical, or newspaper containing defamatory matter gives rise to but one cause of action for libel, which accrues at the time of the original publication, and the statute of limitations runs from that date.

FACTS: Pursuant to a contract with the United States, the Association of the United States Army published a book entitled *Combat Action in Korea.* In the publication the handling of a certain platoon was criticized and it was pointed out that Ogden (P) was the leader of the platoon during certain combat actions. Ogden (P) brought a suit for libel and the Association of the United States Army (D) moved for summary judgment on the ground, among others, that the action was barred by the one-year statute of limitations. The book was published in November 1955, whereas the action was brought on June 25, 1959.

ISSUE: Does the publication of a book, periodical, or newspaper containing defamatory matter give rise to but one cause of action for libel, which accrues at the time of the original publication, with the statute of limitations running from that date?

HOLDING AND DECISION: (Holtzoff, J.) Yes. The publication of a book, periodical, or newspaper containing defamatory matter gives rise to but one cause of action for libel, which accrues at the time of the original publication, and the statute of limitations runs from that date. To say that every sale or delivery of a copy of a publication, if it contains defamatory matter, gives rise to a new cause of action may seem logical from a purely technical standpoint, but to adhere to this doctrine would be to sacrifice reality to strict technical logic. Under modern conditions, the original common-law rule would give rise to an unnecessary multiplicity of suits and would practically destroy the statute of limitations as a statute in response to actions for libel. The court states that the technology of today allows for the printing of millions of copies of a publication daily and to adopt any other rule would lead to an impossible situation. The court adopts the prevailing American doctrine that the publication of a book, periodical, or newspaper containing defamatory matter gives rise to but one cause of action for libel, which accrues at the time of the original publication, and that the statute of limitations runs from that date. It is no longer the law that every sale or delivery of a copy of the publication creates a new cause of action. Defendant's motion for summary judgment granted.

ANALYSIS

The common law was originally that every sale or delivery of a copy of libelous matter was a new publication and, therefore, a new cause of action occurred on each occasion. This court disagrees not in principle with the old common-law rule but rather in light of real issues of modern day living. The court points out the tremendous production capabilities of modern publishers and the effect the application of the common-law rule would have on modern courts in light of these capabilities. To apply the common-law rule today would lead to a multiplicity of suits as well as violate the statute of limitations as to libel.

Quicknotes

LIBEL A false or malicious publication subjecting a person to scorn, hatred or ridicule, or injuring him or her in relation to his or her occupation or business.

STATUTE OF LIMITATIONS A law prescribing the period in which a legal action may be commenced.

New York Times Co. v. Sullivan

Newspaper publisher (D) v. Police commissioner (P)

376 U.S. 254 (1964)

NATURE OF CASE: Civil action for damages for libel.

FACT SUMMARY: The *New York Times* published a full-page advertisement critical of the manner in which the Montgomery, Alabama, police, under Commissioner Sullivan (P), responded to civil rights demonstrations.

RULE OF LAW

A public official may not recover damages for a defamatory falsehood concerning his official conduct unless he can prove that the statement was made with actual malice.

FACTS: On March 29, 1960, the *New York Times* carried a full-page advertisement entitled "Heed Their Rising Voices," placed by several black clergymen of Alabama. The advertisement charged that southern black students engaged in nonviolent demonstrations were "being met by an unprecedented wave of terror by those who would deny and negate" the United States Constitution and Bill of Rights. The advertisement went on to describe certain alleged events in support of this charge, including various actions taken by the police of Montgomery, Alabama. L.B. Sullivan (P), the Police Commissioner of Montgomery, brought a civil libel action against the New York Times Co. (D), claiming that although the advertisement did not mention him by name, it attributed policy misconduct to him by inference. The trial judge instructed the jury that the advertisement was "libelous per se," leaving the New York Times Co. (D) with no defense other than proving the statement true in all respects. Some of the statements were found to be inaccurate descriptions of events that had occurred in Montgomery, and Sullivan (P) was awarded $500,000. The Supreme Court of Alabama affirmed, and the New York Times Co. (D) appealed on grounds of constitutional protection of speech and press.

ISSUE: May a public official recover damages for a defamatory falsehood concerning his official conduct unless he can prove that the statement was made with actual malice?

HOLDING AND DECISION: (Brennan, J.) No. A public official may not recover damages for a defamatory falsehood concerning his official conduct unless he can prove that the statement was made with actual malice. If criticism of a public official's conduct is published without actual malice—that is, without knowledge that it was false and without reckless disregard of whether or not it was false—it is protected by the constitutional guarantees of freedom of speech and press. This qualified privilege to publish defamation of a public office is not limited to comment or opinion, but extends as well to false statements of fact, providing there was no actual malice. Behind this decision is a "profound national commitment to the principle that debate on public issues should be uninhibited, robust and wide-open," and that "right conclusions are more likely to be gathered out of a multitude of tongues, than through any kind of authoritative selection." There would be a pall of fear and timidity imposed upon those who would give voice to pure criticism by any rule that would compel such a critic of official conduct to guarantee the truth of all his factual assertions. In addition, any attempt to transmute criticism of government to personal criticism, and hence potential libel of the officials of whom the government is composed, would be unconstitutional. Reversed and remanded.

ANALYSIS

Prior to the *Sullivan* case, there was a general recognition, at common law, of a qualified privilege known as "fair comment." Criticism of public officials' conduct and qualifications was allowed to be published as a matter of public concern—this much was undisputed. But sharp disagreement existed between state courts: the majority held that the privilege of public discussion was limited to opinion and comment, and a vigorous minority insisted that even false statements of fact were privileged, if made for the public benefit with an honest belief in their truth. The Supreme Court of Alabama was thus following the majority position in the instant case, and the holding of the Supreme Court came as something of a bombshell, termed by Professor Prosser as "unquestionably the greatest victory won by the defendants in the modern history of the law of torts." Since *Sullivan*, the rule has been applied to criminal, as well as civil, libel and has been extended to all public officers and employees, no matter how inferior their position.

Quicknotes

ACTUAL MALICE The issuance of a publication with knowledge of its falsity or with reckless disregard as to its truth.

LIBELOUS PER SE A false or malicious publication that subjects a person to scorn, hatred or ridicule, or that injures him in relation to his occupation or business of such an extreme nature that the law will presume that the person has suffered such injury.

St. Amant v. Thompson

Defamer (D) v. Sheriff (P)

390 U.S. 727 (1968)

NATURE OF CASE: Action for damages for libel.

FACT SUMMARY: In a televised political speech, St. Amant (D) read statements falsely charging Thompson (P), a deputy sheriff, with criminal conduct relating to a union dispute.

RULE OF LAW

In a defamation suit, a public official must prove that the defendant had serious doubts as to the truth of his publication in order to demonstrate actual malice.

FACTS: St. Amant (D) made a televised political speech, during which he read statements made by Albin, a union member, falsely charging Thompson (P), a deputy sheriff, with criminal conduct. Thompson (P) was awarded damages by the trial court in his suit against St. Amant (D) for defamation. The intermediate appellate court reversed the judgment, holding that St. Amant (D) had not acted with the actual malice required by the *New York Times v. Sullivan* rule, 376 U.S. 254 (1964). The Louisiana Supreme Court reversed the appellate court, finding that St. Amant (D) had acted in "reckless disregard" of the truth, in that he had failed to verify the defamatory information given to him by Albin.

ISSUE: In a defamation suit, must a public official prove that the defendant had serious doubts as to the truth of his publication in order to demonstrate actual malice?

HOLDING AND DECISION: (White, J.) Yes. In a defamation suit, a public official must prove that the defendant had serious doubts as to the truth of his publication in order to demonstrate actual malice. The standard for reckless conduct is different from that of mere negligence. "Reckless conduct is not measured by whether a reasonably prudent man would have published, or would have investigated before publishing. There must be sufficient evidence to permit the conclusion that the defendant in fact entertained serious doubts as to the truth of his publication." Only the proof of publication with such doubts will show a reckless disregard for truth or falsity and thus bear the burden of demonstrating actual malice. However, a defendant in a defamation action cannot insure a favorable verdict merely by testifying that he published with a belief that the allegations were true. The finder of fact must be satisfied that the publication was indeed made in good faith. After reviewing the facts in the record, the Court concluded that "by no proper test of reckless disregard was St. Amant's (D) broadcast a reckless publication about a public officer." There was no evidence to indicate an awareness of probable falsity of Albin's statement about Thompson (P). Failure to investigate does not in itself establish bad faith. Reversed and remanded.

ANALYSIS

The holding in the instant case reiterates a point made by the United States Supreme Court in *New York Times v. Sullivan*, in speaking to the evidence that the Times had failed to check the accuracy of the advertisement against the news stories in its own files. The Court held that "evidence against the Times supports at most a finding of negligence in failing to discover the misstatements, and is constitutionally insufficient to show the recklessness that is required for a finding of actual malice." The Supreme Court's retention of the term "malice" has been deplored as "highly unfortunate" by Professor Prosser. In *Henry v. Collins*, 380 U.S. 356 (1965), the United States Supreme Court completely dispensed with the old-fashioned meaning of "malice," holding that actual ill will and a desire to do harm were not sufficient to defeat the constitutional privilege. Yet it chose to cling to the discredited term, though "scienter" would have been more appropriate. The state of mind required by the test of "actual malice" is the same as that required by "scienter" in deceit actions for intentional misrepresentation: actual knowledge of falsity or reckless disregard of the truth. In either instance, where this test is met, liability is established.

Quicknotes

ACTUAL MALICE The issuance of a publication with knowledge of its falsity or with reckless disregard as to its truth.

DEFAMATION An intentional false publication, communicated publicly in either oral or written form, subjecting a person to scorn, hatred or ridicule, or injuring him or her in relation to his or her occupation or business.

LIBEL A false or malicious publication subjecting a person to scorn, hatred or ridicule, or injuring him or her in relation to his or her occupation or business.

Harte-Hanks Communications, Inc. v. Connaughton

Newspaper publisher (D) v. Judicial candidate (P)

491 U.S. 657 (1989)

NATURE OF CASE: Suit for libel by a public figure against a newspaper publisher.

FACT SUMMARY: During an election campaign, a newspaper ran a front-page story against the candidate the newspaper opposed. The story quoted a grand-jury witness's testimony that one candidate tried to bribe her and her sister to testify against a former official in the incumbent candidate's office.

RULE OF LAW

In a defamation suit filed by a public figure, an appellate court must conduct a plenary review of the entire record to confirm whether the plaintiff has shown that the allegedly defamatory statements were made with a reckless disregard for the truth.

FACTS: Connaughton (P) ran for the office of Municipal Judge. *The Journal News*, a local newspaper owned by Harte-Hanks Communications, Inc. (Harte-Hanks) (D), supported Connaughton's (P) opponent, the incumbent in the race. An official in the incumbent judge's office resigned about one month before the election. During a grand-jury investigation of bribery charges filed against the resigned official, one witness testified that Connaughton (P) had tried to bribe her and her sister to testify against the incumbent judge's staff member. One week before the election, *The Journal News* (D) ran a front-page story quoting the grand-jury testimony on Connaughton's (P) alleged attempt to reward persons for testifying against the incumbent judge. Connaughton (P) lost the election and sued the newspaper (D) for libel. At trial, the jury returned a verdict in Connaughton's (P) favor; the trial judge denied Harte-Hanks's (D) motion for judgment notwithstanding the verdict; and Harte-Hanks (D) appealed. The court of appeals affirmed the judgment after considering whether the article was defamatory and false. Harte-Hanks (D) petitioned the United States Supreme Court for further review.

ISSUE: In a defamation suit filed by a public figure, must an appellate court conduct a plenary review of the entire record to confirm whether the plaintiff has shown that the allegedly defamatory statements were made with a reckless disregard for the truth?

HOLDING AND DECISION: (Stevens, J.) Yes. In a defamation suit filed by a public figure, an appellate court must conduct a plenary review of the entire record to confirm whether the plaintiff has shown that the allegedly defamatory statements were made with a reckless disregard for the truth. Under *New York Times v. Sullivan*, 376 U.S. 254, 279-280 (1964), a public figure can prevail in a defamation suit only with clear and convincing proof that allegedly false statements against him were "made with 'actual malice'"—either knowingly or recklessly false. Appellate courts review evidence of actual malice for themselves under a plenary standard to ensure that the constitutionally required convincing clarity of proof is present. The court of appeals applied the correct standard for determining actual malice in this case; any statements in the court's opinion about the newspaper's (D) failure to meet journalistic standards of investigation only supported the ultimate conclusion that the newspaper (D) published the false statements against Connaughton (P) with actual malice—that is, either very aware that the claims probably were false, or with great doubts of their truth. The independence of the court of appeals' review of the evidence, however, deserves a closer look. The evidence must have convincingly shown not only a failure to investigate but also the higher burden that the newspaper (D) had definite reasons to doubt the accuracy of the grand-jury witness's testimony about Connaughton (P). To establish that fact, the court of appeals had to review the evidence in full, for itself, deferring to the jury only on credibility determinations. Here, although the court of appeals reached the correct conclusion—that the statements were published with actual malice—its grounds for that conclusion were too speculative. Whereas the court of appeals held that the jury "could have" determined that actual malice appears in the record evidence, that conclusion inexorably follows when the jury's findings are placed alongside the undisputed evidence. It is undisputed that five other witnesses besides Connaughton (P) denied the false witness's claims against Connaughton (P). It is also undisputed that the newspaper (D) failed to review Connaughton's (P) audio evidence challenging the published statements or to interview a woman whom the newspaper (D) knew to be a crucial witness. The newspaper (D) therefore likely failed to meet standards of journalistic investigation out of a purposeful avoidance of the truth, a likelihood that defeats the newspaper's (D) First Amendment protections under the exacting *New York Times* standard. Affirmed.

ANALYSIS

As the Court observes in *Harte-Hanks*, the constitutional freedom of the press is great but not absolute. The demanding burden of proof in public-figure defamation cases accommodates the public's interest in robust report-

Continued on next page.

ing while preserving the reputation interest of the individual. The relatively onerous burden of review placed on appellate courts in such cases further ensures that the evidence passes, or does not pass, constitutional muster on such important issues.

Quicknotes

BURDEN OF PROOF The duty of a party to introduce evidence to support a fact that is in dispute in an action.

DEFAMATION An intentional false publication, communicated publicly in either oral or written form, subjecting a person to scorn, hatred or ridicule, or injuring him in relation to his occupation or business.

FREEDOM OF THE PRESS The right to publish and publicly disseminate one's views.

LIBEL A false or malicious publication subjecting a person to scorn, hatred or ridicule, or injuring him or her in relation to his or her occupation or business.

PLENARY Unlimited and open; as broad as a given situation may require.

Gertz v. Robert Welch, Inc.

Libeled attorney (P) v. Publisher (D)

418 U.S. 323 (1974)

NATURE OF CASE: Appeal from judgment n.o.v. for the defense in suit for damages for defamation.

FACT SUMMARY: Robert Welch, Inc. (D) published an article accusing Gertz (P) of being a communist in a conspiracy against the police.

RULE OF LAW

(1) The standard of liability for a defamation which a publisher or broadcaster publishes about a private individual is set by the states.

(2) The private defamation plaintiff must prove falsity or reckless disregard for the truth to recover any damages other than compensation for actual injury.

FACTS: A policeman shot and killed a youth. The policeman was convicted of second degree murder. The youth's family retained Gertz (P) as their attorney in a civil action against the policeman. Robert Welch, Inc. (D) published an article in its magazine accusing Gertz (P) of being part of a communist conspiracy against the police and of belonging to two Marxist organizations. Gertz (P) sued Robert Welch, Inc. (D) for libel. Robert Welch, Inc. (D) contended that the article was about a matter of public interest, and, therefore, they were entitled to the protection of the *New York Times* rule, 376 U.S. 254 (1964). The jury awarded Gertz (P) $50,000, but the judge agreed with Robert Welch, Inc., and granted its motion for a judgment n.o.v. The Seventh Circuit affirmed, and Gertz (P) appealed.

ISSUE:

(1) Is the standard of liability for a defamation which a publisher or broadcaster publishes about a private individual set by the states?

(2) Must the private defamation plaintiff prove falsity or reckless disregard for the truth to recover any damages other than compensation for actual injury?

HOLDING AND DECISION: (Powell, J.)

(1) Yes. The standard of liability for a defamation which a publisher or broadcaster publishes about a private individual is set by the states. So long as they do not impose liability without fault, the states may define for themselves the appropriate standard of liability for a publisher or broadcaster of defamatory falsehood injurious to a private individual. This rule recognizes the legitimate state interest in compensating private individuals for wrongful injury to reputation, yet shields the press and broadcast media from the rigors of strict liability for defamation.

(2) Yes. The private defamation plaintiff must prove falsity or reckless disregard for the truth to recover any damages other than compensation for actual injury. The private defamation plaintiff who establishes liability under a less demanding standard than that stated by the *New York Times* (which requires the proof of falsity or reckless disregard for the truth) may recover only damages sufficient to compensate him for actual injury. Actual injury is not limited to out-of-pocket loss; it includes impairment of reputation and standing in the community, personal humiliation, and mental anguish and suffering. The evidence showed that Gertz (P) had not achieved general fame or notoriety in the community, and therefore was not a public figure to whom the *New York Times* standard is applicable. Therefore the trial court erred in entering judgment for Robert Welch, Inc. (D). However, since the jury was allowed to presume damages without proof of fault, a new trial is necessary. Reversed and remanded for further proceedings.

ANALYSIS

This case appears to overrule the plurality in *Rosenbloom v. Metromedia, Inc.*, 403 U.S. 29 (1970), which had stated that the protection of the *New York Times* privilege should be extended to defamatory falsehoods relating to private persons if the statements concerned matters of general or public interest. The *Gertz* opinion states: "The 'publication or general interest' test for determining the applicability of the *New York Times* standard to private defamation actions inadequately serves both of the competing values [protection of the individual v. protection of the press] at stake."

Quicknotes

COMPENSATORY DAMAGES Measure of damages necessary to compensate victim for actual injuries suffered.

DEFAMATION An intentional false publication, communicated publicly in either oral or written form, subjecting a person to scorn, hatred or ridicule, or injuring him or her in relation to his or her occupation or business.

JUDGMENT NOTWITHSTANDING THE VERDICT (JUDGMENT N.O.V.) A judgment entered by the trial judge reversing a jury verdict if the jury's determination has no basis in law or fact.

Dun & Bradstreet, Inc. v. Greenmoss Builders, Inc.

Credit service (D) v. Libeled company (P)

472 U.S. 749 (1985)

NATURE OF CASE: Appeal from award of damages for libel.

FACT SUMMARY: Dun & Bradstreet, Inc. (D), a credit reporting agency, incorrectly reported that Greenmoss Builders, Inc. (Greenmoss) (P) had filed for bankruptcy, which led a jury to award Greenmoss (P) compensatory and punitive damages for libel.

RULE OF LAW

Recovery may be obtained for libel without a showing of actual malice when the statements do not involve a matter of public concern.

FACTS: Dun & Bradstreet, Inc. (D), through the negligence of an employee, notified creditors of Greenmoss Builders, Inc. (P) that Greenmoss (P) had petitioned for bankruptcy. Greenmoss (P) notified Dun & Bradstreet (D) that such was untrue and demanded a correction. A correction was sent; however, Greenmoss (P) felt it was inadequate and sued for libel. It obtained a judgment for compensatory and punitive damages. Dun & Bradstreet (D) appealed, contending no showing of actual malice was made; thus, recovery could not be had. The Vermont Supreme Court reversed the trial court's grant of Dun & Bradstreet's (D) motion for a new trial, and the United States Supreme Court granted certiorari.

ISSUE: May recovery be obtained for libel without a showing of actual malice if the defamatory statements do not concern matters of public concern?

HOLDING AND DECISION: (Powell, J.) Yes. Recovery may be obtained for libel without a showing of actual malice if the defamatory statements do not involve matters of public concern. First Amendment protections extend to speech not of public concern; however, the protection is less stringent than for public speech. The state interest in providing adequate remedies for defamation outweighs this protection; thus, recovery is properly awarded. Affirmed.

DISSENT: (Brennan, J.) The First Amendment requires actual malice be shown to recover for libel where the speech is not of public concern.

ANALYSIS

This case represents a synthesis of the historic decisions in *New York Times v. Sullivan*, 376 U.S. 254 (1964), and in *Gertz v. Robert Welch, Inc.*, 418 U.S. 323 (1974). The first decision dealt with a public figure. The second involved a private figure, but dealt with speech concerning public affairs. Here, we are dealing with a nonpublic plaintiff and nonpublic speech. The Court held that the First Amendment would not intrude in this situation with state common-law principles.

Quicknotes

ACTUAL MALICE The issuance of a publication with knowledge of its falsity or with reckless disregard as to its truth.

COMPENSATORY DAMAGES Measure of damages necessary to compensate victim for actual injuries suffered.

LIBEL A false or malicious publication subjecting a person to scorn, hatred or ridicule, or injuring him or her in relation to his or her occupation or business.

Philadelphia Newspapers, Inc. v. Hepps

Newspaper (D) v. Principal stockholder (P)

475 U.S. 767 (1986)

NATURE OF CASE: Appeal from denial of damages for defamation.

FACT SUMMARY: Philadelphia Newspapers, Inc. (D) published articles linking Hepps (P) to organized crime and refused to disclose its sources at a subsequent trial for libel.

RULE OF LAW

A plaintiff may not recover damages for defamation without showing that the statements are false.

FACTS: Hepps (P) sued Philadelphia Newspapers, Inc. (Philadelphia) (D) for libel for printing stories linking him and his corporation to organized crime. After the trial court refused to instruct the jury about the effect of Philadelphia's (D) exercise of a reporter's shield law, the jury found for Philadelphia (D). The Pennsylvania Supreme Court held that Philadelphia (D) bore the burden of providing the truth of the statements. The United States Supreme Court granted certiorari.

ISSUE: May a plaintiff recover damages for defamation without showing the statements were false?

HOLDING AND DECISION: (O'Connor, J.) No. A plaintiff may not recover for defamation unless he bears the burden of proving that the statements were false. The common-law requirement that the defendant prove the truth of the matter asserted must fall to the constitutional requirement enunciated here. Although the plaintiff in this case is not a public figure, the statements made are of public concern. The burden of proving falsity is no greater than the burden of proving fault and supplies the necessary burden of proof to satisfy the first amendment. Reversed and remanded.

DISSENT: (Stevens, J.) This case overrides the common-law presumption that defamatory speech is false. It gives no weight to the state's interest in protecting the reputation of its citizens.

ANALYSIS

This case focuses on the evidentiary burdens applicable in a defamation case. The Court carefully limited its ruling to the particular facts of this case. It held that the speech must be of public concern for this holding to apply. Thus, a private plaintiff who is defamed on a private matter may still resort to the common law for recovery and evidentiary burdens.

Quicknotes

CERTIORARI A discretionary writ issued by a superior court to an inferior court in order to review the lower court's decisions; the Supreme Court's writ ordering such review.

DEFAMATION An intentional false publication, communicated publicly in either oral or written form, subjecting a person to scorn, hatred or ridicule, or injuring him or her in relation to his or her occupation or business.

Milkovich v. Lorain Journal Co.

Coach (P) v. Publisher (D) and columnist (D)

497 U.S. 1 (1990)

NATURE OF CASE: Appeal from dismissal of a libel action.

FACT SUMMARY: Diadiun (D) wrote a sports column implying that Milkovich (P), a wrestling coach, had lied under oath at a judicial hearing.

RULE OF LAW

Expressions of opinion that imply an assertion of objective fact may be the basis of a libel action.

FACTS: Milkovich (P) was a wrestling coach for a high school in Ohio. In 1974, his team was involved in a fight at a match, and at a subsequent hearing Milkovich (P) was censured for his actions by the athletic association. The order was overturned in a court hearing where Milkovich (P) testified. Diadiun (D), a sports columnist, wrote an article about the situation that stated that Milkovich (P) had lied at the court hearing. Milkovich (P) brought a libel action against Diadiun (D) and the newspaper (D). The Ohio Supreme Court ruled that the column was an opinion and therefore constitutionally protected. Milkovich (P) appealed.

ISSUE: May expressions of opinion that imply an assertion of objective fact be the basis of a libel action?

HOLDING AND DECISION: (Rehnquist, C.J.) Yes. Expressions of opinion that imply an assertion of objective fact may be the basis of a libel action. In *Ollman v. Evans*, 750 F.2d 970 (1984), the court of appeals applied four factors to determine whether a statement was fact or opinion: (1) the specific language used; (2) the verifiability of the statement; (3) the general context of the statement; and (4) the broader context in which the article appeared. This test is improper because although defamation requires a false statement of fact in order to be actionable, expressions of opinion often imply an assertion of objective fact. Simply couching a statement in terms of opinion, such as "In my opinion, Jones is a liar," does not dispel the implication that the speaker has facts on which to base the statement. However, additional separate protection for opinion is not required to ensure the freedom of expression guaranteed by the First Amendment. A libel plaintiff must still prove that a statement of public concern is false as part of his prima facie case. Statements that cannot be reasonably interpreted as stating actual facts are not actionable. Furthermore, statements about public figures and officials must be made with actual malice. These protections are adequate to protect the breathing space necessary to allow writers latitude to write about issues of public concern. Since libel plaintiffs must prove that a statement is false, the verifiability of the statement is the only issue regarding fact and opinion. Diadiun's (D) column carries the connotation that Milkovich (P) committed perjury at the hearing. This is a sufficiently factual statement because it is capable of being proved true or false. Therefore, Milkovich (P) must be allowed to bring a libel action. Reversed.

ANALYSIS

Justice Brennan's dissenting opinion essentially agreed with the majority regarding the standard for determining whether a statement is sufficiently factual to be actionable. However, Brennan argued that Diadiun's (D) column clearly expressed the view that Milkovich (P) had lied given what Diadiun (D) had witnessed at the wrestling match rather than stating that Milkovich (P) had committed perjury.

Quicknotes

LIBEL A false or malicious publication subjecting a person to scorn, hatred or ridicule, or injuring him or her in relation to his or her occupation or business.

Sindorf v. Jacron Sales Co., Inc.

Salesman (P) v. Previous employer (D)

Md. Ct. Spec. App., 27 Md. App. 53, 341 A.2d 856 (1975)

NATURE OF CASE: Action for damages in slander.

FACT SUMMARY: An officer of Jacron Sales Co., Inc. (D) called Sindorf's (P) new employer and advised them that Sindorf (P) might be a thief.

RULE OF LAW

A conditional privilege may be lost where the person who utters the defamation acts with malice or in utter disregard of the truth.

FACTS: Sindorf (P) was employed by Jacron Sales Co., Inc. (Jacron) (D) as a salesman. A dispute arose and Sindorf (P) quit. Sindorf (P) retained some of his inventory as security for commissions due him. Sindorf (P) wrote Jacron (D) that these items would be returned when his commission was paid. Sindorf (P) went to work for Tool Box. Fridkis, a vice-president of Jacron (D), called Brose, Tool Box's president. In the course of conversation as to whether Sindorf (P) had worked for Tool Box prior to resigning, Fridkis said that Sindorf (P) had been fired and was a thief. Sindorf (P) sued for slander and Jacron (D) defended on the basis of privilege. The court directed a verdict for Jacron (D) based on privilege. Sindorf (P) contended that even if the privilege had existed, it was lost based on Fridkis's malice or total disregard of the truth.

ISSUE: May a conditional privilege be lost where the person who utters the defamation acts with malice or in utter disregard of the truth.?

HOLDING AND DECISION: (Orth, C.J.) Yes. A conditional privilege may be lost where the person who utters the defamation acts with malice or in utter disregard of the truth. Privilege is a defense the law allows to defamation actions. It may be absolute or qualified. If the privilege has relatively little social or public significance, it is conditional. Communications between an ex-employer and the new one are conditionally privileged if conducted for a legitimate business or social purpose. Here, Brose and Fridkis were friends and Fridkis had a business purpose for the call. However, even though a conditional privilege exists, it may be lost if the utterance was made with malice or with a total disregard for truth. Here, Fridkis found out early in the conversation that Sindorf (P) had not worked for Tool Box while employed by Jacron (D). He then gratuitously volunteered that Sindorf (P) had been fired and that money and inventory were missing. These statements were false, were not made in response to questions, and appear to have been made to force Sindorf (P) into immediately returning the inventory. The question of malice should have been submitted to the jury. Reversed and remanded for a new trial.

ANALYSIS

An absolute privilege cannot be lost. Most privileges, however, are conditional. If Fridkis had made his statements in response to Tool Box's inquiries, the case might have been decided differently. This would be especially true if there was no spite motive and no attempt to pressure Sindorf (P). It is the socially undesirable motive that destroys the conditional privilege.

Quicknotes

CONDITIONAL PRIVILEGE Immunity from liability for libelous or slanderous statements communicated in the execution of a political, judicial, social or personal obligation, unless it is demonstrated that the statement was made with actual malice and knowledge of its falsity.

DEFAMATION An intentional false publication, communicated publicly in either oral or written form, subjecting a person to scorn, hatred or ridicule, or injuring him or her in relation to his or her occupation or business.

MALICE The intention to commit an unlawful act without justification or excuse.

SLANDER Defamatory statement communicated orally.

Trout Point Lodge v. Handshoe

Canadian hotel (P) v. U.S. public-affairs blogger (D)

729 F.3d 481 (5th Cir. 2014)

NATURE OF CASE: Appeal from summary judgment granted to a U.S. citizen under the Securing the Protection of our Enduring and Established Constitutional Heritage Act (the SPEECH Act) and against Canadian plaintiffs seeking to enforce a Canadian default defamation judgment.

FACT SUMMARY: Various Canadian citizens (collectively "Trout Point" (P)) sought to enforce in U.S. federal court a default defamation judgment (Nova Scotia Judgment) they obtained in Nova Scotia, Canada, against Handshoe (D), a U.S. citizen and public-affairs blogger located in Mississippi. Handshoe (D) succeeded in obtaining summary judgment under the Securing the Protection of our Enduring and Established Constitutional Heritage Act (the SPEECH Act) on the grounds that Trout Point (P) failed to meet its burden under the Act to show that Handshoe (D) had been afforded at least as much protection for freedom of speech in the Nova Scotia action as he would have in a domestic proceeding, or, alternatively, that Handshoe (D) would have been found liable for defamation by a domestic court. Trout Point (P) contended that Handshoe (D) should not have prevailed under the SPEECH Act.

RULE OF LAW

Under the Securing the Protection of our Enduring and Established Constitutional Heritage Act (the SPEECH Act), a default defamation judgment rendered in a foreign country will not be recognized and enforced in U.S. courts where neither the law of the foreign forum, as applied in the foreign proceeding, provides free-speech protection that is coextensive with relevant domestic law, nor the facts, as proven in the foreign proceeding, are sufficient to establish a defamation claim under domestic law.

FACTS: Handshoe (D), a Mississippi citizen, owned and operated *Slabbed.org*, a public-affairs blog. Initially, the blog was hosted by a New Orleans newspaper, the *Times-Picayune*. One of the blog's focuses was on Broussard, a corrupt Louisiana politician. Broussard owned property in Nova Scotia, Canada, near Trout Lake Lodge (P), a hotel property owned and operated by Perret (P) and Leary (P). Handshoe (D) began publishing entries on *Slabbed.org* alleging a link between Broussard and Trout Point Lodge (P), Perret (P), and Leary (P) (collectively, "Trout Point"). After Trout Point (P) informed the *Times-Picayune* that these allegations were erroneous, the Times-Picayune retracted this assertion and issued a correction, and *Slabbed.org* was taken offline. Apparently in retaliation, Handshoe (D), who had found another host for his blog, began an internet campaign to damage Trout Point (P), with derogatory, mean spirited, sexist, and homophobic posts. Trout Point (P) filed suit in the Supreme Court of Nova Scotia (the "Nova Scotia Court"), alleging defamation and related claims. Trout Point's (P) First Amended Statement of Claim asserted that *Slabbed.org's* assertions were directly defamatory and were also defamatory by both true and false innuendo in that they would tend to lower the opinion or estimation of Trout Point (P) in the eyes of others who read the defamatory publications as a series, or alternatively, in parts. Four primary sources of reputational harm were asserted: (1) the linking of Broussard to Trout Point (P), and the implication that its owners were involved in corruption, fraud, money laundering, and other crimes; (2) assertions that Trout Point (P) misled investors and court officials in litigation with the Atlantic Canada Opportunities Agency (ACOA); (3) assertions that Trout Point (P) was a failing business, and that Perret (P) and Leary (P) had a string of failed businesses; and (4) unabashed anti-gay, anti-homosexual rhetoric and rants used to amplify and support the three other "stings." The First Amended Statement of Claim also invoked statements indicating Handshoe's (D) poor opinion of Perret (P) and Leary (P), for example, that they "had Champagne taste on a beer budget," "work as a unit to grift their way through life," and were either "first-class b-tches, common thugs, or plain ol' morons." Trout Point (P) generically alleged that Handshoe's (D) publications were false and malicious. It did not, however, make any specific statements to refute the truth of the individual blog posts at issue. Handshoe (D) did not appear in the Nova Scotia action, and the Nova Scotia Court entered a default judgment against him (the "Nova Scotia Judgment"). The court awarded Trout Point Lodge (P) $75,000 in general damages, and Leary (P) and Perret (P) each $100,000 in general damages, $50,000 in aggravated damages, and $25,000 in punitive damages. It also awarded $2,000 in costs. Trout Point (P) enrolled the judgment in Mississippi state court, and Handshoe (D) removed the case to federal district court. The district court entered summary judgment for Handshoe (D), finding that Trout Point (P) failed to meet its burden under the Securing the Protection of our Enduring and Established Constitutional Heritage Act (the SPEECH Act) to show that "Handshoe was afforded at least as much protection for freedom of speech in [the Nova Scotia] action as he

Continued on next page.

would have in a domestic proceeding or, alternatively, that Handshoe would have been found liable for defamation by a domestic court." The court of appeals granted review.

ISSUE: Under the Securing the Protection of our Enduring and Established Constitutional Heritage Act (the SPEECH Act), will a default defamation judgment rendered in a foreign country be recognized and enforced in U.S. courts where neither the law of the foreign forum, as applied in the foreign proceeding, provides free-speech protection that is coextensive with relevant domestic law, nor the facts, as proven in the foreign proceeding, are sufficient to establish a defamation claim under domestic law?

HOLDING AND DECISION: (Elrod, J.) No. Under the Securing the Protection of our Enduring and Established Constitutional Heritage Act (the SPEECH Act), a default defamation judgment rendered in a foreign country will not be recognized and enforced in U.S. courts where neither the law of the foreign forum, as applied in the foreign proceeding, provides free-speech protection that is coextensive with relevant domestic law, nor the facts, as proven in the foreign proceeding, are sufficient to establish a defamation claim under domestic law. This result comes directly from construing the plain language of the SPEECH Act, which provides that a foreign defamation judgment will be unrecognized and unenforceable unless it satisfies either of two prongs: (1) the defamation law applied in the foreign court's adjudication provided at least as much protection for freedom of speech and press in that case as would be provided by the U.S. federal and state constitutions; or (2), even if such protection was not afforded by the foreign jurisdiction, the defendant would have been found liable of defamation in the U.S. courts. As to the first prong, it is clear that Canadian law provides less protection for speech than U.S. law. Canadian defamation law is derivative of the defamation law of the United Kingdom, which has long been substantially less protective of free speech. The most critical legal difference here is that a Canadian plaintiff, unlike a U.S. plaintiff, need not prove falsity as an element of its prima facie defamation claim. Rather, in Canada, truth is a defense that a defamation defendant may raise and, if so, must prove. Accordingly, Trout Point (P) cannot satisfy the first prong. Trout Point (P) also cannot satisfy the second prong. In Mississippi, the threshold question in a defamation suit is whether the published statements are false. Truth is a complete defense to an action for libel, and the plaintiff bears the burden to prove such falsity. Also, statements that are "substantially true" are not defamatory. Here, the district court concluded that Trout Point (P) failed to prove falsity in the Nova Scotia proceeding. Trout Point (P) argues that this conclusion is erroneous, and that it did prove falsity. However, Trout Point's (P) arguments in this regard are unpersuasive. First, the allegations in the First Amended Statement of Claim—particularly those regarding the falsity of Handshoe's (D) statements—were not particularly well pleaded. The First Amended Statement of Claim was unclear regarding whether all, or just some, of Handshoe's (D) statements were false, and it offered no facts to rebut or undermine most of those statements. Similarly, a Mississippi court could deny a default judgment because the First Amended Statement of Claim did not clearly and specifically allege that each of the relevant statements was false. Second, some of the publications at issue were statements of unverifiable opinion, e.g., that Perret (P) and Leary (P) were a "litigious bunch," and that the Nova Scotia action was "foolish and frivolous." Even if many of Handshoe's (D) posts were offensive, they would not be actionable in Mississippi, which has recognized that "name calling and verbal abuse are to be taken as statements of opinion, not fact, and therefore will not give rise to an action for libel." Finally, a state or federal court in Mississippi could view some of the allegations in the First Amended Statement of Claim as legal conclusions, as opposed to well-pleaded facts. For these three reasons, Trout Point (P) failed to show that the allegations in the First Amended Statement of Claim, standing alone and taken as true, would be sufficient to support a defamation claim in a Mississippi court. Trout Point (P) also asserts that the Nova Scotia Court's finding of facts establish falsity. However, as a threshold matter, the plain language of the SPEECH Act suggests that the purported factual findings of the Nova Scotia Court are irrelevant to the enforceability inquiry. The critical question is not whether the Nova Scotia Court found falsity, but rather whether a state or federal court in Mississippi faced with the allegations in the First Amended Statement of Claim would have done so. Nonetheless, even assuming, arguendo, that the Nova Scotia Court's factual findings have some bearing on the enforceability inquiry, they are insufficient to demonstrate falsity, since the Nova Scotia Court's oral decision did not contain specific findings of fact with respect to the falsity of Handshoe's (D) statements. Trout Point (P) could not identify a single specific allegation in the Statement of Claim that the Nova Scotia Court found was actually false. Rather, the Nova Scotia Court noted generically that some statements were "erroneous," but remained silent as to the truth of others. In sum, a court sitting in Mississippi would not have credited the allegations and evidence on which the Nova Scotia Court based its judgment. While Handshoe (D) asserts that there were insufficient contacts between his posts and Nova Scotia to satisfy U.S. due process, the court need not reach that jurisdictional issue, since Trout Point (P) in any event cannot have its judgment recognized or enforced in the United States. Affirmed.

Continued on next page.

ANALYSIS

Congress enacted the SPEECH Act in 2010 in response to the perceived threat of "libel tourism," a form of international forum-shopping in which a plaintiff chooses to file a defamation claim in a foreign jurisdiction with more favorable substantive law. In enacting the statute, Congress found that by seeking out foreign jurisdictions that do not provide the full extent of free-speech protections to authors and publishers that are available in the United States and by suing United States authors or publishers in those foreign jurisdictions, some persons were obstructing the free expression rights of domestic authors and publishers and chilling domestic citizens' First Amendment interest in receiving information on matters of importance. Before Congress enacted the SPEECH Act, some courts had refused to enforce foreign defamation judgments on First Amendment public-policy grounds, perceiving that the First Amendment would be seriously jeopardized by entry of a foreign libel judgment granted pursuant to standards deemed appropriate in a foreign country but considered antithetical to the protections afforded to the press by the United States Constitution.

Quicknotes

FORUM SHOPPING A situation in which one party to an action seeks to have the matter heard and determined by a court or in a jurisdiction that will provide it with the most favorable result.

CHAPTER 18

Privacy

Quick Reference Rules of Law

Joe Dickerson & Associates, LLC v. Dittmar

Private investigator (D) v. Convicted felon (P)

Colo. Sup. Ct., 34 P.3d 995 (2001) (en banc)

NATURE OF CASE: Suit for invasion of privacy by appropriation of another's name or likeness.

FACT SUMMARY: A private investigator published an article about, and a photograph of, a convicted felon in the newsletter the investigator used to promote his services.

RULE OF LAW

A claim for invasion of privacy by appropriation in Colorado does not require proof of the value of the plaintiff's name or likeness, and an appropriation claim will not lie against a self-promotional article on another person's felony conviction where the defendant asserts a First Amendment privilege.

FACTS: Joe Dickerson (D), a private investigator, investigated Rosanne Dittmar (P) during a divorce case. Dickerson's (D) investigation revealed improprieties in Dittmar's (P) conduct, and Dickerson (D) reported Dittmar (P) to law enforcement officials. Eventually Dittmar (P) was convicted of felony theft for taking bonds from clients of the brokerage firm where she worked. After Dittmar (P) was convicted, Dickerson (D) published an article on her conviction, along with a photograph of her, in the promotional newsletter that Dickerson (D) used to market his investigation service. Dittmar (P) sued Dickerson (D) on several grounds, including invasion of privacy by appropriation of another's name or likeness. Dickerson (D) prevailed in the trial court by summary judgment on all counts of Dittmar's (P) complaint. On the appropriation count, the trial court reasoned that, even if Colorado recognized the tort of appropriation, Dittmar (P) had failed to come forward with evidence on the value of her name or likeness. Dittmar (P) appealed. On the appropriation count, Colorado's intermediate appellate court reasoned that a plaintiff must prove that her name or likeness has value, but that court concluded that Dittmar (P) had shown genuine issues of material fact on other elements of appropriation; accordingly, the intermediate court reversed the trial court's judgment. Dickerson (D) sought further review in the Colorado Supreme Court.

ISSUE: Does a claim for invasion of privacy by appropriation in Colorado require proof of the value of the plaintiff's name or likeness, and will an appropriation claim lie against a self-promotional article on another person's felony conviction where the defendant asserts a First Amendment privilege?

HOLDING AND DECISION: (Bender, J.) No. A claim for invasion of privacy by appropriation in Colorado does not require proof of the value of the plaintiff's name or likeness, and an appropriation claim will not lie against a self-promotional article on another person's felony conviction where the defendant asserts a First Amendment privilege. Invasion of privacy by appropriation is a cognizable claim in Colorado. Unlike section 652C of the Restatement (Second) of Torts and the jurisdictions that follow that section of the Restatement, Colorado does not require a showing that the plaintiff's name or likeness has value; a property-oriented analysis that focuses on value diminishes the more logical focus on the mental anguish that all plaintiffs allegedly experience in claims sounding in appropriation. Accordingly, the elements of appropriation in Colorado are (1) use of the plaintiff's name or likeness by the defendant (2) to benefit the defendant (3) in a way that plaintiff suffered damages (4) caused by the defendant. Dittmar's (P) complaint here is therefore facially sufficient even though it does not allege value. On the other hand, Dickerson's (D) use of Dittmar's (P) name and photograph in his newsletter was privileged, and therefore insulated from suit, because his article was primarily non-commercial speech on an issue of legitimate public concern. See *Cox Broadcasting Co. v. Cohn*, 420 U.S. 469, 492 (1975). The publication of the article and photograph in a newsletter is irrelevant to determining whether the publication was primarily commercial or non-commercial; so is Dickerson's (D) profit motive for publishing the newsletter. Thus, although Dickerson's (D) use of Dittmar's (P) name and likeness clearly had both commercial and non-commercial purposes, the use was primarily non-commercial. Accordingly, the publication was privileged under the First Amendment, and Dittmar's (P) claim for appropriation must fail. Reversed with instructions to reinstate the trial court's entry of judgment for Dickerson (D).

ANALYSIS

In hindsight, the appropriation claim in *Dickerson* seems ill-advised. Dickerson's (D) mixture of commercial and non-commercial purposes is obvious, and the article just as obviously fails to satisfy the narrow definition of commercial speech. See *Central Hudson Gas & Electric Corp. v. Public Service Commn. of New York*, 447 U.S. 557, 561 (1980) ("expression related solely to the economic interests of the speaker and its audience"); *Virginia State Bd. of Pharmacy v. Virginia Citizens Consumer Council*, 425 U.S. 748, 761 (1975) ("no more than propose a commercial transaction"). On the other hand, although Dittmar (P) lost on the merits in *Dickerson*, she and her counsel succeeded in persuading the Colorado Supreme Court to

Continued on next page.

recognize an entirely new cause of action. That is no mean feat, but it also points out the radical redefinition of "success" that the practice of law requires. Note also that attorneys representing clients on similarly weak facts in future cases will have more difficulty discharging their professional responsibilities under, for example, Model Rule of Professional Conduct 3.1 (requiring "meritorious claims and contentions").

Quicknotes

APPROPRIATION The act of making something one's own or making use of something to serve one's own interest.

INVASION OF PRIVACY The violation of an individual's right to be protected against unwarranted interference in his personal affairs, falling into one of four categories: (1) appropriating the individual's likeness or name for commercial benefit; (2) intrusion into the individual's seclusion; (3) public disclosure of private facts regarding the individual; and (4) disclosure of facts placing the individual in a false light.

SUMMARY JUDGMENT Judgment rendered by a court in response to a motion made by one of the parties, claiming that the lack of a question of material fact in respect to an issue warrants disposition of the issue without consideration by the jury.

Sanders v. American Broadcasting Companies, Inc., et al.

Telepsychic (P) v. Undercover reporter (D)

Cal. Sup. Ct., 20 Cal. 4th 907, 978 P.2d 67 (1999)

NATURE OF CASE: Suit for invasion of privacy by intrusion.

FACT SUMMARY: A television journalist posed as a telepsychic and used a hidden video camera and microphone to do an undercover story on a business that gave psychic readings to people who called the company's 900 number.

RULE OF LAW

An employee has a limited expectation of privacy in conversations at his workplace against a reporter's secret videotaping even if coworkers could have seen or heard the conversations.

FACTS: Mark Sanders (P) worked as a telepsychic in the Los Angeles office of Psychic Marketing Group (PMG). As a telepsychic, he performed psychic readings for people who called PMG's 900 number. Several relatively private aspects marked Sanders's (P) workplace: cubicles enclosed on three sides by partitions standing five feet high, a lunchroom apart from the workspace itself, and separate offices for supervisory staff. PMG's policy prohibited access to the workplace by non-employees unless they had permission to enter. Stacy Lescht (D), a reporter for American Broadcasting Companies, Inc. (ABC) (D), secured a job as a telepsychic with PMG so that she could do an undercover story on the company. While she worked as a telepsychic for PMG, she easily heard conversations from nearby cubicles and walkways in the office. Without her coworkers' knowledge or consent, Lescht (D) recorded her conversations with them, including two with Sanders (P), while using a hidden video recorder and microphone. Sanders (P) sued Lescht (D) and ABC (D), alleging one count under section 632 of the California Penal Code and a second count for invasion of privacy by intrusion. The jury found for the defendants on the Penal Code count because workers at PMG could reasonably have expected their conversations not to be private. The defendants then moved to dismiss the claim for intrusion on the same ground. The trial judge denied that motion, reasoning that Sanders (P) had a limited right to privacy against secret videotaping, and the jury returned a verdict against the defendants. The defendants appealed, and the California Court of Appeal reversed, ruling that the findings on the Penal Code count precluded judgment for the plaintiff on the intrusion count as a matter of law. On Sanders's (P) petition for further review, the California Supreme Court ordered the issues confined to determining whether there can be a limited expectation of privacy in a busy workplace.

ISSUE: Does an employee have a limited expectation of privacy in conversations at his workplace against a reporter's secret videotaping even if coworkers could have seen or heard the conversations?

HOLDING AND DECISION: (Werdegar, J.) Yes. An employee has a limited expectation of privacy in conversations at his workplace against a reporter's secret videotaping even if coworkers could have seen or heard the conversations. In California, the tort of invasion of privacy by intrusion has two elements: (1) intrusion into a place, conversation, or matter that is private and (2) the intrusion must highly offend a reasonable person. This Court has never stated that the expectation of privacy in the law of intrusion must be complete or absolute; indeed, this Court's recent decision in *Shulman v. Group W Productions, Inc.*, 18 Cal. 4th 200 (1998), suggested that privacy exists on a sliding scale rather than as an all-or-nothing absolute. Thus, there can be a legitimate expectation of limited privacy, as in workplace conversations overheard by coworkers. Defendants' "complete expectation of privacy" argument therefore fails under case law and in the standard, everyday sense of privacy, even in the workplace. With reference to both senses of privacy, an assessment of privacy in an intrusion analysis must evaluate who is doing the intruding and how they are doing it. Further, the principal cases relied on by defendants, exemplified by *Desnick v. American Broadcasting Companies, Inc.*, 44 F.3d 1345 (7th Cir. 1995), are inapposite. The doctor-patient interaction in *Desnick* cannot control when the conversations occur between coworkers and among the different expectations that such conversations bring. Therefore, the reasonableness of an expectation of privacy in conversations, in workplaces as anywhere else, involves not only the presence of others who could have seen or heard the conversations but also the alleged intruder's identity and the purpose of the alleged intrusion. This holding does not create an automatic expectation of privacy in the workplace; on the contrary, the fact-sensitive rule announced today requires an analysis that will vary from case to case. Furthermore, a media defendant still has every right to try to defeat the offensiveness element of intrusion with reference to the media's legitimate newsgathering function. Reversed and remanded.

Continued on next page.

ANALYSIS

Sanders ends with a lesson in legal analysis straight out of the first semester of law school. This case substantially increases plaintiffs' prospects on intrusion claims against undercover reporting by weakening a strong defense on one element of intrusion (privacy). At the same time, as the court notes at both the beginning and the end of its opinion, media defendants can adjust their trial strategy to negate the other element of intrusion (offensiveness). Plaintiffs prevail only by meeting their burden on *all* essential elements of a claim—a point worth remembering in any area of the law.

Quicknotes

INTRUSION The unlawful entering on to or the taking of possession of another's property.

INVASION OF PRIVACY The violation of an individual's right to be protected against unwarranted interference in his personal affairs, falling into one of four categories: (1) appropriating the individual's likeness or name for commercial benefit; (2) intrusion into the individual's seclusion; (3) public disclosure of private facts regarding the individual; and (4) disclosure of facts placing the individual in a false light.

REASONABLE EXPECTATION OF PRIVACY In order to invoke the Fourth Amendment's protection against unreasonable searches and seizures, an individual must have a reasonable expectation of privacy in respect to the location searched or thing seized.

Hall v. Post

Daughter and adoptive mother (P) v. Newspaper and reporter (D)

N.C. Sup. Ct., 323 N.C. 259, 372 S.E.2d 711 (1988)

NATURE OF CASE: Suit for invasion of privacy by public disclosure of private facts.

FACT SUMMARY: A biological mother returned to the county where she had abandoned her daughter seventeen years before. The local newspaper ran stories on the mother's search and on the subsequent contact between the biological mother and the girl's adoptive mother.

RULE OF LAW

In North Carolina, a plaintiff cannot sue for invasion of privacy by public disclosure of private facts.

FACTS: Rose Post (D) wrote and published an article in *The Salisbury Post* (D) about an ex-carnival worker who was trying to find the biological daughter she had abandoned seventeen years earlier. The story related various details from the biological mother's life: her marriage seventeen years earlier to another carnival worker, the birth and abandonment of their daughter, the father's arrangements seventeen years earlier to leave the child with a babysitter named Mary Hall (P), and the father's later statements that he had formally consented to the child's adoption. The article included a plea to contact the biological mother, who was then staying in the area. The biological mother soon learned the child's name and location. The newspaper then ran a second story by Post (D) two days after her first. The second story identified the child as Susie Hall (P) and Mary Hall (P) as her adoptive mother. The Halls (P) sued Post (D) and the newspaper (D) for invasion of privacy by public disclosure of private facts. Their complaint alleged, in part, that they had fled their home to escape the resulting publicity, and that they both had undergone psychiatric counseling in the stories' wake. [The trial court entered summary judgment for the defendants, and the North Carolina Court of Appeals reversed.] Defendants petitioned for review in the North Carolina Supreme Court.

ISSUE: In North Carolina, can a plaintiff sue for invasion of privacy by public disclosure of private facts?

HOLDING AND DECISION: (Mitchell, J.) No. In North Carolina, a plaintiff cannot sue for invasion of privacy by public disclosure of private facts. The Restatement (Second) of Torts recognizes a tort for public disclosure of private facts that has four elements: (1) publicity, (2) private facts, (3) offensiveness, and (4) illegitimate public concern. This court now declines to adopt such a tort in North Carolina for the same reasons articulated in *Renwick v. News and Observer*, 312 S.E.2d 405 (N.C. 1984), where the court declined to adopt the false-light privacy tort. False-light claims duplicate other causes of action; so do claims for public disclosure of private facts. Moreover, adopting the disclosure tort would only increase the tension between tort law and the First Amendment without returning an appreciable benefit to anyone. Further, the United States Supreme Court has held that even false statements are entitled to some leeway when assessing potential liability. See, e.g., *Hustler Magazine v. Falwell*, 485 U.S. 46 (1988). It is therefore eminently reasonable to conclude that publication of true statements, such as the statements here, should receive at least the constitutional protection to which false statements are entitled. Reversed.

CONCURRENCE: (Frye, J.) The majority reached the correct result but for the wrong reasons. This court should adopt a tort theory that permits non-public figures to recover for wrongful, highly offensive publication of private facts that serve no legitimate public purpose. The U.S. Supreme Court has taken affirmative steps not to decide whether such a tort exists, but the proper resolution of the tension between this new tort and the First Amendment is the middle ground of a "newsworthiness" or "public interest" standard for determining whether private-fact disclosures are constitutionally protected. To minimize any chilling effect from this tort, the threshold question of the legitimacy of the public interest is a question of law for the court. The legitimacy should be measured by the Restatement's standard, which focuses on avoiding "a morbid and sensational prying into private lives for its own sake." In this case, no reasonable juror could find such a prying into the Halls' (P) lives in the challenged stories because the matters clearly were legitimate public issues. Thus, though the private-facts tort should be cognizable in North Carolina, the plaintiffs have failed to meet their evidentiary burden on summary judgment. The majority therefore correctly reverses the court of appeals.

ANALYSIS

If consistency in the law on a country's most fundamental values is a virtue, then the majority's focus on First Amendment issues is clearly the sounder of the two positions in *Hall*. Publication of true statements, in and of itself, should not form a basis for liability in a country in which false statements are protected under the highest court's interpretation of the country's most fundamental law. Under

Continued on next page.

such a rationale, it is at least arguable that the mere adoption of the private-facts tort is a per se violation of the minimum federal standards established by the United States Supreme Court's First Amendment jurisprudence.

Quicknotes

INVASION OF PRIVACY The violation of an individual's right to be protected against unwarranted interference in his personal affairs, falling into one of four categories: (1) appropriating the individual's likeness or name for commercial benefit; (2) intrusion into the individual's seclusion; (3) public disclosure of private facts regarding the individual; and (4) disclosure of facts placing the individual in a false light.

Cantrell v. Forest City Publishing Co.

Wife of accident victim (P) v. Publishing company (D) and reporter (D)

419 U.S. 245 (1974)

NATURE OF CASE: Action for damages for invasion of privacy.

FACT SUMMARY: Eszterhas (D), a reporter, did a follow-up story on the effects of a bridge collapse on the survivors of those who had died.

RULE OF LAW

A reckless disregard of the truth will expose a publisher to liability in an action for invasion of privacy.

FACTS: Cantrell's (P) husband died in a bridge collapse. Forest City Publishing Co. (D) decided to do a follow-up story on the disaster. Eszterhas (D), a reporter, decided to interview the Cantrells (P) to determine the effect that Mr. Cantrell's death had on the family. Eszterhas (D) went to the Cantrell (P) home and interviewed and took pictures of the children. Mrs. Cantrell (P) was not at home. The story, when published, contained many inaccuracies including a so-called interview with and description of Mrs. Cantrell (P). Mrs. Cantrell (P) sued for invasions of privacy in that she and her children were cast in a false light and were exposed to ridicule and pity. The court dismissed the punitive damage issue on the basis that there was no showing of actual malice. It declined to dismiss the entire action and instructed the jury that liability could be found for reckless disregard of the truth. The jury found for Cantrell (P), but was reversed by the appellate court. It felt that the district court's dismissal of the punitive damage issue through a showing of no actual malice was dispositive of the issue since this was necessary for recovery.

ISSUE: Will a reckless disregard of the truth expose a publisher to liability in an action for invasion of privacy?

HOLDING AND DECISION: (Stewart, J.) Yes. It is obvious from the facts that the district court was using "malice" in its common-law meaning when the punitive damage issue was dismissed. The jury was properly instructed that they could find liability for a reckless falsehood or a knowing disregard of the truth. The record contains adequate facts upon which to find that Eszterhas (D) knew that a portion of his story was false and published it in reckless disregard of the truth. For this, both he and Forest City Publishing (D) are liable. Reversed and remanded.

ANALYSIS

This case should be compared with *Gobin v. Globe Publishing Co.*, 531 P.2d 76 (Kan. 1975), and *Cohn v. Brecher*, 192 N.Y.S.2d 877 (N.Y. Spec. Term 1959). In *Cantrell*, the newsworthy value and interest in the story were stale. The embellishments in the story were knowingly false. They were included to make the feature more interesting. Such knowingly false attempts to sensationalize a story abrogate the conditional privilege to inform the public. It would appear that simple negligence would not be sufficient to establish liability. Malice is necessary.

Quicknotes

ACTUAL MALICE The issuance of a publication with knowledge of its falsity or with reckless disregard as to its truth.

INVASION OF PRIVACY The violation of an individual's right to be protected against unwarranted interference in his personal affairs, falling into one of four categories: (1) appropriating the individual's likeness or name for commercial benefit; (2) intrusion into the individual's seclusion; (3) public disclosure of private facts regarding the individual; and (4) disclosure of facts placing the individual in a false light.

PUNITIVE DAMAGES Damages exceeding the actual injury suffered for the purposes of punishment, deterrence and comfort to plaintiff.

Hustler Magazine v. Falwell

Publisher (D) v. Televangelist (P)

485 U.S. 46 (1988)

NATURE OF CASE: Appeal from an award of damages for emotional distress.

FACT SUMMARY: Falwell (P) contended that he could recover for emotional distress caused by a *Hustler* (D) cartoon, even though actual malice had not been shown.

RULE OF LAW

Public figures may not recover for infliction of emotional distress due to an allegedly defamatory act unless actual malice is shown.

FACTS: *Hustler* (D), an adult magazine, printed an ad parody, labeled as such, depicting Falwell (P), a televangelist, as having had sex with his mother and being drunk. Falwell (P) sued for defamation and intentional infliction of emotional distress. The district court directed a verdict for *Hustler* (D) on a privacy invasion count, and the jury found for *Hustler* (D) on the libel count. It awarded Falwell (P) $200,000 for infliction of emotional distress. The court of appeals affirmed holding actual malice standards need not be shown to recover on an emotional distress theory. The United States Supreme Court granted certiorari.

ISSUE: May public figures recover for infliction of emotional due to an allegedly defamatory act unless actual malice is shown?

HOLDING AND DECISION: (Rehnquist, C.J.) No. Public figures may not recover for infliction of emotional distress due to an allegedly defamatory act unless actual malice is shown. The state common-law tort of infliction of emotional distress illustrates a legitimate state interest in the protection of its residents; however, such protection cannot impair First Amendment rights. To allow a recovery for emotional distress in this context would allow First Amendment freedoms to be subverted. Because no actual malice was shown, no recovery could be had. Reversed.

CONCURRENCE: (White, J.) Penalizing publication of parody precludes the free exercise of freedom of press.

ANALYSIS

Actual malice, in the constitutional context of defamation, means the knowledge of the falsity of a statement or a reckless disregard for its truth. In the area of parody, this seems to be inapplicable. No assertion of fact exists to determine whether such was true. However, in the other areas of defamation, this case will have a widespread effect.

Quicknotes

ACTUAL MALICE The issuance of a publication with knowledge of its falsity or with reckless disregard as to its truth.

DEFAMATION An intentional false publication, communicated publicly in either oral or written form, subjecting a person to scorn, hatred or ridicule, or injuring him or her in relation to his or her occupation or business.

Snyder v. Phelps

Father of U.S. soldier (P) v. Church pastor (D)

562 U.S. 443 (2011)

NATURE OF CASE: Appeal from court of appeal's decision to overturn jury verdict in favor of the plaintiff.

FACT SUMMARY: Fred Phelps (D) and other members of the Westboro Baptist Church (D) protested on public property near the funeral of United States Marine Corps Lieutenant Matthew Snyder.

RULE OF LAW

The First Amendment may immunize protesters from tort liability if their speech relates to a matter of legitimate public concern and if the protesters comply with all applicable time, place and manner restrictions relating to public protests.

FACTS: At the funeral of United States Marine Corps Lieutenant Matthew Snyder, Fred Phelps (D), two of his daughters and four of his grandchildren, all members of the Westboro Baptist Church (Westboro) (D), staged a protest against the United States and the military. Westboro (D) had staged such protests at more than six hundred funerals previously. Westboro (D) protested on public land near Mr. Snyder's funeral procession, at the Maryland State House and at the United States Naval Academy. The protesters held signs that read, "Thank God for Dead Soldiers," "God Hates the USA/Thank God for 9/11," and "You're Going to Hell." Prior to the protests, Westboro (D) informed local authorities of its intent to picket. Near the funeral, the protest took place on a 10 × 25-foot space of public land 1,000 feet away from the church where the funeral services were held. Mr. Snyder's father, Albert Synder (P), sued Westboro (D) in federal court for intentional infliction of emotional distress, a state law claim. At his deposition, Snyder (P) testified he could see the tops of Westboro's (D) protest signs as the funeral procession passed but did not hear the protesters. He later saw the protest on the local news the night of the funeral. A jury returned an $11 million verdict for Snyder (P) and Westboro (D) appealed. The court of appeals overturned the verdict on the grounds the First Amendment protected Westboro's (D) speech. Snyder (P) appealed to the United States Supreme Court.

ISSUE: May the First Amendment immunize protesters from tort liability if their speech relates to a matter of legitimate public concern and if the protesters comply with all applicable time, place and manner restrictions relating to public protests?

HOLDING AND DECISION: (Roberts, C.J.) Yes. The First Amendment may immunize protesters from tort liability if their speech relates to a matter of legitimate public concern and if the protesters comply with all applicable time, place and manner restrictions relating to public protests. To prove a claim of intentional infliction of emotional distress, a plaintiff must demonstrate the defendant intentionally or recklessly engaged in extreme or outrageous conduct that caused the plaintiff to suffer severe emotional distress. First Amendment protections are generally at their strongest when relating to speech on matters of public, not private, concern. Debate on legitimate public issues should not be proscribed in any way. Private speech, however, does not enjoy such wide constitutional protections. Speech relating to matters of public concern must relate to any matter of political, social, or other matter of general concern to the community. That determination is performed on a case-by-case basis. Here, the content of Westboro's (D) signs related to matters of public concern: the conduct of the United States and its military and the moral conduct of the country and its citizens. That the protest occurred at a funeral does not make the speech private. Westboro (D) has been protesting military funerals for over 20 years. There is also no evidence of a prior relationship between Westboro (D) and the Snyder family. Lastly, Westboro (D) conducted its protest at a public forum in a peaceful manner. Despite Westboro's outrageous conduct, the First Amendment protects such speech if it relates to a matter of public concern. Affirmed.

DISSENT: (Alito, J.) Westboro's (D) speech in this matter did not relate to matters of public concern. It was a private attack on Lieutenant Snyder simply because he was a member of the United States Marines. Interspersing their comments with speech related to public concern should not shield them from liability for their personal attacks directed at Matthew Snyder. Despite this decision, states remain free to create buffer zones around military funerals without running afoul of the First Amendment. States also have the discretion to remove such private attacks on deceased members of the military from First Amendment protection, even if these private attacks occur in a public space.

ANALYSIS

This was an eight to one decision that underscored the strength of the First Amendment's protections for public speech. While the majority noted that its holding was limited to the facts of the instant case, it also stated that the First Amendment protects speech even if it is outrageous or harmful to certain individuals. The primary goal of

Continued on next page.

the public concern doctrine is to protect one's ability to engage in public discourse.

Quicknotes

FIRST AMENDMENT RIGHTS Rights conferred by the First Amendment to the United States Constitution prohibiting Congress from enacting any law respecting an establishment of religion, prohibiting the free exercise of religion, abridging freedom of speech or the press, the right of peaceful assembly and the right to petition for a redress of grievances.

INTENTIONAL INFLICTION OF EMOTIONAL DISTRESS Intentional and extreme behavior on the part of the wrongdoer with the intent to cause the victim to suffer from severe emotional distress, or with reckless indifference, resulting in the victim's suffering from severe emotional distress.

PUBLIC FORUM Public area so associated with freedom of speech so that restriction of access to it for that purpose is unconstitutional (e.g., sidewalks, streets, parks, etc.).

CHAPTER 19

Civil Rights

Quick Reference Rules of Law

Ashby v. White

Frustrated voter (P) v. Elections officer (D)

K.B., 2 Ld. Raym. 938, 92 Eng. Rep. 126 (1702), H.L., 1 Brown P.C. 62, 1 Eng. Rep. 417 (1703)

NATURE OF CASE: Action for having right to exercise the right to vote.

FACT SUMMARY: Ashby (P) was refused the right to vote in an election by White (D).

RULE OF LAW

A party may recover for wrongfully being denied his right to vote.

FACTS: White (D), an elections official, wrongfully denied Ashby (P) his right to vote in an election. Ashby (P) brought suit against White (D) alleging that he had been damaged. No statutory or common-law cause of action could be found which provided a remedy in such a situation. However, a jury found in favor of Ashby (P). White (D) appealed.

ISSUE: May a party recover for wrongfully being denied his right to vote?

HOLDING AND DECISION: (Lord Holt, C.J.) Yes. A party may recover for wrongfully being denied his right to vote. Ashby (P) had the right to vote. White (D) wrongfully deprived Ashby (P) of his franchise. An injury of this nature damages a party. While no statutory penalty exists, a wrong has been committed. A right without a remedy is no right at all. There must be some method of sanction to enforce the right. For this reason, recovery should be granted to Ashby (P). In no other way can we compensate him for his loss of franchise, and such a decision is necessary to prevent future abuses. [Holt's opinion notwithstanding, a majority of the Court of King's Bench reversed the jury verdict for Ashby (P). Holt was vindicated, however, when the House of Lords subsequently took his side, overturned the King's Bench judgment, and awarded damages to Ashby (P).]

ANALYSIS

A similar rationale to that in *Ashby* was the basis for the passage of the Civil Rights Act of 1964. Where the state refuses to accord rights of citizenship to its citizens, another remedy must be provided. Viewed pragmatically, what remedy does Ashby (P) have? He can't be allowed to vote in an election that is already over. He could seek an injunction to prevent future abuse, but this is hardly an adequate remedy for past misconduct. What damages has Ashby (P) suffered that can be recompensed by money damages? Evidently, White (D) was not terminated from his position. Therefore, Ashby (P) could only sue for punitive damages or seek criminal sanctions.

Quicknotes

PUNITIVE DAMAGES 42 U.S.C. § 2000e-2 makes it an unlawful employment practice to hire or to discharge anyone on the basis of race, color religion, sex, or national origin.

PUNITIVE DAMAGES Damages exceeding the actual injury suffered for the purposes of punishment, deterrence and comfort to plaintiff.

Camp v. Gregory

Aunt (P) v. Caseworker (D)

67 F.3d 1286 (7th Cir. 1995)

NATURE OF CASE: Suit claiming deprivation of liberty in violation of the Fourteenth Amendment.

FACT SUMMARY: Camp (P) brought suit against her nephew's caseworker, Gregory (D), claiming Anthony's substantive due process rights were violated by Gregory's (D) failure to ensure that he was placed in a safe living environment.

RULE OF LAW

A child placed in the guardianship of the state has a due process right not to be placed with a custodian whom the state knows will fail to exercise the requisite degree of supervision over the child.

FACTS: Camp (P) assumed guardianship of Anthony from his mother, who was unable to care for him. She immediately sought appointment of another guardian since she could not provide him with the highly structured care he needed. The state court appointed the Department of Children and Family Services (DFCS) as guardian and Gregory (D) was assigned as Anthony's caseworker. Despite knowledge that Anthony needed a highly structured environment, Gregory (D) returned him to Camp's (P) care. He failed to make any recommendations for an education or guidance program or to follow up on Anthony's progress. In addition he falsely represented to the state court under oath that Anthony was doing fine. Anthony died and Camp (P) brought suit claiming Gregory (D) denied Anthony substantive due process by failing to ensure he was placed in a safe living environment. The district court dismissed and Camp (P) appealed.

ISSUE: Does a child placed in the guardianship of the state have a due process right not to be placed with a custodian whom the state knows will fail to exercise the requisite degree of supervision over the child?

HOLDING AND DECISION: (Posner, J.) Yes. A child placed in the guardianship of the state has a due process right not to be placed with a custodian whom the state knows will fail to exercise the requisite degree of supervision over the child. There are two issues presented here. First is whether the DCFS and Gregory (D) owed a duty to protect Anthony and, second, whether that duty extended to dangers beyond the home. In *DeShaney v. Winnebago County Dept. of Social Services*, 489 U.S. 189 (1989), the Supreme Court held that due process does not require the state to protect a child from abuse by his parents. Gregory (D) argues that *DeShaney* stands for the proposition that he had no duty to protect Anthony from a danger that he nor he state had no role is creating. The fact that the DCFS had been appointed Anthony's guardian, however, is a key distinction from the *DeShaney* case. The DCFS had a cognizable duty to protect Anthony as his guardian. Many jurisdictions have held government officials liable for placing minors in foster homes in which they suffered abuse or neglect. Likewise, other circuits have recognized that public officials may be held liable for damages when they place a child in a foster home knowing or having reason to know the child is likely to suffer harm. Camp (P) moves one step beyond these holdings, claiming that Gregory (D) denied Anthony due process by knowingly returning him to a home that could not guide and supervise him properly. A child placed in the guardianship of the state has a due process right not to be placed with a custodian whom the state knows will fail to exercise the requisite degree of supervision over the child. While the cases acknowledge a difference between the state placing a child with a relative and placing him in a foster home, such distinction is not implicated here. Camp (P) sought the termination of her guardianship because she believed that she was unable to provide Anthony adequate care and supervision. Gregory's (D) and the DCFS's duty to Anthony did not terminate upon the return of Anthony to the Camp (P) household. Thus, the alleged danger Anthony encountered as a result of Camp's (P) failure to properly care for him is properly attributable to Gregory (D). Another issue here is whether Gregory's (D) duty extended to dangers outside the Camp (P) household. Since a parent owes a duty to his child to supervise the child's activities outside the home, the state also has a duty not to place one of its wards with an adult that it knows will not or cannot exercise such supervision. When a DFCS caseworker places a child in a home knowing that the caretaker cannot provide reasonable supervision, and such failure results in injury to the child, the caseworker may he held liable for a deprivation of liberty under the circumstances of the particular case. However, a public official who has deprived someone of their constitutional right is entitled to immunity from an action for civil damages if his actions were objectively reasonable and his conduct does not violate clearly established statutory or constitutional rights of which a reasonable person would have known. While Camp's (P) complaint sufficiently stated a claim for deprivation of substantive due process, Gregory (D) was entitled to qualified immunity. Affirmed.

Continued on next page.

ANALYSIS

The court articulated a narrow range of circumstances under which a DCFS caseworker will be held liable for injuries sustained outside of the home as a result of placing a child with a guardian whom it has reason to know will not provide adequate supervision. Such factors to be considered include the following: (1) the caseworker must have failed to exercise a bona fide professional judgment; (2) the guardian is only expected to provide reasonable supervision; (3) the harm sustained must be reasonably foreseeable; and (4) there must be sufficient causation between the failure to supervise and the resultant injury.

Quicknotes

DUE PROCESS CLAUSE Language found in the Fifth and Fourteenth Amendments to the United States Constitution providing that no person shall be deprived of "life, liberty, or property, without due process of law."

DUTY TO PROTECT/AID A moral duty and not one imposed by law; no liability attaches to those persons who fail to undertake a rescue or otherwise aid a person in need absent a special relationship between them.

REASONABLE PERSON STANDARD The standard of care exercised by a hypothetical person who possesses the intelligence, education, knowledge, attention, and judgment required by society of its members when governing behavior; the standard applies to a person's judgment when determining breach of a duty under the theory of negligence.

Memphis Community School District v. Stachura

School board (D) v. Suspended teacher (P)

477 U.S. 299 (1986)

NATURE OF CASE: Appeal from award of damages for violation of civil rights.

FACT SUMMARY: After Stachura (P) was improperly suspended from teaching, a trial court allowed a jury to award him compensatory and punitive damages based on the importance of the right that the school district (D) violated.

RULE OF LAW

Damages for deprivation of constitutional rights may not be awarded merely for the importance of the rights themselves.

FACTS: Based on his teaching methods, Stachura (P) was suspended from teaching by the Memphis Community School District (D). Stachura (P) sued, contending his constitutional rights had been violated. The district court instructed the jury on punitive and compensatory damages, and instructed it that damages could be awarded based on the importance of the constitutional rights violated. The jury awarded compensatory and punitive damages, the court of appeals affirmed, and the United States Supreme Court granted certiorari.

ISSUE: May damages for deprivation of constitutional rights be awarded merely for the importance of the rights themselves?

HOLDING AND DECISION: (Powell, J.) No. Damages for deprivation of constitutional rights may not be awarded merely for the importance of the rights themselves. Compensatory damages are awarded to compensate. They include out-of-pocket losses as well as intangible losses. The jurors here were asked to put a price on constitutional rights as an abstract concept. This differs from compensation for a deprivation of such right. As a result, the instruction was erroneous. Reversed and remanded.

CONCURRENCE: (Marshall, J.) The majority opinion opens the door to interpretation that damages in a § 1983 case are limited to out-of-pocket injuries. This is not so.

ANALYSIS

The Court rejected Stachura's (P) argument that some constitutional rights are stronger than others. So-called substantive rights, such as freedom of speech, would be given greater importance. The Court declined the invitation to set up a hierarchy of rights that it believed would cause more problems than it would solve.

Quicknotes

COMPENSATORY DAMAGES Measure of damages necessary to compensate victim for actual injuries suffered.

CONSTITUTIONAL TORT Federal law providing a cause of action to any person deprived of his or her constitutional rights under state law.

CHAPTER 20

Misuse of Legal Procedure

Quick Reference Rules of Law

Texas Skaggs, Inc. v. Graves

Store (D) v. Wife of hot check writer (P)

Tex. Civ. App. Ct., 582 S.W.2d 863 (1979)

NATURE OF CASE: Appeal from award of damages for malicious prosecution.

FACT SUMMARY: Texas Skaggs, Inc. (D) contended that it was not liable to Graves (P) for malicious prosecution because the criminal charge did not adequately terminate in her favor, there was sufficient probable cause to bring charges, and no malice was shown.

RULE OF LAW

In order to establish a cause of action for malicious prosecution, a favorable termination of the underlying action must be shown, as well as lack of probable cause to institute the prosecution and malice.

FACTS: Graves (P) left signed blank checks for her husband. Two of the checks were cashed at Texas Skaggs, Inc. (Skaggs) (D) and returned dishonored. Graves (P) paid the checks, yet Skaggs (D) alerted the police. The police arrested Graves (P), but released her after verifying she had paid the checks. Skaggs (D) demanded the charges be filed, but the case was dismissed because the prosecution could not produce the checks as evidence. Graves (P) then sued for malicious prosecution and received an award of $20,000. Skaggs (D) appealed, contending the dismissal did not constitute a favorable termination, it had probable cause to press charges, and insufficient evidence of malice was shown.

ISSUE: In order to establish a cause of action for malicious prosecution is it necessary to show a favorable termination, lack of probable cause, and malice?

HOLDING AND DECISION: (Ray, J.) Yes. In order to establish a cause of action for malicious prosecution, a favorable termination of the underlying action must be shown, as well as lack of probable cause to institute the prosecution and malice. In this case, the criminal action was dismissed for lack of sufficient evidence. Clearly, this constitutes a favorable termination of the case. The jury found that Graves (P) did not know the checks would be negotiated, and that Skaggs (D) had no evidence showing the lack of funds to be knowing or intentional. Malice was found by the jury based upon the insistence to prosecute even after the checks were paid. Affirmed.

ANALYSIS

Malicious prosecution can be charged in cases where the underlying matter was civil or criminal in nature. Because it has a chilling effect on people in having their rights adjudicated, this tort is disfavored in the law. If one element is found lacking, the action will fail. For example, if probable cause to sue or charge the person criminally exists, it matters not that malice is shown, or that the proceeding terminated in favor of the malicious prosecution plaintiff.

Quicknotes

MALICE The intention to commit an unlawful act without justification or excuse.

MALICIOUS PROSECUTION The unlawful civil or criminal prosecution of a party without probable cause.

PROBABLE CAUSE A reasonable basis for believing that a crime has been committed.

Friedman v. Dozorc

Physician (P) v. Adversarial attorney (D)

Mich. Sup. Ct., 412 Mich. 1, 312 N.W.2d 585 (1981)

NATURE OF CASE: Appeal from summary judgment denying damages for malicious prosecution and negligence.

FACT SUMMARY: Friedman (P) contended that Dozorc (D), an attorney who previously sued him, owed a duty of care not to bring suit until reasonable investigation revealed some basis for liability.

RULE OF LAW

An attorney owes no actionable duty of care to an adverse party.

FACTS: Friedman (P) treated Serafin for a urological problem and performed surgery on her. During surgery, Serafin hemorrhaged due to an unknown blood disease. After she died, Dozorc (D) sued him for malpractice on behalf of Serafin's family. Dozorc (D), as plaintiff's attorney, tried the case, presenting no expert testimony that Friedman (P) was negligent. Friedman (P) prevailed and then sued Dozorc (D), contending that he breached a duty owed to Friedman (P) to reasonably investigate the case before bringing suit. Dozorc (D) successfully moved for summary judgment, but the court of appeals reinstated the cause of action for malicious prosecution. Both sides appealed.

ISSUE: Does an attorney owe an actionable duty of care to an adverse party?

HOLDING AND DECISION: (Levin, J.) No. An attorney owes no actionable duty of care to an adverse party. Imposing a duty of this nature would interfere with the attorney's duty to his own client. This would create a conflict of interest that could not be overcome. Further, Friedman (P) showed no special injury that would have allowed a suit for malicious prosecution. To abandon the special injury requirement would open malicious prosecution to any former defendant. As a result, no cause of action was stated. Affirmed in part and reversed in part.

CONCURRENCE: (Levin, J.) The court should fashion a rule that allows successful litigants to recover all costs of litigation and thus lighten the load of wrongful litigation.

ANALYSIS

The English Rule holds that a person must plead and prove special injury, such as to his reputation or person, or an arrest or seizure in order to recover for malicious prosecution. The American Rule does not require a showing of special injury. In this case, no special injury was pled and, thus, because Michigan follows the English Rule, no recovery could be had.

Quicknotes

ABUSE OF PROCESS The unlawful use of the legal process after it has been granted.

DUTY OF CARE A principle of negligence requiring an individual to act in such a manner as to avoid injury to a person to whom he or she owes an obligatory duty.

MALPRACTICE A failure to perform one's professional duties during the course of a client relationship, either intentionally or negligently; or the poor or improper discharge of one's professional obligations.

Grainger v. Hill

Owner of mortgaged vessel (P) v. Lender (D)

C.P., 4 Bing. N.C. 212, 132 Eng. Rep. 769 (1838)

NATURE OF CASE: Action for abuse of process.

FACT SUMMARY: Hill (D) contended that Grainger (P) failed to state a cause of action for abuse of process because he failed to allege that the underlying arrest had been terminated.

RULE OF LAW

An action for abuse of process is not based upon a favorable termination of the underlying proceeding.

FACTS: Grainger (P) owned a boat that he mortgaged to Hill (D). He continued to operate the vessel under the loan agreement. In breach of such agreement, Hill (D) demanded early repayment of the debt. Grainger (P) refused, and Hill (D) had him arrested and held until he gave up possession of the ship. Grainger (P) sued for abuse of process, and a jury verdict was returned in his favor. Hill (D) sought entry of a nonsuit on the basis that Grainger (P) failed to plead and prove that the prosecution had terminated.

ISSUE: Is an action for abuse of process based upon a favorable termination of the underlying action?

HOLDING AND DECISION: (Sir Nicolas Tindal, C.J.) No. An action for abuse of process is not based upon a termination of the underlying action. The tort rests upon the improper invocation of legal process for an ulterior motive. It matters not what or whether the disposition of the underlying action was achieved. Judgment for Grainger (P).

ANALYSIS

This early case illustrates the fundamental difference between the tort of malicious prosecution and abuse of process. Malicious prosecution requires a favorable termination of the underlying case. Abuse of process is available for interlocutory actions that may or may not end the case.

Quicknotes

ABUSE OF PROCESS The unlawful use of the legal process after it has been granted.

INTERLOCUTORY Intervening; temporary; refers to an issue that is determined during the course of a proceeding and which does not constitute a final judgment on the merits.

MALICIOUS PROSECUTION The unlawful civil or criminal prosecution of a party without probable cause.

CHAPTER 21

Misrepresentation

Quick Reference Rules of Law

15. *McElrath v. Electric Investment Co.* Deceit, to be actionable, requires the misrepresentation of some material "existing" (past or present) fact, not mere prediction of future facts; but, if in making said predictions the speaker intends to create in the mind of the recipient this impression that the intention to complete that future act is a present fact in the mind of some party, that is actionable as well. *300*

16. *Hinkle v. Rockville Motor Co., Inc.* A defrauded plaintiff should be allowed to claim out-of-pocket expenses. If the defendant is morally culpable, the representations definite, and the present value ascertainable, then the plaintiff should be permitted to sue for the benefit of the bargain. *301*

Swinton v. Whitinsville Savings Bank

Home buyer (P) v. Seller (D)

Mass. Sup. Jud. Ct., 311 Mass. 677, 42 N.E.2d 808 (1942)

NATURE OF CASE: Action to recover damages for fraudulent concealment.

FACT SUMMARY: Swinton (P) purchased a dwelling house from Whitinsville Savings Bank ("the Bank") (D). The house was infested with termites. The Bank (D) through its salesman knew of the termites and did not disclose this information to Swinton (P) nor was the Bank asked for any such information by Swinton (P).

RULE OF LAW

There is no liability for bare nondisclosure.

FACTS: Swinton (P) purchased a dwelling house from Whitinsville Savings Bank ("the Bank") (D). Swinton (P) alleged that the Bank (D) knew that the home was infested with termites at the time of sale to Swinton (P) and that he (P) had no idea nor any reasonable way at the time to tell whether termites were present or not. Swinton (P) made no allegation of any false statement or representation, or of the uttering of a half-truth that may be tantamount to a falsehood. There was no intimation that the Bank (D) by any means prevented Swinton (P) from acquiring information as to the condition of the house. There was nothing to show any fiduciary relation between the parties. Based upon these facts, the trial court sustained a demurrer in favor of the Bank (D). Swinton (P) appealed.

ISSUE: Is there liability for bare nondisclosure?

HOLDING AND DECISION: (Qua, J.) No. There is no liability for bare nondisclosure. If the Bank (D) were to be found liable on these facts, every seller would be liable who fails to disclose any nonapparent defect known to him in the subject of the sale which materially reduces its value and which the buyer fails to discover. Similarly, it would seem that every buyer would be liable who fails to disclose any nonapparent virtue known to him in the subject of the purchase which materially enhances its value and of which the seller is ignorant. The law has not yet reached the point of imposing upon the frailties of human nature a standard so idealistic as this. Affirmed.

ANALYSIS

This case may be considered a modern one that is based upon very old case law. The rule set down in this case, although still very much operable and in use today, has been eroded from the severity seen here to much more acceptable applications by numerous exceptions that have been created. This case does not represent the modern-day trend, which is toward more of a duty to disclose known material facts. Many states have specific statutes dealing with the subject of concealment in many fields, including that of real estate.

Quicknotes

DEMURRER The assertion that the opposing party's pleadings are insufficient and that the demurring party should not be made to answer.

DUTY TO DISCLOSE The duty owed by a fiduciary to reveal those facts that have a material effect on the interests of the party that must be informed.

FIDUCIARY Person holding a legal obligation to act for the benefit of another.

FRAUDULENT CONCEALMENT The concealing of a material fact which a party is under an obligation to disclose.

Griffith v. Byers Constr. Co. of Kansas, Inc.

Home buyers (P) v. Developer (D)

Kan. Sup. Ct., 212 Kan. 65, 510 P.2d 198 (1973)

NATURE OF CASE: Action by purchasers (P) of new homes to recover damages against real estate developer (D) on theories of implied warranties and fraud.

FACT SUMMARY: Purchasers (P) of new homes in a tract sued the developer (D) of the home sites when they discovered that their lots, because of high saline content, could not be landscaped; the homes had been bought not from the developer (D), but from the building contractor.

RULE OF LAW

A purchaser who has bought a home on a lot that contains sterile soil may recover on a fraud theory from the developer of the lot, even though, in its strict sense, there is a lack of privity between them.

FACTS: Purchasers of new homes (P), who bought from the builder, discovered that the lots on which the homes rested contained high saline soil content, thus making it impossible to landscape the homesites. The saline content did not affect the structural qualities of the homes. Byers Constr. Co. of Kansas, Inc. (Byers) (D), the developer of the lots, had sold the homesites directly to the builder; who in turn had constructed homes on them and sold them to the purchasers (P). These purchasers (P) sued Byers (D) to recover damages on alternate theories of breach of an implied warranty of fitness, and fraud in the concealment of a material matter. Their complaint alleged that Byers (D) had developed and advertised the lots as a choice residential area, that it knew of the soil's saline condition, and that it purposely graded the homesites to prevent them from discovering the presence of salt. The trial court granted summary judgment in favor of Byers (D) on the implied warranty count. It also dismissed the fraud count on the ground that no privity existed between Byers (D) and the purchasers (P). The purchasers (P) appealed.

ISSUE: May a purchaser who has bought a home on a lot that contains sterile soil recover on a fraud theory from the developer of the lot, even though, in its strict sense, there is a lack of privity between them?

HOLDING AND DECISION: (Fromme, J.) Yes. [The court initially holds that the trial court was correct in dismissing the implied warranty count because a real estate developer by subdividing and offering lots for sale as choice residential homesites does not by implication warrant the fertility of the soil of said lots.] This court has already held that where a vendor has knowledge of a defect in property that is not within the fair and reasonable reach of the vendee and that he could not discover by the exercise of reasonable diligence, the silence and failure of the vendor to disclose the defect in the property constitutes actionable fraudulent concealment. There is no reason why this rule should not be extended to a developer of residential lots. The complaint in the present case satisfies the elements of this rule. Furthermore, the fraudulent concealment here is material. A prospective purchaser of a residential building-site would consider the soil condition a material factor in choosing a lot on which to build his home since this factor affects the value and acceptability of the homesite. Finally, the lack of strict privity is immaterial. Liability for fraudulent misrepresentation or concealment extends to the persons or class of persons whom the maker intends or has reason to expect to act or to refrain from action in reliance upon the misrepresentation or concealment. Here, the fact that title was first taken in the name of the builder did not change the identity of those who would be ultimately affected by the fraud—the purchasers (P). The builder was merely acting as a conduit for the passage of title. Reversed as to the dismissal of the fraud count and remanded.

ANALYSIS

Where the fraud action is predicated on intentional tort theory, and the misrepresentation is in the nature of a "continuous deception," the plaintiff need not show that he belongs to a class of persons whom the defendant intended to rely on his assertions. Where a negligent misrepresentation is alleged, the plaintiff must show that he was in that class of persons which was reasonably foreseeable or intended by the defendant to rely. In strict liability cases, no scienter on the part of the defendant need be proved.

Quicknotes

FRAUD A false representation of facts with the intent that another will rely on the misrepresentation to his detriment.

IMPLIED WARRANTY An implied promise made by one party to a contract that the other party may rely on a fact, relieving that party from the obligation of determining whether the fact is true and indemnifying the other party from liability if that fact is shown to be false.

Continued on next page.

NONDISCLOSURE The failure to communicate certain facts to another person.

PRIVITY Commonality of rights or interests between parties.

Derry v. Peek

Company chairman (D) v. Investor (P)

H.L., 14 App. Cas. 337 (1889)

NATURE OF CASE: Action on the case for damages for deceit.

FACT SUMMARY: Peek (P) had purchased shares in Derry's (D) tramway company, which folded after its use of steam and mechanical power was refused by the Board of Trade.

RULE OF LAW

An action in deceit will not lie for a false representation made with an honest belief in its truth.

FACTS: Derry (D) and other directors of a tramway company issued a prospectus, representing their company as authorized by the Board of Trade to use steam or other mechanical power. Peek (P) purchased shares in the company, relying upon the directors' further representation that a considerable savings would result from this technological innovation. The Board of Trade had not, in fact, consented to the use of steam or mechanical power by the company, and refused to do so. "In consequence, the company was wound up" and Peek (P) sued Derry (D). The trial court came to the conclusion that the directors had all believed that the company had the authorization as stated in the prospectus, and that their belief was not unreasonable. On appeal by Peek (P) to the court of appeals, the judgment was reversed on the ground that "while the defendants honestly believed that the statements in the prospectus were true, the statements were made without any reasonable grounds for believing them." Derry (D) appealed to the House of Lords.

ISSUE: Will an action for deceit lie for a false representation honestly believed though on insufficient grounds?

HOLDING AND DECISION: (Lord Herschell, J.) No. An action in deceit will not lie for a false representation made with an honest belief in its truth. It is important to distinguish this action for deceit from a suit for rescission of a contract. Rescission requires proof only of misrepresentation; deceit requires more. Specifically, an action of deceit requires proof of fraud: a misrepresentation made (1) knowingly, or (2) without belief in the statement's truth, or (3) recklessly. Belief in a false statement's truth, as the defendants claim here, always defeats an allegation of fraud. The alleged belief in the truth of a false statement can be tested by examining whether the belief had reasonable grounds and how the witness acquired his alleged belief. This application of the reasonable man standard thus permits a way to assess the witness's state of mind on this point. Reversed.

ANALYSIS

Prior to *Derry v. Peek*, it was generally assumed, by the early text writers at least, that negligent misrepresentation would find a remedy in deceit. But in 1889, the House of Lords clearly identified the action of deceit with intentional misrepresentation, and left merely negligent misrepresentation to be dealt with by an action for rescission of a contract. Although this decision has been condemned as a backward step in the law, the majority of American courts still purport to accept it. In reality, however, most have devised fictions that do allow recovery in deceit for misrepresentation made with less than an actual intent to deceive. It is generally agreed that a wrong motive, as distinguished from a fraudulent intent, is not essential to the tort of deceit.

Quicknotes

DECEIT A false statement made either knowingly or with reckless disregard as to its truth and which is intended to induce the plaintiff to act in reliance thereon to his detriment.

RESCISSION The canceling of an agreement and the return of the parties to their positions prior to the formation of the contract.

International Products Co. v. Erie R.R. Co.

Importer (P) v. Railroad (D)

N.Y. Ct. App., 244 N.Y. 331, 155 N.E. 662 (1927)

NATURE OF CASE: Action for damages for negligent misrepresentation.

FACT SUMMARY: International Products Co (P) insured its imported goods, relying upon Erie R.R. Co.'s (D) misinformation that they were located at Dock F; the goods were later destroyed by fire at Dock D.

RULE OF LAW

An action for damages for negligent misrepresentation will lie where the speaker owes a duty to give correct information.

FACTS: International Products Co. (International) (P), an importer, was expecting a shipment of goods and made arrangements with Erie R.R. Co. (Erie) (D) to receive and store the goods. International (P) desired to insure the shipment after its arrival, and giving this reason for its question, it inquired of Erie (D) where the goods would be stored. Erie (D) replied that the goods were docked at Dock F, from which International (P) inferred that they were already received and stored, and obtained its insurance on this basis. The goods arrived later and were stored at Dock D. They were subsequently destroyed by fire, and International (P) was unable to collect any insurance because of Erie's (D) misdescription. In a suit to recover its loss, International (P) received judgment from the trial court, which was affirmed by the appellate court. Erie (D) appealed.

ISSUE: Will an action for damages for negligent misrepresentation lie where the speaker owes a duty to give correct information?

HOLDING AND DECISION: (Andrews, J.) Yes. An action for damages for negligent misrepresentation will lie where the speaker owes a duty to give correct information. Although the English rule since *Derry v. Peek*, H.L., 14 App. Cas. 337 (1889), was that no cause of action would lie "unless the statement be false to the knowledge of the person making it," the court spoke of New York as already committed to the American, as distinguished from the English, rule. It cited two earlier cases where recovery was allowed on the basis of a negligent statement, but here limited the rule to where a duty exists, if one speaks at all, to give the correct information. To determine whether there is such a duty, there must be knowledge that: (1) the information is desired for a serious purpose; (2) the person to whom it is given intends to rely and act upon it; and (3) if false or erroneous, he will be injured in person or property. In addition, "the relationship of the parties, arising out of contract or otherwise, must be such that in morals and good conscience the one has the right to rely upon the other for information, and the other giving the information owes a duty to give it with care." The court concluded that in such a proper case, words negligently spoken may justify the recovery of proximate damages caused by faith in their accuracy. After discounting as "immaterial" the fact that Erie's (D) negligent answer was not given to serve its own purposes, the court determined that International (P) was entitled to such recovery. Affirmed.

ANALYSIS

Only a minority of American courts have refused to accept *Derry v. Peek*, holding instead that an action for deceit will lie for negligent statements. The prevailing majority have preferred to limit the historical action of deceit and have instead based liability on the negligence action. The instant case was one of the first to carry over negligence from tangible injuries to such economic loss as caused by a negligent misrepresentation. It is generally agreed today that the negligence action is equally appropriate to either type of damage.

Quicknotes

DECEIT A false statement made either knowingly or with reckless disregard as to its truth and which is intended to induce the plaintiff to act in reliance thereon to his detriment.

NEGLIGENT MISREPRESENTATION A misrepresentation that is made pursuant to a business relationship, in violation of an obligation owed, upon which the plaintiff relies to his detriment.

Winter v. G.P. Putnam's Sons

Mushroom eater (P) v. Publisher (D)

938 F.2d 1033 (9th Cir. 1991)

NATURE OF CASE: Appeal from summary judgment in a products liability action.

FACT SUMMARY: Winter (P) relied on a book on mushrooms published by G.P. Putnam's Sons (D) and became critically ill after eating a poisonous mushroom.

RULE OF LAW

Strict products liability is not applicable to the expressions contained within a book.

FACTS: Winter (P) purchased *The Encyclopedia of Mushrooms*, a book published by G.P. Putnam's Sons (Putnam) (D), to help in collecting and eating wild mushrooms. In 1988, Winter (P), relying on descriptions in the book, ate some wild mushrooms that turned out to be poisonous. Winter (P) became so ill he required a liver transplant. He brought a strict products liability action against Putnam (D), alleging that the book contained erroneous and misleading information that caused his injury. Putnam (D) responded that the information in the book was not a product for purposes of strict products liability, and the trial court granted its motion for summary judgment. The trial court also rejected Winter's (P) actions for negligence and misrepresentation. Winter (P) appealed.

ISSUE: Is strict products liability applicable to the expressions contained within a book?

HOLDING AND DECISION: (Sneed, J.) No. Strict products liability is not applicable to the expressions contained within a book. Products liability is geared toward tangible objects. The expression of ideas is governed by copyright, libel, and misrepresentation laws. The Restatement (Second) of Torts lists examples of the items that are covered by § 402A strict liability. All are tangible items, such as tires or automobiles. There is no indication that the doctrine should be expanded beyond this area. Furthermore, there is a strong public interest in the unfettered exchange of ideas. The threat of liability without fault could seriously inhibit persons who wish to share thoughts and ideas with others. Although some courts have held that aeronautical charts are products for purposes of strict liability, these charts are highly technical tools that resemble compasses. *The Encyclopedia of Mushrooms*, published by Putnam (D), is a book of pure thought and expression and therefore does not constitute a product for purposes of strict liability. Additionally, publishers do not owe a duty to investigate the contents of books that they distribute. Therefore, a negligence action may not be maintained by Winter (P) against Putnam (D). Affirmed.

ANALYSIS

This decision is in accord with the rulings in most jurisdictions. See *Alm v. Nostrand Reinhold Co., Inc.*, 480 N.E.2d 1263 (Ill. 1985). The court also stated that since the publisher is not a guarantor of the accuracy of an author's statements, an action for negligent misrepresentation could not be maintained. The elements of negligent misrepresentation are stated in § 311 of the Restatement (Second) of Torts.

Quicknotes

NEGLIGENT MISREPRESENTATION A misrepresentation that is made pursuant to a business relationship, in violation of an obligation owed, upon which the plaintiff relies to his detriment.

STRICT LIABILITY Liability for all injuries proximately caused by a party's conducting of certain inherently dangerous activities without regard to negligence or fault.

SUMMARY JUDGMENT Judgment rendered by a court in response to a motion by one of the parties, claiming that the lack of a question of material fact in respect to an issue warrants disposition of the issue without consideration by the jury.

Hanberry v. Hearst Corp.

Consumer (P) v. Publisher (D)

Cal. Ct. App., 276 Cal. App. 2d 680, 81 Cal. Rptr. 519 (1969)

NATURE OF CASE: Action against publishing company for negligently recommending a product.

FACT SUMMARY: *Good Housekeeping* (D) issued its seal of approval to a pair of slippers which Hanberry (P) claimed were defective.

RULE OF LAW

A party who endorses a product for its own economic gain and for the purpose of inducing the public to buy it may be liable to purchasers, who relying on the endorsement, purchase the product and are injured by it.

FACTS: Hanberry (P) purchased a pair of slippers manufactured by Handal (D). While wearing them, Hanberry (P) slipped on her kitchen floor. Hanberry sued Handal (D) for negligent manufacturing. Hanberry (P) also sued Hearst Corp. (D), publishers of *Good Housekeeping*, which had given its seal of approval for the slippers. Hanberry (P) alleged that Hearst (D) had either not tested the slippers or had been negligent in conducting such tests. Hanberry (P) claimed that she had relied upon the endorsement that it had been given for the purpose of inducing the public to purchase the product and for the economic gain of Hearst (D). Hearst (D) demurred and the court dismissed the complaint against it.

ISSUE: May a party who endorses a product for its own economic gain and for the purpose of inducing the public to buy it be liable to purchasers, who relying on the endorsement, purchase the product and are injured by it?

HOLDING AND DECISION: (Ault, J.) Yes. A party who endorses a product for its own economic gain and for the purpose of inducing the public to buy it may be liable to purchasers, who relying on the endorsement, purchase the product and are injured by it. The issue is triable. Hearst (D) awarded its *Good Housekeeping* seal of approval. Consumers rely upon such representations by reputable allegedly disinterested parties. Hearst (D) issues such seals of approval for its own economic gain. Hearst (D) owes a duty to the public to use proper testing procedures before issuing its seal. These do not represent mere statements of opinion. Hearst (D) held itself out as possessing superior knowledge and special information concerning the slippers. Under such circumstances, Hearst (D) may be liable for negligent misrepresentation if Hanberry's (P) allegations concerning the testing procedure are correct. In any event, the issue is best decided by the trier of fact, not on the pleadings. Hanberry's (P) allegations concerning strict liability and express and implied warranty cannot be maintained since they are only reserved for manufacturers or suppliers to the public. Summary judgment was properly granted as to them. Reversed.

ANALYSIS

Before liability can be found in such cases, it must be alleged and proved that there was reliance on the endorsement. It must have been a significant factor in inducing the purchase. The endorsement must be reasonably specific. In some instances, a products liability theory may be used against an endorser. Hearst's (D) alleged special knowledge is the key point. A mere recommendation would not be actionable unless other special circumstances exist.

Quicknotes

EXPRESS WARRANTY An express promise made by one party to a contract that the other party may rely on a fact, relieving that party from the obligation of determining whether the fact is true and indemnifying the other party from liability if that fact is shown to be false.

NEGLIGENT MISREPRESENTATION A misrepresentation that is made pursuant to a business relationship, in violation of an obligation owed, upon which the plaintiff relies to his detriment.

RELIANCE Dependence on a fact that causes a party to act or refrain from acting.

STRICT LIABILITY Liability for all injuries proximately caused by a party's conducting of certain inherently dangerous activities without regard to negligence or fault.

Richard v. A. Waldman & Sons, Inc.

Homeowner (P) v. Developer (D)

Conn. Sup. Ct., 155 Conn. 343, 232 A.2d 307 (1967)

NATURE OF CASE: Action to recover damages for alleged false representations in connection with the sale of land.

FACT SUMMARY: Real estate developer (D) "innocently" misrepresented to a purchaser of a lot that a structure on the lot was in accordance with local zoning regulations.

RULE OF LAW

An innocent misrepresentation may be actionable if the declarant has the means of knowing, ought to know, or has the duty of knowing, the truth.

FACTS: At the closing date for a real estate transaction, A. Waldman and Sons, Inc. (Waldman) (D), a real estate developer which had contracted with Richard (P) to prepare plans for and construct a house with an attached garage for Richard's (P) use, delivered to Richard (P) a plot plan. This plan showed a side yard of 20 feet as required by local zoning laws. Subsequently, local authorities issued to Richard (P) a certificate of occupancy based on Waldman's (D) survey. Four months later, Richard (P) discovered that the actual side yard of the lot he had purchased was less than three feet away from his neighbor's boundary line, and that the house's location was in violation of zoning laws. In an action by Richard (P) against Waldman (D) to recover damages for false representation, Waldman (D) claimed that the misrepresentation as to the width of the side yard was innocently made. The trial court found that Waldman (D) had falsely and recklessly represented to Richard (P), for the purpose of inducing action, that the premises' side yard was 20 feet and that there was no violation of the zoning regulations. The court further found Richard (P) was induced to rely on these representations that were mistaken, but not innocent. Richard (P) was awarded the difference between the actual value of the property and its value had it been as represented. Waldman (D) appealed.

ISSUE: May an innocent misrepresentation be actionable if the declarant has the means of knowing, ought to know, or has the duty of knowing, the truth?

HOLDING AND DECISION: (Cotter, J.) Yes. An innocent misrepresentation may be actionable if the declarant has the means of knowing, ought to know, or has the duty of knowing the truth. Here, Waldman (D), a real estate developer, had special means of knowing the location of the lot's structure, such being a matter peculiarly relating to its business and one on which Richard (P) was entitled to rely. Neither actual knowledge of the falsity nor fraud or bad faith need be alleged. Furthermore, it is immaterial whether the wrong that can be legally inferred from these facts arises in tort or in contract. Richard (P) may retain the property and recover damages. The misrepresentation here was in the nature of a warranty entitling Richard (P) to a recovery under the contract as for a breach of warranty. Affirmed.

ANALYSIS

There are two important limitations on liability for negligent or "innocent" misrepresentations. First, most jurisdictions require that the maker of the representation be in the business of providing others with information to guide them in certain business transactions. Second, while in a deceit action, the maker will be charged with intending the reliance of all persons who would probably receive the information, in a negligent misrepresentation suit, the maker is liable only if he could have anticipated reliance by the particular plaintiff.

Quicknotes

BREACH OF WARRANTY The breach of a promise made by one party to a contract that the other party may rely on a fact, relieving that party from the obligation of determining whether the fact is true and indemnifying the other party from liability if that fact is shown to be false.

CERTIFICATE OF OCCUPANCY A certificate issued by local government stating that a building is in accordance with local law.

MISREPRESENTATION A statement or conduct by one party to another that constitutes a false representation of fact.

RELIANCE Dependence on a fact that causes a party to act or refrain from acting.

Credit Alliance Corp. v. Arthur Andersen & Co.

Client's lender (P) v. Auditors (D)

N.Y. Ct. App., 65 N.Y.2d 536, 483 N.E.2d 110 (1985)

NATURE OF CASE: Appeal from denial of motion to dismiss action for negligence.

FACT SUMMARY: Arthur Andersen & Co. (D) contended it could not be found liable for negligently preparing financial statements relied upon by Credit Alliance Corp. (P), as they lacked privity.

RULE OF LAW

Accountants may be liable to persons not in privity for negligently preparing financial reports if the accountants knew the report would be relied on for a specific purpose by a known party.

FACTS: Arthur Andersen & Co. (Anderson) (D), accountants, prepared various financial reports outlining the financial situation of L.B. Smith, Inc. Credit Alliance (P), which lent money to Smith based on such reports, sued Andersen (D), contending that the reports were negligently prepared. Andersen (D) moved to dismiss, arguing that in the absence of privity no actionable negligence occurred. The court denied the motion, and Andersen (D) appealed.

ISSUE: May accountants be held liable to persons not in privity for negligently preparing financial reports if the accountants knew the report would be relied upon by that party for a particular purpose?

HOLDING AND DECISION: (Jasen, J.) Yes. Accountants may be held liable to persons without privity for the negligent preparation of financial documents if the accountants knew the report would be relied upon by a person for a specific purpose. In this type of situation, the accountant has a type of relationship with the person that approaches privity. Thus, the duty is recognized. In this case, no evidence was presented indicating Andersen (D) prepared the reports for a specific purpose or that Credit Alliance (P) was to use them. Thus, no duty of care was owed, and no recovery may be had. Reversed.

ANALYSIS

This case was a companion case to *European American Bank & Trust Co. v. Strahs & Kaye*, which was decided at the same time. This decision is an extension of *Ultramares Corp. v. Touche*, 179 N.E. 441 (N.Y. 1931), an opinion by Justice Cardozo. The decision became the seminal case in the area holding that no accountant's liability exists absent privity. As privity became more flexible, it deteriorated as a required element of proof.

Quicknotes

DUTY OF CARE A principle of negligence requiring an individual to act in such a manner as to avoid injury to a person to whom he or she owes a duty.

NEGLIGENCE Conduct falling below the standard of care that a reasonable person would demonstrate under similar conditions.

PRIVITY Commonality of rights or interests between parties.

Citizens State Bank v. Timm, Schmidt & Co.

Bank (P) v. Accounting firm (D)

Wis. Sup. Ct., 113 Wis. 2d 376, 335 N.W.2d 361 (1983)

NATURE OF CASE: Appeal from summary judgment denying damages for misrepresentation.

FACT SUMMARY: Timm, Schmidt & Co. (D) contended that Citizens States Bank (Citizens) (P) could not recover from them as accountants because no privity existed when the reports upon which Citizens (P) relied were negligently prepared.

RULE OF LAW

Accountants may be held liable for the negligent preparation of audit reports to a third party not in privity who relies on the report.

FACTS: Timm, Schmidt & Co. (Trimm) (D), certified public accountants, prepared audit reports on and for Clintonville Fire Apparatus, Inc. (CFA) The report negligently failed to accurately reflect CFA's financial position. Prior to discovery of the problem, Citizens State Bank (Citizens) (P) relied upon the reports in lending CFA money. After the errors were revealed, CFA went bankrupt. Citizens (P) sued Timm (D) to recover the outstanding balance on the CFA debt. Timm (D) successfully moved for summary judgment on the basis that an accountant cannot be held liable to a third party without privity. Citizens (P) appealed.

ISSUE: May accountants be held liable for the negligent preparation of audit reports to a third party not in privity who relies on the report?

HOLDING AND DECISION: (Day, J.) Yes. Accountants may be held liable for the negligent preparation of audit reports to a third party not in privity who relies on the report. Third parties must be able to rely upon financial statements in order to facilitate commerce. It is reasonably foreseeable that a third party would use reports to gauge a company's financial condition preparatory to lending money. In this case, whether the harm caused was reasonably foreseeable was a factual question, and summary judgment was improperly granted. Reversed and remanded.

ANALYSIS

The seminal case in this area is *Ultramares v. Touche*, 174 N.E. 441 (N.Y. 1931). In that case, Judge Benjamin Cardozo held that no liability could attach in this type of case because of the lack of determination in amount, time, and class of liability. Gradually, this case was rejected as the potential plaintiffs became known to the accountant.

Quicknotes

LIABILITY Any obligation or responsibility.

NEGLIGENCE Conduct falling below the standard of care that a reasonable person would demonstrate under similar conditions.

PRIVITY Commonality of rights or interests between parties.

SUMMARY JUDGMENT Judgment rendered by a court in response to a motion made by one of the parties, claiming that the lack of a question of material fact in respect to an issue warrants disposition of the issue without consideration by the jury.

Ultramares Corp. v. Touche

Lender (P) v. Public accounting firm (D)

N.Y. Ct. App., 255 N.Y. 170, 174 N.E. 441 (1931)

NATURE OF CASE: Appeal from denial of damages for fraudulent misrepresentation.

FACT SUMMARY: In reliance upon an audit of Fred Stern & Co. prepared by Touche (D), Ultramares Corp. (P) made several loans to Fred Stern & Co. The audit showed Fred Stern & Co. to be worth $1,000,000, when the company was actually insolvent.

RULE OF LAW

An accounting firm may be held liable for fraudulent representation irrespective of actual knowledge of the fraud.

FACTS: Touche (D), a firm of public accountants, was employed by Fred Stern & Co. to prepare a balance sheet indicating the condition of the business. Touche (D) certified true and to its own knowledge that the balance sheet correctly reflected the financial condition of the business. An employee of Touche (D) entered seventeen fictitious items, totaling $706,000, as "accounts receivable." Touche (D) claims that it did not know about the fictitious entries, but admits that if it had looked, a further investigation would have ensued.

ISSUE: May an accounting firm be held liable for fraudulent representation irrespective of actual knowledge of the fraud?

HOLDING AND DECISION: (Cardozo, C.J.) Yes. An accounting firm may be held liable for fraudulent representation irrespective of actual knowledge of the fraud. If there has been gross negligence, fraud can be inferred. Accountants are held to an especially high standard when certifying the agreement between an audit and entries. Touche (D) invoked the doctrine of "testing and sampling," i.e., random checks that, if found consistent, would show a lack of malfeasance. However, this method was not appropriate here because inspection of the actual invoices was necessary. When Touche (D) certified as to the correspondence between the balance sheets and the accounts, it made a statement as "true to their knowledge," but they had no such knowledge. Therefore, they did not have a sincere or genuine belief that the balance sheet accurately reflected the condition of the business. Reversed and new trial granted.

ANALYSIS

This is a case for fraudulent, rather than negligent, representation. The basis for the court's decision in this case seems to be Touche's (D) certification as to the authenticity of the books when the actual invoices should have been inspected.

Quicknotes

BALANCE SHEET A financial statement reflecting the assets and liabilities of a company on a particular date.

FRAUDULENT MISREPRESENTATION A statement or conduct by one party to another that constitutes a false representation of fact.

Williams v. Rank & Son Buick, Inc.

Buyer (P) v. Used-car dealer (D)

Wis. Sup. Ct., 44 Wis. 2d 239, 170 N.W.2d 807 (1969)

NATURE OF CASE: Action to recover damages for fraud.

FACT SUMMARY: Williams (P) bought what he thought was an air-conditioned car from Rank & Son Buick, Inc. Later, he found it was not air conditioned.

RULE OF LAW

A plaintiff cannot recover for misrepresentation unless his reliance upon the misrepresentation was justifiable.

FACTS: Williams (P) was looking for an air-conditioned car and went to Rank & Son Buick, Inc. (D). A salesman showed him a car and told him it was air-conditioned. Williams (P) also testified that particular car had been so described in an advertisement on which he had relied. However, the evidence was that the advertisement was first published after Williams (P) bought the car. Williams (P) was allowed to take the car for a one-hour test drive, and he did so. Williams (P) testified, however, that it was not until several days later that he discovered that the car was not air-conditioned. Williams (P) was a high school graduate, capable of reading and writing, who operated his own business. Williams (P) brought an action for fraud and was awarded $150.

ISSUE: Can a plaintiff recover for misrepresentation unless his reliance upon the misrepresentation was justifiable?

HOLDING AND DECISION: (Hanley, J.) No. A plaintiff may not recover unless his reliance upon the misrepresentation was justifiable. Courts will refuse to act for the relief of one claiming to have been misled by another's statements, who had opportunity, by the exercise of ordinary observation, to have known of their falsity. Of course, the obviousness of a statement's falsity negates reliance since no one can rely on a known falsity. The intelligence and experience of the plaintiff and the relationship between the parties are factors to be considered in deciding whether the falsity of the statement could have been discovered through ordinary care. Here, Williams (P) was a high school graduate capable of operating his own business. Rank & Son Buick's (D) salesman allowed him to drive and examine the car for a considerable length of time. No great search was required to discover that the car was not air conditioned, and if, as Williams (P) testified, that was of primary importance to him it would seem reasonable for him to have tried the air conditioner. Reversed.

DISSENT: (Wilkie, J.) The falsity of the representation was not so obvious that it could be held as a matter of law that Williams (P) had no right to rely on it.

ANALYSIS

This case demonstrates that in an action for misrepresentation not only must there be reliance, but the reliance must be found to be justifiable under the circumstances. The plaintiff's conduct must not be so unreasonable, in light of information available to him, that the law may say his loss was his own responsibility.

Quicknotes

FRAUD A false representation of facts with the intent that another will rely on the misrepresentation to his detriment.

MISREPRESENTATION A statement or conduct by one party to another that constitutes a false representation of fact.

RELIANCE Dependence on a fact that causes a party to act or refrain from acting.

Italian Cowboy Partners, Ltd. v. Prudential Ins. Co. of Am.

Restaurant business/tenant (P) v. Landlord (D)

Tex. Sup. Ct., 341 S.W.3d 323, 54 Tex. Sup. Ct. J. 822 (2011)

NATURE OF CASE: Appeal from judgment for defendant landlord and defendant property manager in action brought by tenant for rescission of lease and recovery of damages for fraud and breach of the implied warranty of suitability. [The complete procedural posture of the case is not presented in the casebook extract.]

FACT SUMMARY: The Secchis (P), and their restaurant business, Italian Cowboy Partners, Ltd. (Italian Cowboy) (P), contended that they were entitled to rescind a lease Italian Cowboy (P) had entered into with Prudential Insurance Company of America (Prudential) (D), the landlord of a shopping center, because of a persistent sewer gas odor, and that Italian Cowboy (P) was entitled to damages for fraud and breach of the implied warranty of suitability because, inter alia, the restaurant site's property manager, Prizm Partners, had falsely represented during lease negotiations that the restaurant site had no problems with it. Prudential (D) counterclaimed for breach of the lease contract.

RULE OF LAW

(1) Representations are actionable fraudulent misrepresentations of fact, rather than mere opinions, when the circumstances tend to indicate that the person making the representations had special or one-sided knowledge regarding the relevant circumstances.

(2) Even if an expression is an opinion, an expression of that opinion can support an action for fraud when the opinion is based on past or present facts, so that the opinion is based on special knowledge.

FACTS: The Secchis (P), as Italian Cowboy Partners, Ltd. (Italian Cowboy) (P), owners and operators of a restaurant, Italian Cowboy, terminated the restaurant's lease because of a persistent sewer gas odor. In a suit against the landlord, Prudential Insurance Company of America (Prudential) (D), and the property manager, Prizm Partners (D), the Secchis (P) sought to rescind the lease and recover damages for fraud and breach of the implied warranty of suitability. Prudential (D) maintained that rescission was not warranted and sought to recover for breach of contract. The Secchis (P) had successfully owned and operated restaurants for more than 20 years, and identified Keystone Park, a shopping center owned by Prudential (D) and managed by Prizm (D), as a possible site for a new restaurant, Italian Cowboy. Keystone Park housed three successful restaurants and had a vacant restaurant building available for lease. The Secchis (P) began negotiating a potential lease of the vacant restaurant building with Prizm's (D) property management director, Powell. During the lease negotiations, Powell told the Secchis (P) that the building was practically new and had no problems. In particular, Francesco Secchi (P) testified that Powell told him "the building was in perfect condition, never a problem whatsoever." According to Secchi (P), Powell also said, "[t]his is my baby and I was here from the first day when they put the first brick until the last one. The size—it's in perfect condition. There is no problem whatsoever. . . . [it is] a perfect building." Similarly, Jane Secchi (P) testified that Powell told her that "this was a very new building and she had been present at the very beginning of this building and watched it all the way through," that "[i]t was somewhat of her baby," and that "there had been nothing wrong with the place at all." The Secchis (P) began remodeling the property after signing the lease. During this time, the Secchis (P) first heard that a severe odor had plagued Hudson's Grill, the previous tenant. Francesco Secchi (P) also testified that a nearby cinema manager had asked Italian Cowboy's general contractor if he knew of the problematic odor existing in the previous restaurant. Secchi (P) stated that a few days later, "[a] guy with a motorcycle" stopped by the restaurant and said to "be very careful. . . . [there] used to be a place called Hudson's here and they used to serve excellent hamburgers, but there was a very, very bad odor." The trial court listed in its findings of fact three actionable representations made during the lease negotiations: (1) the Secchis (P) were lucky to be able to lease the premises because the building on the premises was practically new and was problem-free; (2) no problems had been experienced with the premises by the prior tenant; and (3) the building was a perfect restaurant site and the Secchis (P) could get into the building for next to nothing. There was also evidence that Powell herself personally experienced the odor and described it as "almost unbearable" and "ungodly." According to its regional manager, Hudson's Grill had even indicated to Powell that it was late in making rent payments because of the odor. Moreover, the odor problem did not appear until a layer of solidified grease was removed from the grease trap. The state's intermediate appellate court, which ruled in favor of Prudential (D), concluded that a binding disclaimer of reliance existed, and, therefore, it did not reach the merits of Italian Cowboy's (P) fraud claims. However, Prudential (D) asserted alternate bases for why Italian Cowboy's (P) fraud claims failed as a matter of law. The elements of fraud are: (1) that a material representation was made; (2) the representation was false; (3) when the representa-

Continued on next page.

tion was made, the speaker knew it was false or made it recklessly without any knowledge of the truth and as a positive assertion; (4) the speaker made the representation with the intent that the other party should act upon it; (5) the party acted in reliance on the representation; and (6) the party thereby suffered injury. Prudential (D) maintained that Italian Cowboy's (P) fraud claims failed as a matter of law because either Powell's representations were statements of opinion (undercutting the first element), or were not known to be false (undercutting the third element). The state's highest court [for civil actions] granted review.

ISSUE:

(1) Are representations actionable fraudulent misrepresentations of fact, rather than mere opinions, when the circumstances tend to indicate that the person making the representations had special or one-sided knowledge regarding the relevant circumstances?

(2) Even if an expression is an opinion, can an expression of that opinion support an action for fraud when the opinion is based on past or present facts, so that the opinion is based on special knowledge?

HOLDING AND DECISION: (Green, J.)

(1) Yes. Representations are actionable fraudulent misrepresentations of fact, rather than mere opinions, when the circumstances tend to indicate that the person making the representations had special or one-sided knowledge regarding the relevant circumstances. Pure expressions of opinion are not representations of material fact, and thus cannot provide a basis for a fraud claim. However, whether a statement is an actionable statement of "fact" or merely one of "opinion" often depends on the circumstances in which a statement is made. Special or one-sided knowledge may help lead to the conclusion that a statement is one of fact, not opinion, and this includes the comparative levels of the speaker's and the hearer's knowledge as among the relevant circumstances upon which the classification of a statement as fact or opinion depends. Here, it defies common sense and any plausible meaning of the word "problem" to infer from Powell's first two representations that in Prudential's (D) "opinion" the sewer gas odor was not a problem for Hudson's Grill. A foul odor is obviously problematic to a restaurant. Additionally, there was evidence that Powell had herself experienced the severity of the odor, that Hudson's Grill had effectively indicated it was having difficulty generating revenue as a consequence of the odor, and that because the odor was not unleashed until a grease trap was uncorked, a reasonable inspection by Italian Cowboy (P) would not have given an indication of the odor. For these reasons, because Powell had knowledge of the odor and its impacts on a restaurant, she had special, superior, and personal knowledge of the odor problem that, as a matter of law, renders her representations actionable and establishes a basis for fraud. Also, legally sufficient evidence existed to demonstrate that she knew her representations were false when she made them.

(2) Yes. Even if an expression is an opinion, an expression of that opinion can support an action for fraud when the opinion is based on past or present facts, so that the opinion is based on special knowledge. Thus, even assuming that Powell's statements are properly considered pure expressions of opinion, Prudential's (D) one-sided knowledge of past facts makes these particular representations actionable under the circumstances. Powell emphasized to Italian Cowboy (P) that she had been working with the restaurant site since its inception, implying that she had personal knowledge of its entire history from her experience—i.e., if there had been something worth mentioning, she would have known about it and mentioned it. Powell's honest representations about her superior knowledge of the site—such as stating that she "was here from the first day when they put the first brick until the last one"—were so intertwined with her other statements that they are actionable, especially given that the persistent odor problem did not appear until a layer of solidified grease was removed from the grease trap, meaning that a reasonable inspection of the premises by Italian Cowboy (P) would not have revealed the problem. Thus, Italian Cowboy (P) did not have access to the same information as Powell. Although Italian Cowboy (P) could have interviewed the former tenant to inquire about prior problems with the property, prospective commercial tenants are not required to undertake such a burden simply to ensure that they can later bring claims arising from their reliance on representations about the property made by a lessor with superior, personal knowledge. Rather, commercial tenants are entitled to rely on the fact that a landlord will not actively conceal material information. Firsthand knowledge—like Powell's—concerning material information—like an odor problem in a restaurant site—is exactly the sort of scenario that demonstrates the sound policy behind the exception allowing an opinion to be actionable under certain circumstances where material information was withheld. Accordingly, even if Powell's representations were opinions, they were actionable, and the evidence sufficiently indicated she knew they were false when made. Because the court of appeals concluded that Italian Cowboy (P) disclaimed reliance, it never reached Prudential's (D) argument as to the factual sufficiency of the evidence supporting Italian Cowboy's (P) fraud claims. Accordingly, because there is no alternative legal basis to render judgment in favor of Prudential (D) on Italian Cowboy's (P) fraud claims, the case is remanded to the court of appeals for further consideration. Reversed and remanded.

Continued on next page.

ANALYSIS

Three dissenting justices in this case focused on language in the lease that stated that "Tenant acknowledges that neither Landlord nor Landlord's agents, employees or contractors have made any representations or promises with respect to the Site, the Shopping Center or this lease except as expressly set forth herein," which was contrasted with the Secchi's (P) petition, which stated that "Italian Cowboy Partners and the Secchis reasonably and detrimentally relied on the representations of Prudential and Prizm that the Premises were suitable for use as a restaurant and were a prime restaurant site." Noting that the Secchis (P) were sophisticated businesspeople, were represented by counsel in their dealings with Prudential (D) and Prizm (D), and had reviewed seven drafts of the lease, the dissenters emphasized that in the lease, Italian Cowboy (P) stated that Prudential (D) and Prizm (D) did not make representations other than those contained in the lease, but that in the petition, Italian Cowboy (P) stated that Prudential (D) and Prizm (D) did make representations, representations that were not contained in the lease. Since the Secchi's (P) statements in the different documents are not reconcilable, and cannot both be true, either representations not contained in the lease were made, or they were not made. Thus, to the dissenters, the lease language should have disposed of the case, since, at the time the lease was inked, the parties unquestionably agreed as to what representations had been made and had not been made. The issue, as the dissenters would have framed it, is whether the law allows a sophisticated party in a commercial transaction, represented by counsel, with full knowledge of all the circumstances, without mistake or duress of any kind, to include in a contract a statement of fact that is important to the other party, and later disavow it as having been false at the time it was made. Of course, the dissenters would have answered in the negative, and would have held Italian Cowboy (P) to the statement it made in the lease.

Quicknotes

BREACH OF WARRANTY The breach of a promise made by one party to a contract on which the other party may rely, relieving that party from the obligation of determining whether the fact is true and indemnifying the other party from liability if that fact is shown to be false.

FRAUDULENT MISREPRESENTATION A statement or conduct by one party to another that constitutes a false representation of fact.

OPINION EVIDENCE Evidence pertaining to the beliefs of the witness rather than to witness' knowledge of the facts.

Vulcan Metals Co. v. Simmons Manufacturing Co.

Buyer (P) v. Manufacturer (D)

248 F. 853 (2d Cir. 1918)

NATURE OF CASE: Action for deceit, on appeal.

FACT SUMMARY: Simmons Manufacturing Co. (D) sold vacuum cleaner manufacturing machines to Vulcan Metals Co. (P) claiming that they were (inter alia) "perfect," and that the vacuum cleaners had never been marketed before.

RULE OF LAW

An opinion is a fact, and when parties are so situated that a buyer may reasonably rely upon the expression of a seller's opinion, the fact that it is an opinion is not a defense to an action in deceit; but, there are some statements that no sensible man takes seriously.

FACTS: Simmons Manufacturing Co. (Simmons) (D) sold Vulcan Metals Co. (Vulcan) (P) machinery for the manufacture of vacuum cleaners. Representations, now challenged by Vulcan (P), were made to the effect that: (1) the vacuum cleaners were "perfect in even the smallest detail," "most economical," "everyone could afford one," "guaranteed perfect satisfaction" etc., and (2) that the vacuum cleaner had never before been put on the market. Vulcan (P) now sues for deceit, charging the representations above were false. Simmons (D) contended that both statements were mere opinion and, therefore, not actionable and they were substantively true since only 60 machines had ever been sold. The trial court directed a verdict for Simmons (D) on each count. Vulcan (P) appealed.

ISSUE: May an action for deceit (misrepresentation) lie where the representations challenged involve mere opinions as well as misrepresentations about a product sold?

HOLDING AND DECISION: (Hand, J.) Yes. An opinion is a fact, and when parties are so situated that a buyer may reasonably rely upon the expression of a seller's opinion, the fact that it is an opinion is not a defense to an action in deceit; but there are some statements that no sensible person takes seriously. Much depends on the relative equality of the parties involved in terms of their ability to know whether a statement is mere "dealer's talk" opinion, or fact statement (the ability to examine merchandise is but one factor in considering this question). Some statements are so patently "dealer's talk" that no sensible person would take them seriously. Here, the statements about the quality of the machines are clearly such "dealer's talk." No sensible person expects anything to be perfect. This is not true of the statement about previous sales, however. There, only the seller has reason to know the relative truth of such statements. Here, the misrepresentation is sufficiently material (to the salability of the vacuum cleaners) to be actionable. The judgment is reversed, with instructions to permit a new trial in the action of deceit.

ANALYSIS

This case points out the general relationship between opinion and misrepresentation or deceit. Note the comparison made by Learned Hand. A political campaign manager or a politician will often make claims that no one really believes (e.g., "I will balance the budget," "I will eradicate poverty"). Such "puffing up" talk is done to show the candidate's intentions; it is not meant to be taken literally. No sensible person would ever rely upon it.

Quicknotes

DECEIT A false statement made either knowingly or with reckless disregard as to its truth and which is intended to induce the plaintiff to act in reliance thereon to his detriment.

MISREPRESENTATION A statement or conduct by one party to another that constitutes a false representation of fact.

PUFFING The communication of an opinion not intended as a representation of fact and upon which an action for fraud or misrepresentation cannot be based.

RELIANCE Dependence on a fact that causes a party to act or refrain from acting.

National Conversion Corp. v. Cedar Bldg. Corp.

Tenant in industrial building (P) v. Landlord (D)

N.Y. Ct. App., 23 N.Y.2d 621, 246 N.E.2d 351, 298 N.Y.S.2d 499 (1969)

NATURE OF CASE: Appeal from affirmance of award for plaintiff in action for fraud and breach of warranty arising from a lease.

FACT SUMMARY: A lease between National Conversion Corp. (Tenant) (P) and Cedar Bldg. Corp. (Landlords) (D) provided that the leased premises were in an unrestricted zone and that the Tenant's (P) use of converting restaurant garbage into fertilizer would not be in violation of the zoning ordinance. The Tenant (P) represented in the lease that it would not produce objectionable odors or gases. Unbeknownst to the Tenant (P), whose attorney had been assured by the Landlords' (D) attorney that the premises were in an unrestricted zone, the premises were actually in an M-1 district, so that Tenant (P) would have had to have made a sizeable investment to comply with the M-1 standards. When Tenant (P) was cited for violations of those standards, after it had altered the premises and installed equipment, it moved out of the premises and sued the Landlords (D) for fraud in the inducement. The Landlords (D) argued that because the Tenant (P) could not have avoided producing objectionable odors or gases, the false representation as to unrestricted zoning by the Landlords (D) and the covenant by the Tenant (P) nullified one another, disentitling the Tenant (P) to remedies for fraud. The Landlords (D) also argued that the Tenant (P), represented by a lawyer, was just as much on notice, as they, the Landlords (D), were, that the premises were located in a restricted zone. Thus, they invoked the rule that one may not charge another with fraud if one knew, or should have known, the actual situation. Finally, the Landlords (D) contended that if they had made a misrepresentation, it was one of law, rather than fact, and that, therefore, fraud could not lie.

RULE OF LAW

A cause of action for fraud in the inducement of a contract is stated where there is a false representation in a contract, the defendant intentionally or recklessly has made false representations either as to its knowledge of the facts or the facts themselves, upon which false statements the plaintiff relies, and the false representation is not an opinion as to the law, but is a statement of fact as to the state of circumstances regulated by law, and is relied on as a statement of fact by the plaintiff.

FACTS: National Conversion Corp. (Tenant) (P) entered a five-year lease with Cedar Bldg. Corp. (Landlords) (D) for industrial premises in New York City (City), for the purpose of converting restaurant garbage into fertilizer. When the lease was entered, both parties were represented by lawyers. The lease contained a representation that the premises were situated in an unrestricted zone, which turned out to be a false representation. In fact, the premises were in an M-1 district for light industrial uses, and the Tenant (P) would have had to have invested a sizeable amount of capital to comply with the requirements and standards of an M-1 district, since garbage conversion would be permitted in an M-1 district provided odors did not become readily detectable at the lot line, and provided various other performance standards not confined to odors were satisfied. The Tenant (P) also covenanted that its operations would produce no objectionable odors or gases. After Tenant (P) altered the premises and installed equipment, but before the initial operation of the enterprise, the City cited the Tenant (D) for zoning violations. Eventually, the enterprise was terminated, the Tenant (P) moved out, and then the Tenant (P) instituted an action for, inter alia, fraud in the inducement against the Landlords (D). At trial, the Tenant (P) was awarded a judgment for $70,086.81, which compensated the Tenant (P) for prior rent paid, the cost of installing equipment, and the cost of removal. The state's intermediate appellate court affirmed. On appeal to the state's highest court, the Landlords (D) argued that because the Tenant (P) could not have avoided producing objectionable odors or gases, the false representation as to unrestricted zoning by the Landlords (D) and the covenant by the Tenant (P) nullified one another, disentitling the Tenant (P) to remedies for fraud. The Landlords (D) also argued that the Tenant (P), represented by a lawyer, was just as much on notice, as they, the Landlords (D), were, that the premises were located in a restricted zone. Thus, they invoked the rule that one may not charge another with fraud if one knew, or should have known, the actual situation. However, the Tenant (P) adduced evidence that when it sought an adjournment of the negotiations for its lawyer to check whether the premises were located in an unrestricted zone, the Landlords' (D) lawyer, who was also one of the principals, said that it would not be necessary, that they (Landlords (D)) "own the property, and we know the area," that it is in an unrestricted zone, and "We [Landlords (D)] guarantee it." (The Landlords (D) denied ever making such statements.) The discussion was resolved only by including the representation in the lease. Thus, the Tenant (P) proved that it had not actually known of the zoning requirement and had relied on what it was told. Finally, the Landlords

Continued on next page.

(D) contended that if they had made a misrepresentation, it was one of law, rather than fact, and that, therefore, fraud could not lie. The state's highest court granted review.

ISSUE: Is a cause of action for fraud in the inducement of a contract stated where there is a false representation in a contract, the defendant intentionally or recklessly has made false representations either as to its knowledge of the facts or the facts themselves, upon which false statements the plaintiff relies, and the false representation is not an opinion as to the law, but is a statement of fact as to the state of circumstances regulated by law, and is relied on as a statement of fact by the plaintiff?

HOLDING AND DECISION: (Breitel, J.) Yes. A cause of action for fraud in the inducement of a contract is stated where there is a false representation in a contract, the defendant intentionally or recklessly has made false representations either as to its knowledge of the facts or the facts themselves, upon which false statements the plaintiff relies, and the false representation is not an opinion as to the law, but is a statement of fact as to the state of circumstances regulated by law, and is relied on as a statement of fact by the plaintiff. As a preliminary matter, regarding the Landlords' (D) argument that the Tenant (P) cannot be entitled to damages for fraud because the Tenant's (P) covenant offsets the misrepresentation regarding the premise's zoning, the two provisions are not contradictory but are reconcilable, and, therefore, do not negate each other. Even in an unrestricted zone, there is an obligation on the part of landowners and users not to permit objectionable odors, and there is also a common-law duty not to maintain a nuisance, so that the Tenant's (P) covenant was a rational inclusion even in a lease covering premises in an unrestricted zone. However, this determination does not resolve the key issue of fraud in the inducement. By proving that the Landlords (D) had persuaded the Tenant's (P) lawyer that it would not be necessary to check whether the premises were located in an unrestricted zone, and that, therefore, the Tenant (P) did not actually know of the true zoning but relied on what it had been told by the Landlord (D), the Tenant (P) made out a classic instance of fraud in the inducement. The Landlords (D) intentionally or recklessly made false representations either as to their knowledge of the facts or the facts themselves. Thus, the Tenant (P) was induced to make a lease for use of the premises for garbage conversion on the representation that the premises were in an unrestricted district. The Landlords (D) also contend that only a misrepresentation of law rather than of fact was involved and, therefore, that fraud could not lie. However, the law recognizes a sharp distinction between a pure opinion of law that may not, except in unusual circumstances, base an action in tort, and a mixed statement of fact as to what the law is or whether it is applicable. The law has outgrown the over-simple dichotomy between law and fact in the resolution of issues in deceit. Instead, a statement as to the law, like a statement as to anything else, may be intended and understood either as one of fact or one of opinion only, depending on the circumstances of the case. The statements in this case, both before the execution of the lease, and in the body of the lease, exemplify an instance in which the statements are not intended or understood merely as an expression of opinion. The Landlords (D) said they knew the premises were in an unrestricted district. This meant that they knew as a fact that the zoning resolution did not restrict the use of the particular premises, and the Tenant (P) understood the Landlords' (D) statement that way. When coupled with the further fact that the Tenant's (P) lawyer was persuaded not to verify the status of the premises on the Landlords' (D) representation, it is equally clear that the Tenant (P) understood the statement to be one of fact, namely, what the zoning resolution covering the area in which the premises were located provided by way of description, map, and requirements. The misrepresented fact was what the zoning resolution contained, by way of description, map, and requirements. The Landlords (D) did not express opinions as to the law itself, but as to matters regulated by law. Moreover, the modern rule extends even further to cover a false opinion of law if misrepresented as a sincere opinion, as in the case of any other opinion, where there is reasonable reliance on the opinion. Additionally, in proper circumstances, there may even be reliance on a fraudulently expressed statement of the law. Arguably, the facts of this case do not require so great a reach, because here the statements were keyed to the underlying data (facts) upon which the applicability of the particular zoning provisions governing the rights of owners and users were to be determined (the law). Consequently, the affirmed findings of fact establish the Landlords' (D) liability for fraud in the inducement. Affirmed.

ANALYSIS

To establish the scienter required for fraud (at least under New York law), a party must advance clear and convincing evidence that the defendant either knowingly or recklessly misrepresented a material fact. Here, the court held that scienter was established where the Landlords (D) "recklessly" made false representations either as to their knowledge of the facts or the facts themselves. Reckless conduct is, at the least, conduct that is highly unreasonable and that represents an extreme departure from the standards of ordinary care to the extent that the danger was either known to the defendant or so obvious that the defendant must have been aware of it. In some cases, an "egregious refusal to investigate the doubtful" may also give rise to an inference of recklessness.

Continued on next page.

Quicknotes

BREACH OF WARRANTY The breach of a promise made by one party to a contract on which the other party may rely, relieving that party from the obligation of determining whether the fact is true and indemnifying the other party from liability if that fact is shown to be false.

FRAUD IN THE INDUCEMENT Occurs when a testator is induced to execute a testamentary instrument as a result of the misrepresentation of certain facts existing at the time of its creation that may have effected the manner in which the testator disposed of his property.

FRAUDULENT MISREPRESENTATION A statement or conduct by one party to another that constitutes a false representation of fact.

SCIENTER Knowledge of certain facts; often refers to "guilty knowledge," which implicates liability.

McElrath v. Electric Investment Co.

Hotel lessee (P) v. Hotel owner (D)

Minn. Sup. Ct., 114 Minn. 358, 131 N.W. 380 (1911)

NATURE OF CASE: Appeal of an order overruling a demurrer to a deceit complaint.

FACT SUMMARY: Electric Investment Co. (D) induced McElrath (P) to lease property on assurances that an electric car line would be constructed on it.

RULE OF LAW

Deceit, to be actionable, requires the misrepresentation of some material "existing" (past or present) fact, not mere prediction of future facts; but, if in making said predictions the speaker intends to create in the mind of the recipient this impression that the intention to complete that future act is a present fact in the mind of some party, that is actionable as well.

FACTS: Electric Investment Co. (D) leased property to McElrath (P) for a term of years. In order to induce the lease, Electric Investment (D) had represented to McElrath (P) that: (1) the Minneapolis, St. Paul, Rochester and Dubuque Electric Traction Co. would complete and operate an electric railway through the area of said property, (2) which would make said property an important resort area, and (3) that McElrath (P) would surely make $1500 per annum from the resort business. McElrath (P) sued claiming deceit. Electric Investment (D) demurred on the grounds that the representations were mere nonactionable predictions of future facts. Upon an overruling of this demurrer, Electric Investment (D) appealed.

ISSUE: Will an action for deceit lie for misrepresentations of future facts (predictions)?

HOLDING AND DECISION: (Brown, J.) No. Deceit, to be actionable, requires the misrepresentation of some material "existing" (past or present) fact, not mere prediction of future facts; but, if in making said predictions the speaker intends to create in the mind of the recipient the impression that the intention to complete the future act is a present fact in the mind of some party, that is actionable as well. In such cases, an existing fact (present intention) has been misrepresented. Here, the general rule applies only to the representation about the area becoming an important resort area, such was a mere prediction, and the demurrer must be granted to that part of the complaint. On the other hand, the representations about the construction of a railway are actionable since they may have misrepresented (this is yet to be proven at trial) the existing fact of the Railroad Co.'s intent to build an electric railroad there. Such is a proper subject for deceit. Affirmed.

ANALYSIS

This case points out the material element in deceit (or misrepresentation) of a "material past or present fact." Only such a fact may be the proper subject of a deceit action. The seeming "exception" above is really no exception at all. Predictions may never be a proper subject for deceit. Misrepresentations, implicit or express, of present intents may always be, however. Ordinarily, a prediction as to events occurring in the future is considered mere opinion. No action will lie for such statements, since it is impossible to "warrant" something that does not exist. An intention, however, does "exist." It may be guaranteed or warranted. As such, it is actionable.

Quicknotes

DECEIT A false statement made either knowingly or with reckless disregard as to its truth and which is intended to induce the plaintiff to act in reliance thereon to his detriment.

DEMURRER The assertion that the opposing party's pleadings are insufficient and that the demurring party should not be made to answer.

MISREPRESENTATION A statement or conduct by one party to another that constitutes a false representation of fact.

Hinkle v. Rockville Motor Co., Inc.

Car buyer (P) v. Dealership (D)

Md. Ct. App., 262 Md. 502, 278 A.2d 42 (1971)

NATURE OF CASE: Action for damages for misrepresentation of a new car.

FACT SUMMARY: Rockville Motor Co. (D) sold, as a new car, a vehicle that had been wrecked previously.

RULE OF LAW

A defrauded plaintiff should be allowed to claim out-of-pocket expenses. If the defendant is morally culpable, the representations definite, and the present value ascertainable, then the plaintiff should be permitted to sue for the benefit of the bargain.

FACTS: Hinkle (P) purchased an allegedly new car from Rockville Motor Co., Inc. (Rockville) (D). Hinkle (P) discovered that the car actually had 2,000 miles on its speedometer. Rockville (D) reduced the purchase price to compensate Hinkle (P). Some four months later, Hinkle (P) found out that the car had been involved in an accident some months before he purchased it. Hinkle (P) brought suit for breach of warranty and misrepresentation. Hinkle (P) alleged that it would cost $800 to return the car to its warranted condition. At the close of testimony, Rockville (D) moved for a directed verdict since Hinkle (P) had failed to produce evidence as to value of the automobile at the time of sale. Therefore, the jury had no facts upon which to render a verdict for damages. The directed verdict was granted. Hinkle (P) appealed on the basis that he was entitled to out-of-pocket expenses for the misrepresentation and that the $800 repair cost was a sufficient showing of value to sustain a jury verdict.

ISSUE: Can a plaintiff recover for misrepresentation only if the value of the misrepresented chattel is proven?

HOLDING AND DECISION: (Barnes, J.) No. A defrauded plaintiff should be allowed to claim out-of-pocket expenses. If the defendant is morally culpable, the representations definite, and the present value ascertainable, then the plaintiff should be permitted to sue for the benefit of the bargain. A majority of states allow recovery for the "benefit of the bargain" if sufficiently proved in order to compensate a plaintiff as though the transaction had been carried out as represented. Other states restrict plaintiff to his "out-of-pocket expenses" to recoup his actual losses. Maryland is a middle-of-the-road state. If the fraudulent representation also amounted to a warranty, plaintiff may recover for the loss of the bargain because a fraud accompanied by a broken promise should cost the wrongdoer as much as the latter alone. Where damages under the benefit-of-the-bargain rule are proved with sufficient certainty, that rule will be employed. Here, the $800 figure to repair the automobile was sufficiently explicit to allow a jury to find that this was the amount of damages sustained and that the car was worth $800 less than the purchase price. Judgment reversed and case remanded.

ANALYSIS

This case outlines the problems associated with establishing damages. A plaintiff may recover his actual loss based on the misrepresentation (out-of-pocket damages) or, if warranted to be of a certain value, then his benefit of the bargain, i.e., the difference between the value of the property and that as represented. In addition, the plaintiff may plead and prove consequential damages. These are losses that are based upon the misrepresentation. Therefore, in *Vezina v. Souliere*, 103 Vt. 190 (1931), the plaintiff was allowed to recover when a supposedly gentle horse kicked him.

Quicknotes

BENEFIT OF THE BARGAIN Calculation of assessing damages in actions for breach of contract measured as the difference between the actual value and the purported value of the goods being bought.

CONSEQUENTIAL DAMAGES Monetary compensation that may be recovered in order to compensate for injuries or losses sustained as a result of damages that are not the direct or foreseeable result of the act of a party, but that nevertheless are the consequence of such act and which must be specifically pled and demonstrated.

MISREPRESENTATION A statement or conduct by one party to another that constitutes a false representation of fact.

CHAPTER 22

Interference with Advantageous Relationships

Quick Reference Rules of Law

Ratcliffe v. Evans

Business owner (P) v. Publisher (D)

C.A., 2 Q.B. 524 (1892)

NATURE OF CASE: Action for injury based on a published falsehood.

FACT SUMMARY: Evans (D) published injurious and false words regarding Ratcliffe's (P) business.

RULE OF LAW

An action for malicious interference with business, based on a published falsehood, will lie even though special damages are not proven.

FACTS: Ratcliffe (P) had carried on a business with his father. Upon his father's death, he continued to operate the business. However, Evans (D), publisher of the County Herald, falsely printed an article stating that the business had ceased existence. Ratcliffe (P) brought suit for damages based on the false and malicious publication and received a judgment. Evans (D) appealed, contending that a judgment could not lie since Ratcliffe (P) was unable to prove special damages.

ISSUE: May an action for malicious interference with business, based on a published falsehood, lie even though special damages are not proven?

HOLDING AND DECISION: (Lord Bowen, J.) Yes. By the very nature of the tort, the plaintiff will often only be able to show general damages. For this reason, an allegation of general damages is sufficient to support the analogous tort of libel. The same should be true where, as here, a false publication is maliciously intended to cause, and actually does cause, damage to the plaintiff. In such a case, proof of general damages will suffice to support the action. Appeal dismissed.

ANALYSIS

The principle of "injurious falsehood," established in the *Ratcliffe* case, is now deemed to include a wide variety of more specific torts arising out of false and malicious statements resulting in a pecuniary loss to another. Some of these torts may still be referred to by other titles, such as trade libel or slander of title.

Quicknotes

INJURIOUS FALSEHOOD A defamatory statement that inflicts actual damage.

LIBEL A false or malicious publication that subjects a person to scorn, hatred or ridicule, or that injures him in relation to his occupation or business.

SLANDER Defamatory statement communicated orally.

SPECIAL DAMAGES Damages caused by a specific act that are not the usual consequence of that act and which must be specifically pled and proven.

Horning v. Hardy

Sellers (D) v. Putative property owners (P)

Md. Ct. Spec. App., 36 Md. App. 419, 373 A.2d 1273 (1977)

NATURE OF CASE: Appeal from nonsuit to injurious falsehood counterclaim.

FACT SUMMARY: The trial court found that the Hardys (P) were privileged to make their damaging assertion regarding their belief that they owned property which the Hornings (D) sought to sell to a third party, thereby breaking off the deal.

RULE OF LAW

The conditional privilege to make a damaging statement when necessary to protect one's economic interests may only be overcome by a showing of constitutional or common-law malice.

FACTS: The Hardys (P) claimed they were the true owners of property the Hornings (D) were in the process of selling. As such, the Hardys (P) filed suit for trespass and ejectment and informed the potential purchasers of the property of their claim. The Hornings (D), in turn, filed a counterclaim based on slander of title and interference with a contract (the purchasers backed out of the deal after being apprised of the Hardys' (P) claim to the property). The trial court found for the Hornings (D) on the original suit, holding that the Hardys (P) had produced no evidence demonstrating their ownership of the property. It additionally found for the Hardys (P) on the counterclaim, holding that they were privileged to protect their asserted interest by informing the prospective purchasers of their claim. The Hornings (D) appealed the adverse judgment on the counterclaim.

ISSUE: May the conditional privilege to make a damaging statement when necessary to protect one's economic interests only be overcome by a showing of constitutional or common-law malice?

HOLDING AND DECISION: (Liss, J.) Yes. The conditional privilege to make a damaging statement when necessary to protect one's economic interests may only be overcome by a showing of constitutional or common-law malice. The tort complained of by the Hornings (D) has been combined and reclassified as the tort of injurious falsehood. It is similar to the tort of defamation, although it differs in that actual damages must be proved in all cases for an action to lie. However, other rules derived from the law of defamation also apply to the tort of injurious falsehood. As such, a true statement, though injurious, is privileged. Furthermore, a plaintiff must show that the false, injurious statement was made negligently by the defendant. Finally, a plaintiff in such an action has a conditional privilege to make a statement, even though it is false and injurious, if he does so to protect an economic interest, such as property ownership, unless he does so with malice, either constitutional (as defined by the *New York Times* case, 376 U.S. 254 [1964]) or common law (spite or ill will). Thus, in the instant case, the Hardys (P) were privileged to assert their ownership claim, although false and injurious to the Hornings' (D) claim, unless it is shown they did so maliciously. The Hornings (D) have not made such a showing, and on the basis of the record, they cannot. Mere failure to properly investigate, as is alleged, does not reach the level of such reckless disregard of the truth as to constitute malice. Affirmed.

ANALYSIS

The law of injurious falsehood in Maryland, applied in the *Horning* case, was defined by Judge Barnes, in the case of *Beane v. McMullen*, 291 A.2d 37 (Md. 1972), as follows: "Injurious falsehood or disparagement . . . consist[s] of the publication of matter derogatory to the plaintiff's title to his property, or its quality, or to his business in general . . . of a kind calculated to prevent others from dealing with him, or otherwise to interfere with his relations with others."

Quicknotes

DEFAMATION An intentional false publication, communicated publicly in either oral or written form, subjecting a person to scorn, hatred or ridicule, or injuring him or her in relation to his or her occupation or business.

DEFENSE OF CONDITION PRIVILEGE A defense to an action for libel or slander asserting immunity from liability for libelous or slanderous statements communicated in the execution of a political, judicial, social or personal obligation, unless it is demonstrated that the statement was made with actual malice and knowledge of its falsity.

INJURIOUS FALSEHOOD A defamatory statement that inflicts actual damage.

NONSUIT Judgment against a party who fails to make out a case.

SLANDER OF TITLE A defamatory statement made with the intent to disparage a party's title to real or personal property.

Testing Systems, Inc. v. Magnaflux Corp.

Equipment manufacturer (P) v. Competitor (D)

251 F. Supp. 286 (E.D. Pa. 1966)

NATURE OF CASE: Action to recover damages for disparagement of property.

FACT SUMMARY: Testing Systems, Inc. (P) and Magnaflux Corp. (D) were competing manufacturers of the same product. Testing Systems (P) alleged that Magnaflux (D) falsely informed Testing Systems' (P) customers that the U.S. Government had found that Testing Systems' (P) products were 40 percent as effective as Magnaflux's (D).

RULE OF LAW

While statements that make an unfavorable comparison of products are privileged, statements that contain specific assertions of unfavorable facts are not privileged and are actionable.

FACTS: Testing Systems, Inc. (P) and Magnaflux Corp. (D) were competing manufacturers of industrial and commercial testing equipment, devices, and systems. Testing Systems (P) alleged that Magnaflux (D) distributed a false report to Testing Systems' (P) current and prospective customers. The report stated that the U.S. government had tested Testing Systems' (P) product and found it to be 40 percent as effective as Magnaflux's (D). It was also alleged that Magnaflux's (D) agent said that Testing Systems' (P) "stuff is no good" and that "the government is throwing them out." Magnaflux (D) contends that it did no more than make an unfavorable comparison of Testing Systems' (P) product with its own.

ISSUE: Is a statement which contains specific assertions of unfavorable facts about a competitor's product protected by the privilege to make statements of unfavorable comparisons of products?

HOLDING AND DECISION: (Lord, J.) No. A statement which makes an unfavorable comparison of products, or which "puffs" or exaggerates the quality of one's own product is not usually actionable. However, there is a difference between saying that one's product is better than another's and asserting specific unfavorable facts. The latter, being an assertion of fact, implies that the party making the statement is fortified with the substantive facts necessary to make it. In this case, Magnaflux Corp. (D) admitted the truth of the allegations. Statements of unfavorable comparison merely express an opinion, the truth or falsity of which is difficult or impossible to ascertain. Magnaflux's (D) statement is an assertion of a specific fact, and hence is not privileged. Further, Magnaflux (D) gave added authenticity to its statements by invoking the authority of the U.S. Government. Such statements and its statement that the government was throwing out Testing Systems' (P) products are not mere comparison and are not protected. Judgment for the plaintiff.

ANALYSIS

As this case demonstrates, general statements of comparison stating that the defendant's products are better than the plaintiff's are privileged so long as they contain no specific assertions of unfavorable facts about the plaintiff's product. The basis for this rule is that the practice of sellers to "puff," boast, or exaggerate as to the excellence of their product over rival products is so well known that purchasers attach little or no importance to such assertions, and so they usually can do no serious harm.

Quicknotes

DISPARAGEMENT OF PROPERTY An untrue statement regarding certain property which denigrates such property and for which an action may lie.

PUFFING The communication of an opinion not intended as a representation of fact and upon which an action for fraud or misrepresentation cannot be based.

Lumley v. Gye

Theatre manager (P) v. Interferer (D)

Q.B., 2 El. & Bl. 216, 118 Eng. Rep. 749 (1853)

NATURE OF CASE: Action to recover damages for interference with a contract.

FACT SUMMARY: Wagner had a contract with Lumley (P) to sing exclusively at his theater for a period of time. Gye (D) knew the conditions of the contract. For the purpose of injuring Lumley (P), Gye (D) enticed Wagner to refuse to perform.

RULE OF LAW
A person who procures a breach of another's contract is liable for damages due to his interference.

FACTS: Lumley (P) and Wagner had contracted that she would perform in Lumley's (P) theater for a period of time during which she would not perform elsewhere without Lumley's (P) consent. Gye (D) knew the conditions of this contract. During the time the agreement was in force, and with the intention of injuring Lumley (P), Gye (D) enticed and procured Wagner to refuse to perform. Due to this enticement and procurement, Wagner did wrongly refuse to perform in Lumley's (P) theater.

ISSUE: Is a person who procures a breach of another's contract liable for damages due to his interference?

HOLDING AND DECISION: (Lord Erle, J.) Yes. A person who procures a breach of another's contract is liable for damages due to his interference. It is clear that an action will lie by a master against a person who procures that a servant should unlawfully leave his service. The master's right of action arises from the wrongful act of putting an end to the relation of employer and employed by the procuring of the servant to break his contract. The same principle is applicable in this case, since the cause of action arises from the procurement of the violation of a right. When this principle is applied to a violation of a right arising out of an employment contract, the nature of the service contracted for is immaterial. In this case, Gye's (D) enticement and procurement of Wagner that caused her to breach her contract with Lumley (P) was a violation of Lumley's (P) right for which Gye (D) should be held liable. It is immaterial that Gye (D) did not act unlawfully in procuring the breach of the contract. His malicious interference with Lumley's (P) rights makes him liable. Judgment for the plaintiff.

ANALYSIS

Lumley v. Gye is the leading modern case allowing recovery in tort for the interference with a contract. It and subsequent cases emphasized that the existence of the contract is something of a property interest in the plaintiff. Interference with such an interest gives rise to a cause of action. Although American courts were reluctant to accept the doctrine in the beginning, now decisions that rejected it have been for the most part overruled. The tort is recognized everywhere except in Louisiana, which continues to hold there is no action for inducing the breach of a contract unless means unlawful in itself are used. Elsewhere, the tort is recognized as to any contract, regardless of its character.

Quicknotes

INTERFERENCE WITH CONTRACTUAL RELATIONS An intentional tort whereby a defendant intentionally elicits the breach of a valid contract resulting in damages.

Bacon v. St. Paul Union Stockyards Co.

Livestock dealer (P) v. Stockyard owner (D)

Minn. Sup. Ct., 161 Minn. 522, 201 N.W. 326 (1924)

NATURE OF CASE: Appeal from demurrer to action for damages for interference with business relations.

FACT SUMMARY: Bacon (P) contended that St. Paul Union Stockyards Co. (D) had wrongfully barred him from the stockyards and had deprived him of his means of livelihood.

RULE OF LAW

The wrongful interference with the contract relations of others causing a breach is a tort.

FACTS: Bacon (P) contended that he was employed by the Drover Livestock Commission Co., engaged in buying, selling and dealing in livestock in St. Paul Union Stockyards Co.'s (St. Paul) (D) stockyards, but that St. Paul (D) had wrongfully, unlawfully and willfully excluded him from its stockyards, had barred and prevented him from carrying on his occupation, and had forbade any person, firm, or corporation from employing him in or near the stockyards. After St. Paul's (D) demurrer to the complaint was sustained by the trial court, Bacon (P) appealed.

ISSUE: Is the wrongful interference with the contract relations of others causing a breach a tort?

HOLDING AND DECISION: (Per curiam) Yes. The wrongful interference with the contract relations of others causing a breach is a tort. Here, the complaint states a cause of action for wrongful interference with Bacon's (P) employment. It appears that Bacon (P) had steady employment, and that St. Paul (D) wrongfully, willfully, and unlawfully prevented him from continuing in that employment. Such conduct is in violation of Bacon's (P) rights. Reversed.

ANALYSIS

As this case indicates, the action of barring an employee from his place of employment may constitute an actionable tort. Related acts that may result in tort liability include restricting the sales of a person's employee, fraudulently inducing a person to breach a contract, and depriving a person of necessary labor.

Quicknotes

DEMURRER The assertion that the opposing party's pleadings are insufficient and that the demurring party should not be made to answer.

INTERFERENCE WITH CONTRACTUAL RELATIONS An intentional tort whereby a defendant intentionally elicits the breach of a valid contract resulting in damages.

Della Penna v. Toyota Motor Sales, U.S.A., Inc.

Automobile wholesaler (P) v. Automobile manufacturer (D)

Cal. Sup. Ct., 11 Cal. 4th 376, 902 P.2d 740 (1995)

NATURE OF CASE: Appeal from reversal of verdict for defendant in claim for interference with prospective economic advantage.

FACT SUMMARY: Della Penna (P), an auto wholesaler who exported cars to Japan for resale, brought action against Toyota Motor Sales, U.S.A., Inc. (D) when it took steps to prevent him from conducting his business.

RULE OF LAW

A plaintiff seeking to recover for interference with prospective economic advantage has the burden of proving that the defendant's interference was wrongful by some measure beyond the fact of the interference itself.

FACTS: Della Penna (P) had a lucrative business in which he bought Lexus cars from U.S. retailers at near retail prices and then exported them to Japan for resale. Toyota Motor Sales, U.S.A., Inc. (Toyota) (D), the maker of Lexus, wanted to prevent imported U.S. Lexus cars from being re-exported to Japan. To try to curb this practice, Toyota (D) compiled a list of offending auto brokers and warned its dealers that those who did business with them faced possible sanctions. As a result, Della Penna's (P) supply of cars dried up. Della Penna (P) brought suit for interference of prospective economic advantage. The judge gave the jury instructions that Della Penna (P) had the burden of showing that Toyota's (D) interference was wrongful "by some measure beyond the fact of the interference itself." The jury returned a verdict for Toyota (D), but the court of appeals reversed, finding that the judge erred in placing the burden on Della Penna (P). The Supreme Court of California granted review.

ISSUE: Does a plaintiff seeking to recover for interference with prospective economic advantage have the burden of proving that the defendant's interference was wrongful by some measure beyond the fact of the interference itself?

HOLDING AND DECISION: (Arabian, J.) Yes. A plaintiff seeking to recover for interference with prospective economic advantage has the burden of proving that the defendant's interference was wrongful by some measure beyond the fact of the interference itself. There is an important distinction between the disruption of an existing contract and the interference with a prospective contract or economic relationship. Courts should firmly distinguish these differences and acknowledge that relationships short of a contract have inherent risks. Della Penna's (P) business, although lucrative, was inherently risky because it was entirely speculative. Della Penna (P) did not have contracts with the dealers he bought from. Therefore, the instruction given by the trial court, that Della Penna (P) had the burden of proving that Toyota's (D) actions were wrongful beyond the fact of the interference, was proper under the circumstances. The judgment of the court of appeals should be reversed, and the trial court's judgment for Toyota (D) should be reinstated. Reversed and remanded.

CONCURRENCE: (Mosk, J.) The majority's reversal of the court of appeals was correct although the rationale was not. The tort of interference with prospective economic advantage can be proven by showing other tortious conduct such as defamation, fraud, or deceit. The majority was wrong in accepting that the instruction given to the jury by the trial court was proper. The formulation of an instruction should not include any reference to motive. However, this error was not prejudicial.

ANALYSIS

Courts faced with cases of interference with prospective economic advantage have developed numerous formulas and tests for determining liability. The Restatement (Second) of Torts § 766B identified a seven-factor balancing test that the California court declined to apply. These factors include: (1) the nature of the actor's conduct; (2) the actor's motive; (3) the interests of the other with which the actor's conduct interferes; (4) the interests sought to be advanced by the actor; (5) the social interests in protecting the freedom of action of the actor and the contractual interests of the other; (6) the proximity or remoteness of the actor's conduct to the interference; and (7) the relations between the parties.

Quicknotes

INTERFERENCE WITH PROSPECTIVE ADVANTAGE An intentional tort whereby a defendant intentionally interferes with a valid business expectancy, resulting in the termination of the expectancy and damages.

Neibuhr v. Gage

Shareholder (P) v. Corporate officer (D)

Minn. Sup. Ct., 99 Minn. 149, 108 N.W. 884 (1906)

NATURE OF CASE: Appeal from order for new trial in an action for fraud.

FACT SUMMARY: Neibuhr (P) contended that he should be allowed to bring suit in tort for Gage's (D) actions in compelling him to transfer stock.

RULE OF LAW

A party injured by duress is entitled to the same remedies available in cases of deceit.

FACTS: Neibuhr (P) possessed 91 shares of stock in Gage, Hayden & Co. (Gage) (D), with a face value of $9,100. Gage (D) accused Neibuhr (P) of grand larceny and threatened to have him convicted unless he transferred the shares to Gage (D). Neibuhr (P) contended that he was innocent, but that Gage (D) had led him to believe that Gage (D) would produce perjured testimony against him in support of the accusation. Under threat of immediate arrest and imprisonment and without opportunity for consultation, Neibuhr (P) transferred the shares. Niebuhr (P) then brought this action to recover damages he suffered by reason of being required to transfer those shares under duress. After the trial judge granted a motion for new trial, both parties appealed.

ISSUE: Is a party injured by duress entitled to the same remedies available in cases of deceit?

HOLDING AND DECISION: (Elliot, J.) Yes. A party injured by duress is entitled to the same remedies available in cases of deceit. As commonly understood, fraud is a wrong accomplished by deception, but duress is a species of fraud in which compulsion in some form takes the place of deception in accomplishing the injury. In both cases, the wrongdoer accomplishes the same wrong and does it with the same bad intent. Reversed; judgment ordered for Neibuhr (P).

ANALYSIS

The remedy of restitution is usually available to victims of conduct that could be labeled duress, fraud, or deception. Restitution will allow the victim to recover any unjust enrichment obtained by the party exercising the duress over the victim. It will also invalidate certain otherwise available defenses, such as consent.

Quicknotes

RESCISSION The canceling of an agreement and the return of the parties to their positions prior to the formation of the contract.

Freeman & Mills, Inc. v. Belcher Oil Company

Accounting firm (P) v. Client (D)

Cal. Sup. Ct., 11 Cal. 4th 85, 900 P.2d 669 (1995)

NATURE OF CASE: Grant of review in breach of contract and bad faith denial of contract action.

FACT SUMMARY: Freeman & Mills, Inc. (Freeman) (P) sued Belcher Oil Company (Belcher) (D) for money owed pursuant to Freeman's (P) providing of accounting services to Belcher (D). Pursuant to litigation, he asserted breach of contract, bad faith denial of contract, and quantum meruit bases for recovery.

RULE OF LAW

There is no tort cause of action for bad faith denial of a contract.

FACTS: Belcher Oil Company (Belcher) (D) retained the Morgan firm to defend it in a Florida lawsuit. Pursuant to a letter of understanding, Belcher (D) was obligated to pay for costs, including accountant fees. Morgan hired Freeman & Mills, Inc. (Freeman) (P) to provide financial analysis and litigation support for Belcher (D) in the suit. Morgan was subsequently discharged and asked for a summary of the work performed by Freeman (P). Freeman (P) was also asked to terminate its work for Belcher (D). Freeman's (P) final statement was for fees of $70,042.50, plus $7,495.63 for costs. Freeman (P) billed Belcher (D), which refused payment. Freeman (P) filed suit against Belcher (D) alleging breach of contract, bad faith denial of contract, and quantum meruit. The jury concluded that Belcher (D) was in breach of contract and denied the existence of the contract. Belcher (D) appealed from the court's corrected judgment. The court of appeals found that no special relationship existed between the parties to justify a tort theory of recovery for bad faith denial of the contract. The court remanded for a retrial limited to the issue of damages under the breach of contract cause of action. This court granted review to resolve confusion regarding its holding in *Seaman's*, 36 Cal. 3d 752, 686 P.2d 1158 (1984), recognizing a tort cause of action for bad faith denial of a contract.

ISSUE: Is there a tort cause of action for bad faith denial of a contract?

HOLDING AND DECISION: (Lucas, C.J.) No. There is no tort cause of action for bad faith denial of a contract. In *Seaman's*, this court established the tort of bad faith denial of contract. Subsequent decisions indicated a reluctance to allow tort recovery for noninsurance contract breaches. The *Seaman's* decision left a number of questions unresolved and resulted in inconsistent decisions. Many court of appeals decisions recognized compelling policy reasons to preclude tort remedies for breaches of contract outside the insurance context. In *Harris*, 14 Cal. App. 4th 70 (1993), the court set forth the following reasons for denying tort recovery in breach of contract cases: (1) the different objectives of tort and contract law; (2) the importance of predictability and stability in contractual dealings; (3) the danger of tort liability (including punitive damages) for every breach of contract; and (4) deference to legislation in making decisions regarding the appropriate remedies. Based on these reasons, *Seaman's* is overruled. Affirmed.

ANALYSIS

There is no tort liability on a party for interference with its own contract. Rather, there must be an independent tort upon which to base liability.

Quicknotes

BAD FAITH Conduct that is intentionally misleading or deceptive.

BREACH OF CONTRACT Unlawful failure by a party to perform its obligations pursuant to contract.

CAUSE OF ACTION A fact or set of facts the occurrence of which entitles a party to seek judicial relief.

LIABILITY Any obligation or responsibility.

QUANTUM MERUIT Equitable doctrine allowing recovery for labor and materials provided by one party, even though no contract was entered into, in order to avoid unjust enrichment by the benefited party.

Nash v. Baker

Wronged wife (P) v. The other woman (D)

Okla. Ct. App., 522 P.2d 1335 (1974)

NATURE OF CASE: Action by wife and minor children for alienation of affection.

FACT SUMMARY: The court dismissed the action of Mrs. Nash's (P) minor children against the woman (D) who enticed their father away from the marriage.

RULE OF LAW

Children do not have a cause of action for any losses sustained through the efforts of a third party to break up the marriage.

FACTS: Mr. Nash had an affair with Baker (D). Mr. Nash left his family for Baker (D) and Mrs. Nash (P) sued for alienation of affection, loss of consortium, adultery, etc., on her own behalf and for her minor children. The children's action was dismissed and a judgment was rendered against Mrs. Nash (P) for her own cause of action. She appealed.

ISSUE: Do children have a cause of action for any losses sustained through the efforts of a third party to break up the marriage?

HOLDING AND DECISION: (Romang, J.) No. Children do not have a cause of action for any losses sustained through the efforts of a third party to break up the marriage. Neither the Constitution nor statute gives any right to children in this area. They have no cause of action for alienation of affection, loss of future income, adultery, loss of consortium, etc. Unless specifically authorized by statute, they may not recover. The court correctly dismissed their action. Judgment affirmed.

ANALYSIS

Nash has several interesting facets. First, the law may not provide a remedy for every wrong. It must be granted by the legislature (statutory), the common law (previous judicial decisions which have not been abrogated by statute), or by the creation of new judicial causes of action. Secondly, the case illustrates an attempt to extend the coverage of existing law to cover claims by the children. In most such situations, courts are hesitant to enter into a quasi-legislative area and prefer to defer to a decision by the legislature if the law is to be changed.

Quicknotes

ALIENATION OF AFFECTIONS A cause of action arising from the willful and malicious interference with a marital relationship.

LOSS OF CONSORTIUM An action brought based on willful interference with the marital relationship.

CHAPTER 23

Torts in the Age of Statutes

Quick Reference Rules of Law

Burnette v. Wahl

Children (P) v. Their mothers (D)

Or. Sup. Ct., 284 Or. 705, 588 P.2d 1105 (1978)

NATURE OF CASE: Appeal from dismissal of action for damages for breach of parental duties.

FACT SUMMARY: Five minor children (P) sought damages from their mothers (D) for emotional and psychological injury caused by abandonment and failure to perform parental duties.

RULE OF LAW

No action lies in tort for breach of parental duties.

FACTS: Burnette (P), as guardian, brought suit on behalf of five minor children, aged two to eight, against their mothers (D) for emotional and psychological injury caused by the failure of the mothers (D) to perform their parental duties towards the children. Among the allegations in the action were claims for violation of an Oregon criminal statute for failure to maintain them, abandonment, and neglect. After the trial court entered orders of dismissal after sustaining demurrers to the complaint, Burnette (P) appealed.

ISSUE: Does an action lie in tort for breach of parental duties?

HOLDING AND DECISION: (Holman, J.) No. No action lies in tort for breach of parental duties. There is a strong state policy, as evidenced by the state criminal statute, of requiring the kind of parental nurturing, support, and physical care of children which the mothers (D) here are alleged to have denied their children. However, it does not follow that it would be wise or judicious to vindicate that policy by a tort action for damages by children against their mothers. If there is ever a field in which juries and general trial courts are ill equipped to do social engineering, it is in the realm of the emotional relationship between mother and child. Affirmed.

DISSENT: (Linde, J.) It is incongruous to hold that the legislature provided for a felony prosecution of parents who egregiously violate a duty toward their children, but that it meant to exclude civil actions on behalf of the maliciously abandoned children for fear of impairing the family unit.

ANALYSIS

The majority opinion in this case was grounded upon the state legislature's actions in creating remedies for the type of conduct involved in this case, and the reluctance of the court to permit judicial interference with the family unit. As the court noted, the legislature had never established a cause of action for a parent's refusal to provide parental services.

Quicknotes

ALIENATION OF AFFECTIONS A cause of action arising from the willful and malicious interference with a marital relationship.

INTRAFAMILY TORT IMMUNITY The immunity of family members from tort liability in actions brought by another member of the family.

OREGON CHILD PROTECTION LAWS The Oregon legislature enacted an array of laws for the purpose of protecting or vindicating children's rights.

Nearing v. Weaver

Spousal abuse victim (P) v. Police officers (D)

Or. Sup. Ct., 295 Or. 702, 670 P.2d 137 (1983)

NATURE OF CASE: Appeal from affirmance of summary judgment for police officers in suit brought under state statute to recover damages for physical and emotional injuries.

FACT SUMMARY: Nearing (P) brought suit against a municipality (D) and police officers (D) under the state's Abuse Prevention Act (Act) for psychological and physical injuries allegedly sustained as a result of the officers' (D) knowing failure to arrest her husband for violation of a restraining order, contending that the officers (D) and municipality (D) were susceptible to liability under the Act over defenses of official discretion and official immunity.

RULE OF LAW

A police officer who knowingly fails to enforce a judicial order issued pursuant to a state statute designed to strengthen legal protections for persons abused by a present or former spouse or a cohabitant may be held liable for resulting psychological and physical harm to the intended beneficiaries of the order, over the defenses of official discretion and official immunity.

FACTS: The state's legislature enacted Abuse Prevention Act (Act) to strengthen legal protection for persons threatened with assault by a present or former spouse or a cohabitant. The means chosen for this purpose included the use of temporary restraining orders, injunctions, and temporary child custody orders, and mandatory provisions for the warrantless arrest upon probable cause of a person believed to have violated such an order. A few years after the Act was enacted, Henrietta Nearing (P) separated from her husband. Several months later, the husband entered her home without her permission and struck her. Henrietta (P) reported the incident to police officer Weaver (D) and her husband was arrested and charged with assault. The following day a court issued an order restraining the husband from bothering Henrietta (P) or her two minor children (P) and from entering their home. The husband continued to enter the home, caused damage to the home, and threatened to remove the children. Henrietta (P) reported the incidents to Weaver (D) and asked him to arrest her husband. He declined on the basis that he had not seen the husband on the premises. The husband repeatedly continued to enter the home, and on one occasion assaulted Henrietta's (P) friend. The police department continued to be unresponsive to Henrietta's (P) reports of continued death threats and actual assaults. Although the police officers to whom she reported these incidents assured her that they would arrest the husband, they did not take any such action. Henrietta (P) then brought suit alleging that she suffered severe emotional distress and physical injuries as a proximate result of the police officers' (D) failure to arrest her husband and that her children (P) suffered acute emotional distress and psychological impairment. The officers (D) denied the allegations and pleaded the affirmative defenses of immunity and discretion. After the trial court granted summary judgment to the police officers (D) and municipality (D), the state's intermediate appellate court affirmed. Henrietta (P) appealed and moved to strike the affirmative defenses and assigned denial of the motion as error. The state's highest court granted review.

ISSUE: May a police officer who knowingly fails to enforce a judicial order issued pursuant to a state statute designed to strengthen legal protections for persons abused by a present or former spouse or a cohabitant be held liable for resulting psychological and physical harm to the intended beneficiaries of the order, over the defenses of official discretion and official immunity?

HOLDING AND DECISION: (Linde, J.) Yes. A police officer who knowingly fails to enforce a judicial order issued pursuant to a state statute designed to strengthen legal protections for persons abused by a present or former spouse or a cohabitant may be held liable for resulting psychological and physical harm to the intended beneficiaries of the order, over the defenses of official discretion and official immunity. Weaver (D) argued that state law does not allow recovery of damages for negligent infliction of emotional distress. The plaintiffs responded that the law does allow recovery of damages for psychic or emotional harm when the defendant's conduct infringes a legal right independent of an ordinary negligence claim. The plaintiff's argument is correct. The issue then is whether the plaintiffs asserted the infringement of a legal right independent of a negligence action, which they did. The duty the officers (D) are alleged to have neglected is not the ordinary common-law duty of care but a specific duty imposed by statute to enforce court orders. Here the risk, the harm, and the potential plaintiff were all foreseen by the legislature; it was not left to a clerk, or a lawyer, or the officers in this case to foresee a possible risk and to form a "reasonable" opinion as to what "due care" might be required to avoid it. Such ad hoc judgments are precisely what the legislature meant to overcome when it enacted the obligation to enforce judicial orders. This does not mean

Continued on next page.

that the obligation creates absolute liability for resulting harm, and officers may still have various defenses under the statute itself, for instance that the defendant officer made a good faith effort to perform, or that the officer was prevented from doing so by one or another obstacle, either factual or legal. Whatever would be a defense under the statute is a defense to civil liability. The Act clearly established a duty on the part of the officers (D) towards the plaintiffs and mandated that the officers (D) arrest and take into custody without a warrant persons whom the officers had probable cause to believe had violated a restraining order that has been served and filed by the court. The Act was passed specifically in response to the failure of police officers to remove persons involved in cases of domestic violence, such as here, to allow the victim to escape immediate danger. The officers (D) claimed that a determination of probable cause is a discretionary function immune from liability. Discretion, however, exists only where responsibility for value judgments and policy choices among competing goals and priorities has been delegated to the officer. Here the Act intentionally negates any discretionary function by the officer by mandating enforcement of the restraining order. The officers' (D) claim of immunity also fails since such immunity provides for a shield against liability for a good faith arrest, not for the failure to make an arrest. Accordingly, both affirmative defenses should have been stricken by the lower courts. Reversed and remanded.

DISSENT: (Peterson, J.) Although the court can create a new tort based on policy considerations, it should not do so in this case, for the following reasons. First, there is no way of knowing how the creation of a new tort will affect the ability of municipalities and counties to enforce the law and recruit and hire competent law enforcement officers, and there is no way of knowing how much a new tort would exacerbate the fiscal problems of the state's cities. Given the prevalence of domestic strife, the effect upon a local government budget could be considerable. There also is no way to know how such a new tort might affect day-to-day law enforcement practices, since the imposition of personal liability on officers and their employers for failure to arrest could result in an inefficient use of scarce police resources in a period of social crisis or high crime. Moreover, since the law at issue is a new law, there is insufficient information to determine whether the creation of a strict liability remedy against public bodies and their peace officers is necessary to vindicate the law's statutory policy. If peace officers are not doing their duty, the legislature should take another look at this area and make the decision as to whether the creation of such a cause of action is necessary, especially since so far the potentially impacted public bodies and their employees have not yet been heard from, either by the legislature or any court.

ANALYSIS

The majority responds to both the dissent and the concurrence in its opinion. In response to the claim that it imposes strict liability, the majority answers that it does not impose liability without fault. The statute simply mandates that the officers respond to the court order. It also rejects the concurrence's contention that damages may not be recovered for mental injuries absent physical injuries since the officers (D) owed a specific duty toward the plaintiff under the statute.

Quicknotes

DISCRETION The authority conferred upon a public official to act reasonably in accordance with his or her own judgment under certain circumstances.

EMOTIONAL DISTRESS Extreme personal suffering that results from another's conduct and for which damages may be sought.

OFFICIAL IMMUNITY Immunity of an official from civil liability for injuries sustained by an individual as a result of actions performed in the discharge of his official duties.

RESTRAINING ORDER An order, similar to an injunction, prohibiting a defendant from certain activities until a hearing regarding an injunction on such activities may be conducted.

Bivens v. Six Unknown Named Agents of Federal Bureau of Narcotics

Suspect (P) v. Federal agents (D)

403 U.S. 388 (1971)

NATURE OF CASE: Suit alleging violation of Fourth Amendment rights.

FACT SUMMARY: Bivens (P), who had been the victim of an unwarranted search for narcotics, brought an action for damages directly under the Fourth Amendment to the United States Constitution.

RULE OF LAW

Monetary damages may be recovered for violations of the Fourth Amendment by federal officials.

FACTS: Bivens (P) brought suit, seeking damages for violation of his Fourth Amendment rights to be free from unreasonable searches and seizures. His complaint stated that several agents of the Federal Bureau of Narcotics (D), acting under claim of federal authority, entered his apartment and arrested him for alleged narcotics violations. The agents manacled Bivens (P) in front of his wife and children and threatened to arrest the entire family. A thorough search of the family residence was then conducted. Bivens (P) stated that the arrest and search were effected without a warrant, and that unreasonable force was employed in making the arrest, and that he had suffered great humiliation, embarrassment, and mental suffering as the result of the agents' unlawful conduct. After the court of appeals affirmed the district court's dismissal of the action, Bivens (P) appealed.

ISSUE: May monetary damages be recovered for violations of the Fourth Amendment by federal officials?

HOLDING AND DECISION: (Brennan, J.) Yes. Monetary damages may be recovered for violations of the Fourth Amendment by federal officials. The Fourth Amendment operates as a limitation upon the exercise of federal power regardless of whether the state in whose jurisdiction that power is exercised would prohibit or penalize the identical act if engaged in by a private citizen. Historically, damages have been regarded as the ordinary remedy for an invasion of personal interests in liberty. Bivens (P) is entitled to recover money damages for any injuries he has suffered as a result of the agents' (D) violation of the Fourth Amendment. Reversed and remanded.

CONCURRENCE: (Harlan, J.) It is entirely proper that these injuries be compensable according to uniform rules of federal law, especially in light of the very large element of federal law which must control the scope of official defenses to liability.

DISSENT: (Burger, C.J.) Legislation is the business of the Congress, and it has the facilities and competence for that task, which the courts do not.

ANALYSIS

This case, a landmark decision, is generally recognized as the first case in which the Supreme Court implied a cause of action arising directly from a constitutional provision. The nature of Bivens's (P) action, though, is nearly identical to that which may be asserted against state officials under the federal civil rights statute, 42 U.S.C. § 1983.

Quicknotes

FOURTH AMENDMENT Provides that persons be secure as to their person and private belongings against unreasonable searches and seizures.

Alexander v. Sandoval

Director of public safety (D) v. Driver's license examinee (P)

532 U.S. 275 (2001)

NATURE OF CASE: Suit to enjoin enforcement of a state policy requiring English-only driver's license examinations.

FACT SUMMARY: A state department of public safety adopted a policy requiring driver's licenses to be administered only in English. A non-English-speaking driver's license examinee sued under Title VI of the Civil Rights Act to enjoin the state department from enforcing the policy.

RULE OF LAW

A private individual cannot sue to enforce regulations promulgated under Title VI of the Civil Rights Act.

FACTS: The Alabama Department of Public Safety, whose director was Alexander (D), accepted federal funds and thus was required to comply with Title VI of the federal Civil Rights Act, 42 U.S.C. 2000d et seq. Section 601 of the statute prohibited the department from discriminating against persons on the basis of race, color, or national origin. Section 602 authorized federal agencies to adopt and promulgate rules to carry out § 601's prohibition on discrimination. The U.S. Department of Justice (DOJ) adopted and promulgated such a rule, proscribing policies that had even the effect of such discrimination. The Alabama Department of Public Safety then adopted a policy requiring that all driver's license examinations be administered in English. Sandoval (P), who did not speak English, filed suit to enjoin enforcement of the English-only policy; he claimed that the DOJ's rule, promulgated pursuant to § 602, created a right for him to sue to enforce the regulation's requirements. The trial court agreed, and it also agreed with Sandoval (P) on the merits of his request for injunctive relief, enjoining Alexander (D) from enforcing the English-only policy. The Eleventh Circuit Court of Appeals affirmed the trial court. Alexander (D) petitioned for review in the United States Supreme Court.

ISSUE: Can a private individual sue to enforce regulations promulgated under Title VI of the Civil Rights Act?

HOLDING AND DECISION: (Scalia, J.) No. A private individual cannot sue to enforce regulations promulgated under Title VI of the Civil Rights Act. The Court may take three aspects of Title VI as given for purposes of this appeal. First, § 601 does create a private right of action. Second, the only discrimination prohibited by § 601 is intentional. Third, the Court will assume in this case that regulations promulgated pursuant to § 602 can apply to groups. Against that backdrop, it is clear that § 601's private right of action cannot include a similar right in the DOJ's regulations promulgated under § 602 because the regulations prohibit conduct allowed by § 601. Thus, if a private right of action exists in the DOJ's regulations, it must derive from § 602. To determine whether § 602 implies a private right to sue, it is improper to refer to the law of implied rights as it existed when Title VI was enacted in 1964. This understanding was superseded, without deviation in the interim, in *Cort v. Ash*, 422 U.S. 66, 78 (1975). Further, the "contemporary legal context" is no more than possible support for the statutory text itself. In this case, the text of § 602 ends the inquiry: It has no rights-creating language, limits federal agencies to "effectuating" § 601, and applies only to the regulated recipients of federal funds, not to the individuals who are protected by § 601. Section 602's methods of enforcement also fail to demonstrate congressional intent to create a private right of action. Sandoval (P) and the Government next would find the private right in the DOJ's regulations themselves, but regulations cannot create rights of action where Congress has not first done so in the empowering statute. Nor have the two most recent amendments to Title VI implicitly "ratified" this Court's implied-rights decisions. Indeed, no case has found the implied right that is essential to Sandoval's (P) argument. Further, the implicit-ratification argument is fundamentally flawed because Congress's inaction on specific portions of a statutory scheme means only that Congress took no action in those areas. It does not mean that Congress has affirmatively approved any of this Court's decisions. Reversed.

ANALYSIS

Sandoval is part of a distinct trend in the Supreme Court to limit judicial recognition of new implied rights of action. A fruitful question to ponder, especially when weighing the possibility of bringing suit under a statutory scheme that does not directly express a right of action, is whether that trend is grounded in the law or in something even more intangible and personal. Justice Stevens, writing in dissent in the 5-4 decision in *Sandoval*, concluded that "today's decision is the unconscious product of the majority's profound distaste for implied causes of action rather than an attempt to discern the intent of the Congress that enacted Title VI of the Civil Rights Act of 1964." 532 U.S. at 317.

Continued on next page.

Quicknotes

PRIVATE RIGHT OF ACTION A fact or set of facts the occurrence of which entitle a party to seek judicial relief.

De Falco v. Bernas

Land developers (P) v. Local government racketeers (D)

244 F.3d 286 (2d Cir. 2001)

NATURE OF CASE: Appeal from a trial court's order vacating a civil jury's award of damages on violations of the federal Racketeer Influenced and Corrupt Organization Act (RICO).

FACT SUMMARY: Local government officials, and people influencing them, conditioned the local government's approval of a land-development project upon the developers' surrender of property and their employment of certain persons.

RULE OF LAW

A private individual cannot successfully enforce the federal criminal RICO statute, 18 U.S.C. 1962(c), unless he proves that the prohibited racketeering conduct was both the factual and proximate cause of his injuries.

FACTS: De Falco and others (P) bought land in Delaware Township, Sullivan County, New York to develop the land. Dirie (D), the Town of Delaware's supervisor and a member of the Town's legislative body, expressly conditioned the Town's approval of the planned development on De Falco (P) allowing Dirie's (D) son to harvest timber on the property. When De Falco (P) entered a logging contract with an out-of-state logging company for the project, Dirie (D) demanded that De Falco (P) dissolve the contract and threatened De Falco (P) with the prospect of losing the approval of the Town's planning board. The Bernas defendants (D) also threatened De Falco (P) with the local government's disapproval of the development project even though they were not officially members of the local government. The Bernas defendants (D), who operated a road-construction business, withdrew gravel from De Falco's (P) property and demanded that De Falco (P) transfer shares in the proposed new business to the Bernas defendants (D). After about seven months, De Falco (P) eventually complied with the demand, but the Bernas defendants (D) escalated their demands by requiring expanded rights to the property's gravel pit, threatening to close down the entire development project if De Falco (P) resisted. De Falco (P) sued. The jury found a violation of the federal RICO statute, 18 U.S.C. 1962(c), and awarded De Falco (P) $1.6 million, as well as $1,000.00 for truck wheels and tires that Dirie (D) had extorted from De Falco (P) for Dirie's (D) son. The trial judge vacated the $1.6 million award, finding that the evidence failed to show sufficient causation between the RICO violations and De Falco's (P) injuries, but the trial judge left the $1,000.00 award intact. De Falco (P) appealed.

ISSUE: Can a private individual successfully enforce the federal criminal RICO statute, 18 U.S.C. 1962(c), unless he proves that the prohibited racketeering conduct was both the factual and proximate cause of his injuries?

HOLDING AND DECISION: (Underhill, J.) No. A private individual cannot successfully enforce the federal criminal RICO statute, 18 U.S.C. 1962(c), unless he proves that the prohibited racketeering conduct was both the factual and proximate cause of his injuries. The evidence at trial established that Dirie (D) and the Bernas defendants (D) did violate 18 U.S.C. 1962(c). That provision of the RICO Act requires that a defendant committed at least two instances of racketeering activity; that the defendants participated in an enterprise, either directly or indirectly; and that the defendants' activities affected interstate or foreign commerce. De Falco (P) met its burden on these essential elements of a RICO claim. First, the Town and the defendants were distinct, as 18 U.S.C. 1962(c) requires. The defendants here were separate and distinct from the Town but used their power to adversely affect De Falco's (P) ability to secure the Town's approval of the development project. As this court has held, see *United States v. Angelilli*, 660 F.2d 23, 30-35 (2d Cir. 1981), the enterprise contemplated by RICO includes governmental units: The statutory language is broad enough to include governments; the Act's substantive goals of combating bribery and extortion are peculiarly applicable to governments, and the legislative history shows that Congress expressly intended for the statutory scheme that contains RICO to apply to governments. Further, Dirie's (D) challenge to RICO's interstate-commerce requirement has no merit because his conduct forced De Falco (P) to break a contract with an out-of-state logging company and because the Town's business regularly touched interstate commerce. De Falco (P) also showed that both Dirie (D) and the Bernas defendants (D) participated in the RICO enterprise. Dirie (D) directly participated in the Town's affairs, and he used his positions to impose extortionate demands upon De Falco (P). The Bernas defendants' (D) participation in the Town's operations was shown by their threats to close down De Falco's (P) project altogether and by a Town official's written reference to the need for the Bernas defendants' (D) approval of the project. The evidence also established that Dirie (D) and the Bernas defendants (D) each engaged in racketeering activity at least twice within a ten-year period. The five acts of extortion allegedly committed by Dirie (D)

Continued on next page.

need not have involved fear of force or violence; fear of economic injury is enough, and the evidence meets that element of extortion here. Further, the Bernas defendants (D) engaged in a pattern of open-ended continuity sufficient to constitute a pattern of racketeering activity. The other way to prove a racketeering pattern, as closed-ended continuity, has always required a period of at least two years in this court. The Bernas defendants' (D) extortions of De Falco (P) over the latter half of 1989 fail to satisfy that requirement; even viewing the evidence most favorably to De Falco (P), which yields a period of eighteen months for the racketeering activities of the Bernas defendants (D), De Falco (P) still has failed to show closed-ended continuity. De Falco (P) has shown open-ended continuity, however, because there was a threat that the Bernas defendants' (D) criminal activities would continue after their proven racketeering activities occurred. Although De Falco (P) thus established a violation of 18 U.S.C. 1962(c), the evidence fails to satisfy RICO's remedies provision, 18 U.S.C. 1964(c). Under that provision's "by reason of" requirement, a defendant's violative conduct must be both the factual and the proximate cause of De Falco's (P) injuries. In this case, De Falco (P) therefore needed to prove that it complied with all requirements for approval of its lots and that no other cause besides the racketeering activities burdened De Falco's (P) sale of the lots. The record contains no such evidence. Accordingly, the trial court correctly vacated the $1.6 million award but incorrectly left the $1,000.00 award intact. Affirmed in part, vacated in part.

ANALYSIS

The plaintiffs in *De Falco* might easily have grounded their complaint on a common-law claim such as intentional interference with a business or economic relationship, particularly with respect to the contract with the out-of-state logging company. A common-law claim, though, would not have included the treble-damages incentives provided under the federal RICO statute. Students should note, though, that civil RICO claims can be temptations that exact a sharp price upon attorneys themselves. The strength of the evidence here on the defendants' violations of 18 U.S.C. 1962(c) minimizes the absence of evidence on causation. It is all too possible, however, for counsel's failure to determine an adequate foundation for civil RICO claims, certainly before filing a complaint, to cause courts to impose strict penalties upon such professionally delinquent attorneys themselves. See, e.g., *Byrne v. Nezhat*, 261 F.3d 1075, 1115 (11th Cir. 2001) ("[p]articularly with regard to civil RICO claims, plaintiffs must *stop and think* before filing them") (quoting *Pelletier v. Zweifel*, 921 F.2d 1465, 1522 (11th Cir. 1991)) (emphasis in original).

Quicknotes

BRIBERY The offering, giving, receiving, or soliciting of something of value for the purpose of influencing the action of an official in the discharge of his public or legal duties.

BURDEN OF PROOF The duty of a party to introduce evidence to support a fact that is in dispute in an action.

CAUSE IN FACT The event without which an injury would not have been incurred.

EXTORTION The unlawful taking of property of another by threats of force.

PROXIMATE CAUSE The natural sequence of events without which an injury would not have been sustained.

RICO Racketeer Influenced and Corrupt Organization laws; federal and state statutes enacted for the purpose of prosecuting organized crime.

TORTIOUS INTERFERENCE WITH CONTRACTUAL RELATIONSHIP An intentional tort whereby a defendant intentionally elicits the breach of a valid contract resulting in damages.

Pulliam v. Coastal Emergency Svcs.

Estate of medical patient (P) v. Hospital (D)

Va. Sup. Ct., 257 Va. 1, 509 S.E.2d 307 (1999)

NATURE OF CASE: **Appeal on the constitutionality of a statutorily proscribed damages cap on recovery for medical malpractice.**

FACT SUMMARY: **An emergency room patient died after being misdiagnosed, but the damage award recovered by her estate was reduced based on a damages cap mandated by statute.**

RULE OF LAW
A statutory cap on medical malpractice damages does not violate the Constitution.

FACTS: Mrs. Pulliam was admitted to the hospital (D) complaining of pain in her legs. She was examined by Dr. DiGiovanna (D) in the emergency room, and discharged after being prescribed a muscle relaxant. Mrs. Pulliam returned later, complaining of weakness in her extremities. She was admitted for further examination, and her condition subsequently worsened, whereupon she was transferred to the intensive care unit. Mrs. Pulliam died, and an autopsy revealed the cause of death as pneumonia and bacterial infection. Her husband (P), executor of her estate, brought suit for malpractice against Dr. DiGiovanna (D) and the hospital (D) vicariously. At trial, Pulliam (P) was awarded a verdict of $2.05 million, which the trial court judge later reduced to $1 million based on a statutorily imposed cap on damages for medical malpractice. Mr. Pulliam (P) filed an appeal, asserting that the trial court committed error by failing to recognize that such a cap was unconstitutional.

ISSUE: Does a statutory cap on medical malpractice damages violate the Constitution?

HOLDING AND DECISION: (Carrico, C.J.) No. A statutory cap on medical malpractice damages does not violate the Constitution. The doctrine of stare decisis does not compel a court to follow a prior decision where there has been error in that decision. The present case requires this court to reaffirm the holding of the court in *Etheridge v. Medical Center Hospitals*, 237 Va. 87, 376 S.E.2d 525 (Va. 1989), a case of similar facts dealing with the constitutionality of a malpractice cap. In *Etheridge*, the court concluded that a medical malpractice cap does not violate any constitutional guarantees. Where flagrant error or mistake existed in the *Etheridge* decision, this court cannot follow its precedent as an aforementioned violation of the doctrine of stare decisis. Pulliam's estate (P) contends that such error does indeed exist, and this court should not be deterred from ignoring the doctrine of stare decisis and reversing *Etheridge* on several independent grounds. We address Pulliam's (P) contention on all grounds and find no merit in plaintiff's (P) arguments that any error existed in *Etheridge* as decided. First, a damages cap is appropriate after a plaintiff has had the proper benefit of a jury trial, contrary to Pulliam's (P) assertion that a new trial is necessary first. Pulliam (P) contends that the cap applied in *Etheridge* was impermissible special legislation. However, the cap as applied in *Etheridge* bears a reasonable and substantial relation to the legislature's objective in protecting the public's health, safety, and welfare. Pulliam (P) next argues that a damages cap is an unconstitutional taking of a plaintiff's property, and the failure of the *Etheridge* court to find such a cap unconstitutional is error. We disagree; a taking only results when the right has vested or accrued to the plaintiff first, which is not the case with malpractice damages. Pulliam (P) asserts that an intermediate level of scrutiny should have been applied in *Etheridge*, rather than the lower-level rational basis test. However, no fundamental right or suspect classification has been implicated in the affirmation of the damages cap as applied in *Etheridge*, which enunciated the correct level of scrutiny. Finally, Pulliam (P) asserts that the damages cap in *Etheridge* violates separation of powers by invading the province of the judiciary. However, we have consistently ruled that the legislature has the power to provide, modify, or repeal a remedy. The court therefore rejects all of Pulliam's (P) arguments. Affirmed.

CONCURRENCE: (Kinser, J.) Without addressing the issue of stare decisis, I agree that a medical malpractice cap creates unnecessary injustice, since it operates to disadvantage those persons who are the most severely injured by negligent health care providers.

ANALYSIS

A cap on damages is a common tool for state tort reform, to limit the windfall recovered by plaintiffs for various policy reasons. In this case, separation of powers is only briefly implicated, but plays a larger role contextually since it is the province of the legislature to vindicate public policy, often avoiding a damages cap to limit the defendant's ability to subsequently calculate how much it could potentially pay and thereby avoid other remedial measures that might be more costly.

Continued on next page.

Quicknotes

MALPRACTICE A failure to perform one's professional duties during the course of a client relationship, either intentionally or negligently; or the poor or improper discharge of one's professional obligations.

STARE DECISIS Doctrine whereby courts follow legal precedent unless there is good cause for departure.

CHAPTER 24

Compensation Systems as Substitutes for Tort Law

Quick Reference Rules of Law

Blankenship v. Cincinnati Milacron Chemicals, Inc.

Employees (P) v. Chemical manufacturer (D)

Ohio Sup. Ct., 69 Ohio St. 2d 608, 433 N.E.2d 572, *cert denied*, 459 U.S. 857 (1982)

NATURE OF CASE: Appeal from affirmance of dismissal of action for work-related injuries resulting from an employer's intentional tortious conduct.

FACT SUMMARY: Blankenship (P) and other employees (P) of Cincinnati Milacron Chemicals, Inc. (Milacron), contended that the workers' compensation system did not bar their suit against Milacron (D) for their injuries resulting from Milacron's (D) intentional tortious conduct.

RULE OF LAW

The workers' compensation system does not bar direct employee suits against employers for intentional torts.

FACTS: Blankenship (P) and other employees (P) of Cincinnati Milacron Chemicals, Inc. (Milacron) brought suit against Milacron (D) for injuries resulting from working conditions. The employees (P) alleged that Milacron (D) knew that such conditions existed, failed to correct the conditions, failed to warn the employees (P) of the damages and conditions that existed, and failed to report the conditions to various state and federal agencies to which they were required to report by law. The employees (P) also alleged that Milacron (D) failed to warn the employees (P) that certain occupational diseases were being contracted and failed to provide medical examinations as required by law. The employees (P) further alleged that Milacron's (D) omissions were intentional, malicious, and in willful and wanton disregard of the duty to protect the health of employees. The trial court dismissed on the basis that the workers compensation system provided the only remedy for such work-related injuries. The state's intermediate appellate court affirmed, and the state's highest court granted review.

ISSUE: Does the workers' compensation system bar direct employee suits against employers for intentional torts?

HOLDING AND DECISION: (Brown, J.) No. The workers' compensation system does not bar direct employee suits for the employer's intentional conduct. Although employers who comply with the state's workers' compensation provisions are not liable for damages at common law or by statute for any injury, or occupational disease, or bodily condition, received or contracted by any employee in the course of or arising out of employment, whether or not such injury, occupational disease or bodily condition is compensable through the workers' compensation system, where an employee asserts a claim for damages based on an employer's intentional tort, the substance of the claim is not an injury received or contracted by any employee in the course of or arising out of employment. The risk of intentional tort is not part of the usual risk occasioned by employment, and an employer's intentional tortious conduct cannot be considered to be in the course and scope of the employment relationship. Thus, such intentional employer conduct falls outside the workers' compensation system. Since an employer's intentional conduct does not arise out of employment, employers do not receive immunity from civil liability for their intentional torts for participating in the workers' compensation system, and an employee may resort to a civil suit for damages resulting from such conduct. Such a holding not only comports with constitutional and statutory requirements but is also consistent with the legislative goals that underlie the workers' compensation statute. The workers' compensation system is based on the premise that an employer is protected from a suit for negligence in exchange for compliance with the Workers' Compensation Act. The Act operates as a balance of mutual compromise between the interests of the employer and the employee whereby employees relinquish their common law remedy and accept lower benefit levels coupled with the greater assurance of recovery, and employers give up their common law defenses and are protected from unlimited liability. However, the protection afforded by the Act has always been for negligent acts and not for intentional tortious conduct. Indeed, workers' compensation acts were designed to improve the plight of injured workers, and to hold that intentional torts are covered under the Act would be tantamount to encouraging such conduct, which cannot be reconciled with the motivating spirit and purpose of the Act. Moreover, the compensation scheme was specifically designed to provide less than full compensation for injured employees. Damages such as pain and suffering and loss of services on the part of a spouse are unavailable remedies to the injured employee. Punitive damages cannot be obtained. Yet, these damages are available to individuals who have been injured by intentional tortious conduct of third parties, and there is no legitimate reason why an employer should be able to escape from such damages simply because the employer committed an intentional tort against an employee. Finally, one of the avowed purposes of the Act is to promote a safe and injury-free work environment. Affording an employer immunity for its intentional behavior certainly would not promote such an environment, because an employer could commit intentional acts with impunity with the knowledge that, at the

Continued on next page.

very most, only its workers' compensation premiums might rise slightly. Reversed and remanded.

DISSENT: (Holmes, J.) Tort actions brought by an employee against an employer should be permitted only in cases where the employer actually intended to injure its employees.

DISSENT: (Krupansky, J.) There should be no judicial creation of an intentional misconduct exception to employers' tort immunity because there is no express exception to such immunity in the Workers' Compensation Act.

ANALYSIS

Most states, Ohio now included, have made allowances for an employer's intentional conduct within their workers' compensation systems. Thus, while actual civil suits may not be brought, increased compensation benefits are paid for the intentional conduct of the employer.

Quicknotes

WORKERS' COMPENSATION ACT The statutory right of an employee to claim fixed benefits (primarily loss of earnings and medical expenses) from her employer for injury or disease arising out of and in the course of employment.

Glossary

Common Latin Words and Phrases Encountered in the Law

A FORTIORI: Because one fact exists or has been proven, therefore a second fact that is related to the first fact must also exist.

A PRIORI: From the cause to the effect. A term of logic used to denote that when one generally accepted truth is shown to be a cause, another particular effect must necessarily follow.

AB INITIO: From the beginning; a condition that has existed throughout, as in a marriage that was void ab initio.

ACTUS REUS: The wrongful act; in criminal law, such action sufficient to trigger criminal liability.

AD VALOREM: According to value; an ad valorem tax is imposed upon an item located within the taxing jurisdiction calculated by the value of such item.

AMICUS CURIAE: Friend of the court. Its most common usage takes the form of an amicus curiae brief, filed by a person who is not a party to an action but is nonetheless allowed to offer an argument supporting his legal interests.

ARGUENDO: In arguing. A statement, possibly hypothetical, made for the purpose of argument is one made arguendo.

BILL QUIA TIMET: A bill to quiet title (establish ownership) to real property.

BONA FIDE: True, honest, or genuine. May refer to a person's legal position based on good faith or lacking notice of fraud (such as a bona fide purchaser for value) or to the authenticity of a particular document (such as a bona fide last will and testament).

CAUSA MORTIS: With approaching death in mind. A gift causa mortis is a gift given by a party who feels certain that death is imminent.

CAVEAT EMPTOR: Let the buyer beware. This maxim is reflected in the rule of law that a buyer purchases at his own risk because it is his responsibility to examine, judge, test, and otherwise inspect what he is buying.

CERTIORARI: A writ of review. Petitions for review of a case by the United States Supreme Court are most often done by means of a writ of certiorari.

CONTRA: On the other hand. Opposite. Contrary to.

CORAM NOBIS: Before us; writs of error directed to the court that originally rendered the judgment.

CORAM VOBIS: Before you; writs of error directed by an appellate court to a lower court to correct a factual error.

CORPUS DELICTI: The body of the crime; the requisite elements of a crime amounting to objective proof that a crime has been committed.

CUM TESTAMENTO ANNEXO, ADMINISTRATOR (ADMINISTRATOR C.T.A.): With will annexed; an administrator c.t.a. settles an estate pursuant to a will in which he or she is not appointed.

DE BONIS NON, ADMINISTRATOR (ADMINISTRATOR D.B.N.): Of goods not administered; an administrator d.b.n. settles a partially settled estate.

DE FACTO: In fact; in reality; actually. Existing in fact but not officially approved or engendered.

DE JURE: By right; lawful. Describes a condition that is legitimate "as a matter of law," in contrast to the term "de facto," which connotes something existing in fact but not legally sanctioned or authorized. For example, de facto segregation refers to segregation brought about by housing patterns, etc., whereas de jure segregation refers to segregation created by law.

DE MINIMUS: Of minimal importance; insignificant; a trifle; not worth bothering about.

DE NOVO: Anew; a second time; afresh. A trial de novo is a new trial held at the appellate level as if the case originated there and the trial at a lower level had not taken place.

DICTA: Generally used as an abbreviated form of obiter dicta, a term describing those portions of a judicial opinion incidental or not necessary to resolution of the specific question before the court. Such nonessential statements and remarks are not considered to be binding precedent.

DUCES TECUM: Refers to a particular type of writ or subpoena requesting a party or organization to produce certain documents in their possession.

EN BANC: Full bench. Where a court sits with all justices present rather than the usual quorum.

EX PARTE: For one side or one party only. An ex parte proceeding is one undertaken for the benefit of only one party, without notice to, or an appearance by, an adverse party.

EX POST FACTO: After the fact. An ex post facto law is a law that retroactively changes the consequences of a prior act.

EX REL.: Abbreviated form of the term "ex relatione," meaning upon relation or information. When the state brings an action in which it has no interest against an individual at the instigation of one who has a private interest in the matter.

FORUM NON CONVENIENS: Inconvenient forum. Although a court may have jurisdiction over the case, the action should be tried in a more conveniently located court, one to which parties and witnesses may more easily travel, for example.

GUARDIAN AD LITEM: A guardian appointed by the court to represent a minor or incompetent person in a legal action.

HABEAS CORPUS: You have the body. The modern writ of habeas corpus is a writ directing that a person (body) being detained (such as a prisoner) be brought before the court so that the legality of his detention can be judicially ascertained.

IN CAMERA: In private, in chambers. When a hearing is held before a judge in his or her chambers or when all spectators are excluded from the courtroom.

IN FORMA PAUPERIS: In the manner of a pauper. A party who proceeds in forma pauperis because of his poverty is one who is allowed to bring suit without liability for costs.

INFRA: Below, under. A word referring the reader to a later part of a book. (The opposite of supra.)

IN LOCO PARENTIS: In the place of a parent.

IN PARI DELICTO: Equally wrong; a court of equity will not grant requested relief to an applicant who is in pari delicto, or as much at fault in the transactions giving rise to the controversy as is the opponent of the applicant.

IN PARI MATERIA: On like subject matter or upon the same matter. Statutes relating to the same person or things are said to be in pari materia. It is a general rule of statutory construction that such statutes should be construed together, i.e., looked at as if they together constituted one law.

IN PERSONAM: Against the person. Jurisdiction over the person of an individual.

IN RE: In the matter of. Used to designate a proceeding involving an estate or other property.

IN REM: A term that signifies an action against the res, or thing. An action in rem is basically one that is taken directly against property, as distinguished from an action in personam, i.e., against the person.

INTER ALIA: Among other things. Used to show that the whole of a statement, pleading, list, statute, etc., has not been set forth in its entirety.

INTER PARTES: Between the parties. May refer to contracts, conveyances, or other transactions having legal significance.

INTER VIVOS: Between the living. An inter vivos gift is a gift made by a living grantor, as distinguished from bequests contained in a will, which pass upon the death of the testator.

IPSO FACTO: By the mere fact itself.

JUS: Law or the entire body of law.

LEX LOCI: The law of the place; the notion that the rights of parties to a legal proceeding are governed by the law of the place where those rights arose.

MALUM IN SE: Evil or wrong in and of itself; inherently wrong. This term describes an act that is wrong by its very nature, as opposed to one which would not be wrong but for the fact that there is a specific legal prohibition against it (malum prohibitum).

MALUM PROHIBITUM: Wrong because prohibited, but not inherently evil. Used to describe something that is wrong because it is expressly forbidden by law but that is not in and of itself evil, e.g., speeding.

MANDAMUS: We command. A writ directing an official to take a certain action.

MENS REA: A guilty mind; a criminal intent. A term used to signify the mental state that accompanies a crime or other prohibited act. Some crimes require only a general mens rea (general intent to do the prohibited act), but others, like assault with intent to murder, require the existence of a specific mens rea.

MODUS OPERANDI: Method of operating; generally refers to the manner or style of a criminal in committing crimes, admissible in appropriate cases as evidence of the identity of a defendant.

NEXUS: A connection to.

NISI PRIUS: A court of first impression. A nisi prius court is one where issues of fact are tried before a judge or jury.

N.O.V. (NON OBSTANTE VEREDICTO): Notwithstanding the verdict. A judgment n.o.v. is a judgment given in favor of one party despite the fact that a verdict was returned in favor of the other party, the justification being that the verdict either had no reasonable support in fact or was contrary to law.

NUNC PRO TUNC: Now for then. This phrase refers to actions that may be taken and will then have full retroactive effect.

PENDENTE LITE: Pending the suit; pending litigation underway.

PER CAPITA: By head; beneficiaries of an estate, if they take in equal shares, take per capita.

PER CURIAM: By the court; signifies an opinion ostensibly written "by the whole court" and with no identified author.

PER SE: By itself, in itself; inherently.

PER STIRPES: By representation. Used primarily in the law of wills to describe the method of distribution where a person, generally because of death, is unable to take that which is left to him by the will of another, and therefore his heirs divide such property between them rather than take under the will individually.

PRIMA FACIE: On its face, at first sight. A prima facie case is one that is sufficient on its face, meaning that the evidence supporting it is adequate to establish the case until contradicted or overcome by other evidence.

PRO TANTO: For so much; as far as it goes. Often used in eminent domain cases when a property owner receives partial payment for his land without prejudice to his right to bring suit for the full amount he claims his land to be worth.

QUANTUM MERUIT: As much as he deserves. Refers to recovery based on the doctrine of unjust enrichment in those cases in which a party has rendered valuable services or furnished materials that were accepted and enjoyed by another under circumstances that would reasonably notify the recipient that the rendering party expected to be paid. In essence, the law implies a contract to pay the reasonable value of the services or materials furnished.

QUASI: Almost like; as if; nearly. This term is essentially used to signify that one subject or thing is almost analogous to another but that material differences between them do exist. For example, a quasi-criminal proceeding is one that is not strictly criminal but shares enough of the same characteristics to require some of the same safeguards (e.g., procedural due process must be followed in a parole hearing).

QUID PRO QUO: Something for something. In contract law, the consideration, something of value, passed between the parties to render the contract binding.

RES GESTAE: Things done. In evidence law, this principle justifies the admission of a statement that would otherwise be hearsay when it is made so closely to the event in question as to be said to be a part of it, or with such spontaneity as not to have the possibility of falsehood.

RES IPSA LOQUITUR: The thing speaks for itself. This doctrine gives rise to a rebuttable presumption of negligence when the instrumentality causing the injury was within the exclusive control of the defendant, and the injury was one that does not normally occur unless a person has been negligent.

RES JUDICATA: A matter adjudged. Doctrine which provides that once a court of competent jurisdiction has rendered a final judgment or decree on the merits, that judgment or decree is conclusive upon the parties to the case and prevents them from engaging in any other litigation on the points and issues determined therein.

RESPONDEAT SUPERIOR: Let the master reply. This doctrine holds the master liable for the wrongful acts of his servant (or the principal for his agent) in those cases in which the servant (or agent) was acting within the scope of his authority at the time of the injury.

STARE DECISIS: To stand by or adhere to that which has been decided. The common law doctrine of stare decisis attempts to give security and certainty to the law by following the policy that once a principle of law as applicable to a certain set of facts has been set forth in a decision, it forms a precedent that will subsequently be followed, even though a different decision might be made were it the first time the question had arisen. Of course, stare decisis is not an inviolable principle and is departed from in instances where there is good cause (e.g., considerations of public policy led the Supreme Court to disregard prior decisions sanctioning segregation).

SUPRA: Above. A word referring a reader to an earlier part of a book. (The opposite of infra.)

ULTRA VIRES: Beyond the power. This phrase is most commonly used to refer to actions taken by a corporation that are beyond the power or legal authority of the corporation.

Addendum of French Derivatives

CHATTEL: Tangible personal property.

CY PRES: Doctrine permitting courts to apply trust funds to purposes not expressed in the trust but necessary to carry out the settlor's intent.

IN PAIS: Not pursuant to legal proceedings.

PER AUTRE VIE: For another's life; during another's life. In property law, an estate may be granted that will terminate upon the death of someone other than the grantee.

PROFIT A PRENDRE: A license to remove minerals or other produce from land.

VOIR DIRE: Process of questioning jurors as to their predispositions about the case or parties to a proceeding in order to identify those jurors displaying bias or prejudice.